Continental Crossroads

D1086872

Continental

Published in cooperation with THE WILLIAM P. CLEMENTS CENTER

FOR SOUTHWEST STUDIES, *Southern Methodist University*

Crossroads

Remapping U.S.-Mexico Borderlands History

Edited by SAMUEL TRUETT *and* ELLIOTT YOUNG

DUKE UNIVERSITY PRESS *Durham and London* 2004

AMERICAN ENCOUNTERS/GLOBAL INTERACTIONS

A series edited by Gilbert M. Joseph and Emily S. Rosenberg

This series aims to stimulate critical perspectives and fresh interpretive frameworks for scholarship on the history of the imposing global presence of the United States. Its primary concerns include the deployment and contestation of power, the construction and deconstruction of cultural and political borders, the fluid meanings of intercultural encounters, and the complex interplay between the global and the local. American Encounters seeks to strengthen dialogue and collaboration between historians of U.S. international relations and area studies specialists.

The series encourages scholarship based on multiarchival historical research. At the same time, it supports a recognition of the representational character of all stories about the past and promotes critical inquiry into issues of subjectivity and narrative. In the process, American Encounters strives to understand the context in which meanings related to nations, cultures, and political economy are continually produced, challenged, and reshaped.

© 2004 DUKE UNIVERSITY PRESS

All rights reserved

Printed in the United States of America

on acid-free paper ⊗ Designed by Amy Ruth Buchanan

Typeset in Carter & Cone Galliard by Tseng Information Systems Inc.

Library of Congress Cataloging-in-Publication Data appear on the

last printed page of this book.

2nd printing, 2006

Contents

DAVID J. WEBER

Foreword

In the last decades of the twentieth century, American historians discovered America. Students of colonial English America, who had seldom looked across the Appalachians, began to gaze westward. In the great expanse that stretched to the Pacific they found other colonial powers—France, Spain, and Russia—and a multitude of Native American peoples with their own stories to tell. At the century's end, historian Alan Taylor summed up this new, more expansive colonial history in his magisterial *American Colonies*. Meanwhile, as historians of English colonial America looked westward, a new generation of historians of the American West looked to the east and began to apply the concerns of "mainstream" American historians to their region. With probing studies of race, class, ethnicity, gender, and the environment, the new western historians blurred the boundaries between regional and national history and moved the locus of American history westward. By the end of the twentieth century, then, American history had caught up with American manifest destiny. It had become transcontinental.

The scholars represented in this collection of essays suggest that American history should not stop at the nation's edges. They make a case that American history should be transnational as well as transcontinental. In the largest sense, they suggest that any nation's borderlands cannot be understood solely within the framework of national history because forces from both sides of a border shape the lives of borderlands residents.

Continental Crossroads focuses on the modern U.S.-Mexico borderlands, where a boundary line seems to separate two dissimilar cultures and economies. Created in 1848 and modified in 1854, the international boundary ran initially through sparsely populated country, its coordinates clearer on the map than on the ground. In the twentieth century, however, the physical line became more clearly defined and defended, particularly by the United States. Mexicans who crossed the line illegally in search of new opportunities in *el norte* risked arrest, deportation, and, in the worst of cases, death from exposure to the elements or from the inhumane and criminal negligence of smugglers.

Yet, if the international boundary came to be a serious barrier, it did not become an insurmountable obstacle. Radio and television transmissions ignore it completely, as do air and water, some of it polluted. Capital, commodities, and people—black, brown, red, and white—all find ways across, legally or illegally. Like boundaries elsewhere in the world, the U.S.-Mexico border has not so much separated people as drawn them to it—and beyond. In human terms, the U.S.-Mexico borderlands extend northward to places like Chicago and Milwaukee, home to substantial numbers of Mexican nationals and ethnic Mexicans by the end of the twentieth century. At the same time, the borderlands also extend southward to San Miguel de Allende and Guadalajara, with their long-standing colonies of Anglo-American expatriates and retirees.

Some of the forces that have pushed and pulled people across the U.S.-Mexico border lie beyond the control of a single nation state. In the post-NAFTA era, for example, some Mexican farmers cannot make a living because their market is flooded with low-priced corn imported from the United States and subsidized by its government. Unable to find remunerative work at home, displaced rural workers make the risky crossing into the United States, where they provide a source of cheap labor that some Anglo-Americans regard as essential. Other Mexicans stop short of crossing the border, but move north to work in assembly plants, or maquiladoras, south of the line. There, higher wages in the maquiladoras are matched by a higher cost of living, forcing these new borderlands residents to move into squalid, dangerous slums. As the companies who built the maquiladoras find cheaper labor in other parts of the world, they close the assembly plants and move on, leaving behind unemployed and displaced workers, some of whom cross into the United States in search of the opportunities that eluded them south of the border. In these, and many other ways, transnational forces deeply affect Mexicans and Anglo-Americans on both sides of the border—as they have peoples everywhere. These forces have been unusually unsettling in the U.S.-Mexico borderlands, however, where the economy of a developing nation meets the economy of the richest country on the planet.

In their brilliant introduction to *Continental Crossroads*, editors Samuel Truett and Elliott Young review historians' debates about the U.S.-Mexico borderlands. They ask how we might construct new narratives that take transnational as well as national forces into account for the history of Mexico as well as the United States. Neither they nor the historians they have invited to contribute to this innovative volume offer glib answers. They do ask provocative questions and tell stories about a remarkable range of borderlands topics and peoples. Some, like the U.S. Border Patrol, are familiar historical actors, but others, like blacks fleeing the post-Reconstruction South for northern Mexico or Chinese immigrants moving into Sonora and Baja California, are little known. At the hands of these skilled researchers, writers, and thinkers, the "remapping" of the history of the U.S.-Mexico borderlands takes us into new and interesting terrain toward a destination yet to be determined.

Acknowledgments

This book began as a series of informal conversations between Andrés Reséndez, Alexandra Stern, Samuel Truett, and Elliott Young at meetings of the Latin American Studies Association, the Pacific Coast Branch of the American Historical Association, and the Conference of Mexican, United States, and Canadian Historians. As we shared insights and stories from our respective journeys across northern Mexico and the U.S. Southwest, we began to realize that we were part of something larger than ourselves. It took us a while to understand what this common ground was, and what, exactly, tied our work together. This book is part of this ongoing discussion. We offer few definitive conclusions, but we hope to have posed larger questions that others will find useful as they explore this place and idea called the borderlands.

A project such as this requires the fortitude and patience of many people. First, we would like to thank Andrés Reséndez and Alexandra Stern, who were part of the original gang of four, and remained trusted advisors throughout the process. Second, we would like to thank the contributors to this volume for offering us creative and original works, engaging in exciting intellectual exchange, offering valuable advice on the introductory essay, responding to our suggestions and editorial advice, and keeping to the deadlines. Third, we owe a great debt of gratitude to David Weber, who has been a steadfast supporter of the project from the very beginning. David not only wrote an elegant foreword but also generously arranged and financed a special manuscript symposium at the William P. Clements Center for Southwest Studies at Southern Methodist University. We would also like to thank Sherry Smith, Karl Jacoby, and Benjamin

Johnson, who offered invaluable advice in helping us to organize this symposium.

The Clements Center symposium allowed the contributors to meet face to face for a memorable weekend and to engage regional scholars and an astute public. After years of virtual conversations and editing, it was a delight to have warm bodies to connect with the digital prose. The symposium—which included a series of presentations and public engagements—reminded us of the intellectual energy and feisty debates that borderlands history can inspire. It is rare for an academic symposium to end with beads of sweat forming on foreheads, but such is the nature of a field in ferment. We thank the public participants for traveling hundreds of miles to participate in these discussions. We offer special thanks to Andrea Boardman, Ruth Ann Elmore, and the rest of the generous staff at the Clements Center for their flawless organization and good cheer. We would also like to thank David Weber and the Clements Center for their subvention of the maps and production of the final book. We hope it will be worth their generous support.

The anonymous readers at Duke University Press provided invaluable comments on the manuscript and motivated us all to rethink our essays and the ways they spoke to one another. We also owe special thanks to Bárbara O. Reyes, Raúl Ramos, and Luis Alvarez for their close readings of penultimate drafts of the introductory essay. We thank Valerie Millholland and Miriam Angress at Duke University Press, who helped us navigate the potentially treacherous waters of a multiauthor volume with patience and wisdom, and Natalie Hanemann, who drew the maps. Finally, Gilbert Joseph wisely advised us to send the manuscript to Duke University Press in the first place and continued to give valuable support throughout the long publication process.

We hope that this volume will open up new dialogues between Latin Americanist, U.S. West, and Chicana/o historians, anthropologists, literary critics, and cultural studies scholars. Rather than enforce new fences and borders, we want to build bridges. We will have succeeded if our readers, like us, discover new colleagues and friends in a variety of different fields, and become themselves new world border crossers.

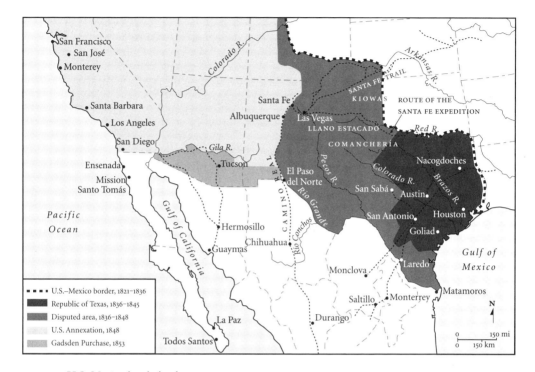

U.S.-Mexico borderlands, 1821–1854.

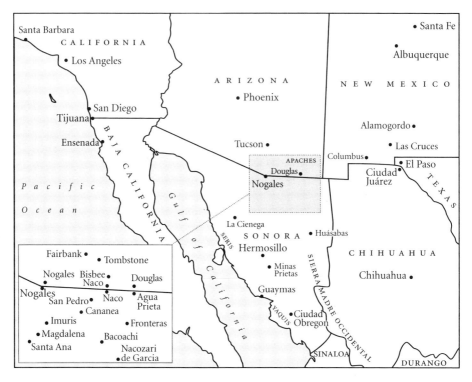

U.S.-Mexico borderlands after 1848 (western half).

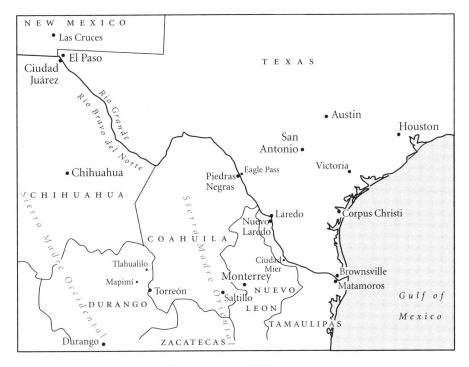

U.S.-Mexico borderlands after 1848 (eastern half).

Introduction

Making Transnational History:

Nations, Regions, and Borderlands

It has been two decades since anthropologist Eric Wolf warned us against succumbing too easily to the siren's song of national history. Empires, nations, and ordinary people, Wolf proposed in 1982, have long been part of a transnational "bundle of relationships" shaped by migration, the expansion of world markets, and the rise and fall of imperial regimes. "These are familiar facts," he insisted, yet "historians, economists, and political scientists [still] take separate nations as their basic framework of inquiry."[1] Today, as we peer into the new millennium, Wolf's critique of national history seems more compelling than ever. People, things, and information seem to be moving more than ever across borders, while older national entities are both disintegrating and reintegrating themselves into such entities as the European Union, the Non-Aligned Movement, MERCOSUR, and the Free Trade Area of the Americas. As contested and fragile as these entities are, they remind us that globalization and transnationalism are reshaping our lives in profoundly new ways. To understand these transformations, we must find ways to see beyond the nation, even as we keep the nation in focus.

This need is especially acute for historians, who have traditionally had a special affection for national borders. Whether we start with Christopher Columbus, Jamestown, or the Aztec empire, our history is often told as a narrative of events that shaped us as citizens of a specific nation. If we consider that this has long been the central work of history—to create "imagined communities" of fellow citizens—then we should hardly be surprised.[2] Yet if we look beyond these selective traditions, we discover a multiplicity of worlds that history forgot. This is particularly true in the

U.S.-Mexico borderlands. Ever since the border was mapped in 1854, the borderlands have supported a complex web of historical relationships that transcended—even as they emerged in tandem with—the U.S. and Mexican nations. Residents of the borderlands often see their history differently. In ways, the stories they tell are local or regional subsets of national history, in other ways they are quintessentially national, and in others they completely transcend the nation. Yet these stories are characterized most of all by their absence from mainstream Mexican and U.S. history; we know little about them.

Studying the U.S.-Mexico borderlands allows one to engage these hidden stories while reflecting critically on the process of territorialization that coincided with the rise of nation-states. Territoriality, argues historian Charles Maier, is the key development of the modern era.[3] National borders are where territorialization becomes real, where physical markers and barriers are erected, and agents of the state regulate the movement of people, goods, and information. As many of the essays in this volume show, the state's ability to control U.S.-Mexican border space was relatively weak until the second decade of the twentieth century, and even then this control was more dream than reality. Struggles to delimit and define national and ethnic identity in the borderlands exposed the incoherency of the imagined bounded space of the nation. By understanding contradictions between the ideal nation and social reality at the point that national identity was being forged, we can better historicize the nation. What have nations meant for those living at (or moving across) their most tangible territorial limits, and how can the histories of these continental crossroads help us rethink the world we live in today?

Border Approaches

If the power of national history has pushed the borderlands to the margins, it does not mean that historians have ignored the U.S.-Mexico borderlands. For Latin American, Chicana/o, Native American, Spanish borderlands, and western U.S. historians who have devoted their careers to the study of the border region, there is little that is truly *new* about borderlands history. This collection, moreover, suggests that their insights *have* begun to percolate into the mainstream, especially during the last two decades. The contributors to this collection hail from some of the most established centers of Latin American, Chicana/o, and U.S. West history north of the border, and the shared conversations we have engaged in as graduate students and faculty members have been possible not only due to the pathbreaking work of our mentors and their generations, but also because our respective fields have matured to the point that cross-field conversations feel *natural*. In short, we have reached a turning point in borderlands history where Latin American, Chicana/o, western U.S., and other historians have begun to reap the common harvests of years of work at the crossroads of their respective fields.

For years, the term "borderlands history" conjured up romantic stories of Indians, missionaries, and soldiers on the northern frontier of New Spain. This association began in 1921, when U.S. historian Herbert Eugene Bolton published *The Spanish Borderlands: A Chronicle of Old Florida and the Southwest*.[4] Using Mexican and Spanish archives, and building on an earlier generation of work by San Francisco bookseller Hubert Howe Bancroft and others, Bolton hoped to forge a Hispanic counterpart to Frederick Jackson Turner's foundational narrative of the U.S. frontier, while challenging a deep legacy of black legend–inspired thought that pushed Spanish America to the margins of early U.S. history.[5] By the early 1930s, the history of the "Spanish Borderlands" enjoyed enormous popularity as Bolton's students—104 Ph.D.s and 323 M.A.s—carried the field to other schools, while the publication of *The Spanish Borderlands Frontier* in 1970 by Bolton protégé John Francis Bannon brought the field to a newer generation.[6] These historians did more than simply rewrite frontier history from a Hispanic perspective. As Richard Griswold del Castillo argues, they "awakened scholars to the importance of the Mexican frontier as a historical bridge between Anglo and Latin America."[7]

Bolton's historical vision soon bumped up against alternative border approaches. During the 1930s, contemporaries of Bolton such as Carlos E. Castañeda and George I. Sánchez began writing histories of ethnic Mexican culture and identity, and scholars such as Carey McWilliams and Américo Paredes followed suit in the 1950s.[8] These histories often took place in the borderlands, and even made references to the Spanish frontier, but they focused less on frontier processes, per se, and more on ethnic Mexican communities in the United States. With the rise of a new cohort of Chicano scholars in the 1960s and 1970s, this scholarship shifted onto new political ground. Rodolfo Acuña, Juan Gómez-Quiñones, Albert Camarillo, and others, writing in the context of the Chicano Movement, focused on the historical foundations of racism, discrimination, and exploitation, while underscoring processes of identity and community formation. By the early 1980s, these and other Chicana/o scholars (along with some of their non-Chicano colleagues) began to leaven their stories with the conceptual insights of social history, placing Mexican-origin populations in the U.S. Southwest within a broader history of ethnic, race, class, gender, and power relations.[9]

Chicana/o scholars embraced a historiographical legacy that had little to do with Bolton and the Spanish borderlands, but the fact that these historians shared "borderland" terrain brought some scholars to reflect on the distinctions between the two fields. Many Chicano historians felt that Spanish borderlands scholars celebrated and institutionalized a "white" story of Spanish colonists while ignoring, often demonizing, the *mestizo* past.[10] The fact that the Boltonian narrative ended before the creation of the actual border further limited its appeal to Chicano scholars. It was this later borderlands, mapped by force of conquest over Mexican homelands, that Chicano scholars took as their relevant tradition. Rodolfo Acuña's 1972 tale of conquest and colonialism, for instance, began with the U.S. invasion of Texas, while Juan Gómez-Quiñones started in the twentieth century, with the rise of new ethnic Mexican identities and political struggles.[11] With Chicano history, the borderlands also shifted spatially. This was the result of a focus not only on the lands taken in 1848 but also on Aztlán, the mythical Aztec homeland, which many Chicanos associated with the U.S. Southwest.[12] Places like Louisiana and Florida, former Spanish lands that had also been subject to U.S. conquest, were too far removed from these particular points of reference to matter as much in the new Chicano history.

Borderland distinctions also emerged in the ways historians told stories. Whereas Bolton and his heirs told celebratory tales of the "frontiering genius" of the Spanish, and some Hispanic scholars—using the same heroes—penned epics of an enduring "Spanish-American" culture, Chicano historians wrote more radical stories of political, economic, and social subordination under U.S. rule, highlighting imperialist U.S. visions of Mexico and Mexican-origin peoples. These differences between borderlands narratives, some felt, established arbitrary chronological distinctions. Historian Ralph Vigil, for instance, urged Chicana/o scholars to connect their stories to the frontier past. "Mexican-American history still remains a part of the history of the Borderlands, where two frontiers collided, and a fusion, which is still in progress, began," he wrote in 1973.[13]

Meanwhile, Donald Worcester, one of Bolton's last students, chided Spanish borderlands scholars for failing to embrace work in Chicana/o history. "The Spanish Borderlands have expanded and are still expanding," he proposed three years later, "yet the horizons of borderlands historians have remained limited to the colonial era."[14]

A path-breaking effort to bridge this divide was David J. Weber's 1982 book, *The Mexican Frontier, 1821–1846*.[15] Boltonian and Chicano scholars alike embraced Weber's analysis of the understudied decades of northern Mexico before the U.S.-Mexican War. Some historians began to drop "Spanish" from "borderlands history" to include this later frontier era, and once scholars bridged this temporal gap, possibilities for dialogue across fields grew.[16] In the decade that followed, Chicana/o scholars such as Ramón Gutiérrez, Rosaura Sánchez, and Antonia Castañeda applied new approaches to race, ethnicity, and gender from Chicana/o and Latin American history to the colonial borderlands.[17] They were joined by U.S. and Mexican historians—led by Cynthia Radding, Frank de la Teja, Cheryl E. Martin, Leslie S. Offutt, Ana María Alonso, Ross Frank, Susan Deeds, Cecilia Sheridan, James Brooks, and others—who wove ethnohistory, ethnic and gender studies, economic and environmental history, and cultural studies into an increasingly multivocal portrait of New Spain's northern frontier.[18] Drawing on shared political, intellectual, and methodological concerns, tied to recent approaches to postcolonial and subaltern studies, recent Chicana/o and "Spanish" borderlands historians have come, in this fashion, to find remarkable common ground between their fields.

Yet older boundaries have proven resilient. In the mid-1990s, the editors of this volume joined an online discussion list on Spanish borderlands history. The list owners chose to limit all discussions to the region's history before 1900—a curious closing date, since Spanish borderlands history traditionally closes in 1821 (or in 1848, if one follows Weber's effort to include Mexican rule in the region). When we queried participants about these temporal parameters, we were surprised to discover how passionately they argued to maintain a boundary between the "Spanish" past and later histories of ethnic relations and immigration. Even though they could not clearly explain why 1900 should mark the watershed, they did feel a divide was appropriate.[19] In short, even with common ground emerging between Chicana/o and Spanish borderlands history, the divide between "frontier" and "modern" borderlands—floating somewhere over the nineteenth century—still exerts enormous power over the scholarly imagination. This may be an effect of residual political boundaries between Chicana/o and borderlands history (i.e., dividing a "Spanish" past from twentieth-century ethnic relations), but it is also because borderland narratives remain tied to national periodizations, often determined by historical processes and events thousands of miles from the borderlands.

This tendency to harness borderlands history to the centralizing logic of the nation also explains why few scholars see common ground between the histories of the Mexican North and U.S. Southwest after the border was mapped in the mid-nineteenth century.[20] If one wants to learn, for instance, what happened to the Spanish colonial province of the Pimería Alta after the 1854 Gadsden Purchase, one must turn to separate histories written for audiences who often have little sense of history on *el otro lado*. Towns of the former Pimería Alta, such as Tucson, Arizona, and Magdalena, Sonora, are bound together even today by family, religious festivals, and migration, but owing to historiographical divisions that segregate the colonial from the national, and the U.S. from Mexico, few historians or their audiences understand how or why.[21] The organizational logic of national narratives, in other words, has come to exert a profound impact on the way we envision the past: we imagine the mid-nineteenth century as a point of spatial and narrative rupture, whereas, for many border people, it marked the beginning of years of negotiation between colonial, national, regional, and global coordinates that were—despite the U.S. annexation of land and people—anything but fixed.

To recover the hidden relationships between borderland histories, then, one must also turn to the regional historiographies of the American Southwest and Mexican North. By the late nineteenth century, the Southwest was already starting to emerge as a distinct place in the American mind.[22] Local "pioneer" historical societies often led the way with popular tales of the defenders of the Alamo, pioneers and outlaws, and the Apache wars. Echoing Frederick Jackson Turner, most of these histories focused on Anglo-Americans, yet the idea of the region's distinctiveness from the rest of the Turnerian West also began to emerge during this same period, as railroad corporations and local boosters attempted to make the region an exotic haven for tourists, and Americans also began to celebrate "Hispanic" and Native American pasts of New Mexico, California, and Arizona. This effort was later bolstered in the early twentieth century by

Herbert Eugene Bolton's effort to institutionalize a Hispanic alternative to the national frontier myth.[23]

Yet even though Southwestern history was being rapidly produced, there was little interest in connecting local pieces into a regional narrative, as Turner and others had done for the American West. " 'Southwest,' alone or with qualifying adjectives," historian Burl Noggle notes, "almost defies definition," and it was precisely this ambiguity, geographer Richard Francaviglia adds, that made the Southwest appealing.[24] Historians contributed to this ambiguity. Some highlighted the unique power of land to shape traditions, others emphasized a "heroic triad" of Indian, Hispanic, and Anglo-American cultures, and others made the region a laboratory for the study of cultural pluralism, dependency, assimilation, and incorporation. Few studies, with the exceptions of D. W. Meinig's *Southwest: Three Peoples in Geographical Change* (1971) and Thomas D. Hall's *Social Change in the Southwest, 1350–1880* (1989) tried to join the pieces of this history into a larger temporal or geographical whole.[25] Histories written at the scale of states or localities continued to dominate the field. Historians studied Texas, New Mexico, Arizona, and California but were less concerned about asking what tied Austin, Albuquerque, Tucson, and San Diego together within a larger "southwestern" narrative.

Indeed, these places were much more likely to find common ground in the broader history of the American West, owing largely to the fact that scholars after Turner reinforced the idea of western significance and exceptionalism in the American imagination. Even when the so-called New Western historians began to unweave the Turnerian fabric in the 1980s, historians still found it easy to imagine the American West as a larger regional whole. They contested its precise boundaries and qualities but found its conceptual and institutional moorings stronger than ever.[26] What made the West so coherent, especially in contrast to the Southwest? The answer, perhaps, lies in the relationships of these two regions to the nation. The West is a regional subset of the nation, but it has often stood in for the nation itself. It was a proving ground of national expansion and state making, and under the guidance of men such as Frederick Jackson Turner and Theodore Roosevelt, it became the wellspring of American exceptionalism. By contrast, Americans imagine the Southwest, as they imagine most other U.S. regions, as a dependent subset of the nation. Its lack of a historical center—especially in contrast to the "national" West—points again to the centralizing forces in the production of U.S. historical identity.[27]

The tendency of Americans to see southwestern history as somewhat inchoate and subordinate to national history has its counterpart in the way many Mexican historians see the Mexican North. In ways, the North exerts a mythical power not unlike that which the American West holds in the United States. The *Norteño*, a rugged and self-reliant (if also provincial) archetype of Mexican masculinity, has a place in the national imagination that is similar to that of the cowboy north of the border. The Mexican North was known not only as a land of military might (symbolized by a frontier tradition of Indian fighters and revolutionaries) but also as a pragmatic and progressive region conditioned by proximity to the United States. And as historians such as Miguel León-Portilla and Barry Carr note, it was the tough, pragmatic, and progressive North that produced the dynasty of leaders that rebuilt Mexico in the decade after the Mexican Revolution.[28] Yet like the Southwest, the North has more often than not found itself at the frontiers of centralizing historiographical efforts to *forjar patria* from the perspective of Mexico City. Without a Frederick Jackson Turner to bring popular images of the North to the scholarly center, Mexican history has tended to relegate the region to the margins. The history of the North, explains historian Cuauhtémoc Velasco, traditionally reflects a colonial scheme in which Mexico's "regions were oriented politically and economically towards the heart of the nation."[29]

The significance of the North began to shift in the late 1960s, as historians began to assign more value to the "many Mexicos" that persisted through centralizing regimes of the nineteenth and twentieth centuries. From isolated research in the 1970s, to more institutionalized work in the 1980s and 1990s, historians such as Friedrich Katz, Hector Aguilar Camín, Luis Aboites Aguilar, Mario Cerutti, Ana María Alonso, Daniel Nugent, Sergio Ortega Noriega, Miguel Tinker Salas, Victor Orozco, Paul Vanderwood, Juan Mora-Torres, and others have begun to flesh out a more clear understanding of northern Mexican history from a range of local, state, and subregional perspectives.[30] This work, especially compared to that on the U.S. West, is distinguished by its flexible approach to region. Even though many historians articulate a vision of a separate "northern" identity, their works rarely address the region in its entirety; they tend to focus on particular states or groups of states (the Mexican Northwest, the Mexican Northeast, Monterrey and its regional "ambit," etc.).[31] This may reflect the uneven nature of a history that is only now gaining institutional support, but it also reflects the fact that unlike the U.S. West—which was being tied together by railroads at precisely the moment that it was being imagined as a region—the Mexican North has always been divided by geography into provinces that were linked more tightly to Mexico City than to each other. In short, although the idea of the North is strong in Mexico, it is a notion that tends to be powerfully diffracted across a structurally "subregional" historical reality.

Rather than sidestepping these various regional traditions because they lack clear-cut commensurability, borderlands historians need to find ways to incorporate them into a broader field of inquiry. By interweaving insights of Spanish borderlands and Chicana/o history with western U.S., southwestern U.S., and northern Mexican history, we can open up new transnational dialogues about frontiers, regions, and their historical relationships. For instance, recent scholars of northern Mexico, following the lead of historian Friedrich Katz, have thought about colonial, regional, and ethnic relations in ways that remind us of Turner's frontier thesis. Some see the North as a unique place where a masculine warrior tradition, cross-class cooperation, and democratic institutions emerged from the crucible of colonial Indian wars and the "open frontier." By putting this work into dialogue with "new western" critiques from the U.S. side of the border, historians of the Mexican North might engage in efforts to disentangle the history of the Mexican North from the rhetoric of Norteño politics.[32] Likewise, western historians can benefit greatly from the relatively open-ended and flexible models of regions and subregions found in the work of Mexican historians such as Mario Cerutti and Sergio Ortega Noriega.[33] The absence of a Frederick Jackson Turner for the Mexican North has, perhaps, freed scholars south of the border to explore alternative regional patterns in ways that could, in turn, help historians of the U.S. rethink the "many Americas" north of the border.

If borderlands history finds its place amid a wide range of frontier, regional, and ethnic histories, it has also been shaped since the 1960s by the rise of poststructuralism. Whereas Bolton and his students once focused on institutions such as the *presidio* and the mission, and reified subjects such as the conquistador and missionary, poststructuralist analyses have highlighted culture and hybrid identities.[34] The deconstructionist methods and postmodern theories of literary critics and philosophers provided powerful tools with which to question a master narrative that paid short shrift to Indians, mestizos, Chicanos, women, and a host of other subjects. The introduction of these new subjects implied more than just adding new chapters about various ethnic and sexual minorities to an ever-expanding corpus of border history; it demanded a fundamental rethinking of the meaning of the borderlands and of history in general.

Scholars have taken up this challenge in a variety of disciplines and have thus deepened our understanding of race, ethnicity, gender, and their historical relationships to the borderlands. Critical analysis of race and ethnicity became a key part of borderlands scholarship with the emergence of Chicano studies. Turning triumphalist narratives—in which Anglo-American pioneers defeated "savage" Indians and Mexicans—on their head, Chicano historians such as Rodolfo Acuña showed how Anglos violently destroyed what had been a relatively harmonious society. These foundational Chicano counternarratives were, some have argued, "by and large implicitly nationalist in origin."[35] More complex studies of racial, gender, and ethnic identity have, in subsequent decades, exploded myths of monolithic ethnic communities, either good or evil, and revealed highly diversified and fractious identities.[36] This is evident not only in Chicana/o history and literary studies, but also in revisionist approaches to the so-called Spanish borderlands. James Brooks, for example, reorients older tales of Spanish, mestizo, and Indian difference by focusing on hybrid racial relations anchored in slavery and kinship, and bringing these relations forward into the national era.[37]

In shifting our situational frame, we have begun to recover histories of ethnic and racial groups that were often missing from traditional borderland narratives. Led by such pioneers as Edward H. Spicer, scholars of Native America have fleshed out a history of native peoples that rivals that of other border cultures.[38] Recently, native scholars have added critical depth to this scholarship with histories written from the perspective of such groups as the Yaqui and Tohono O'odham.[39] Neil Foley brought African Americans into the borderland milieu with his path-breaking book *White Scourge*, which complicated the white-black racial dyad that undergirds much of U.S. history.[40] Asian American scholars Evelyn Hu-DeHart, Erika Lee, and Lawrence Fong, for their part, placed border Chinese in transnational perspective, thereby challenging the white-mestizo-Indian triad that has been assumed to reign throughout Mexico.[41] Sharing this multivocal borderlands terrain are religious refugees such as Mormons and Mennonites, immigrants from Europe, Asia, and the eastern United States such as Italians, Serbs, Ukrainians, Germans, Russians, Japanese, African Americans, and immigrant native groups such as Kickapoos and Mixtecs, not to mention the mixture of rural people who are often treated by scholars as ethnic groups on one side of the border, and peasants on the other.[42]

But one needs to do more than simply add new groups to the mix. We follow the lead of scholars who question the racial categories that keep us from understanding what Gary Nash calls the "hidden history of mestizo America."[43] "The idea of an absolute cleavage between African, white, and Native American is false," writes Jack Forbes, "as is the notion of a 'two-caste' society."[44] The essays in this volume add to efforts to undo monolithic views of Anglos and Mexicans, and give voice to silenced mestizo identities.[45] Yet they also explore the basic fact that the border has served for years as a locus for the *reinforcement* of boundaries marking the body politic, whether expressed in national, racial, or gendered terms. From both U.S. and Mexican perspectives, the border has been a site where white men could renew their virility and articulate a "primitive masculinity" that reinforced both national and racial boundaries. Even into the twentieth century, the border was associated with racial and gender codes associated with a "frontier" legacy of European American men defending against "nomadic" Indian communities such as the Comanches and Apaches. In northern Mexico, a similar portrait of strong-willed (often white) pioneers who survived arid deserts, "indios barbaros," and Yankee invaders—and who later served as a "revolutionary" vanguard—inflected national identity, even if in a regionally specific way.[46]

These identities emerged at precisely the moment at the turn of the century when statesmen and capitalist elites were subordinating and domesticating the periphery. They therefore served the nation and national elites at the expense of the border, even as they bolstered border identities. This process of appropriation continues even to this day as multinational corporations such as Taco Bell encourage customers to "make a run for the border," and metropolitan intellectuals and artists cash in on the caché of the borderlands in New York, Los Angeles, and Mexico City.

This legacy of simultaneously crossing and reinforcing borders, and supporting—while also locally and regionally reconfiguring—nationalizing and modernizing practices, speaks directly to the increasingly global and fragmented world that border people inhabit today. In his seminal essay on migratory circuits that connect Aguililla, Michoacán, to Redwood City, California, anthropologist Roger Rouse writes that "it is the circuit rather than any one locale that constitutes the setting in relation to which Aguilillans orchestrate their lives."[47] This sense of living in two places at once is what Nestór García Canclini finds in Latin America in the 1980s and 1990s, "where traditions have not yet disappeared and modernity has not yet completely arrived."[48] Yet even as new transnational circuits and strategies reorient border lives, the nation stays as strong as ever. Likewise, the ongoing and simultaneous presence of the modern and "traditional," in what Rouse has described as the "social space of postmodernism," is not an anomaly, but rather a hallmark of U.S.-Mexican relations.[49] Borderlands history can help us better understand today's border crossings by highlighting contradictions between the multiplicity of social spaces that coexisted and contended even as the nation captured the minds, bodies, and territories of its emerging citizenry.

In all these ways, borderlands history has come to find its center in increasingly complex and expansive stories. Much of this flows directly from exciting new trends in Chicana/o, U.S. West, Spanish borderlands, and Mexican history. With luck, historians will see the essays in this collection as contributions to ongoing developments in each of these fields. Rather than suggest an alternative to these fields—after all, many of us call ourselves Chicana/o, Latin American, U.S., and regional U.S. historians, and research and publish within these "home" fields—we seek to remap borderlands history as a *meeting place* of these fields. Indeed, conversations between scholars in these fields *on their own terms*, whether in the archives, in published work, or at multifield conferences such as the one that the William P. Clements Center for Southwest Studies at Southern Methodist University hosted for the authors of this collection, will yield greater results than efforts to see borderlands history as a special field apart. When Chicana/o, Latin American, and western U.S. historians pool their insights on frontiers, state making, immigration, and ethnic history, the results are often contested—as we have learned in our collaborations here—but they promote a model of scholarly dialogue that seems appropriate for a world in which borders and their respectful crossings are more important than ever.

Telling Border Stories

The prospect of weaving these strands together in a coherent narrative framework is daunting, and some might say impossible. We admit at the outset a respect for multiple stories. For as long as the borderlands remain home to many communities, historians will need to make space for multiple historical voices that make different, often contradictory, claims on the past. We have already discussed some of the discord among early Spanish borderlands and Chicano narratives. Likewise, native historians will tell different stories than those writing about Norteño Apache fighters, and "Hispanos" in New Mexico may find it hard—even troublesome—to think of their history as part of the same borderlands universe as *campesinos* or immigrant *maquila* workers in Baja California. Historians of Chinese, African American, and Mormon settlements in the U.S. Southwest and northern Mexico, for their part, may write for audiences who see the borderlands as peripheral to larger ethnic, cultural, and diasporic traditions. How can historians engage these stories, while at the same time challenging and transcending the boundaries that have traditionally given them meaning?

We offer no easy answers to these questions. Historians might *start*, however, by looking for common denominators. What historical processes helped shape both the U.S. Southwest and northern Mexico? Perhaps the most compelling place to begin is with the nation itself, for despite their differences, all border people share a legacy of distance and isolation from the national centers of the United States and Mexico. This history of living at the frontiers of the body politic is a long one, beginning centuries before independent nations emerged on the American scene. Few border people considered themselves peripheral—most saw their own communities as central—but empires and nations mattered, and part of what made frontiers and borders distinctive was their position at the edges of states and state making. Thus a useful starting point for borderlands history is to ask what happened when fuzzy and mobile frontiers—first of empires, then nations—gave way to more fixed national boundaries. And no less importantly, what happened when people and places at the frontiers of state rule and power began to find themselves at a new crossroads *between* those nations that sought to contain them?

These questions are even more intriguing because both Mexican and U.S. scholars have pondered them, yet never together and never in the same way. Historian Friedrich Katz, for instance, placed Mexican frontiers and borders within a larger regional narrative in 1981. Until the late nineteenth century, he wrote, the northern border states of Sonora, Chihuahua, and Coahuila were "frontier" provinces, marked among other things by their political and economic isolation from Mexico City. Yet by the century's end, the influx of U.S. capital and the expansion of Mexican state power into the northern periphery had transformed the frontier into the "border." "What had once been largely beyond the reach of any country," he argued, "was now within the reach of two countries at once."[50] More than the border itself, new relationships brought nations together. Inspired by visions of a new "modern" age, statesmen, entrepreneurs, and capitalists in the United States and Mexico made laws, investments, and transnational alliances to facilitate the flow of technology, capital, and workers across the border. As "modernizing" elites dispossessed community lands, push into the transnational wage sector joined pull, as uprooted rural people began to seek new wage opportunities on both sides of the border. As the frontier became the border, in other words, people found themselves caught in a new web of transnational relationships, which changed what it meant to be a resident of the Mexican North.

In 1993, western historians William Cronon, George Miles, and Jay Gitlin offered a similar way of thinking about frontiers and borders from a U.S. perspective. Like Katz, they were seeking to connect an earlier frontier history—which Frederick Jackson Turner declared "closed" in the 1890s—to a later twentieth-century regional history. Rather than preserving the disjuncture between older and newer stories, they proposed that historians study how frontier America "became western."[51] Katz's "frontier-to-border" and Cronon, Miles, and Gitlin's "frontier-to-region" narratives charted similar plotlines, underscoring parallel processes of incorporation that tied the Mexican and U.S. peripheries to emerging nations and global markets. Yet where Katz saw these economic and political changes as border phenomena that moved northern Mexico onto a new transnational stage, western historians remained trapped within a nation-bound paradigm. Even though the West had also been connected to two nations by political alliances and circuits of labor and capital, western historians deemphasized these linkages; Mexicans became significant only when they crossed the border. The fact that these migrants were also part of a broader cultural, economic, and political history of Mexico seemed to matter less to scholars working from what was—and what remains—a largely a priori notion of regional history.[52]

Latin Americanist Jeremy Adelman and U.S. historian Stephen Aron attempted to move beyond this nation-centered vision in their important, but much-contested, 1999 essay "From Borderlands to Borders."[53] Adelman and Aron also saw a shift in economic, cultural, and political relationships in the nineteenth century, but saw it as part of a larger continent-wide transition from imperial to national America. Borderlands between North American empires and native peoples had been fluid throughout the eighteenth century, they argued, but this changed in the early nineteenth century, when "colonial borderlands gave way to national borders." As newly independent "states of North America enjoyed unrivaled authority to confer or deny rights to peoples within their borders," they went on to propose, "borderlanders became 'ethnics'—minorities distinguished by phenotype or language from the 'national' majority." In other words, with the rise of the hegemony of American nation-states, borderlands became "bordered" lands, and history was, from that point forward, nationally and ethnically bounded.[54]

This argument—that the rise of American nation-states drew the curtain on earlier borderland encounters and transformations—echoed an argument that Howard Lamar and Leonard Thompson had made two decades earlier.[55] In their classic study *The Frontier in History*, Lamar and Thompson revised Frederick Jackson Turner's notion of the "closing" frontier for use in comparative frontier contexts. Frontier processes come to an end, they argued, "when one group establishes political power over the other"; after this, the history of a given region became "relations of ethnicity and class within a single society."[56] Both visions of the periphery—Adelman and Aron's continental epic of hardening borders, and Lamar and Thompson's comparative tale of closing frontiers—build on similar ideas of hegemony. Once nation-states are able to map out and police their borders, the argument runs, people follow suit. Whether they have become part of a single society, or a national minority (or majority), the human subjects of these narratives shed their frontier skins and embrace new identities and histories grounded in a nation-bound "ethnicity."

If Cronon, Miles, and Gitlin exclude Mexico from their "western" story, Adelman and Aron go farther. Their vision of an increased national bounding of American space is diametrically opposed to Katz's idea of the postfrontier "border" as a place linked to two nations at once. As a narrative, the "borderlands-to-borders" scheme is compelling, but it lacks a firm evidentiary base. Adelman and Aron never cross the border between colonial and national histories long enough to show how nations actually go about the business of "fixing" and transforming border society. And if recent scholarship on the relationship between states and border people in northern Mexico is an indication, history undermines Adelman and Aron's claims as much as it supports them. Daniel Nugent and Ana María Alonso have demonstrated how peasants in Chihuahua used frontier-based claims to land and power to challenge the hegemonic power of the state in the twentieth century, thereby forging alternative political and ethnic identities to resist those imposed on them from the center.[57] In a similar vein, Evelyn Hu-DeHart and Josiah Heyman show how Yaquis and Mexicans used the border to cross back and forth between the transnational waged world and rural villages in Mexico, evading conventional ethnic, national, and class categories for years.[58] Demonstrating how difficult it was for state and national elites to "fix" identity and history by simply drawing borders, these scholars propose that, if anything, such mappings further blurred the boundaries of ethnicity and power.

Nation formation and the expansion of world markets, in short, transformed North American frontiers, but how they did so, and what categories of borderlands or "bordered lands" emerged from the transformation remains one of the most complex and unresolved issues of borderlands history. It is most important to recognize the *diversity* of narratives that can carry one across the frontier and "postfrontier" divide. If anything, the fact that these stories can take very different trajectories should alert us to the pitfalls of bounding this terrain too tightly. Borderland historians should instead seek more open-ended tales, since from one specific borderlands history to the next, they will likely find elements of each of the plotlines discussed so far. Considering these narratives in the aggregate, one factor that stands out, perhaps above all, is the dynamic tension between forces that create (regionally or nationally) "bordered" places, and those that transnationalize, or put people and places in "reach of two nations at once." By underscoring this basic tension between division and connection, we can study what Michiel Baud and Willem Van Schendel call the "paradoxical character" of borderlands. "Borders create political, social, and cultural distinctions," Baud and Van Schendel explain, "but simultaneously imply the existence of (new) networks and systems of interaction across them."[59]

As we develop more open-ended narratives, we should still be sensitive to turning points in borderlands history. Adelman and Aron have already sketched in broad strokes one of the most basic of these: the transformation of America from a meeting ground of natives and newcomers to a land of independent nations. In the Mexican North and U.S. Southwest, this shift gave rise to what Andrés Reséndez describes elsewhere as a tension between rituals and profits, as frontier residents repositioned themselves simultaneously within newly emerging national identities and transnational commercial networks.[60] The U.S.-Mexico War must figure at least as prominently, since it not only resulted in a newly divided frontier but also cast a shadow over U.S.-Mexican border relations for decades to come. Following the Treaty of Guadalupe Hidalgo and Gadsden Purchase, efforts by the United States and Mexico to incorporate their adjoining peripheries gave rise to a legacy of social conflict and resistance. Cross-border alliances in the Apache wars, and efforts to subdue such "bandits" as Juan Cortina in South Texas and Henry Crabb in Sonora, were part of a larger effort by statesmen and economic elites to remove "obstacles" to both transnational development and liberal nation making.[61]

Increasingly, Mexicans and Americans would approach the border future through twin lenses of "progress" and "modernization." Beginning in the 1880s, an industrial age of railroads and large-scale capitalist development systematically brought the "periphery" more in touch with the "center," as the borderlands entered what was known in Mexico as the Porfiriato (named after President Porfirio Díaz), and in the United States as the Gilded Age. From 1880 to 1910 in Mexico, the transnational connections discussed by Friedrich Katz amplified the tensions between national identities and transnational market ties that characterized the borderlands since the early nineteenth century, and gradually made these tensions more modern. In Mexico this modernizing circuitry, which connected the border region more intimately to both Mexico and the United States, was grounded in new fiscal reforms, the opening of the border to investment, the dispossession of land, and the rise of a national police to maintain at least the appearance of law and order.[62] Similar processes of dispossession, "modernization," and surveillance began to unfold north of the border.[63] By the twentieth century, modernizing visions were dominant in the American Southwest and Mexican North, while the border itself—increasingly a magnet for capital, labor, and resources—seemed less and less capable of bounding national space.

But with new connections came new boundaries. Already by the 1890s, Mexicans along the border and elsewhere had begun to resist the new political and economic order, often steered by the same liberal and "modernizing" forces that brought racial, economic, and political injustice to the borderlands in the first place. Revolts among Garzistas in South Texas,

Teresitas in Tomochíc, Chihuahua, and Nogales, Arizona, and "Las Gorras Blancas" in northern New Mexico in the 1890s gave way to other forms of resistance, including labor strikes among Mexican miners in Clifton, Arizona, in 1903 and Cananea, Sonora, in 1906, and the parallel expansion of new networks of "revolutionaries" in exile in the United States.[64] In 1910, winds of discontent in Mexico erupted into the Mexican Revolution, which created a new series of social, political, and economic boundaries in the borderlands. From the perspective of U.S. capitalists, the Revolution created a new landscape of disorder that motivated many U.S. corporations and families to flee Mexico for the safety of the United States.[65] Along with revolutionary battles, the flight of capital further "unsettled" Mexico for those who stayed behind.

If the military and economic dislocations of the Mexican Revolution closed earlier pathways of capital and labor, they opened new corridors of migration to the far north, as migration of Mexicans into the United States reached a new high. Many immigrants were refugees of the new political and economic regime, but some were transnational agents of revolution who used their position in the United States to bring social and political justice to Mexico. These border crossings were important not only for revolutionary exiles such as the Flores Magón brothers but also for the broader poetics of struggle—the *corridos*, newspaper essays, and new revolutionary ideas and identities—that they helped generate. "The discourse of the revolution knew no boundaries," notes Emma Pérez.[66] Meanwhile, the revolution helped incorporate the northern periphery even more fully into the Mexican center. Revolutionary leaders Pancho Villa and Pascual Orozco brought the north to the center as warrior heroes in the early years of the twentieth century, and in the 1920s Sonoran leaders Álvaro Obregón and Plutarco Calles took the reins of the Mexican presidency, applying northern traditions of pragmatism and "progress" to the reconstruction of the Mexican state.[67]

A central plank of postrevolutionary visions was the renewal of economic ties to the United States, ties that formerly benefited Obregón and Calles as entrepreneurs and statesmen, and which now promised to help renew national power. Meanwhile, industrial development in the U.S. Southwest during the 1920s pulled more Mexican workers north across the border. Yet just as new corridors of capital and labor seemed to be knitting the borderlands back together, new forms of nativism began to take root on both sides of the line. In the U.S. Southwest, nativism coincided with new forms of bureaucratic control, as efforts to limit immigration between 1917 and 1924 (not always targeted at Mexicans) were joined by the formation of the U.S. Border Patrol in 1924. Meanwhile, in northern Mexico, xenophobic sentiments during the earlier years of the Mexican Revolution were refocused in the 1920s against the Chinese, sentiments that would eventually lead to their expulsion from Sonora in the early 1930s.[68] As some border people were excluded on the basis of race, others became subjects of efforts to incorporate local ethnic groups into the body politic. In Mexico, José Vasconcelos employed the concept of "the cosmic race" to incorporate rural Indians and mestizos into the postrevolutionary state, while reformers in the border state of New Mexico drew explicitly on Vasconcelos's model to incorporate rural Indians and Hispanos into a new multicultural vision of national identity.[69]

By the 1930s, nationalism, cultural and economic incorporation, and bureaucratic state making converged to map new divisions in the U.S.-Mexico borderlands. Nativist sentiments and economic anxieties in 1930 motivated the repatriation of Mexicans from the U.S. Southwest, while the continental downswings of the Great Depression cut deeply into the economic bonds between northern Mexico and the U.S. Southwest. U.S. mining and agricultural enterprises in Mexico shut down, expelling workers into the surrounding countryside. Meanwhile, by the late 1930s, Mexico and the United States moved state making to a new nationalistic and bureaucratic level under the Cárdenas and Roosevelt administrations. In many ways, it was as if the borderlands between nations—perennially fluid and porous to movements from one side to the other—were finally starting to harden into the clearly marked boundaries that appeared on most national maps. For a while, the borderlands had seemingly become "bordered" lands. But it would only be for a while. With the onset of World War II, booming wartime markets, and the new Bracero program in the 1940s, Mexican migrants flowed north, while U.S. capitalists took advantage of the improved economic climate in Mexico (and new invitations to foreign investors) to create new transnational enterprises. As closed doors swung open again, and as capital, people, and things began to move across space more profoundly than ever, the borderlands would enter new, uncertain storied terrain.

These larger transnational processes, from the 1820s to the 1940s, underpin what we propose as the "formative" era of modern borderlands history. In this era of ferment, marked by a simultaneous opening and closing of borders, the borderlands assumed their present shape. Historians who wish to understand how borders in our new global era are simultaneously fading and growing stronger than ever may do well to look at this history, for the contemporary tug of war between the transnational and national in the borderlands has a much deeper history than many scholars realize. By plotting a rough chronology of these formative changes, we seek to orient the reader rather than canonize turning points in borderland history. The essays in this volume will, in fact, work as much to complicate this narrative as to reinforce it. Although we have put these essays in rough chronological order, we have organized them primarily around common themes and points of potential dialogue. Some offer new lenses for looking at old stories. Others focus on subjects that have been ignored or glossed over in previous histories. Together, they suggest the wide range of ways that readers can approach the transnational American past, while offering a starting point for future research in this fascinating scholarly crossroads.

Part One, "Frontier Legacies," looks at two borderlands at the cusp of the colonial and national periods—Texas and California—and challenges our assumptions about these transnational frontiers. Raúl Ramos debunks the stereotype that Indians and Mexicans in Texas were always fighting each other, demonstrating how Tejanos in Béxar (today San Antonio) developed more sophisticated strategies of peace and cooperation that stood in contrast to earlier colonial and later U.S. Indian policies. This carefully rendered portrait of ethnic relations forces us to rethink popular images of frontier "fighting culture" in the Mexican North. In a similar revisionist vein, Louise Pubols notes that the tendency to let Mariano Guadalupe Vallejo's story of opportunism and destruction reflect the Californio elite in general negates legacies of "hard-earned adaptation and persistence" pursued by other clans such as the de la Guerra family of Santa Barbara. Far from being opportunists who sold out their people, the de la Guerras refashioned relations of patriarchy to sustain Californio political power for decades after the U.S. conquest. Both authors urge us to rethink frontier stories by revisiting ethnic relations. It is not that Vallejo did not make a fatal miscalculation when he welcomed Anglo interlopers to California or that Tejanos did not fight Indians, but rather that scholarly and popular visions have not fully reflected the richness and heterogeneity of Mexican responses to the others they encountered in the frontier between nations.

Part Two, "Borderland Stories," examines the many literary worlds that emerged in the nineteenth-century borderlands and complicates Benedict Anderson's notion of the imagined national community by asking what other kinds of communities and competing literary traditions were forged in the borderlands. Bárbara Reyes focuses on competing narratives of native woman Bárbara Gandiaga's role in the murder of a Dominican priest in Baja California in 1803, showing how patriarchal groups reconstructed her actions and identity for distinct ends. Colonial authorities told tales that criminalized Gandiaga, and justified their control over the native population, but fifty years later, Baja Californianos reappropriated her as an anticlerical heroine in local stories that bolstered new forms of national power in the borderlands. Andrés Reséndez's study of how Mexicans, Indians, and Anglo-Americans produced alternative narratives about the 1841 Santa Fe Expedition further complicates our view of literary traditions in the early national borderlands. Even though some groups had power to disseminate their views more widely, others effectively employed competing literary forms—from broadsides to winter counts—to extract power and meaning from shifting regional conditions. Moving to a global scale, Elliott Young looks at travel narratives by border journalist and revolutionary Ignacio Martínez, arguing that his treatment of European imperialism and anticolonial struggles in Asia and Africa helped him articulate alternative visions of modernity at the border. A political exile who sought legitimization in the global marketplace, Martínez brought the world home to the border in ways that challenged Anglo-American and European models, while reproducing many of the assumptions that undergirded imperialism.

Part Three, "Transnational Identities," examines less visible border crossers, such as African Americans, Chinese, and Europeans, that challenge the "brown-white" ethnoracial dyad that many see as paradigmatic of the borderlands. Grace Delgado's study of Chinese merchants and laborers in the Arizona-Sonora border region, and Karl Jacoby's examination of an African American colony in northern Mexico, reveal a more complex racial picture of the borderlands. These alternative stories complicate our understandings of labor and racial ideologies in a transnational setting, but they also offer a richer portrait of the motivations and personal histories that led people to move back and forth across the line. Samuel Truett's inquiry into the transnational life and times of Russian-German-Mexican-American gendarme Emilio Kosterlitzky adds new national bearings to the mix. Whether their point of origin was China, the U.S. South, or Russia, these people and their histories expand our vision of borderland possibilities and limitations. African American entrepreneur William H. Ellis could "pass" as Mexican or Cuban, but African American colonists he led into Mexico from Alabama faced more rigid boundaries of race and class. Likewise, as Grace Delgado notes, Chinese merchants often used their class standing to cross national borders closed to Chinese laborers, while in other instances, crossings were based more on race or local political alliance. Finally, Samuel Truett shows how customs guard and officer Emilio Kosterlitzky—who migrated from Russia to Mexico, and later as a political exile to the United States—negotiated transnational space along twin axes of power and identity. An enforcer of ever-hardening borders between the United States and Mexico, his proper national place remained ambiguous and subject to profound negotiation.

Part Four, "Body Politics," demonstrates how, by the early twentieth century, the borders of national, ethnic, and gendered bodies were being remapped in profoundly new and modern ways. This reflected an ongoing tension between the opening and closing of borders—increasingly policed, the borderlands never became truly *bordered* lands—but it also revealed new relationships between gender, ethnicity, and the nation-state. Benjamin Johnson and Alexandra Stern study these relationships against a backdrop of state efforts to domesticate the borderlands by quelling rebellions and patrolling boundaries. Johnson explores tensions between Tejano Progressives and those who backed a racial rebellion in 1915 known as the Plan de San Diego uprising. While this revolt was the last armed rebellion by Mexican Americans in Texas, the later rise of civil rights and more militant political movements after the 1920s suggests that the "order" that had been established by the state and its associated elites remained tenuous and vulnerable to challenge. For their part, Tejano Progressives took these boundary disputes as a starting point for mapping out a new place *within* the United States. Stern turns to the Anglo-American community, and particularly to the Texas Rangers and the U.S. Border Patrol. Just as Mexican revolutionaries were being tamed in South Texas, the Rangers' primitive masculinity and martial ideals were being domesticated in the 1920s under the new Border Patrol. This compassionate masculinity, associated with the rise of the welfare state, signaled even greater intervention of the state in domestic life as well as on the border. Both these essays suggest that campaigns to patrol the boundaries between the United States and Mexico and to protect a vulnerable, feminized nation—as well as ethnic communities *within* the body politic—are persistent features of the borderlands, much like the enduring political rhetoric of order, disorder, invasion, and containment that links the border to its "frontier" past even today.

The contributors to this volume ultimately take wide-ranging pathways in and out of the continental crossroads. Readers will observe differences and even contradictions among the essays. However, all of the authors address one central issue: the construction and negotiation of borderlands identity. Perhaps this is because it is precisely the nation's edge where difference from others is marked out with fences, gates, and other signs and systems of control. It is, after all, upon entering and exiting nations that one is required to produce a document (usually a passport) declaring one's official identity.

When we look at identity in the borderlands, what we find is not a simple story of Mexicans on one side and North Americans on the other, or even a simple story of South-North or East-West relationships. Instead, we discover a multiplicity of overlapping and competing histories not only of Mexicans and Anglo-Americans but also of Californios, Tejanos, Sonorenses, native peoples, African Americans, Asian Americans, and European Americans. When these different American groups met in the borderlands, the encounter was sometimes peaceful, often violent, and always contested. As we follow their stories, we encounter a complex web of human trajectories leading North, South, East, and West. This collection not only suggests multiple pathways into this complex historical terrain—often challenging long-held assumptions about the borderlands and their histories—but it ultimately offers new road maps and compass bearings for our ongoing transnational journeys into the greater American past.

Notes

1 Eric R. Wolf, *Europe and the People without History* (Berkeley: University of California Press, 1982), 3–4.

2 See Benedict Anderson, *Imagined Communities: Reflections on the Origin and Spread of Nationalism* (London: Verso/NLB, 1983).

3 Charles S. Maier, "Consigning the Twentieth Century to History: Alternative Narratives for the Modern Era," *American Historical Review* 105 (June 2000): 807–31.

4 Herbert Eugene Bolton, *The Spanish Borderlands: A Chronical of Old Florida and the Southwest* (New Haven: Yale University Press, 1921). Bolton's scholarship was known before 1921, but this book gave "borderlands" history its name.

5 David J. Weber, "Turner, the Boltonians, and the Borderlands," *American Historical Review* 91:1 (February 1986): 66–81, and Albert Hurtado, "Parkmanizing the Spanish Borderlands: Bolton, Turner, and the Historians' World," *Western Historical Quarterly* 26:2 (Summer 1995): 149–67.

6 John Francis Bannon, *The Spanish Borderlands Frontier, 1513–1821* (New York: Holt, Rinehart, and Winston, 1970).

7 Richard Griswold del Castillo, "New Perspectives on the Mexican and American Borderlands," *Latin American Research Review* 19:1 (1984): 199. This was true in a very literal sense, since Bolton's students went on to become leading scholars in both U.S. and Latin American history, with some working in both fields.

8 See, for example, Carlos E. Castañeda, *Our Catholic Heritage in Texas, 1519–1936* (Austin: Van Boeckman-Jones Co., 1936–58); George I. Sánchez, *Forgotten People: A Study of New Mexicans* (Albuquerque: University of New Mexico Press, 1940); Carey McWilliams, *North from Mexico: The Spanish-Speaking People of the United States* (New York: Greenwood Press, 1968 [1950]); and Américo Paredes, *"With His Pistol in His Hand": A Border Ballad and Its Hero* (Austin: University of Texas Press, 1959).

9 See David G. Gutiérrez, "The Third Generation: Reflections on Recent Chicano Historiography," *Mexican Studies/Estudios Mexicanos* 5:2 (Summer 1989): 281–96, and "Significant to Whom? Mexican Americans and the History of the American West," in *A New Significance: Re-Envisioning the History of the American West*, ed. Clyde A. Milner II (New York: Oxford University Press, 1996), 67–89, for discussion of these trends. See, for key examples of this work, Juan Gómez-Quiñones, "Research Notes on the Twentieth Century," *Aztlán* 1 (Spring 1970): 115–32; Rodolfo Acuña, *Occupied America: The Chicano's Struggle for Liberation* (San Francisco: Canfield Press, 1972); Mario Barrera, *Race and Class in the Southwest: A Theory of Racial Inequality* (Notre Dame: University of Notre Dame Press, 1979); Albert Camarillo, *Chicanos in a Changing Society: From Mexican Pueblos to American Barrios in Santa Barbara and Southern California* (Cambridge: Harvard University Press, 1979); Mario T. García, *Desert Immigrants: The Mexicans of El Paso, 1880–1920* (New Haven: Yale University Press, 1981); Ricardo Romo, *East Los Angeles: History of a Barrio* (Austin: University of Texas Press, 1983); Thomas E. Sheridan, *Los Tucsonenses: The Mexican*

Community in Tucson, 1854–1941 (Tucson: University of Arizona Press, 1986); Sarah Deutsch, *No Separate Refuge: Culture, Class, and Gender on an Anglo-Hispanic Frontier in the American Southwest, 1880–1940* (New York: Oxford University Press, 1987); David Montejano, *Anglos and Mexicans in the Making of Texas* (Austin: University of Texas Press, 1987); Robert R. Álvarez Jr., *Familia: Migration and Adaptation in Baja and Alta California, 1800–1975* (Berkeley: University of California Press, 1987), and Vicki L. Ruiz, *Cannery Women, Cannery Lives: Mexican Women, Unionization, and the California Food Processing Industry, 1930–1950* (Albuquerque: University of New Mexico Press, 1987).

10 See Manuel Patricio Servín, "California's Hispanic Heritage: A View into the Spanish Myth," *Journal of San Diego History* 19 (1973): 1–9, and the response of Ralph Vigil, "The Hispanic Heritage and the Borderlands," *Journal of San Diego History* 19 (1973): 33, 38–39, as well as the discussion of these works in *New Spain's Far Northern Frontier: Essays on Spain in the American West, 1540–1821*, ed. David J. Weber (Dallas: Southern Methodist University, 1979), 117–18.

11 Acuña, *Occupied America*, and Gómez-Quiñones, "Research Notes."

12 John R. Chávez, *Lost Land: The Chicano Image of the Southwest* (Albuquerque: University of New Mexico Press, 1984), 129–55.

13 Ralph H. Vigil, "The New Borderlands History: A Critique," *New Mexico Historical Review* 48:3 (July 1973): 200.

14 Donald E. Worcester, "The Significance of the Spanish Borderlands to the United States," *Western Historical Quarterly* 7 (January 1976): 5–18. Worcester earned his M.A. under Bolton and went on to earn his Ph.D. at Berkeley in 1947 immediately after Bolton retired, so I call him a Bolton student here in a somewhat loose sense.

15 David J. Weber, *The Mexican Frontier, 1821–1848: The American Southwest under Mexico* (Albuquerque: University of New Mexico Press, 1982).

16 David J. Weber, "John Francis Bannon and the Historiography of the Spanish Borderlands: Retrospect and Prospect," *Journal of the Southwest* 29 (Winter 1987): 331–63.

17 Ramón A. Gutiérrez, *When Jesus Came, the Corn Mothers Went Away: Marriage, Sexuality, and Power in New Mexico, 1500–1846* (Stanford: Stanford University Press, 1991); Rosaura Sánchez, *Telling Identities: The Californio Testimonios* (Minneapolis: University of Minnesota Press, 1995); and Antonia I. Castañeda, "Presidarias y Pobladoras: Spanish-Mexican Women in Frontier Monterey, Alta California, 1770–1821" (Ph.D. diss., Stanford University, 1990).

18 Cynthia Radding, *Wandering Peoples: Colonialism, Ethnic Spaces, and Ecological Frontiers in Northwestern Mexico, 1700–1850* (Durham: Duke University Press, 1997); Jesús F. de la Teja, *San Antonio de Béxar: A Community on New Spain's Northern Frontier* (Albuquerque: University of New Mexico Press, 1995); Cheryl English Martin, *Governance and Society in Colonial Mexico: Chihuahua in the Eighteenth Century* (Stanford: Stanford University Press, 1996); Leslie S.

Offutt, *Saltillo, 1770–1810: Town and Region in the Mexican North* (Tucson: University of Arizona Press, 2001); Ana María Alonso, *Thread of Blood: Colonialism, Revolution, and Gender on Mexico's Northern Frontier* (Tucson: University of Arizona Press, 1995); Ross Frank, *From Settler to Citizen: New Mexican Economic Development and the Creation of Vecino Society, 1750–1820* (Berkeley: University of California Press, 2000); Susan M. Deeds, *Defiance and Deference in Mexico's Colonial North: Indians under Spanish Rule in Nueva Vizcaya* (Austin: University of Texas Press, 2003); Cecilia Sheridan, *Anónimos y desterrados: La contienda por el "sitio que llaman de Quauyla," siglos XVI–XVIII* (México, D.F.: CIESAS: M.A. Porrúa Grupo Editorial, 2000); and James Brooks, *Captives and Cousins: Slavery, Kinship, and Community in the Southwest Borderlands* (Chapel Hill: University of North Carolina Press, 2002). Also see the recent essays by these authors and others in Robert H. Jackson, ed., *New Views of Borderlands History* (Albuquerque: University of New Mexico Press, 1998).

19 This discussion list, known as "Spanbord," is remarkably cutting edge in its crossing of other borders, notably that between professional historians and archaeologists.

20 To be fair, Mexicans and Americans also have difficulties imagining common ground in the Spanish borderlands, a notion that resonates more with North Americans than with Mexicans. See José Cuello, "Beyond the 'Borderlands' is the North of Colonial Mexico: A Latin Americanist Perspective to the Study of the Mexican North and the United States Southwest," *Proceedings of the Pacific Coast Council of Latin American Studies* 9 (1982): 1–24, but see the call to counter this trend in Cuauhtémoc Velasco, "Historiografía de un territorio perdido," *Historias* 40 (April–September 1998): 21–27.

21 For the Pimería Alta, one might start with James E. Officer, *Hispanic Arizona, 1536–1856* (Tucson: University of Arizona Press, 1987). After 1856, one might turn to Stuart F. Voss, *On the Periphery of Nineteenth-Century Mexico: Sonora and Sinaloa, 1810–1877* (Tucson: University of Arizona Press, 1982), and Thomas E. Sheridan, *Arizona: A History* (Tucson: University of Arizona Press, 1995). A book that examines some of the links between these otherwise distinct narrative domains is James S. Griffith, *A Shared Space: Folklife in the Arizona-Sonora Borderlands* (Logan, Utah: Utah State University Press, 1995).

22 See Richard Francaviglia, "Introduction," in *Essays on the Changing Images of the Southwest*, ed. Richard Francaviglia and David Narrett (College Station: Published for the University of Texas at Arlington by Texas A&M University Press, 1994), and Burl Noggle, "Anglo Observers of the Southwest Borderlands, 1825–1890: The Rise of a Concept," *Arizona and the West* 1:1 (1959): 105–31.

23 For a discussion of these elements in the creation of the idea of the Southwest, see Charles H. Montgomery, *The Spanish Redemption: Heritage, Power, and Loss on New Mexico's Upper Rio Grande* (Berkeley: University of California Press, 2002).

24 Noggle, "Anglo Observers," 105, Francaviglia, "Introduction."

25 Ross Calvin, *Sky Determines: An Interpretation of the Southwest* (New York: Macmillan, 1934); Paul Horgan, *The Heroic Triad: Essays in the Social Energies of Three Southwestern Cultures* (New York: Holt, Rinehart and Winston, 1970); Evon Z. Vogt, *People of Rimrock: A Study of Values in Five Cultures* (Cambridge: Harvard University Press, 1966); Edward H. Spicer and Raymond H. Thompson, eds., *Plural Society in the Southwest* (New York: Interbook, 1972); Richard White, *The Roots of Dependency: Subsistence, Environment, and Social Change among the Choctaws, Pawnees, and Navajos* (Lincoln: University of Nebraska Press, 1983); Howard R. Lamar, *The Far Southwest, 1846–1912: A Territorial History* (New Haven: Yale University Press, 1966); Montejano, *Anglos and Mexicans*; Edward H. Spicer, *Cycles of Conquest: The Impact of Spain, Mexico, and the United States on the Indians of the Southwest, 1533–1960* (Tucson: University of Arizona Press, 1962); D. W. Meinig, *Southwest: Three Peoples in Geographical Change* (New York: Oxford University Press, 1971); and Thomas D. Hall, *Social Change in the Southwest, 1350–1880* (Lawrence: University Press of Kansas, 1989).

26 See discussion, for instance, in Walter Nugent, "Where Is the American West?' Report on a Survey," *Montana, The Magazine of Western History* 42 (Summer 1992): 2–23.

27 The only other U.S. region that has such a clear position in the American mind is the American South, which holds that place largely because of slavery and the Civil War, two issues that struck to the very core of national identity.

28 Miguel León-Portilla, "The Norteño Variety of Mexican Culture: An Ethnohistorical Approach," in *Plural Society in the Southwest*, ed. Edward H. Spicer and Raymond H. Thompson (New York: Interbook, 1972), 77–114, and Barry Carr, "Las peculiaridades del norte mexicano, 1880–1927: Ensayo de interpretación," *Historia mexicana* 22 (January–March 1973): 320–46.

29 Velasco, "Historiografía de un territorio perdido," 21–22.

30 Friedrich Katz, *The Secret War in Mexico: Europe, the United States, and the Mexican Revolution* (Chicago: University of Chicago Press, 1981); Hectór Aguilar Camín, *La frontera nómada: Sonora y la Revolución Mexicana* (México: Siglo Veintiuno Editores, 1977); Luis Aboites Aguilar, *Norte precario: Poblamiento y colonización en México, 1760–1940* (México: El Colegio de México, Centro de Estudios Históricos: Centro de Investigaciones y Estudios Superiores en Antropología Social, 1995); Mario Cerutti, *Burguesía, capitales e industria en el norte de México: Monterrey y su ámbito regional (1850–1910)* (México: Alianza Editorial; Monterrey: Facultad de Filosofía y Letras de la Universidad Autónoma de Nuevo León, 1992), Ana María Alonso, *Thread of Blood*; Daniel Nugent, *Spent Cartridges of Revolution: An Anthropological History of Namiquipa, Chihuahua* (Chicago: University of Chicago Press, 1993); Sergio Ortega Noriega, *Un ensayo de historia regional: El noroeste de México, 1530–1880* (México: Universidad Nacional Autónoma de México, Instituto de Investigaciones Históricas, 1993);

Miguel Tinker Salas, *In the Shadow of the Eagles: Sonora and the Transformation of the Border during the Porfiriato* (Berkeley: University of California Press, 1997); Victor Orozco, *Las guerras indias en la historia de Chihuahua* (México: Consejo Nacional para la Cultura y las Artes, 1992); Paul Vanderwood, *The Power of God against the Guns of Government: Religious Upheaval in Mexico at the Turn of the Nineteenth Century* (Stanford: Stanford University Press, 1998); and Juan Mora-Torres, *The Making of the Mexican Border: The State, Capitalism, and Society in Nuevo León, 1848–1910* (Austin: University of Texas Press, 2001). For an overview of historiographical trends, see Velasco, "Historiografía," but also see Thomas Benjamin, "Regionalizing the Revolution: The Many Mexicos in Revolutionary Historiography," in *Provinces of the Revolution: Essays on Regional Mexican History, 1910–1929*, ed. Thomas Benjamin and Mark Wasserman (Albuquerque: University of New Mexico Press, 1990), 319–57, for the rise of the "many Mexicos" paradigm.

31   See, for instance, Cerutti, *Burguesía, capitales e industria*; Ortega Noriega, *Ensayo de historia regional*; and José Cuello, *El norte, el noroeste y Saltillo en la historia colonial de México* (Saltillo: Archivo Municipal de Saltillo, R. Ayuntamiento de Saltillo, 1990).

32   The application of Turnerian thought to the Mexican North can be found in the work of Friedrich Katz, e.g., *Secret War in Mexico*, 18–21. Katz students Daniel Nugent and Ana María Alonso have also carried similar assumptions into their more recent ethnohistories of Chihuahua. See Nugent, *Spent Cartridges*, and Alonso, *Thread of Blood*. Nugent and Alonso have acknowledged and historicized the political bases of state-centered (as well as popular) visions of norteño history, yet what is still needed is a rigorous examination of the role that regional political rhetoric has played in promoting these visions. A good step in this direction can be found in Stuart Voss's history of nineteenth-century Sonora and Sinaloa, *On the Periphery of Nineteenth-Century Mexico*.

33   Cerutti, *Burguesía, capitales e industria*, and Ortega Noriega, *Ensayo de historia regional*.

34   Gloria Anzaldúa, *Borderlands/La Frontera = The New Mestiza* (San Francisco: Aunt Lute Books, 1987); Jose Limón, *Dancing with the Devil: Society and Cultural Poetics in Mexican-American South Texas* (Madison: University of Wisconsin Press, 1994); Claire Fox, *The Fence and the River: Culture and Politics at the U.S.-Mexico Border* (Minneapolis: University of Minnesota Press, 1999); Roger Christopher Rouse, "Mexican Migration to the United States: Family Relations in the Development of a Transnational Migrant Circuit" (Ph.D. diss., Stanford University, 1989); Caren Kaplan, Norma Alarcón, and Minoo Moallem, eds., *Between Woman and Nation: Nationalisms, Transnational Feminisms, and the State* (Durham: Duke University Press, 1999); Pablo Vila, *Crossing Borders, Reinforcing Borders: Social Categories, Metaphors, and Narrative Identities on the U.S.-Mexico Frontier* (Austin: University of Texas Press, 2000); and Emma

Pérez, *The Decolonial Imaginary: Writing Chicanas into History* (Bloomington: Indiana University Press, 1999).

35 Alex Saragoza, "Recent Chicano Historiography," *Aztlan* 19:1 (1990): 9.

36 The differences between Acuña's first (1972) and third edition (1988) of *Occupied America* illustrate the move within the scholarship toward an increasingly complex view of the Mexican American community. Two recent works that reflect the complexities of border race, class, and gender identities are Deena J. González, *Refusing the Favor: The Spanish-Mexican Women of Santa Fe, 1820–1880* (Oxford: Oxford University Press, 1999), and Linda Gordon, *The Great Arizona Orphan Abduction* (Cambridge: Harvard University Press, 1999).

37 Brooks, *Captives and Cousins.*

38 For some of the best work in this area, see Spicer, *Cycles of Conquest,* Edwin R. Sweeney, *Cochise, Chiricahua Apache Chief* (Norman: University of Oklahoma Press, 1991); William B. Griffen, *Apaches at War and Peace: The Janos Presidio, 1750–1858* (Albuquerque: University of New Mexico Press, 1988); William L. Merrill, *Rarámuri Souls: Knowledge and Social Process in Northern Mexico* (Washington, D.C.: Smithsonian Institution Press, 1988); Bernard Fontana, *Of Earth and Little Rain: The Papago Indians* (Tucson: University of Arizona Press, 1989); Thomas Kavanagh, *Comanche Political History: An Ethnohistorical Perspective, 1706–1875* (Lincoln: University of Nebraska Press, 1996); and Evelyn Hu-DeHart, *Yaqui Resistance and Survival: The Struggle for Land and Autonomy, 1821–1910* (Madison: University of Wisconsin Press, 1984).

39 See, for instance, Anita Endrezze, *Throwing Fire at the Sun, Water at the Moon* (Tucson: University of Arizona Press, 2000), and Frances Manuel and Deborah Neff, *Desert Indian Woman: Stories and Dreams* (Tucson: University of Arizona Press, 2001). Much of this native history comes to us more in the form of memory and poetics than in the scholarly "etic" form of most nonnative histories of native groups.

40 Neil F. Foley, *The White Scourge: Mexicans, Blacks and Poor Whites in Texas Cotton Culture* (Berkeley: University of California Press, 1997).

41 See essays by Hu-DeHart, Fong, and others in *The Chinese Experience in Arizona and Northern Mexico* (Tucson: Arizona Historical Society, 1980); Erika Lee, *At America's Gates: Chinese Immigration during the Exclusion Era, 1882–1943* (Chapel Hill: University of North Carolina Press, 2003); and Grace Delgado, "In the Age of Exclusion: Race, Region, and Chinese Identity in the Making of the Arizona-Sonora Borderlands, 1863–1943" (Ph.D. diss., UCLA, 2000).

42 See, for instance, B. Carmon Hardy, "The Mormon Colonies of Northern Mexico: A History, 1885–1912" (Ph.D. diss., Wayne State University, 1963); Kelly Lynn Hedges, "Plautdietsch and Huuchdietsch in Chihuahua: Language, Literacy and Identity among Old Colony Mennonites in Northern Mexico" (Ph.D. diss., Yale University, 1996); Gabriel Trujillo Muñoz, *Kitakaze (viento del norte): Los japoneses en Baja California* (Mexicali, B.C.: Ed. Larva, 1997); Rosalie

Schwartz, *Across the Rio to Freedom: U.S. Negroes in Mexico* (El Paso: Texas Western Press, 1975); James S. Griffith, *Southern Arizona Folk Arts* (Tucson: University of Arizona Press, 1988); Felipe A. Latorre, *The Mexican Kickapoo Indians* (Austin: University of Texas Press, 1975); and Michael Kearney, "The Effects of Transnational Culture, Economy, and Migration on Mixtec Identity in Oaxacalifornia," in *The Bubbling Cauldron: Race, Ethnicity, and the Urban Crisis,* ed. Michael Peter Smith and Joe R. Feagin (Minneapolis: University of Minnesota Press, 1995), 226–43.

43 Gary B. Nash, "The Hidden History of Mestizo America," *Journal of American History* (December 1995): 941–64.

44 Jack D. Forbes, "The Manipulation of Race, Caste and Identity," *Journal of Ethnic Studies* 17 (Winter 1990): 14.

45 Ramón Gutiérrez pointed in this direction in "Beyond Black and White: New Models for Understanding Race in the United States," Arthur L. Throckmorton Lecture, Lewis and Clark College, 7 February 2000.

46 See, for instance, Alonso, *Thread of Blood*, but also see Gail Bederman, *Manliness and Civilization: A Cultural History of Gender and Race in the United States, 1880–1917* (Chicago: University of Chicago Press, 1995).

47 Roger Rouse, "Mexican Migration and the Social Space of Postmodernism," in *Between Two Worlds: Mexican Immigrants in the United States,* ed. David Gutiérrez (Wilmington: Scholarly Resources, 1996), 254.

48 Néstor García Canclini, *Hybrid Cultures: Strategies for Entering and Leaving Modernity* (Minneapolis: University of Minnesota Press, 1995), 1.

49 Rouse, "Social Space of Postmodernism."

50 Katz, *Secret War in Mexico,* 7.

51 William Cronon, George Miles, and Jay Gitlin, "Becoming West: Toward a New Meaning in Western History," in *Under an Open Sky: Rethinking America's Western Past,* ed. William Cronon, George Miles, and Jay Gitlin (New York: Norton, 1992), 3–27.

52 Historian Richard White acknowledges this problem, writing, "the boundaries of the American West are a series of doors pretending to be walls." Richard White, *"It's Your Misfortune and None of My Own": A New History of the American West* (Norman: University of Oklahoma Press, 1991), 3. Yet few historians have passed through these doors in systematic ways. For a promising first step, see Paul Sabin, "Home and Abroad: The Two 'Wests' of Twentieth-Century United States History," *Pacific Historical Review* 66 (August 1997): 305–35.

53 Jeremy Adelman and Stephen Aron, "From Borderlands to Borders: Empires, Nation-States, and the Peoples in Between in North American History," *American Historical Review* 104:3 (June 1999): 814–41. See critiques of Adelman and Aron in the subsequent forum in *American Historical Review* 104:4 (October 1999): 1222–39.

54 Adelman and Aron, "Borderlands to Borders," 816–17, 840–41.

55 Leonard Thompson and Howard Lamar, "Comparative Frontier History," in *The Frontier in History: North America and South Africa Compared*, ed. Howard Lamar and Leonard Thompson (New Haven: Yale University Press, 1981), 3–31.

56 Ibid., 10.

57 Daniel Nugent and Ana María Alonso, "Multiple Selective Traditions in Agrarian Reform and Agrarian Struggle," in *Everyday Forms of State Formation: Revolution and the Negotiation of Rule in Modern Mexico*, ed. Gilbert M. Joseph and Daniel Nugent (Durham: Duke University Press, 1994), 209–46.

58 Josiah Heyman, *Life and Labor on the Border: Working People of Northeastern Sonora, Mexico, 1886–1986* (Tucson: University of Arizona Press, 1991), and Hu-DeHart, *Yaqui Resistance and Survival*.

59 Michiel Baud and Willem Van Schendel, "Toward a Comparative History of Borderlands," *Journal of World History* 8:2 (Fall 1997): 211–42.

60 Andrés Reséndez, *Changing National Identities at the Frontier: Texas and New Mexico, 1800–1850* (Cambridge: Cambridge University Press, 2004).

61 For the Apache wars, see Shelley Bowen Hatfield, *Chasing Shadows: Indians along the United States–Mexico Border, 1876–1911* (Albuquerque: University of New Mexico Press, 1999), and Sweeney, *Cochise*. For Juan Cortina and Henry Crabb, see Joseph Allen Stout, *The Liberators: Filibustering Expeditions into Mexico, 1848–1862, and the Last Thrust of Manifest Destiny* (Los Angeles: Westernlore Press, 1973), and Jerry D. Thompson, ed., *Juan Cortina and the Texas-Mexico Frontier, 1859–1877* (El Paso: Texas Western Press, 1994). For efforts to remove these obstacles, see David M. Pletcher, *The Diplomacy of Trade and Investment: American Economic Expansion in the Hemisphere, 1865–1900* (Columbia: University of Missouri Press, 1998), 79–91.

62 See Tinker Salas, *Shadow of the Eagles*, Mora-Torres, *Making of the Mexican Border*; John H. Coatsworth, *Growth against Development: The Economic Impact of Railroads in Porfirian Mexico* (DeKalb: Northern Illinois University Press, 1981); Robert H. Holden, *Mexico and the Survey of Public Lands: The Management of Modernization, 1876–1911* (DeKalb: Northern Illinois University Press, 1994); Paul J. Vanderwood, *Disorder and Progress: Bandits, Police, and Mexican Development* (Lincoln: University of Nebraska Press, 1981); and Samuel Truett, *Transnational Dreams: Transforming the U.S.-Mexico Borderlands* (New Haven: Yale University Press, forthcoming).

63 See Montejano, *Anglos and Mexicans*; Lamar, *The Far Southwest*; Sheridan, *Arizona*; William DeBuys, *Enchantment and Exploitation: The Life and Hard Times of a New Mexico Mountain Range* (Albuquerque: University of New Mexico Press, 1985); and Malcolm Ebright, *Land Grants and Lawsuits in Northern New Mexico* (Albuquerque: University of New Mexico Press, 1994).

64 For these conflicts, see Elliott Young, *Catarino Garza's Revolution on the Texas-Mexico Border* (Durham: Duke University Press, 2004), Paul J. Vanderwood,

The Power of God against the Guns of Government: Religious Upheaval in Mexico at the Turn of the Nineteenth Century (Stanford: Stanford University Press, 1998); Robert J. Rosenbaum, *Mexicano Resistance in the Southwest: "The Sacred Right of Self-Preservation"* (Austin: University of Texas Press, 1981); Gordon, *The Great Arizona Orphan Abduction*; and W. Dirk Raat, *Revoltosos: Mexico's Rebels in the United States, 1903–1923* (College Station: Texas A&M University Press, 1981).

65 Linda B. Hall and Don M. Coerver, *Revolution on the Border: The United States and Mexico, 1910–1920* (Albuquerque: University of New Mexico Press, 1988).

66 Pérez, *Decolonial Imaginary*, 56.

67 See Katz, *Secret War*; Friedrich Katz, *The Life and Times of Pancho Villa* (Stanford: Stanford University Press, 1998); Raat, *Revoltosos*; Hall and Coerver, *Revolution on the Border*; Aguilar Camín, *Sonora y la revolución mexicana*; Nugent, *Spent Cartridges*; and Alonso, *Thread of Blood*. For northerners and state making during the 1920s, see Carr, "Las peculiaridades del norte," and Héctor Aguilar Camín, "The Relevant Tradition: Sonoran Leaders in the Revolution," in *Caudillo and Peasant in the Mexican Revolution*, ed. D. A. Brading (Cambridge: Cambridge University Press, 1980).

68 See discussions of changing American notions toward (and efforts to control) immigration in David G. Gutiérrez, *Walls and Mirrors: Mexican Americans, Mexican Immigrants, and the Politics of Ethnicity* (Berkeley: University of California Press, 1995), and Lawrence A. Cardoso, *Mexican Emigration to the United States, 1897–1931* (Tucson: University of Arizona Press, 1980). For anti-Chinese campaigns, start with Leo Michael Dambourges Jacques, "The Anti-Chinese Campaigns in Sonora, Mexico, 1900–1931" (Ph.D. diss., University of Arizona, 1974), and José Jorge Gómez Izquierdo, *El movimiento antichino en México (1871–1934): Problemas del racismo y del nacionalismo durante la Revolución Mexicana* (México: Instituto Nacional de Antropología e Historia, 1992), but also see Lee, *At America's Gates*, esp. 151–87.

69 Suzanne Forrest, *The Preservation of the Village: New Mexico's Hispanics and the New Deal* (Albuquerque: University of New Mexico Press, 1989).

✳ *Frontier Legacies*

Finding the Balance:

Béxar in Mexican/Indian Relations

We should all live with the peace and security like the beautifully feathered birds that fly through the air livening the fields, and we should destroy the thieving birds that stir up trouble. —CHEROKEE CAPTAIN GUONIQUE, translated by Francisco Ruiz, 10 January 1823.[1]

In my opinion, the southern Lipans (Apache) are the most cruel of all the barbaric nations I know . . . I have been told by some of these Indians that they sometimes eat those they kill in war. —FRANCISCO RUIZ, *Report of Observations and Additional Information about Indians living in the Department of Texas*, 1828.[2]

In these accounts in the epigraphs above, Francisco Ruiz, the Indian commissioner for the Mexican Department of Texas, presented two indigenous groups as almost polar extremes. Ruiz's contact with a Cherokee leader emphasized peace and cooperation, while his notes on the Lipan Apache culture stressed war and barbarism. Depictions of indigenous people in narratives of the Spanish colonization of northern New Spain frequently raise these and other binomial opposites. In these stories, indigenous groups were either civilized or barbarous, made peace or war, hindered settlement or assimilated into missions. Indigenous people figured in with a larger set of obstacles to settlement on the frontier, including environment, geography, economic conditions, and the Spanish empire itself. Taking a closer look at the establishment of relations, both peaceful and bellicose, between a variety of indigenous groups and the citizens of a borderland settlement such as Béxar, Texas (present-day San Antonio) provides one way to move beyond binomial categories. Attention to indigenous relations at the local level helps us to understand these contacts as part of a more complex network of interests and identities. When seen in this light, relations with indigenous groups served not as a hindrance but a significant advantage in constructing Bexareño civil society and developing negotiating strategies with other actors, such as the Mexican state and Anglo-American immigrants.

For Bexareños, life on the frontier meant being aware of indigenous people on a daily basis.[3] While this awareness occasionally took the form of direct contact through trade or violence, indigenous people mainly affected the lives of Tejanos by controlling large portions of Texas, thus limiting Spanish colonization and movement. The focal period of this study examines indigenous relations at a critical juncture as Spanish colonial power waned and American economic and demographic pressure loomed. As the Mexican independence movement grew in strength in the early nineteenth century, colonial power on the frontier declined, leaving Tejanos on their own to establish security with the diverse and expanding number of indigenous groups in Texas. More than just an "Indian fighter" culture, Tejanos also participated in an ongoing search for negotiated peace with the people of the region.[4] The fierce and frequent violent interactions made a siege mentality among Bexareños and other Tejanos understandable and peace efforts more remarkable. The inhabitants of the border region craved stability and turned to town leaders to carry on the efforts started by the colonial government. In fact, the negotiations and treaties described in this essay point to a larger shift in the project of the region from colonization and settlement to state building.

Béxar's location on the far reaches of the colonial frontier, its sizable population, and its regional economic importance put the town at the center of the effort to forge contact, if not coexistence, with the indigenous people of Texas. A wide range of interactions, from violent to commercial, emerged from a combination of the cultural and political differences among tribes. While this essay does not attempt to provide a comprehensive account of these relations, especially from the indigenous perspective, it provides a general overview of Tejano approaches to establishing some stable arrangement with the inhabitants of the region. Tejano policies toward Indians took into account both the history of previous policies and their own limited understanding of indigenous culture. Rather than reacting to violence or imposing their will on the indigenous groups, leaders in Béxar set up a complex system of treaties, gift giving, and trade along with military enforcement that shaped their community and political organization.

Paying close attention to the dynamics of relations with indigenous groups from only one town instead of the entire region or nation highlights the complexities and deep social impact of this element of border life. While regional approaches are important in developing a general sense of the indigenous contact of the times, they gloss over the way these relations fit into a wide variety of other social relationships internal and external to the locality. A focus on the local level reveals the importance of social hierarchies within the town as well as the other negotiations townspeople were simultaneously undertaking.

By making and maintaining peace and trading with indigenous people, local Bexareño leaders increased their social status within their community. Furthermore, the absence of Spanish authority bolstered their position, allowing them to negotiate directly between the Mexican state and Anglo-American immigrants. At the risk of understating the frequently violent nature of Mexican/Indian relations, an examination of peaceful negotiations and contacts provides insight into another set of considerations and issues facing inhabitants of the borderlands. In the process of surviving in the frontier, Bexareños lived on the balance between several extremes: between war and peace of encroaching nations, between force and treaty with indigenous people, and between trust and suspicion in international and local trade. But the outcomes of these negotiations were not wholly in their hands. Indigenous political and cultural systems defined the parameters of peace and undoubtedly affected Mexican society in Béxar.

*   *   *

Bexareño Francisco Ruiz's activity among the indigenous groups of Texas illustrates the complexity of relations between Mexicans and Indians. After the royalist victory at the Battle of Medina in 1813 and the reestablishment of the Crown's authority in Texas, many insurgent Tejanos fled northward out of Béxar. An active Mexican insurgent, Francisco Ruiz is thought to have lived with and among Comanche groups until Mexican Independence.[5] Except for along the strips of highway to Nacogdoches and San Sabá, indigenous people occupied most of the province of Texas to the north and west of Béxar. This land, sometimes called "Comanchería" by Mexicans after its most populous indigenous group, provided an anonymous and safe haven for rebels escaping the reach of the Spanish military.

Reports coming back to Spanish officials in Béxar and to Arredondo in Monterrey located Ruiz and other insurgents hiding out in the hinterlands around Nacogdoches in 1814.[6] The Spanish government feared these insurgents would unite with other rebels living in the United States or with indigenous tribes to mount another attack on the capital of Texas. While the reports never identified a new movement, they mentioned the commerce and treaties established between the northern groups, such as the Comanche, and Ruiz and his fellow insurgents. Later descriptions of Comanche culture by Ruiz suggest his relationship with the Comanche extended beyond trading, perhaps to include living in the Comanche camp for a lengthy time. In return, Comanches provided every courtesy to Ruiz and helped him survive through rough times living on the frontier. Later, he used his connections to individuals and knowledge of Comanche culture to serve as the Indian Commissioner in Texas for the Mexican government. During the early years of the Republic, Commissioner Ruiz produced a detailed description of various indigenous groups living in Texas, with emphasis on Comanche culture, and crafted several peace treaties with many of these tribes.

Ruiz's actions during this period take on added significance when we note his status as one of the only two Tejano signatories of the Texas Declaration of Independence in 1836. In other words, Francisco Ruiz often took a lead role in negotiating with other groups, whether indigenous or Anglo-American. Taking on such responsibility to broker relations often fell to notable families among the town elites. As one of the town elite, Ruiz maintained his social standing by staying instrumental in forging relations with outsiders such as Indians and Anglo-Americans. As Louise Pubols notes in her essay in this volume, political power in colonial and early national Mexico relied on patriarchal family social structures. Patriarchy and status in these communities transcended typical class identifiers such as wealth to include reliance on reciprocity and benevolence to maintain status. Francisco Ruiz, then, represents an element of the local Béxar elite who maneuvered among and negotiated between Mexicans, Indians, and Anglos in Texas.

Ruiz's stay among Comanche groups contradicts general portrayals of

Comanches as wild, violent savages, intent on killing or enslaving any non-Comanche person.[7] The historical record thus suggests a much more complex picture. Ruiz's friendship with Comanches came not as an anomaly but a result or by-product, of an Indian policy initiated by the Crown in the eighteenth century and continued by Bexareños. Initially, Catholic missions and military presidios formed the first line of contact with indigenous groups. By the mid-eighteenth century, conversion among the sedentary tribes and armed conflict with nomadic tribes reached the limit of their effectiveness. Some Spanish government officials also turned to gifts and treaties with northern tribes to negotiate peace between the many indigenous peoples on the frontier. By the end of the colonial period, the Mexican insurgency siphoned away funds for these gifts, along with other elements of the Spanish colonial frontier apparatus. By independence in 1821, the Catholic missions were secularized and the system of presidios left with skeleton crews. Tejanos reestablished the level of relations initiated by the Spanish government but tailored trade and treaties to suit their needs. Tejano arrangements differed from Spanish colonial policy by allowing indigenous groups greater amounts of trade and movement. At this point, Tejanos reduced their reliance on a central authority for their Indian policy, reflecting the federalist bent Mexican nationalism took in Texas.[8]

Missions and Mestizaje

An examination of Mexican relations with indigenous groups in Texas during the late colonial and early national period reveals many of the cultural and ideological roots of Tejano attitudes toward indigenous people. While the experiences of Francisco Ruiz with Comanches demonstrate close contact, most Tejanos avoided or feared Indians. Fear and conflict created a siege mentality in frontier towns, leading to what has been called an "Indian fighter" ethos among Spanish colonists.[9] Labeling Tejanos "Indian fighters," though, detracts from the full extent of their relations with and attitude toward indigenous groups. While violence undoubtedly existed between Tejanos and indigenous groups, trading alliances and the security of diplomatic overtures led Tejanos to continue the policy of negotiation started by Spanish officials.

The end of the Spanish colonial government elevated the role of local Tejano elites in preserving peace and security in the region. Through this role, Tejanos began to develop two significant aspects of their political identity: autonomy from the central government authorities and the ability to negotiate across cultures. Early-nineteenth-century Indian policy figured prominently in aspects of Tejano ideology relative to the rise of the Mexican nation-state. Autonomy and cultural negotiation are recurrent themes in Béxar during this period, also seen through the dominance of federalist political ideology in Béxar or policies toward other immigrants, especially Anglo-Americans.

Tejano interest in forging a secure frontier arose from their desire to see their province prosper. At the turn of the nineteenth century, an official from Chihuahua emphatically noted, "Population is the central point where all plans must be rooted." [10] The plan outlined that increased numbers of citizens in the provinces would both spur commerce and industry and secure the territory from encroaching Anglo-American interests. But the largest impediment to reaching these goals was the difficulty in establishing a lasting and stable peace with the indigenous tribes of the land.

Any analysis of Spanish, and later Mexican, relations with the indigenous people of the region must also take into consideration the multitude of tribes and family groups of indigenous people encountered by the colonists coming north from Mexico. Broad generalizations about Mexican-Indian relations obscure the complexity of this interaction and the historical variations in contacts between different tribes. [11] Edward Spicer notes, "Although direct resistance was a universal reaction to contact with the Whites, it did not always come first. There were many tribes whose first reaction was one of friendly curiosity and there were others who sought the advantage of alliance with the Spaniards, or later with Anglo-Americans, against Indian enemies." [12] Spicer's suggestion that relations with each tribe should be seen as historically specific underscores the wide variety of experiences between Mexicans and Indians in nineteenth-century northeastern Mexico. The diversity of this task is made even more difficult by the numerous tribes present in that region. Cecilia Sheridan's research into early colonial settlements among these groups found up to 822 distinct peoples. [13]

Generations of historians have studied and characterized the Spanish conquest of the New World and the effect and impact it had on the indigenous people. [14] The experience of conquest and colonization in Mesoamerica took a different form from that in the northern colonial settlements, principally as a result of the cultural differences between indigenous peoples as well as the region's distinct environment. As historian Vito Alessio Robles noted of the peoples of the Mexican northeast, "These Indians were completely different than those that the Spanish encountered on the central plateau and on large parts of both coasts . . . but none of [these studies of the conquest] considers the special conditions encountered by Spaniards in the northeast of Mexico."[15] Instead of *mestizaje* and the *encomienda*, colonial officials developed a policy of Indian relations employing missions and the military.[16] Sheridan characterizes Spanish colonization among indigenous peoples in the north as an incomplete or stunted version of the rapid version that took place in central Mexico.[17]

Mexican colonists constructed their own categories to understand Indian cultures, distinguishing between tribes beyond the classic binary characterizations of *indios bárbaros* (barbarous Indians) and *indios civilizados* (civilized Indians). Generally, *civilizado* implied conversion to Catholicism, along with acculturation to Spanish manners. Several Mexican observers of the time wrote lengthy descriptions of the Indians of the Northeast, and in most cases made specific distinctions between these groups. One of these commentators from Béxar, Juan Antonio Padilla, reported on the "customs, habits and modes of life" of the barbarous tribes of Texas in 1819.[18] Within the category of barbarous, Padilla divides his report into two groups of tribes, friendly and hostile.[19] He lists sixteen tribes under "friendly nations," led primarily by the Caddo, and six under "hostile nations," with the Comanche and Lipan Apache most prominent. Regarding the Caddo, Padilla writes, "Considering the fact that they are heathens, the moral customs of these natives are good, since they are not ambitious like the Comanches nor deceitful like the Lipanes."[20] Padilla's distinction between barbarous tribes complicates simple classifications such as *bárbaro* or *civilizado* to a gradation of social and cultural markers. Armed with a more detailed understanding of indigenous cultures, frontier Mexicans attempted to create peaceful coexistence in Texas. Forging treaties and restraining military force would test the limits of these definitions.

More than a century after contact between the Indians of northern Mexico and the Spanish government, nineteenth-century government policy attempted to continue several successful patterns from the eighteenth century. Colonial officials, most from the ranks of the military, found gift giving and diplomacy produced longer peaceful periods at a lower cost than military expeditions. However, changes in the social and political landscape shaped by both Anglo-American westward expansion and environmental limitations made the balance struck at the end of the eighteenth century much more difficult to maintain.[21]

Beginning in the eighteenth century, Spanish colonial authorities constructed a chain of missions and presidios northward, into Texas, reaching to the Louisiana border. The location of these frontier institutions reveals their dual purpose, to establish the Spanish presence in the frontier against foreign governments and to control the indigenous people in the region. They aimed at laying the groundwork for civilian colonization of the region. Franciscan missionaries established the first permanent mission along the San Antonio River in 1718 with the founding of San Antonio de Valero.[22]

Subsequently, Franciscans built five more missions down the San Antonio River. The missions, and a presidio established by San Antonio de Valero, provided a basis for the settlement of families of Canary Islanders and the founding of Béxar in 1731. Beyond Béxar, Spanish interest in Indian relations turned to the more organized and less familiar Lipan Apache and Comanche tribal groups to the west. In 1757, Franciscan missionaries founded San Sabá mission in a brief and unsuccessful attempt to convert and colonize Apache people to the west of Béxar.[23]

Ideally, the missions were to attract indigenous people to live on the grounds, convert them, and bring them into Spanish civilian life. Once completely "reduced," the mission would revert to secular, or civilian, status as a parish church in the town. The missions began their secularization in April 1793, with the distribution of mission lands to the "native Christians of San Antonio de Valero."[24] The remaining missions secularized that year, but Franciscans continued to function as missionaries among the indigenous population, resulting in a partial secularization. The Mexican government legislated full secularization in 1823, completing the process of land distribution in the area around Béxar.

Secularization implied the incorporation of the converted indigenous population into Spanish civil society.[25] Incorporation thus suggests the disappearance of difference among indigenous groups and between colonist and native. Hinojosa and Fox have commented, "The secularization of the missions undoubtedly contributed to a blending of different groups into San Fernando [de Béxar]."[26] Even after secularization, though, self-identification as Indian continued. Census records from 1820 contain the self-identified categorization, or quality, of *Indio, Mestizo, Coyote,* or *Espa-*

TABLE I. January 1, 1820 Census of Béxar.

Barrio	Spaniard	Mestizo	Indian	Other*	Total
Valero	285	108	63	19	475
Sur	272	14	123	53	462
Norte	314	197	45	5	561
Laredo	68	0	7	22	97
Total	939	319	238	99	**1595**
%	58.9%	20.0%	14.9%	6.2%	

Source: *Residents of Texas: 1782–1836* (San Antonio: University of Texas Institute of Texan Cultures, 1984), 153–84.

*Other includes the categories listed as Negro, Mulatto, Coyote, Genízaro and Europeo.

ñol with the names of the families of Béxar.[27] (See table 1). The missions themselves maintained their status as barrios within the city's jurisdiction. This appears in the large number of people identified as *Indio* in the southern section of town where most of the missions were located. But, through secularization of the missions, tribal or group identification by mission Indians all but disappeared.[28] The degree of identification with local indigenous groups might explain the dramatic difference in identification with *Mestizo* in the northern and Valero sections of Béxar. The full impact of indigenous integration on the construction of concepts of ethnicity among Tejanos remains to be more fully explored.[29]

Yet these census categories and various terms for indigenous people do point to a more fluid employment of identity in region. As other essays in this volume note, identities in the borderlands were marked by fluidity rather than hardened distinctions. Identities in Béxar continued a similar trend both through self-identification by Bexareños and external categorization of indigenous people. But this period also witnessed the reorientation of other identities that affected the way Tejanos interacted with indigenous people. The ideology of the developing Mexican nation-state reached Béxar. While local interests drove much of the Indian policy, their actions also addressed the needs of the larger region and nation. This larger perspective of the nation did not correlate with the local view of Tejanos as "Indian fighters."

Spanish colonial officials developed what one historian called the "frontier colonial apparatus" to foster a secure and stable environment receptive to further northern migrations.³⁰ Using presidial detachments of soldiers, military commanders crafted a system of threat and reward to negotiate a peaceful equilibrium with the nomadic tribes of the North.

The larger civilian population living in the *Provincias Internas de Oriente* by the middle of the eighteenth century required Spanish officials to take more concerted and decisive steps to establish peaceful relations with the nomadic indigenous groups in the region. Decades had passed since the establishment of the mission system in Coahuila and Texas, and while many indigenous groups settled in these communities, most remained in their *rancherías* and continued their lives on the plains. Although Mexican colonists and indigenous groups lived in largely separate places, tensions constantly arose between them. It became clear that more active steps on the part of Spanish officials, especially within the military, would be required to create a climate in the region favorable to increased Mexican settlement.

State Defines the Extremes: An Eighteenth-Century Ideological Spectrum

In 1784, the governor of Texas, Don Domingo Cabello, wrote a report suggesting a policy toward the Lipan Apaches and other indigenous groups of the northeast.³¹ Along with the recommendations, the report also included a brief history of relations with indigenous people in the region and a copy of an inquiry conducted by Teodoro de Croix beginning in 1777. Cabello described the early years of Spanish settlement with indigenous groups in the northeastern provinces as relatively harmonious. "Having established these two Presidios [La Bahía del Espíritu Santo and San Antonio de Béxar] with all the support necessary, the first colonists enjoyed an unstated tranquillity since the many Indian Nations that were situated within the territory of this Province were of very good temperament."³² The Spanish colonists and missionaries carried out their mercantile and religious contact with the surrounding indigenous people.

According to Cabello's narrative of the region, the calm ended in 1723, when a group of Lipans killed a *vecino* from Béxar near the town. Cabello marked this as a turning point in the region, writing, "This deed . . . reduced the colonists and Indians of this province into a major distress. . . . Since the aforementioned Lipans set foot into these territories, they have stained it with human blood."³³ Cabello attributed the Lipan change of heart to their own battles with Comanches to the north and west. It would take twenty-six years of battles on the northern frontier before the Spanish government reached a general peace treaty with the Lipan. In the treaty, signed on August 19, 1749, the Lipan noted they would treat any Spaniard they came across as a friend and brother, and the Spanish agreed likewise.[34] An exchange of captives took place after the ceremony. The Lipan increased their presence in the region, in some cases interacting to a greater degree with some of the indigenous groups. Cabello notes that the Lipan absorbed the Jumano group, settling in their lands between the Rio Grande and the Nueces.[35]

Once again, the relative peace of the region fell apart as Lipan attacks increased around 1765. Cabello wrote, "Since the year 1765 it should be labeled the sad period of the break out of war by the Lipan throughout the province of Coahuila. A time when neither a stone, weed nor plant could be found without human blood on it."[36] Cabello again attributed the increased militancy among the Lipan to increased fighting between the Lipan and Comanche. Nevertheless, by 1772 the Spanish managed to craft a peace treaty with many of the indigenous people now inhabiting the region, including certain factions of the Comanche.[37] The Comanche chief made clear the diversity among the larger group, therefore limiting the scope of people he represented beyond his own immediate group. Cabello noted the Comanche captain "could not guarantee for the others of his Nation, because it was composed of many captains, and he did not know if they would agree with what he has done." Meanwhile, Lipan groups continued raiding Spanish settlements, roughly along the triangle from Béxar to La Bahía to Laredo.

Cabello concluded with strong condemnation of the Lipan and against negotiating any treaties with the group. Not only did he distrust Lipans to uphold the treaty but he suggested initiating a punitive military campaign against the entire group.[38] He couched his proposal in biblical terms, comparing it to King Saul's war against the Amalekites. As the Amalekites were idol worshipers, "the Lipans are even more so, and along with being so by their essence they are infinitely full of superstitions, sorcery and diabolical witchcraft, traitors to our King and declared enemies of the human race," Cabello wrote.[39] He then extensively outlined the military tactics necessary to carry out his campaign, attacking from the south and pinning the Lipan against the Comanche lands.

But, not all Norteños shared Cabello's opinions about the Apache.

Cabello's beliefs belong on one end of a wide spectrum of attitudes held by Mexicans toward Apaches and indigenous people in general. The views of José Cortés stood at the other end of that spectrum. Cortés, a lieutenant in the Royal Corps of Engineers, provided a much more sympathetic portrayal of the Apache in his *Memorias*.[40] Like Cabello, Cortés also held the safety and well-being of the inhabitants of the *Provincias Internas* as his goal in interacting with Apaches. But, rather than treating relations with Apaches as a lost cause, Cortés described a rational Apache culture, which fought for justifiable reasons. Cortés felt through mutual cultural understanding, and the establishment of trade with the Apache, the future of the region would be safe and bountiful.

Cortés stressed a material interpretation to explain Apache actions over a biological or cultural imperative. He wrote, "in order to bring them out of the mountains and keep them in settlements, it is vital to provide them aid to cover their major needs."[41] He believed many of the tensions between Spaniards and Apache arose out of unintended hunting and land disputes. Cortés also conveyed a complex understanding of the diversity of the Apache culture. In a sense, Apache served as a loose term to describe the people of a common language group. Cortés noted this but added that Apache rancheria occasionally united to advance a common goal.

Cortés then turned his attention to Comanches on the northern frontier, writing in a complimentary tone. Regarding Spaniards entering Comanche camps, he noted, "He who travels through their lands is lodged, regaled, and treated with the greatest friendship. From the moment the traveler arrives they take charge of caring for his horses and baggage, and if anything is missing at the time of his departure they detain him until it turns up. . . . On their departure they provide them with an escort to accompany them to the place where the escort can be relieved by warriors and guides from another *ranchería*."[42] Ruiz's stay with Comanches during the insurgency makes sense in light of these comments. As Ruiz's later statements make clear, with the proper respect and protocol, peaceful and prosperous relations did exist between Mexicans and Comanches. Cortés echoed the basis of these relations and contradicted negative reports, writing, "They always tell the truth, understand hospitality, and in general their customs are less barbarous than those of the Apaches."[43] He continued his assessment of Comanche trustworthiness, stating, "In their dealings with the Spanish they display notions of honor and of the most rigid justice."[44] By calling Comanche people honorable, Cortés made contracts and treaties possible and elevated Comanche status vis-à-vis other peoples of the region.[45]

Cabello's and Cortés's analyses of the Apache exemplify the broad spectrum of views held by leaders in the North. While opinions between Norteños varied regarding how to interact with indigenous people, policy decisions nevertheless had to be made. But these policies should be examined both at the level of proclamations made by officials and at the level of everyday actions taken by the residents of Béxar and other frontier towns.

Negotiating Peace in Béxar—Gift Giving

Elizabeth A. H. John's research on relations between indigenous people in the North and Spanish government officials lays out many of the chief policy objectives and decisions from the seventeenth and eighteenth centuries. She notes both the success the Spanish had in making treaties with the Comanche and the difficulty they experienced in understanding and negotiating with Apaches.[46] The Spanish military also set up a system of providing Comanches with gifts and housing. Finally, a system of punishments and accountability between Comanche and Spanish against transgressions of the treaties was agreed on.

Usually, the treaties with the Comanche involved establishing a relationship with several designated leaders and decorating them with the regalia of generals.[47] These treaties extended to all the towns and outposts in the Provincias Internas, but they didn't necessarily account for the heterogeneity and conflict within a given indigenous group. For instance, many of the treaties discussed by John involved Comanche groups around Santa Fe and Chihuahua, a distinct political group from those occupying the region northwest of Béxar. Spanish officials in Texas and Coahuila crafted their own treaties with these Comanche groups, but they didn't necessarily coincide with the treaties between Comanches and colonists farther west. These differences led to the appearance of Comanche treaty transgressions when someone from another group would steal from or kill a colonist during a treaty period. Nevertheless, Spanish officials developed a sufficiently sophisticated sense of the Comanche culture to differentiate between the eastern and western Comanche groups. In one letter from 1819, for example, the Commandante General of the Provincias Internas de Occidente informed the governor of New Mexico of military plans against the eastern Comanche. He asked the governor to meet with the western Comanche leaders to explain the situation and tell them the actions were not against their people.

Through gift giving and peaceful overtures, Tejanos worked to forge relationships with various indigenous groups in the region. Regarding Comanche relations, John notes, "Tejanos traveled freely into the Comanchería to hunt and to trade; Comanche families came routinely to trade and visit at San Antonio de Béxar. There, eastern Comanches received the crown's annual treaty presents, and some Comanches formed personal friendships with San Antonians that proved useful in troubled times."[48] These sorts of contacts coincided with Comanche values important to establishing mutually trustworthy relations. John adds, "Visiting was a vital component of Indian friendships and unstinting hospitality a prime value in Indian cultures. Reciprocity was important."[49] Table 2 demonstrates the material dimension of this reciprocity between Bexareños and indigenous people in their hinterland. The lack of Comanche statements regarding gift giving makes their interest in this exchange more difficult to ascertain. It has been suggested that various Comanche groups used this trade to solidify their domain over other indigenous groups in the region.[50]

Municipal officials in Béxar maintained detailed records of the goods exchanged with the visiting tribes. These records permit the reconstruction of the cycle of visiting and gift giving over the course of a year. Table 2 lists the number of people visiting Béxar each month, with the largest attendance coming in the summer months. While fewer Comanche visitors came to Béxar in the winter months, records show a greater amount of meat delivered as gifts as the weather turned colder. Fewer Comanche entered Béxar despite the proximity of their winter camp to town.

Perhaps most telling of the degree of trust built by these visits is the amount of gunpowder that exchanged hands. Spanish officials gave Indians gunpowder, presumably for use in hunting, without fear of it being used in attacks against Spanish colonists. More importantly, gunpowder allowed Comanche hunters the means to participate in the borderlands trading economy.[51] The goods and tools gained both through gift giving and raiding increased the wealth of Comanche groups who in turn traded these goods with the increasing number of Anglo-American colonists making their way westward.

Comanche people reciprocated Tejano actions by supporting hunting and trade expeditions in the region, as well as later providing a hideout

TABLE 2. Indian Gifts Presented in Béxar for 1807.

	Visitors	Trade Value	Cattle	Meat lbs.	Gunpowder
Jan	159	216	9	156	1
Feb	97	58	1	760	0
Mar	138	106	1	988	50
Apr	164	665	15	260	0
May	156	210	2	580	1
June	342	500	29	730	0
July	626	1150	50	204	0
Aug	256	571	16	1044	0
Sept	24	133	3	530	0
Oct	250	350	17	1016	15.5
Nov	10	11	0	144	0
Dec	76	143	2	1120	0
Totals:	2298	4113	145	7532	67.5

Source: Béxar Archives, passim. documents covering 1807.

for insurgents. John describes one hunting incident in 1803, when 130 Bexareños rode into the Comanchería to hunt buffalo.[52] Comanches provided the hunters with shelter and guides and even tended their horses during the expedition. During the Republic era, Bexareños relied on these contacts in exploring the possibility of joining with the Santa Fe trade.[53]

Creating peace in Texas occasionally took larger efforts than gift giving as Spanish officials negotiated treaties with neighboring groups. The establishment of peace with Oso Ballo, a Comanche leader, in Chihuahua in 1811 provides an example of the beliefs and methods for carrying out these negotiations.[54] A report of the treaty informed officials in Béxar of the agreement. A key element of the report established the scope of Oso Ballo's authority, describing him as the "captain" of the Yamparica tribe within the alliance of Western Comanches. This specificity suggests an understanding by Spanish officials of the complexity of Comanche leadership and alliances. The report noted that Oso Ballo first received a large medallion to distinguish his leadership and pay respect and reminded Béxar officials to maintain the flow of gifts Comanches had grown to expect: "I urge you to keep in mind the importance of not failing to keep in store the items the Indian Nations have grown accustomed to receive;

for if it occurs, grave consequences of a large magnitude would come about. Take every measure to easily, securely and quickly acquire the necessary articles."[55] Ultimately, any peace treaty crafted between the Spanish and these groups required a continuation of gift giving. These gifts not only established peace but also led to other benefits for the colonists. One came in the form of information and warnings from Comanche people about potential attacks from other indigenous groups. In December 1811, a "Capitancillo," or junior captain, of the Comanches named El Sordo rode into Béxar with three others to inform authorities of potential raids against Béxar by the Tahuallares and Tahuacanos tribes.[56]

These reports also pointed to fears and uncertainty about maintaining this carefully crafted peace, especially as rebellion against the Crown spread through the nation. Funds and personnel were turned to fighting the insurgents, and in turn, insurgents used newly created rifts with indigenous groups against royalists. The advice from Chihuahua regarding peace with Chief Oso Ballo might have sprung from a desire to maintain secure relations with indigenous people while fighting the insurgency. Additionally, insurgents relied on and manipulated their connections with indigenous groups to continue their movement against the colonial government.[57] In the case of Béxar, many insurgents fleeing the city after royalists recaptured it sought refuge in Comanche camps.[58]

Balance under Pressure

The insurgency and Mexican independence threatened the delicate equilibrium with indigenous people crafted by the royal authorities. Initially, the rebellion diverted funds from the peace effort. Independence completed the Spanish abandonment of the frontier, leaving the Mexican government and local officials to form their own Indian policy. Historian Luis Aboites Aguilar points to this shift as a significant moment in the rise of local elites and the larger federalist effort.[59] While his study focuses principally on Sonora, his observations suggest a link between local self-reliance in regard to Indian relations and the development of local political autonomy. Such autonomy facilitated raising complaints against the newly formed Mexican state, as well as strengthening regional political identity. A similar pattern appears in Béxar where Bexareño efforts to maintain peaceful relations are typical of the late colonial and early national periods. Indeed, this phenomenon was not a problem unique to Texas, as

Kristine L. Jones observes in her examination of the effects of independence on indigenous relations in the Argentine Pampas.[60]

Tejanos continued many of the policies and practices of governance from the Spanish colonial system, including maintenance of Indian relations. As Elizabeth A. H. John notes, "In fact, the Mexicans would revive their colonial legacy: an imperfect peace, mutually useful to Comanches and Spaniards, infinitely preferable to war, and never comprehensible to the United States."[61] Almost immediately after Independence, the Mexican government in Saltillo supported the peaceful elements of John's "imperfect peace." In a letter to Governor Victor Blanco dated November 16, 1821, the mayor of Monclova, Antonio Elosua, related reports of peace treaties with the major nomadic tribes in Béxar: "I have just received the probable good news of the state of negotiations with the Comanche and Lipan Apache to strike a peace so greatly desired by the inhabitants of this region, with the first sign of their inclination for peace being the arrival in Béxar of two of their sons, Captains (Chief) Quiase and Menchaca."[62] These contacts probably existed as a result of links forged during the insurgency.

Elosua's description of the meeting and his subsequent policy toward the Comanche and Lipan Apache indicate the imperfect nature of these relations. He continued,

> And even though it is impossible to achieve the desirable end of total pacification of these Tribes, as numerous as they are belligerent, I have decided to send you a Proclamation, a draft of which is included, and command all Chiefs and Commanders on the frontier as I currently advise, to prevent their subordinates and their subordinates from undertaking any armed attacks upon the Indians that reside in this region unless they are approached in full battle gear, and even in that case wait until they fire their weapons first. But before all else, attempt to communicate and tell them an Independent system has been reestablished over the empire and they should not make war on us as we shall not initiate on our part.[63]

Elosua's attention to his army's behavior during the inevitable conflicts to come underscores his concern with a larger peace, despite occasional violence. The small skirmishes would not derail the overall peace these leaders sought. Blanco emphasized the tactical high ground with his emphasis on not initiating combat and using dialogue when possible. Nevertheless, the letter conveys a sense of futility in ending all violent clashes. Local leaders questioned the policy of negotiation as Indian attacks on Mexicans continued over the next decade.[64] What appear as violations of treaties or agreements to Mexican settlers more likely resulted from misunderstanding or not knowing the motives of various groups. Despite understanding something of Comanche political and social structure, Mexican officials could not have known all the trading and political interests Comanche had been developing over the years.[65]

Along with Elosua's orders to his subordinates, the Mexican government continued to negotiate treaties with the indigenous groups on the frontier. General Herrera forwarded his report on recent treaty activity to the new Mexican monarch Iturbide on August 17, 1822.[66] He commented on a meeting between the government and two Lipan Apache chiefs, Cuelga de Castro and Yolcha Pocarropa. The Lipan leaders agreed to return all captives and prisoners and keep a general peace; in return, the Mexican government agreed to drop all claims against the tribe. While these treaties marked a significant goal of the newly formed imperial government, the implementation and maintenance of peace required a full-time administrator.

Negotiating Peace in Béxar—Comanche Treaty of 1822

As noted earlier, Francisco Ruiz played an important role in shaping Indian/Mexican relations in the post-Independence period. His contact with Comanche groups during the insurgency established trust and an understanding between Comanche leaders and himself. As an official Indian agent, with the rank of lieutenant colonel, Ruiz set off into the frontier in 1822 to bring back a more complete peace treaty.

The official newspaper of Iturbide's government, the *Gaceta del Gobierno Imperial de Mexico*, reported on the meetings Ruiz held with Comanche leaders in March. The conference lasted three days, with over five thousand Comanche in attendance, including, "the principal chiefs, captains and elders."[67] The discussions mainly took place between Ruiz and Pitsinampa, an elder respected among the Comanche. Pitsinampa negotiated with Ruiz and frequently turned to the assembled Comanche who would vote on what action to take. Ruiz emphasized that his government was not the Spanish but rather the Mexican nation, with "a native Emperor."[68] The conference resulted in a fourteen-point treaty between the Comanches and the Mexican government, covering a variety of issues ranging from captives to trade.

The Comanches elected chief Guonique to travel to Mexico City to sign the treaty. The first item dealt with the central object of the meeting, the establishment of peace. It stated, "There will be perpetual peace and friendship between both nations: all hostilities of all sorts will end, and all that occurred during the Spanish reign will be forgotten."[69] The next items returned all captives who so desired and set up an alliance to protect the frontier against hostile tribes or foreign invasion, including foreign explorers. Item eight placed Béxar at the center of the new alliance and item twelve designated a Comanche interpreter to live in Béxar monitoring all relations. Item eight read, *The Comanche will only practice trade in Béxar*, their merchants traveling there by public roads and under the direction of a chief held accountable for damages caused, and with a passport granted with the Emperors seal: Mexicans will do likewise when they enter into the land of the Comanche."[70] The careful delineation of trading procedures indicates fear persisted among Mexicans, despite the declaration of peace. The treaty even specified which goods each side would participate in trading.

The final item established a scholarship for twelve Comanche youth to be educated in Mexico City every four years. The Comanche youth would learn "to practice the arts and sciences and once they have been instructed, return so that their Nation in this way will become civilized and educated." While local concerns and immediate social networks shaped the form indigenous interactions took, Tejano actions also found their way as part of the national liberal project underway in Mexico after independence. In a sense, the Mexican state took over the conversion project initiated by Catholic missions in the previous centuries. The treaty Ruiz brokered exceeded the peace for gifts relationship initiated by the Spanish; it also demanded more personnel and resources to succeed, two things in short supply on the northern frontier.

While the negotiations occurred under the authorization of the Mexican government, local efforts took on greater importance into the first decade of the new peace. Bexareño support for the deal appears, for instance, through a complaint lodged by José Antonio Navarro in the name of Juan Cortés of Nacogdoches in 1823.[71] Navarro, a prominent vecino, demanded the Mexican government compensate Cortés for over one thousand pesos given to Francisco Ruiz during his negotiations with Comanche and Lipan Apache. The money went specifically toward gifts for the two groups. While Cortés eventually received his reimbursement in 1828, his decision to lend the money demonstrated his interest in seeing the establishment of peace. The loan also indicated how much the process of making peace demanded participation and even leadership by local elites.

Béxar's location as the winter camp for Comanche groups made it a natural place to center Comanche/Mexican relations. Cortés's need to enlist the services of Navarro in Béxar from his home in Nacogdoches illustrates Béxar's place in the hierarchy of official power. The northeastern hinterlands of Béxar developed economically and socially as indigenous groups continued to stream into the region and trade with Anglo-Americans, both legal and illegal, increased.

Triangulating the Balance: Francisco Ruiz and Peter Ellis Bean

Soon after Ruiz negotiated the Comanche treaty in 1822, another agent joined him to aid in carrying out his duties. An Anglo-American resident from the Louisiana/Texas frontier region, Peter Ellis Bean, worked alongside Ruiz to maintain positive relations with the ever-increasing numbers of indigenous groups. Their work straddled the areas between the plains cultures of the Comanche and Lipan Apache, and the Wichita, Caddo, and migrant cultures of the Tawaconis, Waco, Cherokee, and Kickapoo. Both Ruiz and Bean employed their experiences trading and living with the area's tribes to gain their trust and learn their customs.[72]

Bean and Ruiz frequently negotiated treaties together. Ruiz describes one such meeting between the Quichas [Wichita] and Bean and himself.[73] They sought to enlist the aid of the Quichas to broker a peace with the Tawakoni and Waco people. Their efforts succeeded in establishing relations with the two groups in June 1827.[74] These treaties often fell through, as was the case with the Tawaconis and Waco pact. By 1829, Ruiz, Bean, and empresario Stephen Austin led a punitive campaign against the camps of these tribes.[75]

Of all the tribes Ruiz and Bean treated with, the Cherokee practiced a form of diplomacy most recognizable to them.[76] Like several other tribes, Cherokee groups migrated into northeastern Texas in the early nineteenth century in order to avoid Anglo-American westward expansion.[77] Their experiences in trade and war with Anglo-Americans led to a sophisticated diplomatic culture led by a chief for war and diplomacy.[78] Furthermore, Cherokee leaders crafted alliances with other migrant tribes in the area, permitting them to broker settlements with Mexican agents.[79] A meeting between Bean and the Cherokee leadership illustrates the role of the Cherokee in this relationship.

On July 2, 1828, Bean held a meeting in Nacogdoches with several local Indian tribes to sign a peace treaty. The tribes, led by several Cherokee chiefs, included members from the Shavano, Kickapoo, Delaware, Alabama, Nabadache, Ainais, and Cawshatta groups. They sat around a buffalo robe with the Mexican representatives and smoked a peace pipe. The speeches made by the Indian chiefs emphasized their desire to live in the Mexican nation and their friendly feelings toward Mexicans.[80] The context for that meeting around the buffalo robe was the westward march of Anglo-American settlement that had forced these tribes to move to East Texas in 1819 in the first place.

After ceremonial dances, the war and diplomacy chief for the Cherokee stood up and spoke. "It has been twenty moons since we smoked the peace pipe with our Mexican brothers," he stated, "and we desire to be together as one people, and share the same sympathies as our Mexican brothers, and we should never go back on our promises."[81] The chief went on to describe the treaties Bean brokered with the Tawakonis and the Wacos for both the Mexican government and the Cherokee group. While suspicious of the sincerity of the Tawakonis and Waco peace, the Cherokee chief reaffirmed his trust in the arrangement established with the Mexican nation.[82] A Shavano chief echoed these sentiments when he spoke next. "I have heard what my Cherokee brothers have had to say and their word is good," said Piedra Negra, "We are red men and know nothing beyond what we think in our heads. We have traveled a long distance to this Nation, searching for the Mexicans, and they have received us like brothers and we should be honest men." Piedra Negra emphasized the importance of working this new land when he continued, "we do not want to live lost in the prairie like other tribes. . . . These lands are good to those who work them; but those who do not work will always be hungry and he and his woman will be naked and their children will be thieves."[83]

Without delving into the beliefs and culture of these tribes or the sincerity of their overtures, we can say that the proceedings between the Cherokee and the Mexican representative exemplify the new direction of Mexican/Indian relations from their origins in the late eighteenth century policy of gift giving. Tejanos had to contend with an increased number of different tribes as Anglo-Americans pushed their civilization westward. Anglo-American colonists had already established numerous settlements near these tribes by the time of the 1828 treaty. These treaties also raise questions over how land and territory figured into Mexican visions of settlements in Texas. In other words, did they grant privileges to Cherokee, Comanche, and other groups in return for peaceful relations? Colonization laws put in place by the Mexican government in 1824 created a mechanism for indigenous groups to apply for land grants.[84] Mexican efforts not only kept a general peace with the tribes but also aimed to keep Anglo-American colonists from resorting to vigilante attacks against these indigenous groups.

The balancing act begun by the Spanish government in the northern frontier gave way to a series of brokered alliances and treaties designed to maintain peace and security in the region. The sheer number of different cultures Tejanos faced when constructing this arrangement suggests the complexity of this task. One U.S. State Department agent mentioned at least thirty distinct tribes in his listing of the indigenous population of Texas, a population he calculated to be almost 10,000 in 1827.[85] Directives from Mexico City could not possibly have dictated every action taken by Tejano agents. Rather, it was their experiences living in the frontier region that determined the range of relations they crafted rather than any policy dictated from the center.

Balances

By entering into a material and sometimes social relationship with the indigenous people of Texas, Bexareños followed a path similar to that of other colonists throughout the Mexican borderlands and the Americas in general. Indeed, historians examining these varieties of contact now start from the assumption that this contact operates as a two-way street, clearly shaping the internal structure and ideology of both actors involved. The idea of serrano culture introduced by Ana Alonso and Daniel Nugent exemplifies this process for colonial Chihuahua.[86] To the north, Richard White describes this ideological interchange with the concept of a "middle ground."[87] To the south, Kristine L. Jones puts the raiding cultures of the Southern Cone at the center of the nation-state building process. As caciques and caudillos took over the shift from raiding to trading, she writes,

"Local and regional elites assumed greater prominence and played import roles in building the new American states."[88] The creativity of these local elites to assert their power soon came under pressure in Texas as Anglo-American immigrants streamed into the district.

Indigenous groups were acutely aware of the new set of problems Tejanos would soon face. As several of the migrant tribes indicated to Spanish and Mexican authorities, negotiating with Mexico was preferable to the treatment they received at the hands of Anglo-Americans. Once American colonization of Texas was complete, the relative stability offered indigenous groups under Mexican Texas evaporated. Anglo-Americans entered Texas with a preconceived idea about Indians while lacking much prior contact with Mexicans. Occasionally Anglo-Texans linked their beliefs and stereotypes of Indians to those they held of Mexicans. This happened either generally by noting the indigenous side of mestizaje with references to a "mongrel race," or specifically with claims of conspiracy such as the so-called Córdova Rebellion in 1838, which involved Cherokee.[89]

Those Spanish and Mexicans close to Indian policy were the first to witness expansionist aspects of Anglo-American political culture. With foreboding, José Cortés noted in 1799, "we must fear the expansion of their [American] borders. . . . The developments that will emerge in time will bear out my fearful warnings, and then the consequences will be more tragic."[90] Thirty years later, José de las Piedras noted firsthand the effects of American expansion from his post in Nacogdoches. De las Piedras witnessed dozens of tribes and thousands of indigenous people streaming into Texas, leading him to conclude that "the view of the Government of the North is to remove the Indians of their various states at any cost, and bring them into this Republic."[91] He felt powerless to stem the migrations, noting the cover wilderness provided as well as the scant resources assigned to him. Securing the frontier for Spain and then Mexico became a principal goal of Indian policy, and Tejanos decided that to do so necessitated inviting Anglo-Americans to settle the rest of the region.

Tejanos also had an extensive history with indigenous people, one that resulted in a different policy. As Elizabeth A. H. John comments, "One of the tragedies of Texas history was the distrustful Anglo-American Texans' failure to avail themselves of the San Antonio community's well-developed skills in dealing with Indians and its established avenues of communication with Indian communities."[92] Tejanos not only created a policy for their specific situation but demonstrated a deep knowledge of the differences and peculiarities of the wide variety of Indian tribes in the region. Treaties and negotiations with the Comanche varied immensely from those with the Cherokee. Tejanos often dealt with tribes at war with each other.

Tejanos' interactions with the tribes of Texas were predicated on a system of cultural meaning developed during the late eighteenth century and early nineteenth century.[93] These meanings changed along with the politics and economics of the region, but the process of defining other groups and basing policy on those definitions continued throughout the century. Tejanos varied their definitions of indigenous people along several spectrums, from barbarous to civilized and from friend to enemy. Ultimately, the act of defining another group of people involved self-definition by Tejanos and other Mexicans in the North. The political and social events of the nineteenth century tested the limits of those definitions between Mexican and Indian, and later between Anglo-Mexicans and Americans.

The entire set of interactions should be analyzed over the nineteenth century to get a sense of the wide range of Indian-white interactions and the various influences Mexicans, Anglo-Americans, and Indians exerted on one another.[94] While Spanish relations with northern Indian people up to the mid-eighteenth century transpired with little interference from Anglo-American colonists, the following period witnessed greater pressures on these relations on both the Spanish and Native Americans. David J. Weber writes, "Few historians, however, have understood the extent to which American expansion upset the delicate balance between independent Indian peoples and pobladores in Mexico's Far North, from Texas to California."[95] By the same token, Anglo-American relations with Native Americans in the Southwest occurred after several centuries of Native American interaction and negotiation with Spanish missionaries, officials, and settlers.

Practical considerations drove Tejanos' efforts to secure peace in their region, while their ability to do so also depended on continuing, albeit in altered forms, Spanish colonial presidios and missions. Ultimately, Indian violence hindered the economic development and settlement of Texas. The threat of Indian attacks limited trade possibilities and kept people from migrating into the region. While larger towns managed to protect themselves, violence turned the hinterlands into uncontrolled and unproductive territory. But that violence also needs to be put into the context of increasing Anglo-American threats both to indigenous groups and Mexican colonists.

The waning and eventual termination of Spanish oversight of the northeastern frontier allowed Tejanos to take a greater role in shaping Indian policy. While Tejanos continued many of the practices initiated by the Spanish, their experiences on the frontier, especially after the insurgency, tailored their efforts to relate to tribal differences and the economic demands of the region. These actions influenced two elements of Tejano political identity: greater regional autonomy vis-à-vis the centralist state, and the importance of regional stability in light of increased cultural variety.

But the specter of violence never disappeared from the region, and as a result treaties fell apart and attacks occurred with frequency in some years. Tejanos learned to live with a degree of tension and danger tempering their autonomy and stability. That allowance for uncertainty permitted the latitude necessary to craft these kinds of treaties. It also illustrates how Tejano frontier life involved direct contact with many different cultures, entailed the ever-present possibility of violence, and required the flexibility, savvy, and determination to craft a secure peace for prosperity.

Notes

1   *Gaceta del Gobierno Imperial de México*, 30 January 1823, 1:14, 53.

2   José Francisco Ruíz, *Report on the Indian Tribes of Texas in 1828* (New Haven: Yale University Library, 1972), 7.

3   "Bexareño" is the Spanish term for resident of Béxar, later San Antonio, Texas. The term "Tejano" will be used for the Mexican inhabitants of Texas and "Norteño" for the residents of Northern Mexico.

4   Ana María Alonso, *Thread of Blood: Colonialism, Revolution, and Gender on Mexico's Northern Frontier* (Tucson: University of Arizona Press, 1995), 46.

5   See introduction by John C. Ewers, Ruiz, *Report*, 1.

6   "Sumaria contra los yndividuos que se hallan en lo interior de esta provincia . . ." Don Feliciano Ramírez, Juez Fiscal, La Bahía, October 1814, Béxar Archives (BA).

7   Many books describe Indian violence on the frontier. See, e.g., Rupert Norval Richardson, *The Comanche Barrier to South Plains Settlement: A Century and a Half of Savage Resistance to the Advancing White Frontier* (Glendale, Calif.: Arthur H. Clark, 1933); Mildred P. Mayhall, *Indian Wars of Texas* (Waco: Texian Press, 1965).

8 For a larger treatment of the question of nationalism in Texas, see Raúl A. Ramos, "From Norteño to Tejano: The Roots of Borderlands Ethnicity, Nationalism, and Political Identity in Béxar, 1811–1861" (Ph.D. diss., Yale University, 1999); Andrés Reséndez, "Caught between Profits and Rituals: Native Contestation in Texas and New Mexico" (Ph.D. diss., University of Chicago, 1997); Omar S. Valerio-Jimenez, "Indios Bárbaros, Divorcees, and Flocks of Vampires: Identity and Nation on the Rio Grande, 1749-1894" (Ph.D. diss., UCLA, 2001).

9 Alonso, *Thread of Blood*, 30–36. Ironically, the war skills employed by colonists to fight Indians came from those groups themselves.

10 José María Cortés y de Olarte and Elizabeth Ann Harper John, *Views from the Apache Frontier: Report on the Northern Provinces of New Spain* (Norman: University of Oklahoma Press, 1989), 34.

11 Elizabeth A. H. John provides one of the best histories of Indian relations but covers mostly the eighteenth century and areas west of Texas; see *Storms Brewed in Other Men's Worlds: The Confrontations of Indians, Spanish, and French in the Southwest, 1540-1795* (Lincoln: University of Nebraska Press, 1981). In *The Indians of Texas: From Prehistoric to Modern Times* (Austin, University of Texas Press, 1961), William W. Newcomb presents the most comprehensive treatment of Texas Indians but concentrates on their tribal histories with only one brief chapter on the relations Indians carried out with European colonists. Edward Spicer also covers the period in his overview of both Mexican and American Indian policies; see *Cycles of Conquest: The Impact of Spain, Mexico, and the United States on the Indians of the Southwest, 1533–1960* (Tuscon: University of Arizona Press, 1962). Historians of Mexico have touched on the subject more often; see e.g., Cuauhtémoc Velasco Avila, "Historiografía de una frontera amenazada: Los ataques comanches y apaches en el siglo XIX," in *Indio, nación y comunidad en el México del siglo XIX* (México: Centro de Estudios Mexicanos y Centroamericanos/ Centro de Investigaciones y Estudios Superiores en Antropología Social, 1993), and David B. Adams, "Embattled Borderlands: Northern Nuevo León and the Indios Bárbaros, 1686–1870," *Southwestern Historical Quarterly* 95 (2 October 1991): 205–20.

12 Spicer, *Cycles of Conquest*, 16.

13 Cecilia Sheridan, *Anónimos y desterrados: La contienda por el "sitio que llaman de Quauyla," siglos XVI–XVIII* (México: CIESAS, 2000), 353.

14 See, among many, Eric R. Wolf, *Sons of the Shaking Earth* (Chicago: University of Chicago Press, 1959); and David J. Weber, *The Spanish Frontier in North America* (New Haven: Yale University Press, 1992).

15 Vito Alessio Robles, *Coahuila y Texas en la época colonial* (Mexico City: Editorial Cultura, 1938), 422–23. Weber, *Spanish Frontier*, describes these differences in greater detail for those reaches of the Spanish colony now in the United States.

16 The encomienda, or labor tax on the indigenous people, existed in other parts of the northern regions, especially New Mexico. But it never took hold in Texas.

17 Sheridan, *Anónimos y desterrados*, 7.

18 Juan Antonio Padilla, "Report on the Barbarous Indians of the Province of Texas," trans. Mattie Austin Hatcher, "Texas in 1820," *Southwestern Historical Quarterly* 22 (July 1919).

19 Padilla, "Report," 47.

20 Ibid.

21 David J. Weber, "American Westward Expansion and the Breakdown of Relations between Pobladores and 'Indios Bárbaros' on Mexico's Far Northern Frontier, 1821–1846," in David J. Weber, *Myth and the History of the Hispanic Southwest* (Albuquerque: University of New Mexico Press, 1988).

22 Carlos Eduardo Castañeda, *Our Catholic Heritage in Texas, 1519–1936* (New York: Arno, 1976), 5:40; Félix D. Almaráz, "San Antonio's Old Franciscan Missions: Material Decline and Secular Avarice in the Transition from Hispanic to Mexican Control," *The Americas* 44:1 (July 1987): 1. Jesus F. de la Teja, "Indians, Soldiers, and Canary Islanders: The Making of a Texas Frontier Community," *Locus* 3:1 (Fall 1990): 81.

23 Robert S. Weddle, *The San Sabá Mission: Spanish Pivot in Texas* (Austin: University of Texas Press, 1964). In 1758, Comanches burned down the mission and killed several missionaries and Apaches living there. The attack has mainly been attributed to Apache-Comanche conflict. Those Apache living in the mission were thought to be seeking Spanish protection from Comanche attacks.

24 Almaráz, "Franciscan Missions," 2.

25 Weber, *Spanish Frontier*, 306.

26 Gilberto M. Hinojosa and Anne A. Fox, "Indians and Their Culture in San Fernando de Béxar," in Gerald Eugene Poyo and Gilberto Miguel Hinojosa, eds., *Tejano Origins in Eighteenth-Century San Antonio* (Austin: University of Texas Press, 1991), 119.

27 "General Census Report of the City of Béxar and its Missions: Barrios Valero, Sur, Norte, Laredo, Jan. 1, 1820," in University of Texas Institute of Texan Cultures at San Antonio, *Residents of Texas, 1782–1836* (San Antonio: University of Texas Institute of Texan Cultures, 1984).

28 While more work remains to be done on Indian identification in the late colonial/early national period, Lisbeth Haas, *Conquests and Historical Identities in California, 1769–1936* (Berkeley: University of California Press, 1995), describes the continuity of a new identity as mission Indians lasting into the twentieth century among the people of San Juan mission in Orange County.

29 Sheridan, *Anónimos y desterrados*, and Cynthia Radding, *Wandering Peoples: Colonialism, Ethnic Spaces, and Ecological Frontiers in Northwestern Mexico, 1700–1850* (Durham: Duke University Press, 1997), both use the concept of ethno-

genesis to describe the complex process of ethnic identity category development throughout the colonial period.

30 Luis Aboites Aguilar, "Poblamiento y estado en el Norte de México, 1830–1835," in *Indio, nación y comunidad*, 303–13.

31 Cabello Domingo, "Ynforme del Governador de Texas sobre pazes de los Apaches Lipanes en la colonia de Nuevo Santander." Béxar, 30 September 1784, Archivo General de la Nación (AGN), Provincias Internas, v.480 (University of Texas Transcripts) Center for American History, University of Texas (CAHUT).

32 Cabello, "Ynforme," 102–3.

33 Ibid., 105.

34 Ibid., 112.

35 Ibid., 115–16. See also William W. Newcomb, *The Indians of Texas: From Prehistoric to Modern Times* (Austin: University of Texas Press, 1961), 233–34, on the absorption of the Jumano by the Lipan. Newcomb notes the Jumano were left weak by a failed early attempt by Spanish missionaries to convert indigenous people along the Rio Grande. He believes the Jumano had little choice but to become part of the Lipan Apache group sometime around 1715.

36 Cabello, "Ynforme," 117.

37 Ibid., 129. He lists the groups as Taboayazes, Guachitas, Taguacanes, Flechasos, Yzcanis, Quitchas, Caodachaos, and Tancagues.

38 Ibid., 143.

39 Ibid., 144.

40 José Cortés, *Report on the Northern Provinces of New Spain, 1799*, ed. Elizabeth A. H. John, trans. John Wheat (Norman: University of Oklahoma Press, 1989).

41 Ibid., 28.

42 Ibid., 82.

43 Ibid.

44 Ibid.

45 For a discussion of the nature of seventeenth- and eighteenth-century honor on the New Mexico frontier, see Ramón A. Gutiérrez, *When Jesus Came, the Corn Mothers Went Away: Marriage, Sexuality, and Power in New Mexico, 1500–1846* (Stanford: Stanford University Press, 1991), 175–80.

46 John, *Storms Brewed*, 664–716. Also see Elizabeth A. H. John, "A Cautionary Exercise in Apache Historiography," *Journal of Arizona History* 25 (Autumn 1984).

47 Joaquín Real Alencaster, Governor of New Mexico, to Commandant General of the Interior Provinces, "Report on Comanche Affairs, 20 November 1805," in Marc Simmons, *Border Comanches: Seven Spanish Colonial Documents, 1785–1819* (Santa Fe: Stagecoach Press, 1967).

48 Elizabeth A. H. John, "Nurturing the Peace: Spanish and Comanche Cooperation in the Early Nineteenth Century," *New Mexico Historical Review* 59:4 (1984): 347.

49 Elizabeth A. H. John, "Independent Indians and the San Antonio Community," in Poyo and Hinojosa, eds. *Tejano Origins*, 126.

50 Pekka Hämäläinen, "The Western Comanche Trade Center: Rethinking the Plains Indian Trade System," *Western Historical Quarterly* 29 (Winter 1998): 485–513.

51 William B. Griffen, *Utmost Good Faith: Patterns of Apache-Mexican Hostilities in Northern Chihuahua Border Warfare, 1821–1848* (Albuquerque: University of New Mexico Press, 1988), 7. Griffen notes the importance of the secure trading space created in the military peace establishments. "In effect, they maintained a partnership with Mexicans who also became active participants in the larger network of regional trade."

52 John, "Nurturing," 351.

53 Andrés Reséndez discusses the Santa Fe trade in chapter 4 of this volume.

54 John, "Nurturing," 363–64. Nemesio Salcedo to Governador Interino de Texas (Simon Herrera), Chihuahua, 17 September 1811, BA.

55 Salcedo to Herrera, BA.

56 Simon Herrera, Béxar, 15 December 1811, BA.

57 John, "Nurturing," 364–65.

58 Ibid., 365.

59 Aguilar, "Poblamiento y estado," 310–11.

60 Kristine L. Jones, "Comparative Raiding Economies," in Donna J. Guy and Thomas E. Sheridan, eds., *Contested Ground: Comparative Frontiers on the Northern and Southern Edges of the Spanish Empire* (Tucson: University of Arizona Press, 1998), 107.

61 John, "Nurturing," 365.

62 Antonio Elosua, Mayor of Monclova, to Victor Blanco, 16 November 1821, Archivo General del Estado de Coahuila (AGEC).

63 Ibid.

64 Rafael González to Antonio Elosua, Saltillo, 24 January 1826, AGEC, Morelos; In the letter, the Governor González, of Coahuila y Texas, explains to the military commander of the region, Elosua, that the vecinos of Nava were armed in reponse to the resurgence of Indian attacks. The residents comment that they have been "reduced to a state of misery and chaos." Also see Jorge Chávez Chávez, "Retrato del Indio bárbaro: Proceso de justificación de la barbarie de los Indios del septentrión mexicano y formación de la cultura norteña," *New Mexico Historical Review* 73:4 (1998): 400–401.

65 Hamalainen, "Western Comanche Trade Center."

66 Herrera, n.p., 17 August 1822, Beinecke Library, Yale University.

67 *Gaceta del Gobierno Imperial de México*, 30 January 1823, vol. 1, no. 14, p. 51.

68 Ibid., 52.

69 Ibid.

70 My emphasis.

71 Felipe de la Garza to Colonel D. José Félix Tres Palacios, 11 October 1823, Western Americans Collection, Beinecke Library, Yale University.

72 Ruiz goes into great detail on the living, fighting, and religious aspects of Comanche culture. *Report on the Indian Tribes of Texas in 1828*, 7.

73 Ruiz, Nacogdoches, 14 April 1827, BA.

74 Nacogdoches, 13 July 1827, BA.

75 Béxar, 13 April 1829, BA.

76 Dianna Everett, *The Texas Cherokees: A People between Two Fires, 1819–1840* (Norman: University of Oklahoma Press, 1990).

77 Everett, *Texas Cherokees*, 11, notes reports of Cherokee, Chickasaw, and Shawnee as early as 1807. Also, Antonio Cordero to Nemisio Salcedo, Béxar, 30 October 1807, Béxar Archives Translations, v.30, 139, describes a request by the Conchate to settle in Texas. Salcedo writes, "After setting forth their ancient vassalage, their loyalty to our king, and the disdain with which they look upon the seduction of the American government, [they stated that] the object of their visit firstly to request permission for the main tribe . . . to move to the place where they are living."

78 Everett, *Texas Cherokees*, 5, 57. Everett goes into detail on the relations between Mexico and the Texas Cherokee, particularly explaining the Cherokee perspective on their actions.

79 Everett, *Texas Cherokees*, 73, notes the Cherokee carried this sort of policy in their negotiations with the Republic of Texas in 1836, calling the groups "associated bands."

80 Letter from Peter Ellis Bean to Gen. Manuel de Mier y Terán, 11 July 1828, from AGN, Guerra y Marina, transcribed, AGN transcripts v. 329, CASUT, 303–6.

81 Ibid., 303. The political chief was most probably Gatunwali ("Hard Mush") as noted in Everett, *Texas Cherokees*, 57.

82 Everett notes the Cherokee often fought against the Tawankawa and Waco; *Texas Cherokees*, 60.

83 Ibid., 305.

84 Everett, *Texas Cherokees*, 31.

85 Dickson to Clay, Bexar, 1 July 1827, National Archives–Department of State, Dispatches from U.S. Consuls in Texas, 1825–1844.

86 Alonso, *Thread of Blood*, and Daniel Nugent, *Spent Cartridges of Revolution: An Anthropological History of Namiquipa, Chihuahua* (Chicago: University of Chicago Press, 1993).

87 Richard White, *The Middle Ground: Indians, Empires, and Republics in the Great Lakes Region, 1650–1815* (New York: Cambridge University Press, 1991).

88 Jones, "Comparative Raiding Economies," 107.

89 Generally see David J. Weber, *Myth and the History of the Hispanic Southwest* (Albuquerque: University of New Mexico Press, 1988). With respect to the Córdova Rebellion, see Everett, *Texas Cherokees*, 90–93.

90 Cortés, *Report*, 42.

91 José de las Piedras to Manuel de Mier y Terán, Nacogdoches, 20 December 1829, AGN, Guerra y Marina, AGN Transcripts, v.329, CASUT.

92 John, "Independent Indians," 135. One note of indifference by Anglo-Texans appears in a letter from a government official in San Antonio in 1838. W. H. Patton wrote, "Dear Sir, there is nothing new here except that we have had the Comanches in town some days and I am sorry to state that they left before general Johnston arrived and I think there was but little done with them." W. H. Patton to R. A. Irion, San Antonio, 7 February 1838, Texas State Archives: Republic Era (TSA: Republic).

93 Recent scholarship by Jesús F. de la Teja has emphasized the influence of Indian cultural practices on the daily lives of Tejanos. See Jesús F. de la Teja, "Discovering the Tejano Community in 'Early' Texas," *Journal of the Early Republic* 18 (1998).

94 On westward expansion, see David J. Weber, "Mexico's Far Northern Frontier, 1821–1854: Historiography Askew," and "American Westward Expansion," in Weber, *Myth and the History of the Hispanic Southwest*.

95 Weber, "Pobladores and Indios," 121. "Poblador" means colonist.

Fathers of the Pueblo:

Patriarchy and Power in Mexican

California, 1800–1880

On a quiet Sunday in June 1846, General Mariano Guadalupe Vallejo awoke at dawn to the sound of hammering blows on the front door of his home in Sonoma. Vallejo, one of the richest men in California, and his wife Francisca peered through the curtains of their *casa grande* to see a motley buckskin-clad collection of American trappers, horse thieves, and runaway sailors milling about the plaza. Taking the time to dress in his military uniform, Vallejo at last ordered his servants to unlatch the heavy wood door, and admit the men—an armed party from John Frémont's camp. Through an interpreter, a representative declared their intent to arrest Vallejo and seize Mexican army weapons and supplies for the cause of Californian "independence." Vallejo, a native-born Californio, assured them that he sympathized with plans to make California an American protectorate, then gave them the keys to his arsenal. While he wrote out terms of surrender, Vallejo had breakfast prepared for the hungry rebels.

Vallejo, the friend of American settlers in the North, soon found himself in jail at Sutter's Fort without charges or trial. Meanwhile, those left to guard Sonoma raised a hand-sewn flag, bearing a single star, the likeness of a bear, and the phrase "California Republic." These "Bear Flaggers," although they acted without official sanction, were quickly incorporated into the United States Army after July 7, 1846, when Commodore John Drake Sloat of the Pacific Squadron took Monterey and announced the war between the United States and Mexico.[1] Before long, the fleet was joined by U.S. Army forces marching overland from New Mexico. Overpowered, Californians finally capitulated on January 13, 1847. Over the next forty years, the hospitable Vallejo lost his power in California's government to hostile newcomers, and his fortune and enormous ranchos to American creditors; he died so poor that his estate could not cover his funeral expenses.[2]

This story of Mariano Guadalupe Vallejo often serves as the classic example of elite Californio attitudes and experiences during the Mexican-American War, and of Californio decline after the war.[3] Its appeal comes from how closely it seems to follow the classic arc of conquest tales: an enlightened (or greedy) leader of a "traditional" society holds his hand out in welcome to conquerors but finds himself betrayed and suffers the sad but inevitable decline of an older way of life in the face of progress. Told this way, Vallejo, and all Californios, appear to have had little understanding of American legal and economic systems, watching helplessly as the new arrivals stripped them of land, money, and representation. The initial betrayal by elite individuals like Vallejo is blamed for the subsequent fragmentation of the Mexican community, and the losses of the postwar years.

But does this tragic figure of Mariano Guadalupe Vallejo really best represent the Californio experience? The de la Guerra family, Vallejo's cousins in the south, offer a new way to look at the conquest of California. With an entire family as the subject of study, we can see beyond the story of a single striving man pouring tea for his conquerors. Instead, we can perceive the deep and enduring patterns of patriarchy and political authority in Mexican California, and the many options within them for resistance, adaptation, and persistence across the war years.

In the southern counties of California, Californios also eventually lost most of their wealth and influence but did so after a remarkably long period in power. The de la Guerra family and their supporters, for example, were powerful enough to control city and county government in Santa Barbara for more than two decades after the war. At any given time in the 1850s, 1860s, and even 1870s, the de la Guerras or their allies could be found holding office as sheriff, justice of the peace, mayor, city council member, county supervisor, district judge, state assemblyman, or state senator. They ran election tables, held the majority on the grand jury, and dominated the Democratic Party's county committee.

The de la Guerras did not gain their powerful posts at the expense of nonelite Mexicans, but indeed with their support and assistance. Well into the American period, the Californio and Mexican community of the region continued to share with the de la Guerras a notion of the body politic as patriarchal family. The de la Guerra brothers held power because their supporters generally accepted the public face de la Guerras together presented—an enactment of the benevolent community patriarch, a role that their father had originally established under the Spanish and Mexican flags.[4] Townsfolk expected and demanded from their de la Guerra "fathers" the reciprocal support and defense they believed was owed to them. Elites who stepped outside this role found themselves stripped of public authority.

The Mexican Era: Patriarchy as a Language of Authority

The origins of postwar Californio political strategies lie in the years before the Mexican-American War, when Santa Barbarans first learned to think of de la Guerras as their legitimate rulers. José de la Guerra, a military officer and merchant, arrived in California under Spanish rule in 1801, and once posted to Santa Barbara, used his family connections and noble Spanish birth to establish himself quickly as the region's leading man. He became captain of the presidio, with a jurisdiction that stretched south one hundred miles to Los Angeles, and was the wealthiest and best-connected trader in town. Within a few years, Santa Barbarans of all classes began to publicly express his position in the community in the terms of family relations. "We turn to you as a loving father," a group of Los Angeles townswomen wrote to de la Guerra in a petition of 1822.[5] A foreign visitor of the 1830s noted, "All the people of Santa Barbara looked upon him as patriarch of their little community."[6] For the Mexicans of California, these were not empty words of praise but a metaphor that summoned a deep and shared language of power that they and their parents had brought with them from Spain and neighboring regions of Mexico.

Ideally, Spanish colonial society was composed of a hierarchy of corporations (such as the nobility, clergy, military, and Indians), each with their own function and privileges, or *fueros*. Society maintained coherence and stability because no one could exist outside this order; in theory, individuals would know their place in it and submit willingly. This ideal, in turn, was expressed in laws which shaped the social order. As the Council of the Indies expressed it in 1806, "a graduated system of dependence and subordination sustains and insures the obedience and respect of the last vassal to the authority of the sovereign."[7]

Patriarchy—the submission of women to men and children to their father—formed the underlying logic of this entire system. The nuclear family, headed by a husband and father, was the basic unit on which everything else rested. Ideally, the king ruled and provided for his subjects as a benevolent father did for his family, while individual men maintained the social order by acting as the king's representative in the family, governing women and children.[8] In other words, patriarchy in Spanish and Mexican California was not simply an ideology of male dominance over women. The notion of fatherhood played a critical role in how Californians understood authority and the structure of their entire society.[9]

It would be wrong, however, to describe patriarchy as a system that existed outside of the human relationships that sustained it. It was not a thing imposed, but a set of relationships and assumptions under continual negotiation. To put it a different way, being the "father of the town" was not something de la Guerra *was*, it was something he *did*. Among the men of his generation, de la Guerra was remarkably successful in positioning himself at the head of Santa Barbara's social hierarchy through the first half of the nineteenth century. The work of his wife María Antonia Carrillo, his children, and their servants enabled de la Guerra to maintain this role in the community, while every member of that community argued the terms under which they would accept him as their benevolent patriarch.

In 1827, Commander de la Guerra was called upon to produce a census of his district, and he noted a total population of 4,008, including the Indians at the five nearby missions.[10] José de la Guerra acted as a "father" to these Santa Barbarans on two levels. First, he demonstrated command and physical dominance, the mastery through strength of will understood by Californio men to be an expression of the natural authority of a father over his children. But in the eyes of Spanish Mexicans, men who commanded by fear and force or who used their wealth only to benefit themselves were little more than self-aggrandizing tyrants. True masculine virtue derived from fulfilling obligations to dependents.[11] With wealth and a large extended family, men like José de la Guerra could do this on a grand scale.

Family ties structured the political and business worlds and made such concentration of wealth possible. María Antonia Carrillo, like many creole wives across Latin America, connected her immigrant husband to her father and brothers.[12] As presidial commander, de la Guerra placed his Carrillo brothers-in-law in government posts. In turn, the Carrillos oversaw José de la Guerra's business operations in Los Angeles. Other trading partners, military officers, and government officials were linked to the de la Guerras through marriage or the "spiritual kinship" of godparenthood. Mexico's legal system reinforced the family economy over individual interests and sheltered family assets from risk.[13] Patriarchs like de la Guerra sat at the center of a dense web of relations, with recognized authority over a large, multifamily alliance. Skilled men knew when to call in certain favors and when to grant them, and they knew how to use the obligations of kinship to promote their own interests and those of their families. Drawing on these extraordinary resources and connections, de la Guerra had the capacity to prove his worth as "father of the Pueblo."

José de la Guerra's household befitted a man of his standing. Originally, the de la Guerras lived within the walls of the Santa Barbara presidio, but by 1828 a fine new house was nearing completion nearby. A one-story U-shaped adobe, it had one wing devoted to housing merchandise, one central section with large public dining and entertaining rooms and a corner office, and one wing of connecting bedrooms.[14] From a bench in the center of the veranda, José could watch for ships laden with his merchandise to drop anchor in the harbor below. In a town where every other family made do with one or two cramped rooms, the de la Guerra house stood out: large, secure, and impressive. The building itself projected José de la Guerra's status as a dominant patriarch and householder. Upon this stage, servants, family, and dependents created and negotiated this role with de la Guerra.

In the kitchen, back yards, and storerooms, María Antonia Carrillo de la Guerra managed the large staff of mostly Indian servants and kept the household humming. The de la Guerras fashioned adult servants into childlike dependents by using nicknames rather than their given names, clothing them in cheap cotton, and requiring some to sit on the floor with the children of the family.[15] For both elite men and women, the ability to command the labor of others served as a marker of status, but the image of loyal dependents was of equal importance. José worked to appear as a master who protected and cared for his servants, providing food, shelter, clothing, and a powerful advocate as a father would.[16] In at least one case, de la Guerra seems even to have arranged a servant's marriage.[17]

Most servants gave outward signs of submission but demanded material benefits in turn. Most de la Guerra servants were unconverted or "gentile" Indians, but the few mission neophytes among them could exploit the tensions of having two "fathers"—one in the de la Guerra household and another set at the mission. Some used de la Guerra's "protection" to obtain release from the labor demands of the missions. Others employed mission authority to escape de la Guerra's household. Juan, a neophyte and de la Guerra servant, for example, abandoned his work in the de la Guerra house in 1816 and rode to the Mission La Purísima on a new bay horse. Father Payeras refused de la Guerra's demand to send the neophyte back, telling him, "he is going to his own, for they have sent for him."[18]

In several cases, the de la Guerra family formalized the parental relationship to their servants through *compadrazgo*, or godparentage, further increasing their responsibility for the material and spiritual welfare of their charges. Outsiders, too, used spiritual kinship to find a place in de la Guerra's house, and with that, a chance to improve their situations. De la Guerra took in convicts sent north from Mexico, for example, and sailors who jumped ship to start new lives in California.[19] Such spiritual kinship gave the patriarch the right to keep an eye on the behavior of otherwise rootless people. Godchildren also owed their sponsors deference, and as a consequence, having many godchildren conferred honor and prestige. But, in return, godparents could not shirk their responsibilities without losing honor.

A man's honor also depended in part on his ability to protect the women of his household from any hint of sexual dishonor, and as a result "troublesome" or "shameful" women formed a noteworthy subset of the de la Guerra household dependents. In June of 1813, for example, American ship captain George Washington Ayres was expelled for smuggling and left behind his Hawaiian companion Margarita Gégue. The de la Guerra family took in the unmarried Margarita and baptized her under the sponsorship of María Antonia. Margarita used her connections and protected status to establish her virtue in the eyes of the community and became the respectable wife of a soldier four years later.[20] Over the course of de la Guerra's life, several women like this took advantage of a stay in the de la Guerra house to restore or maintain their honor, particularly when they had no husband or father of their own. In frontier California, only the wealthy could afford multiroom houses to shelter women from the offenses of the world.[21]

José de la Guerra's paternal authority and obligations extended beyond the dependents living in his house to cover the entire communitywide "family" of soldiers and settlers. Because Santa Barbara, unlike Los Angeles, was a presidial town organized around a military post, the first settlers knew de la Guerra best as *El Capitán*.[22] Of the 529 non-Indians residing in town in 1827, more than half were soldiers and their families. As *habilitado*, or quartermaster, and then commander, José de la Guerra was charged with providing for his troops, and as a successful merchant was able to do a much better job of it than many other officers. Of course, he took a profit from provisioning the troops, but he also made sure to offer charity to needy soldiers, widows, and orphans.[23] His shrewdest move came in 1817, when he persuaded the government to grant the presidio a "royal" ranch north of Santa Barbara to supply its soldiers with horses, beef, and cash from sales of hides and tallow.[24] Because de la Guerra fulfilled what they saw as his obligations to them, many former soldiers continued to show deference and loyalty to their former captain well after military law had obliged them to.

After independence in 1821, Mexico City abandoned support for the army of the northern frontier. As Santa Barbara's economy shifted from military supply to trade and ranching production, de la Guerra increasingly relied on his commercial interests to reinforce the foundation of his role as town "father." José de la Guerra represented the market to Santa Barbara and Los Angeles settlers, and his power over family and household economies was profound. According to the census, most townsfolk subsisted on their "scanty crops of wheat, beans, Indian corn, and some other vegetables," but nearly everyone ran up debts at de la Guerra's retail store, buying imported and processed goods like cotton cloth, ready-made shoes, and chocolate. In a cash-poor economy, settlers struggled to settle their accounts with labor, otter fur, a few dozen hides, or a sack or two of tallow.[25] Only a few owned their own land; those lucky enough to own cattle grazed them where they could and processed the hides and tallow for the foreign markets, but again de la Guerra inserted himself, acting as middleman to the foreign traders, and taking a cut of the profits.[26]

Landless and debt-ridden settlers may well have muttered under their breaths that the Captain's economic dominance came at their expense. In the public world, de la Guerra, with the aid of his household, had to work hard to overcome this perception. As he had with individuals in his household, José de la Guerra took on the role of *padrino*, or godfather, to the congregations of San José, Mission San Juan Bautista, and Los Angeles, ensuring that each one had a proper building and a well-outfitted priest. Young couples also sought out de la Guerra to act as padrino to their marriages, receiving gifts of wedding clothes and a hosted reception in return. De la Guerra not only donated clothing to young couples but he also could be called upon for small loans, holiday gifts, medical aid, education, and help during natural disasters. In this role, too, his wife often acted on behalf of her husband, taking on the role of godmother, tending to the sick, and handing out gifts.[27]

Prior to the Mexican-American War, José de la Guerra spent decades exercising military command and acquiring wealth but also creating the public impression that he used his connections, rank, and wealth as a father would for his household. As he provided for his family, so he took care of the material needs of his servants, godchildren, cousins, and other dependents. As he sheltered his wife and daughters from shame, so he protected the virtue of other women. As he tended to the morality, education, and health of his family, so he ensured the development of others under his wing. Because he succeeded so well in answering the demands of the community, de la Guerra took on the authority of a legitimate patriarch in their eyes.

This moral authority, in turn, secured for de la Guerra the consent of those he governed, for "good" fathers earned the right to make the rules and settle disputes within their households. Under Spanish rule and into the Mexican era, de la Guerra, as the military commander, was the supreme governmental authority in Santa Barbara and Los Angeles, trying civil cases and answering petitions. But, as one visitor remarked in 1820, his authority seemed to extend beyond statute: "the people look upon him as the absolute ruler of the district, and his counsels and judgments are sought and followed to the letter."[28] Widows asked de la Guerra to mediate with those who owed them money, and mothers petitioned him to intercede with lower authorities on behalf of their sons.[29]

De la Guerra often distributed favors unevenly, especially when his responsibilities to one set of dependents, the soldiers of Santa Barbara, conflicted with the jurisdictional and economic claims of another, the civilian settlers of Los Angeles. For example, in December of 1819, the *regidores* and thirty citizens of Los Angeles signed a petition complaining that de la Guerra had unlawfully taken communal property from the pueblo and granted it to two individuals, Talmates and Machado.[30] This feud continued after independence, as de la Guerra and his allies repeatedly refused to recognize the authority of the civilian government of Los Angeles, and Angelenos refused to pay overdue military taxes.[31]

In the context of this dispute, settlers resisted and made demands using the language of patriarchy and power, playing rival authorities in the military and civil government against each other. In February of 1822, for example, five women of Los Angeles together carefully wrote out a petition to the commander. Their husbands had been convicted by the *alcalde* of "coarse deeds," and as result, the women feared losing their homes and the tools of their trades.[32] "Prostrating ourselves at Your Mercy's feet with the most profound respect and submission," they wrote, "we turn to you as loving father to give us the best consolation."[33] The threat was implied— public disgrace if de la Guerra turned them down, with proof that he was unfit to govern as a "loving father."

A more fundamental danger to de la Guerra's position—indeed to that of all patriarchs—arrived with theories of liberalism in the late 1820s. As Bárbara Reyes shows in her discussion of Baja California in this volume, liberalism challenged traditional sources of authority like the Church, patriarchs, and the military. With this ideology to guide them, second-generation Californians pressed for the distribution of mission lands and a measure of political independence from Mexico in the 1830s. But in Alta California, their rebellion went only so far. Young Mariano Guadalupe Vallejo became one of the most ardent of the reformers, and in a typical maneuver, arrived from Monterey in January of 1839 to restructure the government and military of Santa Barbara, and to weaken José de la Guerra. But the soldiers and officers of the presidio, who placed their loyalties with the "father" who had provided for them, refused the new regime. Within a week, the guardhouse was full of recalcitrant soldiers, and most of the officers were under arrest; Vallejo was forced to concede defeat.[34] In the end, California's second generation rejected the facets of liberalism which challenged paternal authority, and the patriarchal family remained firmly entrenched: a critical institution in the economy and government of Mexican California, and a foundation of a social hierarchy based on paternalism and patronage.[35] Bigger challenges were yet to come.

War Years: Reinventing Patriarchy

In the 1840s, José de la Guerra was looking forward to a comfortable retirement. He had amassed a considerable fortune, including over 200,000 acres of ranchlands, orchards, and vineyards. His eldest sons, José Antonio, Francisco, and Pablo had already taken positions in territorial government. In 1846, the Mexican-American War jeopardized all this. How Californios adapted and transformed Mexican-era patterns over the course of the war, the military occupation that followed, and the boom of the Gold

Rush would determine their ultimate ability to survive in the second half of the century under American rule. In the end, successful elites continued to depend on local patriarchal relations of power, integrating them into a new national regime.

During the war, American military rule upset Mexican power structures. The occupying forces quickly instituted authority at California's territorial level. But, unlike the situation Raúl Ramos describes in Texas, Americans in Southern California, without overwhelming numbers, could only establish their local authority imperfectly. The resulting instability offered the de la Guerras room to emerge as local and statewide leaders while also giving rival Californio men in Santa Barbara the opportunity to challenge de la Guerra dominance. Brothers Pablo and Francisco negotiated constantly between resistance and accommodation, finding ways to serve as representatives of Californio interests within the American system, as they developed local reputations as opponents of that regime.

Unlike Mariano Guadalupe Vallejo, members of the de la Guerra family joined most Californios in opposing American conquest during the war.[36] The day Commodore Sloat of the Pacific Squadron raised the American flag over Monterey, in July of 1846, Customs Administrator Pablo de la Guerra refused to hand over the customs house and treasury and later escaped to join the rest of the California government officers and military, regrouping in the south.[37] His brother Francisco was already calling men to arms along the road from Santa Barbara south to San Buenaventura.[38] Californios recaptured Los Angeles and the rest of the southland in September. Fearing further resistance in the north, American occupying forces in Monterey captured Pablo and younger brother Miguel de la Guerra in early November and held them with no trial or charges for several months.[39]

Although the battles fought on California soil cost the local population only a few deaths and brought them victory at San Pascual on December 6, it was too difficult to keep the war effort going without reinforcements from Mexico. At last, the Californios were forced to sue for peace, and de la Guerras came forward to represent the conquered; on January 11, 1847, Francisco de la Guerra and Francisco Rico met with John Frémont outside Los Angeles. Even in defeat, the de la Guerras negotiated terms. The Treaty of Cahuenga, signed on the 13th, assured Californios the rights of American citizens: life, property, and freedom of movement. In exchange, the men pledged to lay down their arms for the duration of the war.[40] For the next three years, California was ruled by an American military government, before being accepted as a state in 1850.

De la Guerras had resisted American dominance in war, and after the war they took up posts in the American government without fully recognizing its right to govern them. They first did so by securing a leading role in Santa Barbara's civil government. Under military rule, the position of the alcalde carried over into the American era, becoming the only judicial post in the territory under the governor.[41] On May 9, 1847, shortly after the New York Volunteers landed in Santa Barbara, Pablo de la Guerra and his cousin Luís Carrillo were elected First and Second Alcaldes, respectively, of the Santa Barbara district.[42] Governor Stephen Watts Kearny gave official approval to the election of de la Guerra and Carrillo, with the only requirement that they swear an oath to uphold the U.S. Constitution.[43] They refused. Yet so strong was their perceived power over Santa Barbara's Californio community, and so great the American fear of local resistance, that Pablo de la Guerra and Luís Carrillo were permitted, even encouraged, to serve for the rest of the year.[44]

As the Americans consolidated power statewide heading into 1848, they clamped down on such compromises to their authority at the local level. Throughout the year, two new local elections were called, and failed, as de la Guerras refused to run or serve, and other citizens protested the legality of the process.[45] In this moment of instability, their cousin Pedro Carrillo moved in to break the domination of the de la Guerra family over Santa Barbara politics. In February of 1848, he accepted Governor Mason's appointment as alcalde and swore loyalty to the United States. The de la Guerras had preserved their perceived autonomy, but for the first time their principles cost them official roles in territorial and local governance.

The new Santa Barbara alcalde, Pedro Catarino Carrillo, was a nephew and godson of José de la Guerra's wife María Antonia Carrillo. From his blood and spiritual kinship with the de la Guerras, Carrillo might have been expected to support their efforts to preserve Californio property and political autonomy in Santa Barbara. Instead, he chose to risk losing de la Guerra protection for his own alliance with the American authorities and the independent power that might give him. Santa Barbara's crisis of authority came to a head in April of 1848 with what has come to be known as the "Lost Cannon Affair," a sequence of events that exposed the ragged edges of de la Guerra dominance while providing the family with the opportunity to reclaim public and American recognition of that authority.[46]

Earlier that spring, through rumor and backstage political maneuvers, *Alcalde* Carrillo was currying American favor and trying to damage the position of his cousins. De la Guerra men and their associates had been overheard hatching a counterrevolt in a local tavern, Carrillo quietly told the Americans. Francisco de la Guerra and Andrés Pico protested that they were simply planning an expedition against suspected cattle and horse thieves, but the authorities immediately ordered them to put away their arms and disband.

On April 5, 1848, the stakes grew dramatically higher. A six-pound cannon disappeared from the beach at Santa Barbara, and nervous American authorities immediately began a full-scale investigation. Over the next month, Captain Francis J. Lippitt of the First New York Volunteers called Pedro Carrillo and his informants to testify about the "uprising." One by one, they changed their stories. José Genaro Alvarez, for example, the clerk at the tavern, swore he only heard the accused men talking about a horse race and attempts to foil horse rustlers.[47] With the mysterious disappearance of the cannon, what had started as Pedro Carrillo's potentially effective attempt to weaken the de la Guerras' reputations backfired. Lippitt's investigation brought the tactic of rumor and scandal into the harsh light of public scrutiny. In the process, he exposed its practitioners to the knowledge and retribution of the de la Guerras. Santa Barbara's dominant family ultimately emerged even more powerful than before.

Indeed, despite the fact that the de la Guerra brothers no longer held public office, the American authorities continued to recognize their ultimate sway over the region during this affair. The de la Guerras eventually persuaded American military authorities that they had taken no direct role in the theft of the cannon, but they could not dislodge the conviction that, as the recognized leaders of the Californio community, they knew and were protecting those who had taken it. William Tecumseh Sherman, representing the governor, ordered Francisco de la Guerra to find out who stole the gun and why, warning if he did not that "some influential men in your midst will have to suffer a penalty."[48] Francisco refused.

Various accounts survive of what might "really" have happened to the cannon, but one of the most convincing, perhaps, was told years later by a Californio loyalist. "The plan to steal the cannon," José E. García revealed, "was conceived by Don José Antonio de la Guerra, eldest son of Captain de la Guerra, and José Lugo, or 'Chato'." Along with García and other conspirators, they buried the cannon at the beach with the intent to use it "in case of an opportunity for a revolt against the Americans." In other words, if García is to be believed, Captain Lippitt had been quite right to trust Pedro Carrillo and suspect a Californio uprising. And, as it turns out, Sherman had also been right to pinpoint Francisco de la Guerra as someone with knowledge of Californio resistance. The day after the heist, García claimed, he and the others attended mass, and "while we were there, Don Francisco de la Guerra called us aside and took us to a room and very seriously told us that the Americans were very angry about the cannon and we should be very careful not to tell anyone about it."[49] As much as Francisco opposed collaboration, he may also have acted within Californio society to contain those oppositional elements (even his eldest brother) who he knew would trigger strong reprisals from the nervous American occupiers.

The de la Guerras could not maintain their authority in the community simply by squelching rivals; during the military occupation their power continued to derive from the "good" patriarch's moral authority to govern. In the end, one final negotiation sealed this status in the eyes of both the Americans and the town. Unable to identify the culprits or force town leaders to give up the cannon, governor Mason ordered a general fine of $500, levied on townsfolk according to their relative wealth. De la Guerras stepped forward to accept this punishment on behalf of the town. Colonel Jonathan Drake Stevenson, headquartered in Los Angeles, arrived in Santa Barbara in June of 1848; a private meeting with Pablo de la Guerra was the first item on his agenda. Pablo warned the colonel that the people of Santa Barbara resented this tax but would pay out of respect for the family. He then suggested a way to resolve the issue.

Stevenson delayed the immediate call for the assessment, and on July 3 he relocated his headquarters to Santa Barbara, bringing his regimental band. The musicians entered town that evening playing Spanish music and marched immediately to the de la Guerra house, attracting a crowd along the way. While the band serenaded the family, Stevenson called on Pablo to pay his official respects. The next morning, the band took up its concert again at the house, and the townsfolk who attended the day-long fiesta turned in their portion of the fine. That evening, the family held a ball for Santa Barbara's high society in honor of Stevenson, and the next morning on the officer's departure the elder José de la Guerra gave a speech.[50] All of this—the music, open fiesta, elite ball, and public speeches—served to give Californio residents reason to feel that they were not paying a fine out of coercion but in honor of the leading Californio household. Likewise, the de la Guerras, with this ability to negotiate such a display from the Americans, reconfirmed their own status among both elite and nonelite Californios. That month, Alcalde Pedro Carrillo submitted his resignation, refused to pay the fine, and was punished by having some of his property seized.[51]

In the unstable moment of occupation, Californios faced a range of choices in their attempts to claim political authority. Some, like Pedro Carrillo, attempted to improve their position through cooperation with the Americans. Others, like José Antonio de la Guerra and José "Chato" Lugo, opted for another chance at armed resistance. Pablo and Francisco de la Guerra, by continuing to engage the Californio community in their publicly acknowledged role of "Town Father," skillfully negotiated a middle way to emerge as celebrated representatives of that community. This patriarchal relationship became the basis, once voting rights were secured, of a de la Guerra political machine that would last for another generation.

Postwar Politics

Once California had been officially annexed to the United States, the de la Guerra brothers quickly determined that if they were to stay in power they would need to integrate the older system of paternalism and reciprocity with the new one of American-style electoral politics. Working behind the scenes or acting outside the authority of the provisional American government would no longer work once California's state government had been established. If their continuing power under American rule was to be determined by election, the first order of business, then, was to ensure that de la Guerra supporters and dependents would continue to have the power to keep de la Guerras on top.

This power came in the form of voting rights, and the most active and respected son, Pablo, became the voice for Californio citizenship rights when he was chosen to represent Santa Barbara in the state constitutional convention in September of 1849. Early in the proceedings, Charles Botts of Virginia proposed limiting suffrage to only the "white" Mexicans who had become citizens by the terms of the Treaty of Guadalupe Hidalgo. Pablo de la Guerra rose to encourage the delegates to understand clearly "the true significance of the word 'White.' Many citizens of California have received from nature a very dark skin," he argued, "nevertheless, there are among them men who have heretofore been allowed to vote, and not only that, but to fill the highest public offices. It would be very unjust to deprive them of the privilege of citizens merely because nature had not made them White."[52] Unlike the Americans, Californios considered one's public racial identity as somewhat fluid, and only one part of a calculation that allowed those of darker skin or non-European ancestry—the majority of the state's native-born population—to be recognized as something other than Indian or African and to exercise political rights. As one Anglo was forced to admit, in California, "men who have Indian blood in the veins are not for that reason Indians."[53] Botts's language eventually passed, but the category of Mexican "whites" remained a slippery one in practice.

Meanwhile, Pablo de la Guerra insisted that all laws, decrees, regulations, and provisions of the state be published in both English and Spanish. "They cannot obey laws unless they understand them," he argued.[54] This guarantee of bilingual government passed the convention unanimously and provided the foundation not only for compliance to the law but for full participation in Santa Barbara's local government by non-English-speaking Californios. The delegates sent California's first constitution to the voters on October 11, 1849, and threw themselves a grand ball. After the festivities, Pablo returned home, and a little over a month later learned of more good news: he had been elected Santa Barbara's only state senator.[55]

Yet even with voting rights and a pueblo that had reaffirmed the de la Guerra family's authority in the war years, the de la Guerra men had good reason to question their ability to maintain power within a system of electoral politics. From 1848 to 1850, in the heat of the Gold Rush, California's non-Indian population rose from 15,000 to nearly 93,000, and the overwhelming majority of the newcomers were young men of voting age.[56] This rush of new immigrants had no tie to the ranching economy or to Californio families, and de la Guerras feared that the rootless young men would feel no loyalty to or dependence on the Californio elites. Pablo de la Guerra, watching hordes of immigrants overwhelm his northern cousins, worried, "what will become of us in a republican state whose majority of inhabitants are a rabble? God save us."[57] Luckily for de la Guerra, the rabble majority stayed in the north for the next twenty years. The biggest infusion to the southern population in these years came from Sonora, married into the Californio families, and spoke the same language of authority and patriarchy.[58]

For the Californios and Mexican immigrants of Santa Barbara, loyalty to family, community, and the local leaders came to mean loyalty to the Democratic Party. During the 1850s and 1860s, machine politics and a patriarchal family structure made an excellent fit. The methods of party politics complemented the uniquely Californio style of kin networks and patriarchal leadership. Everyone knew that any de la Guerra brother spoke for them all. In 1852, for example, Pablo told supporters that his younger brother Antonio María "has been elected to the Senate in my place."[59] Ten years later, Antonio María smoothly coordinated brother Pablo's run for the district judgeship and delegated the legwork to his brothers and nephews, who canvassed the voters and appealed to kin loyalty to secure votes.[60] At times, the coordination of the brothers and their machine edged into outright fraud. Preprinted ballots, a common machine tool, were distributed through kin networks, and a de la Guerra usually served as election table "inspector."[61]

Kin networks and family loyalties helped de la Guerras to run their campaigns, but the fit of machine politics and the Californio family model did not end there. The American patronage system also replicated Mexican-era models of reciprocity and obligation, allowing de la Guerras the means to reward supporters with employment. As an enticement during the 1860 election, Governor Downey told Pablo, "if you succeed in carrying the Southern Counties I will promise you that the Democracy will give you anything you may want hereafter."[62] The steady income of patronage jobs became increasingly important as the ranching economy slid into decline in the late 1850s. De la Guerras used the possibility of such rewards to keep supporters in line. In 1857, Pablo instructed his brother Antonio María to let "Raymundo" know he had blown his chances for a sure $2,000 a year by voting against the Democrats, "since if it were not for this we believe that we might have been able to obtain for him the Customs."[63] Likewise, the Californio constituency did not hesitate to call the de la Guerras greedy despots in public if the family appeared to be using patronage only for themselves and not the whole community. In the election of 1863, for example, Francisco de la Guerra warned his brothers that "Pedro" of San Buenaventura had organized his friends and family to work against the de la Guerras and was telling them "that we wanted it all for ourselves, that among public employees and candidates there were ten of our family."[64]

To maintain the appearance of the paternal and open-handed generosity essential to their political success, de la Guerras gave supporters more than the rewards of patronage; they also continued the more informal and personal public charity and hospitality of their father. This became especially critical in election seasons. Throughout the war and the Gold Rush, the family had moved strongly to protect its assets and adapt to changing markets, preserving the resources necessary to act as benevolent patriarchs. With extensive ranches and cash reserves, they could afford the charitable gestures that became key campaign tools. During an 1855 race, for example, younger brother Joaquín supervised affairs at the San Julián Ranch, distributing "fat cows" to "the party men" for barbecues and gifts.[65] After the 1863 campaign, Antonio María reported that "holy gold was scattered in handfuls."[66] With victory secured, supporters often pushed for an even grander show of generosity; in 1861 when Pablo rose to the post of lieutenant governor, townsfolk organized a party at the de la Guerra house, knowing that the family would have to foot the bill or lose legitimacy. "It was necessary to agree," Antonio María grumbled, "since these devils already had contracted the musicians and invited various families."[67]

Once in office, the de la Guerras used their public roles to defend the interests of Californios. With many family members to hold down offices in the city, county, and state, the de la Guerra machine had a distinct advantage in pursuing its agenda. At the local level, the de la Guerra brothers usually formed the majority on the city council and the county board of supervisors. Land rights were at the core of Californio autonomy and identity, and the brothers promoted the ranching economy by setting low property taxes on large landowners. But they also defended Californio religion, language, and culture by enforcing the use of Spanish in government and schools, and by ensuring that traditions of horse racing, gambling, dancing, and drinking remained legal on Sundays.

Because they continued to rely on Mexican-era family dynamics, de la Guerras in local government could count on a family ally in Sacramento to carry out this agenda. Even as early as 1851, Mayor Francisco de la Guerra knew that he could demand that the city council send him their resolutions in Spanish, because it was his brother Pablo who had placed that regulation in the state constitution.[68] As mayor or county supervisor, Antonio María and Francisco de la Guerra frequently sent to their state senator—brother Pablo—requests for legislation to set up new schools, regulate sheep pasturage, fund road construction, and establish mail service.[69] During the drought of 1861, Antonio María toured the district and reported to Pablo that "several" of his constituents "have spoken to me to see if you may pass some law protecting the Rancheros."[70] In some cases, de la Guerras in local office even went so far as to draft the state legislation themselves.[71]

In the 1850s and 1860s, the primary threat facing most Californios was an effort on the part of many incoming Americans to seize lands that they considered the spoils of war, even though the Treaty of Guadalupe Hidalgo had guaranteed Mexican property rights. As state senator, Pablo de la Guerra worked especially hard to kill various bills which would have supported the rights of squatters.[72] In one impassioned speech, he claimed his prerogative to speak for all Californios, "those who were abandoned and sold by Mexico. . . . They have no voice in this Senate, except that which is now so weakly speaking in their favor. . . . I have seen old people, sixty and seventy years old, crying like children because they had been cast out from the hearths of their ancestors."[73]

It is telling, perhaps, that in this speech Pablo de la Guerra refers to his elders "crying like children," for as a Californio leader, he continued not only to act but to think of his role as a paternal one. During the sessions of the land claims court, set up in 1851 to determine the legality of Mexican deeds, Californios were frequently accused of perjury and denied their claims. De la Guerra defended the "rustic" vaqueros, the cowboys and ranch hands who made such poor witnesses. The court of law, the slick-talking lawyers, the poor translators, "all this," he told a friend, confused the *vaqueros*, "as it would confuse a fearful child." But his countrymen, Pablo asserted, trusted him as "their organ, their support and their protector."[74]

Ultimately, then, political control in the American era rested on American citizenship rights and machine-style politics, overlaying an older order of patriarchal politics. Because they continued to play the role of the benevolent patriarch so well, and because they skillfully organized extended family networks, the de la Guerras could command an organized bloc of Californio voters. Local Californios, in turn, insisted that de la Guerras fulfill the paternal obligations that gave them the moral authority to govern. "All united," Julio Osuna wrote Pablo from San Diego, "we are preparing to serve you as the 'Champion' of our race."[75]

This state of affairs did not sit well with many incoming Anglos, particularly those with neither family ties to Californios nor a stake in the ranching economy. "When they are united," New England immigrant Charles Huse groused, "they can elect whomever they wish."[76] Unable to overcome the de la Guerra machine and gain access to public office, some de la Guerra opponents turned to other measures, some legal and some not quite so.

Many educated and privileged American migrants into California expected a situation similar to other areas of the West, where they could rise quickly through local government. In southern California, however, they soon ran into the wall of the de la Guerra Democracy. In 1869, for example, Walter Murray lost to Pablo de la Guerra in the race for district judge. Still smarting, an incensed Murray made public accusations of electoral fraud. While allegations like these may have had some truth to them, they were seldom met with a positive response, particularly from a county board of supervisors and board of canvassers made up of de la Guerras. In this case, charges were dismissed, and Pablo claimed victory.[77]

Other opponents did not stand on such formalities of the law. After Cornelius R. V. Lee, for example, lost the mayoral election of 1855 to Pablo de la Guerra, he formed the vigilante group the Santa Barbara Mounted Rifles. By then, Antonio María had taken his brother's place as mayor, and he disarmed the Riflemen to protect accused criminals from being taken out of the jail and lynched. But it soon became apparent that, like the similar Committee of Vigilance in San Francisco, the real target of the Mounted Rifles was not Santa Barbara's outlaw element but the Democratic machine itself. Intimidation, rather than electoral politics or the legal system, was the weapon of choice. Long-time resident William Streeter later remembered that Pablo de la Guerra was "summoned" to a meeting of the Riflemen "and warned against retaining in his employ certain Californians or Mexicans who were known to be bad characters."[78] And when notorious highwayman Jack Powers escaped from custody in February of 1857, the vigilance committee immediately blamed de la Guerras, again for supporting the criminal element. This time, the threat was more explicit: "they had their meetings," Antonio María reported to Pablo, "in which according to reliable reports it was proposed to lynch me and Francisco."[79]

In the charged atmosphere of the 1850s, the de la Guerras worked to prevent a "race war," not just defeating Anglo opposition but also, as they had in the Lost Cannon Affair, keeping more militant elements of the Mexican population from acting out and provoking harsh recrimination.

In 1859, for example, a group of local Anglos lynched Francisco Badillo and his son, poor men suspected of stealing cattle for their family's table. Enraged, a group of native Californians and Sonoran immigrants hunted down and beat the vigilantes. Not long after, one investigator reported, "the larger part of the American citizens of the town assembled at a house near the Landing," and let Pablo de la Guerra know "that they held him . . . responsible."[80] Hoping to show the town's residents that his authority was impartial, Pablo spoke both to the assembly of Americans and to the Californios and Mexican immigrants embroiled in the incident. Because of his mediation, the four Mexicans responsible for beating the vigilantes agreed to leave town, at least for a little while, and Santa Barbara's racial tensions subsided.[81]

*   *   *

A number of factors conspired to bring an end to the de la Guerra political dynasty and to local Californio political power in the 1870s. Although the de la Guerras had been able to hold on to their ranches through the land claims courts after the war, they lost most of their land in the 1860s when a drought pushed over the first domino of debt and foreclosure. They had long since given up the trading business. By the early 1860s, the family had lost most of the material base they had depended on to enact the public role of the generous patriarch. Still, for a decade after the de la Guerra family had passed out of the core of Santa Barbara's economy, the solid bloc of the de la Guerra Democracy held firm because as elected officials the brothers could still deliver patronage and advocate for the interests of their constituency.

More critical, as it turned out, was the erosion of a voting base that continued to speak a common language of patriarchy. The "rabble" Pablo had feared arrived at last when a real estate and tourist boom in the early 1870s pulled in a massive influx of new Anglo citizens and tipped the balance of the voter rolls.[82] By 1870, for the first time, census takers recorded a majority of non-Spanish surnames in the county. The new voters had no memory of the family's role as town patriarch, and unlike the Sonoran settlers of the 1850s, had no interest in learning it.

Yet, even with a weakened de la Guerra family and a majority Anglo population, a local understanding of political authority and patriarchy ran deep. Ironically, Republican developer Thomas R. Bard adopted the language and tactics himself in order to split the Californio vote and finally break the Democratic machine in Santa Barbara County. While involved in protracted court cases to gain control of de la Guerra ranches Simi, Las Posas, and Conejo, Bard befriended the Camarillo family of San Buenaventura and persuaded the daughters to recruit male relatives and friends for his 1867 election.[83] Bard used his own ranches in Ventura to win over what he termed "the Spanish element." In 1873, he wrote a friend, they "were at first inclined to go back upon us but the contribution of a fat cow at my expense for a jolly time on the day before the election promised to give us 1/2 their vote."[84] Despite the ranchero pose, once in power Bard and other Republicans passed laws that favored commercial development and the breakup of Mexican ranching estates.

Fat cows did not win over everyone. In 1871, a final call for unity appeared in the *Santa Barbara Press*: "We are all native Californios, . . . we have lived more or less as brothers," R. Espinoza pleaded. "The Democratic Party, has been and will always be the party that offers more guarantees to the native Californians and to our race."[85] But it was too late. The 1873 county and city elections resulted in the almost complete defeat of Californio candidates and the end of a political system based on a carefully cultivated and shared acceptance of de la Guerra brothers as local patriarchs. From their father's early years playing the role of town patriarch, through the upheavals of the war years, and under American rule, the de la Guerras and their dependents had continually reinvented the very idea of the "Father of the Pueblo." It was not Californio greed, ignorance, or betrayal that brought their rule to an end, but the dwindling numbers of those who spoke the language of Mexican patriarchy.

Notes

1 Hubert Howe Bancroft, *History of California*, vol. 5, *1846–1848* (San Francisco: History Company, 1884–1890), 109–21, 145–50; Neal Harlow, *California Conquered: The Annexation of a Mexican Province, 1846–1850* (Berkeley: University of California Press, 1982), 97–105; Alan Rosenus, *General M. G. Vallejo and the Advent of the Americans* (Albuquerque: University of New Mexico Press, 1995), 108–19; Lisbeth Haas, "War in California, 1846–1848," in *Contested Eden: California Before the Gold Rush*, ed. Ramón Gutiérrez and Richard J. Orsi (Berkeley: University of California Press, 1998), 331–55.

2 Rosenus, *General M. G. Vallejo*, 234.

3 Most recently, Ken Burns used Vallejo for this purpose in his PBS documentary *The West*, and Vallejo is the primary example in the book that accompanied

the series, Geoffrey C. Ward, *The West: An Illustrated History* (Boston: Little, Brown, 1996), 88–90, 110, 152, 392–93.

4   A number of scholars have explored the regions of the Southwest where Mexicans managed to retain power into the American era, but none have fully explored the public language of patriarchy employed in these areas, its roots in the Mexican era, or its constant renegotiation between leaders and supporters. See Evan Anders, *Boss Rule in South Texas: The Progressive Era* (Austin: University of Texas Press, 1982), xii–xvi; Albert Camarillo, *Chicanos in a Changing Society: From Mexican Pueblos to American Barrios in Santa Barbara and Southern California, 1848–1930* (Cambridge: Harvard University Press, 1979); Juan Gómez-Quiñones, *Roots of Chicano Politics, 1600–1940* (Albuquerque: University of New Mexico Press, 1994), 234; and Leonard Pitt, *The Decline of the Californios: A Social History of the Spanish-Speaking Californians, 1846–1890* (Berkeley: University of California Press, 1966).

5   Luisa Barelas, Demetria Ramires, Juana Ygnocencia Reyes, Ma. Luisa Reyes, and Baleriana Lorensana to José de la Guerra, Los Angeles, 1 February 1822, folder 1000, de la Guerra Papers, Santa Barbara Mission Archive-Library, Santa Barbara, California. Further references to the archive will be in the form SBMAL, except for further references to this collection which will be in the form DLG (folder number). Unless otherwise noted, translations from the Spanish are my own.

6   Alfred Robinson, quoted in Joseph A. Thompson, *El Gran Capitán: José de la Guerra* (Los Angeles: Cabrera and Sons, 1961), 166.

7   Council of the Indies, quoted in Lyle N. McAlister, "Social Structure and Social Change in New Spain," *Hispanic American Historical Review* 43:3 (August 1963): 364.

8   Silvia Marina Arrom, *The Women of Mexico City, 1790–1857* (Stanford: Stanford University Press, 1985), 76–77.

9   On the continuation of this colonial social order into the Mexican era, see Rosaura Sánchez, *Telling Identities: The Californio Testimonios* (Minneapolis: University of Minnesota Press, 1995), 101; and John Lynch, *The Spanish American Revolutions 1808–1826* (New York: Norton, 1986), 321–33, 347–49.

10   José de la Guerra, Santa Barbara Presidio, 20 July 1827; Departmental State Papers, 5:2–7, Bancroft Library; see also Auguste Duhaut-Cilly, "Duhaut-Cilly's Account of California in the Years 1827–28," trans. Charles Franklin Carter, *California Historical Society Quarterly* 8:2 (June 1929): 130–66.

11   On patriarchy in late colonial and early republican Mexico, see Ana María Alonso, *Thread of Blood: Colonialism, Revolution, and Gender on Mexico's Northern Frontier* (Tucson: University of Arizona Press, 1995); Virginia Marie Bouvier, *Women and the Conquest of California, 1542–1840: Codes of Silence* (Tucson: University of Arizona Press, 2001); Richard Boyer, *Lives of the Bigamists: Marriage, Family and Community in Colonial Mexico* (Albuquerque: University

of New Mexico Press, 1995); Antonia Castañeda, "Presidarias y Pobladoras: Spanish-Mexican Women in Frontier Monterey, Alta California, 1770–1821" (Ph.D. diss., Stanford University, 1990); Albert L. Hurtado, *Intimate Frontiers: Sex, Gender and Culture in Old California* (Albuquerque: University of New Mexico Press, 1999); Cheryl English Martin, *Governance and Society in Colonial Mexico: Chihuahua in the Eighteenth Century* (Stanford: Stanford University Press, 1996); Douglas Monroy, *Thrown among Strangers: The Making of Mexican Culture in Frontier California* (Berkeley: University of California Press, 1990); Genaro M. Padilla, *My History, Not Yours: The Formation of Mexican-American Autobiography* (Madison: University of Wisconsin Press, 1993); Rosaura Sánchez, *Telling Identities*; Patricia Seed, *To Love, Honour, Obey in Colonial Mexico: Conflicts over Marriage Choice, 1574–1821* (Stanford: Stanford University Press, 1988); and Steve J. Stern, *The Secret History of Gender: Women, Men, and Power in Late Colonial Mexico* (Chapel Hill: University of North Carolina Press, 1995).

12 On the role of women in merchant families, see Susan Migden Socolow, *The Merchants of Buenos Aires, 1778–1810* (Cambridge: Cambridge University Press, 1978); and David A. Brading, *Miners and Merchants in Bourbon Mexico, 1763–1810* (Cambridge: Cambridge University Press, 1971).

13 For the literature on the "family economy" of late colonial and early republican Mexico, see Edith Couturier, "Women in a Noble Family: The Mexican Counts of Regla, 1750–1830," in *Latin American Women: Historical Perspectives*, ed. Asunción Lavrin (Westport, Conn.: Greenwood Press, 1978); John Kicza, "The Great Families of Mexico: Elite Maintenance and Business Practices in Late Colonial Mexico City," *Hispanic American Historical Review* 62:3 (1982): 429–57; John Tutino, "Power, Class, and Family: Men and Women in the Mexican Elite, 1750–1810," *The Americas* 39:3 (January 1983): 359–81; and David W. Walker, *Kinship, Business and Politics: The Martínez del Rio Family in Mexico, 1824–1864* (Chicago: University of Chicago Press, 1981), 55.

14 Michael Imwalle, "Comprehensive Archaeological and Architectural Investigation of the Casa de la Guerra" (unpublished document, Santa Barbara Trust for Historical Preservation, 1994).

15 For a list of servant nicknames, see one provided in 1921 by a granddaughter of José de la Guerra. Fr. Joseph Thompson, "Casa de la Guerra," SBMAL, 5. On the use and meaning of seating and ready-made cotton clothing, see William Dane Phelps, *Alta California 1840–1842: The Journal and Observances of William Dane Phelps, Master of the Ship "Alert,"* intro. and ed. Briton Cooper Busch (Glendale, Calif.: Arthur H. Clark, 1983), 178; and Lisbeth Haas, *Conquests and Historical Identities in California, 1769–1936* (Berkeley: University of California Press, 1995), 52.

16 Most likely, de la Guerra paid his servants with a mix of goods and cash; no records survive.

17 Santiago Argüello to José de la Guerra, San Diego, 22 April 1817, DLG 56, trans. Mary Bowman, vol. 1, letter no. 127, pp. 88–89. Two volumes of translations of the de la Guerra papers were done by Bowman for the California Historical Survey from 1917 to 1919, prior to the deposit of the collection in the Santa Barbara Mission Archive Library. Copies of these translations are now available at this archive. Further references to these translations will be in the form: Bowman (volume), (letter number), p. (no.).

18 Fr. Mariano Payeras to José de la Guerra, Mission Purísima, no month, 1816, DLG 769 (trans. Bowman 2, 135, p. 110).

19 Hubert Howe Bancroft, *History of California*, vol. 2, *1801–1824* (San Francisco: History Company, 1884–1890), 277. In January of 1816, the American ships the *Albatross* and the *Lydia* were captured, and part of their crews taken prisoner, including the captain's twenty-year-old "Negro" slave, "Bob." Captain de la Guerra allowed any who wished, to remain in Santa Barbara. María Antonia de la Guerra and her eldest son José Antonio became padrinos to the ex-slave rechristened Juan Cristóbal. With this act, Juan Cristóbal/Bob transformed himself from slave to free citizen. Santa Barbara Baptismal Records, vol. 1, no. 552, 16 August 1819, SBMAL.

20 Bancroft, *History of California*, 2: 269–70.

21 Martin, *Governance and Society*, 139–42.

22 From 1815 to 1827, de la Guerra served continuously as the presidial commander at Santa Barbara, then periodically as acting commander. Bancroft, *History of California* 2: 570–73; 3: 650–51.

23 For example, Juan Martiarena to José de la Guerra, Monterey, 18 December 1816, DLG 642 (trans. Bowman 1, 124, p. 87).

24 Bancroft, *History of California* 2: 574.

25 For example, see small accounts collected in DLG 210 and DLG 1049; and Antonio María Ortega to José de la Guerra, Rancho Refugio, August 1825, DLG 744 (trans. Bowman 1, 307, p. 203). On indebtedness to merchants, see Haas, *Conquests and Historical Identities*, 53.

26 José del Carmen Lugo, "Life of a Rancher," *Historical Society of Southern California Quarterly* 32:3 (September 1950): 216, 230.

27 As Raúl Ramos notes in his essay in this volume, elites also could successfully extend patriarchal notions of command and reciprocity to their relationships with those outside Mexican communities. Just as the local elites of Texas fought with and gave gifts to the various native peoples of Texas, José de la Guerra disciplined and rewarded gentile and mission Indians in California.

28 Del Castillo Negrete, Journal of 1820, quoted in Thompson, *El Gran*, 162.

29 María Rufin Hernandez to José de la Guerra, Santa Barbara, 14 February 1821, DLG 29 (trans. Bowman 1, 185, p. 124); Fr. José Señan to José de la Guerra, Mission San Buenaventura, 26 September 1821, DLG 904 (trans. Bowman 2, 482, p. 388).

30 Bancroft, *History of California* 2: 354.

31 Thompson, *El Gran*, 79–80; Gov. Luis Argüello to José de la Guerra, Monterey, December 4, 1823, DLG 51 (trans. Bowman 1, 256, p. 156); José Palomares and José Antonio Carrillo to José de la Guerra, Los Angeles, March 10, 1825, DLG 766 (trans. Bowman 1, 297, p. 193); Domingo Carrillo to José de la Guerra, Santa Barbara, 9 April 1834, DLG 137 (trans. Bowman 1, 403, p. 271); Tomás Antonio Yorba to José de la Guerra, 22 August 1834, DLG 1037.

32 An *alcalde* performed the duties, more or less, of a justice of the peace and mayor.

33 Luisa Barelas, Demetria Ramires, Juana Ygnocencia Reyes, Ma. Luisa Reyes, and Baleriana Lorensana to José de la Guerra, Los Angeles, 1 February 1822, DLG 1000.

34 Bancroft, *History of California*, 3: 581–83.

35 The challenge of liberalism is more fully discussed in Louise Pubols, "The de la Guerra Family: Patriarchy and the Political Economy of California, 1800–1850" (Ph.D. diss., University of Wisconsin, Madison, 2000).

36 On the wartime resistance of Californios, see Haas, "War in California."

37 Bancroft, *History of California* 5: 235.

38 Pío Pico to Francisco de la Guerra and Antonio Rodríguez, Commissioners, Santa Barbara, 23 June 1846, DLG 788.

39 Bancroft, *History of California* 5: 363; Angustias de la Guerra Ord, *Occurrences in Hispanic California*, trans. and ed. William H. Ellison and Francis Price (Washington, D.C.: Academy of American Franciscan History, 1956), 61.

40 Bancroft, *History of California* 5: 403–5; Haas, "War in California," 343–45.

41 Harlow, *California Conquered*, 265–66.

42 Bancroft, *History of California* 5: 631.

43 Theodore Grivas, "*Alcalde* Rule: The Nature of Local Government in Spanish and Mexican California," *California Historical Society Quarterly* 40:1 (March 1961): 23.

44 Bancroft, *History of California* 5: 631. At almost the same time, José de la Guerra went one step further, reactivating his Spanish citizenship on 1 May 1847. Cesareo Lataillade to José de la Guerra, Santa Barbara, 13 July 1847, DLG 576.

45 Bancroft, *History of California* 5: 631. Anastacio Carrillo, "Proclamation," Santa Barbara, 8 January 1848 (translation only, Bowman 1, 537, p. 357).

46 Thompson, "Casa"; and DLG 125.

47 Testimony of José Genaro Alvarez, Santa Barbara, April 18, 1848, DLG 125. (trans. Thompson, "Casa," 67). Other informants included Bernarda Ruiz and her son Juan Rodríguez.

48 William Tecumseh Sherman to Francisco de la Guerra, Monterey, 12 April 1848, DLG 125.

49 José E. García, "Episodios Históricos de California," 1878, BANC MSS C-D 85, Bancroft Library, trans. Francis Price, quoted in Thompson, "Casa," 86–88.

50 "A Fourth of July in Santa Barbara in the Year 1848," copy in Thompson, "Casa," 79–83.

51 Bancroft, *History of California* 5: 587, 631. Jonathan Drake Stevenson to José de la Guerra, receipt for $45, Santa Barbara, 4 July 1848, DLG 125.

52 Pablo de la Guerra, quoted in J. Ross Browne, *Report of the Debate in the Convention of California, on the Formation of the State Constitution, in September and October, 1849* (Washington, D.C.: John T. Powers, 1850), 63.

53 Lansford W. Hastings, quoted in Browne, *Report*, 64.

54 Pablo de la Guerra, quoted in Browne, *Report*, 273.

55 Joaquín Carrillo, prefect of the District of Santa Barbara, to Pablo de la Guerra, Santa Barbara, 24 November 1849, DLG 148.

56 Tomás Almaguer, *Racial Fault Lines: The Historical Origins of White Supremacy in California* (Berkeley: University of California Press, 1994), 26, 70.

57 Pablo de la Guerra to Antonio María de la Guerra, Santa Barbara, March 10, 1853, DLG 416.

58 By 1860, 40 percent of the Spanish-speaking population in Santa Barbara had come recently from Mexico. Camarillo, *Changing Society*, 25–26.

59 Pablo de la Guerra to H. E. Robinson, Santa Barbara, 13 January 1852, DLG 415.

60 Antonio María de la Guerra to Pablo de la Guerra, Santa Barbara, 16 October 1863, DLG 351.

61 Antonio María de la Guerra to Pablo de la Guerra, Santa Barbara, 13 October 1863, and 1 November 1863, DLG 351.

62 John Gately Downey to Pablo de la Guerra, Sacramento, 10 September 1860, DLG 245.

63 Pablo de la Guerra to Antonio María de la Guerra, Sacramento, 15 January 1857, DLG 416.

64 Francisco de la Guerra to Pablo de la Guerra, Simi, 23 August 1863, DLG 368.

65 Joaquín de la Guerra to Antonio María de la Guerra, San Julián, 15 October 1855, DLG 373.

66 Antonio María de la Guerra to Pablo de la Guerra, Santa Barbara, 23 October 1863, DLG 351.

67 Antonio María de la Guerra to Pablo de la Guerra, n.d., ca. January 1861, DLG 351.

68 Francisco de la Guerra to President of the Santa Barbara City Council, Santa Barbara, 6 January 1851, DLG 352.

69 Pablo de la Guerra to Antonio María de la Guerra, Senate, 15 March 1856, DLG 416; Board of Supervisors, Antonio María de la Guerra president, to Senator Pablo de la Guerra, Santa Barbara, 7 February 1861, DLG 896.

70 Antonio María de la Guerra to Pablo de la Guerra, Santa Barbara, 29 April 1861, DLG 351.

71 Pablo de la Guerra to Antonio María de la Guerra, Sacramento, 17 March 1860, DLG 416.

72 Pablo took particular satisfaction in defeating one squatter's bill in 1855, telling his brother Antonio María, "Yesterday has been a day of great triumph for me and for all of the Californios." Pablo de la Guerra to Antonio María de la Guerra, Sacramento, 14 April 1855, DLG 416.

73 Pablo de la Guerra, quoted in *El Clamor Publico* (Los Angeles), Saturday, 26 April 1856, 1.

74 Pablo de la Guerra to Numa Hubert, Santa Barbara, 22 August 1860, DLG 426, (trans. Nancy Appelbaum).

75 Julio Osuna to Pablo de la Guerra, San Diego, 3 March 1864, DLG 752.

76 Charles Huse, quoted in Camarillo, *Changing Society*, 23.

77 Santa Barbara County Board of Supervisors, Minute Book B, 25 and 26 October 1869, 200–201.

78 William A. Streeter, "'Recollections of Historical Events in California, 1843–1878' of William A. Streeter," ed. William H. Ellison, *California Historical Society Quarterly* 18:2 (June 1939): 261.

79 Antonio María de la Guerra to Pablo de la Guerra, Santa Barbara, 11 February 1857, DLG 351 (trans. Joseph Hall).

80 James Henry Carleton, Brevet Major in U.S. Army to Major W. W. Mackall, Assistant Adjutant General, Fort Tejon, 5 October 1859, quoted in Cameron Rogers, ed., *A County Judge in Arcady: Selected Private Papers of Charles Fernald, Pioneer California Jurist* (Glendale, Calif.: Arthur H. Clark, 1954), 119.

81 Camarillo, *Changing Society*, 21–22; Rogers, *County Judge in Arcady*, 115–21.

82 The railroad did not arrive in Santa Barbara until 1887; travelers came by sea or stage from Los Angeles. On the postwar demographic changes, see Camarillo, *Changing Society*, 41–46.

83 Almaguer, *Racial Fault Lines*, 88.

84 Thomas Bard to J. P. Green, August 1873, quoted in Almaguer, *Racial Fault Lines*, 89.

85 R. Espinoza, letter dated 4 September 1871, printed in the *Santa Barbara Press*, 9 September 1871, quoted in Camarillo, *Changing Society*, 44.

✳ *Borderland Stories*

Race, Agency, and Memory in a

Baja California Mission

T he most significant accomplishment of conquest, argues David Gutiérrez, is the dominant forces' ability to provide a set of narratives that describe, explain, and justify the domination of one group over others.[1] As a theater of multiple conquests, led first by the Spanish and then the Mexican and American nation-states, the borderlands provide a unique and compelling context for exploring this dynamic across time. How, within this contested terrain, did stories inflect conquest and domination, and to what extent did they cross the temporal boundaries of colonial and national regimes?

In this essay, I address these questions through an analysis of narratives about a thirty-four-year-old native woman, Bárbara Gandiaga, whom colonial authorities convicted in 1806 of conspiring to kill a Dominican friar at Mission Santo Tomás in Baja California. There were several accounts of the murder, including the official version, as constructed by colonial authorities, and a legend that was recovered by a Peruvian immigrant in Baja California in the late nineteenth century.[2] I examine these two versions of Gandiaga's story not simply as contrasting narratives but as reflections of competing hegemonic discourses. They operate at the threshold of two narrative domains: that of the colonial Dominican project in Antigua California, and that of anticlerical Reformist discourse in Baja California. By examining how the narrative of Bárbara Gandiaga and the murder at Mission Santo Tomás later underwent a discursive transformation during the nineteenth century, we can gain important insights into the ambivalent and ever-shifting relationship between hegemonic discourse, popular memory, and gendered agency in the colonial and postcolonial border-lands.[3]

These reconstructions of Bárbara Gandiaga's story must also be placed against the geographical backdrop of colonial and early national Baja California. Antigua California emerged as an exceptionally isolated area, even when compared to neighboring provinces in far northern New Spain and Mexico.[4] The distinctiveness of this frontier region was manifest in the narratives of early settlers that carried over, albeit somewhat transformed, when colonial Antigua California became national Baja California in the early nineteenth century. Most importantly, these narratives were framed predominantly in local terms, relying on—and responding to—regionally specific networks, processes, and events that had as much to do with social relations on the edges of imperial and national authority as they did with efforts to imagine empires and nations.

Murder at Mission Santo Tomás

Indian resistance to the Baja California missions took the form of rebellion, large-scale flight, and even the murder of missionaries. Two such murders took place at Santo Tomás de Aquino in 1803. Father Miguel López died that January from what the authorities initially thought suspicious, but then dismissed as natural, causes. It was after López's assistant Father Surroca was found in May, brutally beaten to death, that the colonial authorities began to connect the deaths.[5] Bárbara Gandiaga, and several native men were eventually charged with conspiracy to commit murder, arrested, and held prisoner at San Vicente.[6] Lieutenant José Ruiz, commander at the San Vicente garrison, took statements from the accused Indians regarding Father Eudaldo Surroca's murder, which were subsequently used in the judicial proceedings against them for the first murder (that of Miguel López). In her testimony, Gandiaga denied direct involvement in the murder, yet the missionaries not only charged her with conspiracy to murder both priests but also considered her the intellectual author of both murders.[7]

Lieutenant José Ruiz set out to gather the facts regarding the Surroca murder. Upon arriving at Santo Tomás he was taken to view the friar's body. He reported that he found abrasions on Surroca's head and knees and scratches on his neck. Upon compiling the various witnesses' testimonies and the suspects' statements, Ruiz was able to ascertain that on the night of Surroca's murder, eighteen-year-old Lázaro Rosales removed a nine-year-old mission page, Carlos Aparicio, from where he was sleeping, ostensibly near the friar's quarters. As they were leaving, the page saw thirty-two-year-old Alexandro [*sic*] de la Cruz lurking in the shadows.[8] Upon returning, Rosales and de la Cruz entered Surroca's room. Lázaro went in first and grabbed Surroca by the neck. Alexandro followed and grabbed Surroca to hold him down. Reportedly, Bárbara Gandiaga was getting a candle, and Juan Miguel Carrillo, a twenty-four-year-old Indian who was Gandiaga's mate, was at the outside door serving as a lookout. According to the men's testimony Bárbara then entered the room and grabbed Surroca by the genitals. During the struggle Surroca fell from the bed and struck his head on the wall. When they confirmed that Surroca was dead they lifted him, positioned him on the bed facing the wall, and covered him.[9]

The following morning, twenty-two-year-old Melchor Gutiérrez, a mission Indian, ran into Lázaro, who was scurrying from the friar's dwelling. Rosales told Gutiérrez that he had killed the friar because Gandiaga had ordered him to do so. Gutiérrez also testified that he knew of another occasion when Gandiaga had ordered the death of a gentile Indian who was known to practice witchcraft.[10] Juan Miguel Carrillo, another mission Indian, was also interrogated. He said he had overheard a conversation between Rosales and Gandiaga, in which Rosales commented to Gandiaga that no one knew they had killed the missionary. Twenty-year-old mission Indian Nicolasa Carrillo also testified that Gandiaga had told her that she, along with Rosales and de la Cruz, had killed the missionary.[11]

Gandiaga denied all accusations against her. According to her testimony she had little, if any, participation in the matter, and the men were responsible for the death of the friar. Rosales, by contrast, not only implicated her as the mastermind of the murder but also testified that after the crime was committed Gandiaga ordered them to clean Surroca's bloodied face and change his clothing so there would be no indication of foul play. While the men were changing the priest, she reportedly closed the window so they would not be seen from the outside. When they had finished, Gandiaga took some supplies from the pantry and left with the men.[12]

During the investigation the male suspects attempted to clear themselves and others of the crime, stating that Gandiaga instructed them to not implicate her in the murder and to blame others for the crime. Reportedly Gandiaga ordered twenty-four-year-old Mariano Carrillo to blame

Rosales and another Indian (who was later cleared of all charges). Gandiaga also told Alexandro de la Cruz to keep her name out of the investigation. De la Cruz also testified that Juan Miguel Carrillo had not taken part in the murder, that Gandiaga had implicated him because she was angry that Carrillo had implicated *her* in the crime. Thus, reportedly, Gandiaga pointed the finger at her mate, Juan Miguel, out of revenge. According to the men, Gandiaga wanted Surroca killed to make way for a better missionary. In addition, Gandiaga was upset with the priest because he had given gifts to some of the women in the choir. Apparently after Gandiaga complained, Surroca scolded her, threatened her with a lashing, and sent her to the *ranchería* to eat with the rest of the Indians.[13]

Having completed the investigation and determined the culpability of Lázaro Rosales and Alexandro de la Cruz, Commander Ruiz submitted his findings to Governor José Joaquín de Arrillaga at Loreto. He noted at the time that findings against the other suspects would be completed soon thereafter. Ruiz also indicated that new testimony taken from Gandiaga revealed foul play in the death of Father Miguel López. He ended his report with the statement that "the Indian Bárbara has a diabolical spirit." But by September of that year, Governor Arrillaga instructed Lieutenant José Pérez Fernández to take charge of the investigation, since Ruiz's findings included irregularities and nullified much of the proceedings. Thus, the lieutenant went about reinterviewing the suspects and established that the male suspects confirmed Gandiaga's role in the murder as conspirator and instigator of Surroca's murder. Gandiaga stood firm in her denial of the accusations.[14]

As suspicion had been raised regarding the death of the second missionary, Father López, the authorities embarked on an investigation of this second death. Gandiaga told Commander Ruiz that she first heard of the death of Father Miguel López from one of the missionary's pages, an Indian boy named Juan de Dios. She had then asked Mariano Carrillo how Father López had died. Mariano began by explaining that Juan Miguel Carrillo, a relative, had gotten drunk and struck the son of the *mayordomo*. The mayordomo had complained to the friar, who ordered that Juan Miguel be shackled and punished.[15] News later trickled back to Lázaro Rosales that Juan Miguel had been locked in the single men's quarters. When Lázaro heard of Father López's intent to punish Juan Miguel, he decided to help free him. Two other Indians, a sixteen-year-old male named

Miguel and a twenty-four-year-old male named Thomas [*sic*] Arrillaga, were sleeping in the single men's quarters when Lázaro entered to let Juan Miguel out. It was then—Mariano later told Gandiaga—that Lázaro and Juan Miguel decided to kill the friar.[16]

Shortly after Juan Miguel and Lázaro left the men's quarters, they proceeded to Father López's quarters. Juan Miguel hid under a large table in the main room while Lázaro, who also served as the mission cook, took the evening meal to López. Apparently the friar became enraged because the meal was not to his liking and proceeded to threaten Lázaro, telling him that he would be severely punished the following day. Lázaro left the room and told Juan Miguel that he too would be punished. Juan Miguel had been sick and was unsure that he and Lázaro would be able to overpower the friar without assistance, so the two men found Mariano Carrillo and convinced him to help them kill López. Once they were in the friar's room, the scuffle ensued. Juan Miguel sat on top of López while Mariano strangled him. Father López struggled and pleaded for forgiveness. Mariano responded: "you are not forgiven, when you want to punish *you* do not forgive."[17] Afterward, to be sure López was dead, they wrapped a cloth belt that Lázaro was wearing tightly around the friar's neck. Then they carefully placed him on the bed to appear as if he were asleep.[18]

The scuffle woke up two young boys, Juan de Dios and Ildefonso, who worked as pages for Father López. They were, as was their custom, sleeping under the friar's cot. They awoke to find Lázaro, Juan Miguel, and Mariano sitting on the friar's bed; by then López was dead. When they realized what had happened, they tried to run. The men caught the boys and told them "they had better keep quiet" long enough to give the men time to escape. After a few hours, they were to inform others at the mission that the friar had passed away. Fearing for their lives, the boys initially followed the men's instructions. Juan de Dios believed Lázaro fully capable of having committed the crime; once, when he had been shackled and punished, Lázaro had told him that one day he would kill the friar.[19] Ildefonso also kept quiet, and it was only later, when questioned by the authorities, that the boys revealed what they knew.[20]

After considering the testimony, the authorities charged Mariano, Juan Miguel, and Lázaro with conspiracy to murder López. All three men vehemently denied the charge. In none of the statements taken by Commander Ruiz was Gandiaga mentioned as being present at the time of the murder, nor did anyone describe her as a participant in the plan to execute the crime. Nevertheless, along with the men, she was charged with conspiracy in murdering the friar.

By the time authorities were reaching a decision on López's case, Mariano, Juan Miguel, Lázaro, and Gandiaga, along with Alexandro de la Cruz, had already been arrested and charged for the May 1803 murder of Father Eudaldo Surroca.[21] Lieutenant José Pérez Fernández of the Loreto presidio was commissioned to take depositions for the Surroca case. Of these, Lázaro Rosales's testimony was the only one that supposedly identified Surroca's murderer. When asked, "do you know why you are imprisoned," Lázaro replied that he was in jail because [he] took the life of the missionary father.[22] The others consistently denied the charges, and although others eventually implicated Juan Miguel Carrillo and Alexandro de la Cruz, by all accounts Gandiaga neither participated directly nor was she involved in the planning of the murder. Yet she did confirm her knowledge of the men's intention to kill Surroca, and she placed herself—after the fact—at the murder scene. During what may have been an attempt to escape after the murder, she was instructed by Juan Miguel to get supplies and clothing from the mission pantry, and in the process she saw Father Surroca's lifeless body in his quarters.[23] For this marginal participation, she was charged and convicted as a conspirator. Along with Lázaro Rosales and Alexandro de la Cruz, Gandiaga was sentenced to death by hanging.[24]

Soon afterwards Juan Miguel died from an illness contracted in jail, and Lázaro and Alexandro de la Cruz were executed.[25] Some of the key witnesses died as well. This added to the difficulty of determining Gandiaga's role in López's murder by the time the proceedings on this second case were reviewed for final adjudication, and the colonial state would fill this gap as it saw fit. With few witnesses left alive, and no corroborating testimony to support Gandiaga's position, she was charged—along with Mariano Carrillo—as a conspirator and was suspected by the mission authorities to be the instigator of the murder.[26]

What was at stake in the construction of the case against the Indians, especially against Gandiaga? There is a striking absence in the judicial record of any compelling or justifiable motive for the murders. The missionaries did not appear to have carried out any severe, unwarranted, or unprovoked brutal punishment against the Indians prior to the murders, nor was there evidence of sexual misconduct. Instead, the official story that emerges from the judicial proceedings is one of an irrational and immoral action ostensibly committed by merciless and ruthless savages against their missionaries.

The scribe at Mariano Carrillo's deposition for the López murder wrote that Carrillo emphasized his testimony with demonstrative gestures, including thumping his chest with his fist. This depiction paints a portrait of a fiery, quasi-savage character "naturally" inclined to the heinous act of murder. The steadfast refusal by the accused Indians to admit their guilt, for its part, demonstrated an apparent lack of remorse, or what the missionaries might have construed as a lack of Christian conscience. For the colonial authorities, this revealed an unrelentingly deceitful posture on the part of the Indians, who may have simply feared the fatal consequences of an admission of guilt.

Yet the authorities' decision to place intellectual authorship of both the crimes on Gandiaga is somewhat puzzling. It risked the possibility of bringing into the investigation any number of dynamics, sexual or otherwise, between the friars and the Indian woman. The fact that her testimony offered no such link, in fact, would have made it difficult for the authorities to demonstrate any clear reason for her involvement in the conspiracy. Seen another way, the lack of clear motivation renders her participation as the peak of illogical, irrational, and/or treacherous behavior.[27]

The judicial record depicts Gandiaga, moreover, as alternately a passive, marginally involved woman who merely followed the lead and instructions of her mate and male counterparts in the case of the López murder, and as a treacherous, manipulative, vengeful, and diabolical woman in the case of Surroca's murder. Some of the military and civilian officials reviewing the case, however, viewed Gandiaga differently. Lieutenant Ruíz claimed that Gandiaga was incapable of the charges against her. He requested a protector for Gandiaga and defending attorneys for the Indian males. Juan José Monroy, the defending attorney, petitioned for clemency in the case against Gandiaga, alleging that she was only a child incapable of maliciousness in the commission of the murder. Yet even this dissenting opinion bolstered the racist and gendered stereotypical assumptions behind the judicial process: Indian women were either childlike and incapable of malicious or sophisticated—albeit criminal—thinking, passive followers of their aggressive and bellicose male cohorts, or manipulative, vengeful, diabolical females.[28]

The colonial authorities had no qualms about attempting to utilize the events for the purposes of consolidating, if not regaining, control over the

Santo Tomás Indian population. In fact, shortly after the Surroca murder investigation began there was mass flight of Indians fearing broad, indiscriminate, and brutal retaliation as a consequence of the murder.[29] At the missionaries' urging, the civilian authorities agreed to recommend conviction of the accused Indians for the murder of Friar Surroca. On December 18, 1805, Viceroy Jose de Iturrigaray decreed this verdict and sentenced Gandiaga, Rosales, and de la Cruz to be hanged until dead; their heads and right hands were to be cut off and displayed in a public site as an assertion of their crime.[30] This gruesome sentence was meant to thwart any plans of retaliation against the missionaries by the mission's Indian population and preclude any possible future insurrections.

Antigua California and the Dominican Frontier

In order to understand the willingness of the missionaries to construct a case against Gandiaga and the Indians, and to seek the most severe punishment for their alleged actions, it is important to understand the precariousness of mission life in this frontier setting. The establishment of missions in Antigua California was entrusted first to the Jesuit order in the late 1600s.[31] Jealousy over Jesuit control of lands and Indians in the Americas, along with court intrigue and political maneuverings in Spain, eventually led to the ouster of Jesuits from the New World in 1767. In Baja California, authorities subsequently replaced Jesuits first with Franciscans and then with Dominicans. The Dominican Fathers of the Holy Order of Preachers assumed control of the Antigua California missions in 1773.[32] Not unlike the other *Provincias Internas*, the colonization of the Californias was characterized by geographic and political isolation. This situation was particularly acute in Antigua California because the colonial authorities were reluctant to invest in its missions or settlement.[33]

The arid conditions of the Dominican frontier, the semi-nomadic lifestyle of the indigenous groups who inhabited the region, and the isolation and lack of financial support from the Viceroyalty contributed to the difficulties these missionaries faced in successfully building a self-supporting mission economy.[34] In order to equalize the population and the resources, the missionaries frequently moved Indians to other parts of the peninsula, sometimes separating children from their parents in the process to increase their power over these neophytes. The local indigenous population frequently resisted this forced relocation policy.[35]

It was under these precarious conditions that the Dominicans built the Mission of Santo Tomás de Aquino.[36] Bárbara Gandiaga was among the Indian women who were taken from their families to work and live in the Santo Tomás Mission. Although it is not exactly clear to which indigenous group Gandiaga belonged, she may have been a member of the Kumiais, a nearby group.[37] Along with other Indians, Gandiaga was probably instructed in Christian beliefs and rituals and forced into daily routines and practices that promoted strict observance of Spanish patriarchal values and Christian mores.[38] Unmarried indigenous men and women at Mission Santo Tomás were assigned segregated sleeping quarters (where they would be locked up during the night), as well as gender-specific tasks.[39] Conditions were far from benign. The Dominicans in Baja California, notes historian Lucila León Velasco, were known for the severe punishments they meted out to those who "broke mission rules regarding sexual behavior, labor and compliance with church attendance."[40]

The mission economy, wherever it did flourish, succeeded as a result of the exploitation of indigenous labor. The missionaries of Baja California attempted to transform what were mostly hunting and gathering populations into more sedentary farming populations and, thus, into more "stable" sources of labor power.[41] They sought further control through corporal punishment; floggings and lashings were a common occurrence for even minor infractions of mission routines and Catholic ritual.[42] Despite these coercive measures, Indians across the Californias resisted colonial transformation and control. Indian resurrections were not uncommon, and the missionaries' domination over the Indian population was always fragile. The geographic isolation, harsh climate, lack of viceregal support, and continued indigenous resistance all made for a hostile environment and unstable and precarious conditions. That two murders were committed in one mission within the span of four months must have created an environment of severe panic and ominous foreboding of further criminal acts, which might explain the zealousness with which the missionaries sought punishment against Gandiaga and her cohort.

The Legend of Bárbara Gandiaga

By the mid-nineteenth century, Baja California had experienced, along with the rest of Mexico, the national defeat of Spanish colonial rule. This was followed by a liberal reform movement whose leaders sought to construct a discourse that reflected a more enlightened approach to race relations combined with new "liberal" views of church and state. It was in this context that the second story of Gandiaga came to light.

The second story of Bárbara Gandiaga was discovered among the memoirs of South American adventurer Manuel Clemente Rojo (1820–1900), who traveled to California during the Gold Rush.[43] A native of Peru, Rojo journeyed to Mexico as a self-described adventurer, not unlike many international miners who had heard of the gold riches that were to be found in California. During the trip north, Rojo and an associate were shipwrecked off the western coast of Baja California near the Bahía de Todos Santos. Rojo's partner continued north on foot while Rojo stayed behind to safeguard the salvaged load. During his short stay in the Ensenada region he met and befriended residents of the area, including local soldiers, civilians, and Indians. Rojo returned to Baja California in 1856 after a brief stay in Alta California and settled for a decade in the southern region of the Baja California peninsula, in La Paz, and later in the community of Todos Santos. He later moved to the northern region of the peninsula in 1865 and lived in a variety of locations including Santo Tomás.

Over the years, Rojo wrote his memoirs, which included reminiscences about those people who befriended him, mestizos and Indians alike, and about those with whom he developed long-standing relationships and associations. It is through recollections from these, as he called them, "respectable old men"—who either lived during Gandiaga's time or had heard about this Indian woman—that we get a fuller understanding of her life's narrative.[44]

Gandiaga was remembered as a young indigenous maiden of inordinate beauty, sixteen or seventeen years old in 1794, who was taken and literally imprisoned by the missionaries.[45] She reportedly trained to sing in the choir, and for this purpose was scurried from the *convento* to the father's cell for choir practice, as well as to the kitchen to cook for the missionaries.[46] However, one day "*Padre* Lázaro" took Gandiaga to his cell after she had imbibed of the mission wine and became unconscious; after this he never again allowed her to leave the kitchen area, nor to see her friends and family. Gandiaga's sleeping quarters were transferred to a pantry adjacent to both the kitchen and the friar's cell. Thereafter, Gandiaga became Padre Lázaro's personal cook. Subsequently, mission residents heard muffled screams that emanated from Gandiaga's quarters during the night. They were described as "sounds Bárbara might make as if she were defending herself while being forced against her will." In addition, Bárbara Gandiaga was said to be terribly afraid of the Padre, not only for his purported practice of "controlling the bodies and minds of the indigenous youth," but also because he treated the indigenous population of the area inhumanely. He was known for his beatings of those who ran away from the missions or refused to submit to mission rules.[47]

According to this legend, two (or three) indigenous men attempted to free Bárbara Gandiaga from her bondage, only to be caught in the act by the friar. Responding to a series of loud voices and noises, several soldiers from the *cuartel* rushed to the room. Gandiaga was found standing above the body of the friar, bloody knife in hand. At that point other alarmed mission residents entered the room. When asked, "Who killed the *fraile*?" Gandiaga is said to have responded, "I did," almost at the same time as the Indian men cried out, "We did." In this telling of the events, the colonial authorities found Gandiaga and her "co-conspirators" guilty and condemned them to hang. Their bodies were to be left hanging in the middle of the mission courtyard until they rotted and were either consumed by buzzards or left to fall in putrefied pieces to be eaten by rodents or other scavenging animals.[48]

Baja California's Anticlericalism

Not unlike the other newly independent Latin American nations, Mexico in the 1820s and 1830s was undergoing a process of nation building. This process required newly minted narratives that highlighted the virtue of the new regimes and created new binary models of heroism and sedition. Thus it is not surprising that stories like that of Gandiaga attempted to attribute the ills of the fledgling nation to those aspects of its colonial heritage that it purportedly proposed to overcome, among them the dominance of the Catholic Church. These discursive underpinnings were particularly salient in the emerging context of Mexican liberalism. Liberalist philosophy and views in Mexico took legislative shape during the *Reforma* period (1854–67) and culminated with the *Leyes de Reforma*. But incipient expressions of liberal thinking and debate appear as early as the 1820s, with José María Luis Mora (1794–1850), considered one of the major liberal theorists of the pre-Reforma period. Mora helped shape the early structure and orientation of Mexican liberalism, among other things calling for free trade and a repudiation of the country's Spanish colonial past. Anti–Catholic

Church sentiment was also a characteristic expression of liberalism in the 1830s, and 1840s, as the "presence of this vast property-holding institution, which absorbed a large percentage of the liquid capital of the country and which lived as a separate juridical entity, was particularly intolerable."[49] To be sure, there were many differences among liberal thinkers and politicians regarding this issue; however, Reforma legislation gave considerable attention to anticlerical issues such as clerical control of education, natural resources and land, and Catholic religious and judicial privilege.[50]

Anticlerical sentiment had existed from the onset of the mission period in the Californias. For the most part it emerged from the competition among clerical, military, and civilian colonials for access to the indigenous populations in this borderland area. The missionaries were first to formally complain to the viceregal authorities regarding sexual abuse and other improprieties committed by both military and civilian personnel in the region.[51] But the issue of who controlled the Indians, and their labor, was a source of conflict as well.[52] Relations between miners and missionaries could also be antagonistic. During the late eighteenth century, miners were often dependent on the missions for agricultural products and other foodstuffs, and they frequently complained of the missionaries' lack of economic support and accused them of avarice in their business dealings.[53]

Ownership and use of the peninsula's most arable land was another issue that strained relations between the civilian population and the missionaries. In California as early as 1825, José María Echeandía, one of the first *jefe políticos* of the region during the postindependence period, proposed the redistribution of cultivable mission land to the mission Indians. Not surprisingly, the Dominicans resisted this. The order to secularize the missions of the Californias came soon thereafter (1830) and was followed (1834) by the sale of productive agricultural lands formerly claimed by missions.[54] Many civilian settlers claimed the Dominican friars were not the most capable administrators of mission lands; in fact, many friars were seen as having personally benefited from mission production. Even where lands were redistributed, Dominicans still maintained control of some of the most fertile.[55] Ultimately some of the most arable lands did transfer over to private ownership, though for the most part many of the Dominican missions were simply left in ruins, as a result of drought, lack of resources, abandonment, out-migration of native populations, and the sacking of missions by Indians and civilians alike.

Given this local history, it is not surprising that anticlerical discourse and policies formulated by liberal thinkers from the center resonated with many Baja Californianos. Yet to better understand the relationship of anti-clerical thought to the legend of Gandiaga, one needs also to examine Manuel Clemente Rojo's particular brand of liberalism.[56] For it is Rojo's investment in Baja California's economic, social, and political success that may shed light on his interest in rediscovering and documenting this legend.

Manuel Clemente Rojo's Liberalism

After settling in Baja California in 1865, Rojo became a well known and respected resident, ultimately holding several positions as educator, historian, and high-ranking public official, serving as local congressional delegate, district judge, secretary of state for the Jefe Político of the peninsula, and as interim Jefe Político. He was also instrumental in the founding of public schools throughout the region; he helped create a government-sponsored elementary school system and a teacher-training college, the Escuela Superior Hidalgo, and the Colegio Superior de Comercio. Rojo's dedication to promoting education at one point led Porfirio Díaz to appoint him teacher of the Escuela Nacional de Niños de Santo Tomás.[57]

Rojo's political and intellectual contributions to Baja California also extended to the establishment and reconstruction of many public archives and the founding of the Biblioteca del Partido. He also wrote several ethnographic, sociopolitical, and natural narratives of the region. His *Apuntes históricos de la frontera de la Baja California* not only recorded flora, fauna, and development of settlements in the peninsula but also described the social and cultural relations between missionaries and Indians and the dynamics of missionization, resistance to colonial domination, and community building.[58] Rojo's desire to record the life, customs, and beliefs of the indigenous peoples and early mestizo settlers of the peninsula, as well as his investment in the political, social, and economic development of Baja California, in many ways mirror the liberal policies which promoted the construction of a superstructure that would support a new political and economic course for the nascent republic.[59]

The Indians Rojo came in contact with on the peninsula were, in his assessment, peaceful and capable of friendship if treated well. His portrayal of Indian punishment during the mission period is a scathing indictment of the brutal and inhumane treatment that passed as Dominican discipline.

Rojo records a conversation with Don Francisco Xavier Gastélum (one of the respected old Baja Californianos who befriended him and whom he interviewed) in which Gastélum claimed that the Dominican priests were responsible for all the colonial Indian rebellions, because of their practice of forcibly baptizing Indians against their will, making them work too hard, and treating them poorly. Rojo notes that through Gastélum he met an Indian (Jatñil), described as the leader of an insurrection intended to kill a missionary of Mission Guadalupe. In his recollection of this meeting Rojo gives no indication of feeling fear; instead he relates that he felt rather flattered when the Indian introduced him to his wife as a friend.[60] Such encounters may have informed his treatment of Dominican-Indian relationships in his *Apuntes históricos*, which paints a picture of cruel and merciless Dominicans whose treatment of the Indians led to a violent uprising in 1808.

The legendary version of Bárbara Gandiaga's life and actions, as told by the Baja Californianos and documented by Rojo, is significantly different from what is found in the official judicial documents.[61] It is a version congruous with the anticlerical, reformist sentiments of Rojo's times, and even more significantly of Rojo's own liberalist views. The legend offers an explanation of the murder as justifiable given the reportedly brutal treatment of the Indians at Santo Tomás by the Dominican missionaries and the confinement and abuse of Gandiaga by her missionary priest. The particular segment of the story when the Indians are discovered after the murder acquires significance because the storytellers are ascribing a certain amount of agency to Gandiaga's response to the question "Who did it?" Her actions are not only deemed justifiable; her admission of the act, given the legendary circumstances of her life at the mission, would be seen as exculpatory. Her alleged incarceration in the mission, the missionary's attempt at keeping her from contacting her family, and the sexual violence alluded to in the legend: any one of these acts could be considered sufficient reason for her desperate act for freedom. That Gandiaga is found with the dagger in her hand only credits her with a sense of valor and dignity of heroic proportions.

A Gendered Agency

Bárbara Gandiaga and her alleged co-conspirators' guilt or innocence may not be the most significant issue here. The killing of the friars may very well have been a retaliatory act of violence on the part of the Indians. However, the viceregal government was compelled to judge her case in relation to the broader state of colonial affairs and especially the precariousness of life in Baja California. The Church for its part provided no space for sanctuary or recourse for defense of Gandiaga since the mission institution was not only the locus of the act but also one of the coercive entities reviewing her case.[62]

Little is known about Gandiaga's daily life in the mission. No official records attest to any injury, physical or otherwise, committed against her. Current scholarship has, however, clearly established that for native women and their communities, the arrival of soldiers and priests in the Californias ushered in an era of unprecedented violence and social change, and that the initial imposition of Spanish colonial power centered on women through the violent extortion of sex as a tool of the colonial project for control and domination.[63] Yet such violence is notoriously difficult to find in the official record; the practice of veiling the violent and sexually aggressive behavior of missionaries, and soldiers, was often condoned, if not sanctioned.[64] In the case of Bárbara Gandiaga, the colonial judicial record contained no details of physical and sexual abuse, and yet the space produced by this absence—regardless of what actually took place at Mission Santo Tomás—later became fertile ground for legend and folklore.

Equally interesting is the way in which Bárbara Gandiaga's agency was constructed in the contrasting discourses. Two separate patriarchal groups were vying for "control" of Gandiaga's story. First there are the colonizers in the form of the Church, who along with the juridical prosecutors were invested in making Gandiaga a case of exemplary punishment for the maintenance of social control among the indigenous population.[65] It is obvious that Gandiaga's actions challenged and undermined the missionaries' authority. That the missionaries charged her as a co-conspirator, and accused her of being the "instigator" and "principal author" of the murders, affords her, if only symbolically, the role of chief aggressor. Ironically, the colonial authorities construct her agency in an archetypically feminine way—on one hand as a vengeful temptress and manipulator of men, and on the other as a submissive female victim. In the colonial discourse, she was seen as a "diabolical" temptress whose power came from manipulating her male cohort; she was not only a conspirator but also conceived of, planned, and ordered her co-conspirators to execute the crime. This stereotypically feminine construction of Gandiaga was possibly the only way that the authorities could conceive of a woman—an indigenous woman at that—participating in a murder conspiracy, an affront that required that the transgressor(s) be dealt with in the harshest of manners.[66]

The subsequent legend provides a similar construction of Bárbara Gandiaga's gendered agency. This second patriarchal group, the "respectable old men" whom Rojo interviewed, reconstructs Gandiaga in a feminine way by representing her as a victimized "young and beautiful woman." Although her actions are linked to a larger masculine conspiracy that collectively provides the broader subordinate group a sense of agency, Gandiaga is symbolically empowered when she is discovered wielding the murder weapon herself. In this scenario she is the righteous heroine, who through this epic act reclaims her virtue.

Thus both patriarchal groups were bent on constructing a gendered agency for her, representing it for different ends, of course, in the public narrative of the judicial proceedings and, subsequently, in the hegemonized oral history. Gandiaga's actions unfolded at a time when the missionaries were still the colonial authorities in the region. The oral history, in turn, was constructed during a dynamic, changing political period when the newly independent society and government was solidly in the process of nation building, creating the kind of discourse that reflected its newly independent philosophy and politics. Gandiaga's agency is thus contained in the colonial legal discourse of her case and only later restored, and redefined, in the public memory of a reformist Baja California society.

The actual events of Bárbara Gandiaga's life in the borderlands matter, but perhaps more important are the ways her story was recast and reconfigured across multiple generations. What these narratives tell us in the end is that Baja California's early political development, rooted in the colonial experience, responded to the unique characteristics of geographic isolation and lack of support from the colonial, and later national, center. In addition, the fact that the narratives were defined and constructed during different hegemonic periods supports Jean Franco's assertion that the imaginary nature of these patriarchal master narratives serves to control the interpretation of events and portray stereotyped, racialized, and gendered notions of women's actions and lives that ultimately bolster prevailing social hierarchies.[67]

Notes

1 David Gutiérrez, "Significant to Whom?: Mexican Americans and the History of the American West," in *A New Significance: Re-Envisioning the History of the American West*, ed. Clyde A. Milner II (Oxford: Oxford University Press, 1996).

2 There are several versions of the murder. One narrative has Gandiaga murdering the missionary in a fit of jealousy, rendering the murder a crime of passion, and obfuscating justifiable cause for it. A second narrative frames the murder as retaliation against brutal treatment of the Indians, making it a justifiable act of rebellion, a rendering consistent with the anticlerical sentiments of the early national period. Another version, which appears in several statements, including Gandiaga's, suggested that the Indians murdered the missionary as a preemptive strike, fearing harsh punishment for an attack committed against the son of a mission servant.

3 The primary sources used in this essay are copies of the original manuscripts from the Archivo Nacional de la Nación, Fondo Provincias Internas in Mexico City, and are housed at the Instituto de Investigaciones Históricas, Universidad Autónoma de Baja California, Tijuana, Baja California, México (hereafter referred to as AGN, IIH-UABC). All texts in English from these sources are my translation.

4 Unlike other parts of this frontier, Baja California was not considered a practical, and certainly not a profitable, venture. Early Jesuit mission interest and efforts relating to Baja California went largely unsupported by New Spain's government, forcing the Jesuit missionaries to create a fund built by private donations to begin, and sustain, the mission project. This particular approach to the development of Baja California, and the distinct peninsular shape of the region created an acute sense of isolation that prevailed during the region's national period and beyond.

5 As a result, Surroca's murder, which occurred four months after Lopez's, was actually investigated first. Father Rafael Arviña's correspondence to Father Fermín Lasuén dated 18 June 1803, in Albert B. Nieser, *Las fundaciones misionales dominicas en Baja California, 1769–1822* (Mexico, B.C.: Universidad Autónoma de Baja California, Colección Baja California: Nuestra Historia, 1998), 209. Fr. Rafael Arviña, president of the Dominican Fathers in the frontier, reported in a letter to Father Fermín Lasuén of the Franciscan order in Alta California that he had been notified of Fr. Eudaldo Surroca's death, believed to have occurred in a violent way and perpetrated by four Indian domestics. Father Arviña's letter contained a postscript, notifying Father Lasuén of the death of Father Miguel López.

6 The male suspects included Lázaro Rosales, Mariano Carrillo, Juan Miguel Carrillo, and Alexandro de la Cruz. There are at least three accounts, or versions, of the events. According to the judicial records the first murdered friar

is identified as Miguel López. The judicial records also name a second victim, Friar Eudaldo Surroca. Other records, such as the memoir of Manuel Clemente Rojo, refer to the murdered missionary as Padre Lázaro. A third version of the events appears in David Zárate Loperena, "Testimonios de Santo Tomás: La muerte del Padre Eudaldo Surroca: 1803," *Memoria del X simposio de historia regional* (Ensenada, B.C.: Universidad Autónoma de Baja California, Asociación Cultural de Liberales en Ensenada, Periódico Vivir en Ensenada, 1991).

7   Arviña's letter quoted in Engelhardt, *Mission and Missionaries in California*.

8   David A. Zárate Loperena, "*Testimonio de Santo Tomás: La Muerte del Padre Eudaldo Surroca en 1803*." Paper presented at the twenty-eighth Simposio de la Asociación Cultural de las Californias, Rosarito, B. Cfa., June, 1990, published in *Apuntes para la historia regional: Antología de David A. Zárate Loperena*, Centro de Investigaciones Históricas, Universidad Nacional Autónoma de México. From "Causa criminal seguida a resultas de haberse encontrado muerto en su cama a r.p. Eudaldo Surroca, Ministro de la Misión de Santo Tomás en la Antigua California," 1804. Californias, vol. 59, exp. 8, AGN, p. 3.

9   "Declaración de Lázaro Rosales," "Declaración de Alexandro de la Cruz," "Declaración de Juan Miguel Carrillo," in Zárate Loperena, *Testimonios*, 43–45.

10 "Declaración de Melchor Gutiérrez," in ibid., 45. Gutiérrez stated that Gandiaga ordered the death of the gentile who was about to be baptized. The motive for this event is unclear.

11 "Declaración de Juan Miguel Carrillo," Declaración de Nicolasa Carrillo," in ibid.

12 "Declaración de Lázaro Rosales," in ibid.

13 "Declaración de Mariano Carrillo," "Declaración de Alexandro de la Cruz," in ibid, 46–47.

14 Juan Manuel Ruiz, "Nuevos testimonios sobre la muerte del P. Miguel López A.," to J. J. Arrillaga, San Vicente, 29 August, 1803, in Zárate Loperena, *Testimonios*, 48. My translation.

15 Gandiaga statement, AGN, IIH-UABC, f. 2, dated 26 November 1803; and Mariano Carrillo statement, f. 6, AGN IIH-UABC.

16 Miguel's (no last name) statement, AGN, vol. 18, exp. 13, IIH exp. 2.2, f. 31, dated 5 December 1803; Thomas Arrillaga's statement, f. 37–38, dated 27 December 1803, and Gandiaga's statement, f. 3, AGN, IIH-UABC.

17 Gandiaga statement, f. 3, AGN, IIH-UABC.

18 Gandiaga statement, f. 3, AGN, IIH-UABC.

19 Juan de Dios's (no last name) statement, AGN, vol. 18, exp. 13, IIH exp. 2.2, fs. 28–29, dated 5 December 1803, AGN, IIH-UABC.

20 Ildefonso's (no last name) statement, AGN, vol. 18, exp. 13, IIH exp. 2.2, f. 30, dated 5 December 1803, AGN, IIH-UABC.

21 "En la causa seguida contra Bárbara Gandiaga, Lázaro Rosales y Alexandro de

la Cruz . . ." AGN, vol. 18, exp. 13, IIH exp. 2.2, f. 54, dated 11 June 1806, AGN, IIH-UABC.

22 Lázaro Rosales's statement, AGN, vol. 18, exp. 13, IIH exp. 2.2, f.40–1, dated 26 January 1804, AGN, IIH-UABC.

23 Gandiaga's statement, fs. 22–27, AGN, IIH-UABC.

24 Gandiaga, Rosales, and Cruz sentence decree. AGN, vol. 18, exp. 13, IIH exp. 2.2, fs. 56–58, AGN, IIH-UABC.

25 Rosales and Cruz were shot and not hanged because reportedly at the time of execution there was no executioner available.

26 Nieser, *Las fundaciones misionales*, 211. Mariano Carrillo, an Indian who had lived approximately six years at the mission, testified while detained at the garrison of San Vicente, charged with conspiracy to commit the López murder, that he had a conversation with Bárbara Gandiaga about the crime after the fact but that she was not involved in the murder. Mariano Carrillo also vehemently denied any involvement in the murder. In his testimony, he validates Gandiaga's statement regarding her innocence. In addition, Juan de Dios indicated in his statement that subsequent to the murder he had related all that he knew to Gandiaga. Both he and Ildefonso, the other page, thereby additionally corroborated Gandiaga's testimony. However, it was decreed that there was sufficient cause to believe that Mariano Carrillo carried out the murder and that Gandiaga was involved in the conspiracy. Carrillo was subsequently found guilty of Father López's murder and sentenced to six years hard labor at the presidio of Loreto. See Mariano Carrillo statement, f. 6, and Mariano Carrillo's sentence decree, AGN, vol. 18, exp. 13, IIH exp. 2.2 f. 85, dated 20 June 1808, AGN, IIH-UABC.

27 That the authorities revisited López's death and declared it a murder (after the Surroca event) could have served the purpose of dispelling suspicions of improper conduct on the part of Friar Surroca, i.e., one murder might arouse suspicion about the dynamics of the missionary/Indian relationship; two murders can be portrayed as a concerted threat to the entire mission project. I would like to thank Carmen Nocentelli-Truett for pointing this out to me.

28 The Indian males are similarly perceived; Pedro Montes de Oca, inspector of the *Audiencia*, agreed with defending attorney, Juan José Monroy, who attributed minor status to the Indians for reasons not of their age but rather their perceived mental capacity. In Nieser, *Las fundaciones misionales*, 210, from *Causa criminal*.

29 Ruiz informed Governor Arrillaga that he was forced to temporarily suspend the investigation of Surroca's murder owing to the need to take troops to capture the fleeing Indians and to pacify the region. This reportedly took approximately two months. From *Causa criminal*, in Zárate Loperena, *Testimonios*, 43.

30 Nieser, *Las fundaciones misionales*, 211.

31 W. Michael Mathes, "Descubrimientos y expediciones," *Ensenada: Nuevas apor-*

taciones para su historia, Mexicali, B.C., UABC, 1999), 53. The missionary period in the Californias takes place from 1697 to 1849.

32 According to the agreement approved, and signed, by Fray Rafael Verger, the Guardian of the College of the Propagation of Faith of San Fernando (the Franciscan order), and Fray Juan Pedro de Iriarte, the head of the Holy Order of Preachers (the Dominicans), the "Dominican Fathers [would] take charge of the old missions of Baja California and the Frontier Mission of San Fernando de Velicatá . . . to the boundaries of the Mission of San Diego . . . the Fathers of the College of San Fernando [would] maintain the establishment they occupy from said port of San Diego following the road to Monterrey, the Port of San Francisco, and farther beyond," in Engelhardt, *Missions and Missionaries*, 510. In the geohistorical context of peninsular California at the end of the eighteenth century, the area located in the northwestern part of the peninsula, and the missions that were built there by the Dominicans, became part of what is known as the Dominican Frontier (Mario Alberto Magaña, "Indígenas, misiones y ranchos durante el Siglo XIX," in *Ensenada: Aportaciones*, 84).

33 Although, for the most part, the establishment of the missions in the Californias was an undertaking only nominally supported by the Crown through the Viceroys' fiscal administrations, financing was largely secured by other Jesuit endeavors and private donations to the Fathers of the Society of Jesus' Pious Fund. According to Stuart F. Voss, *On the Periphery of Nineteenth-Century Mexico, Sonora and Sinaloa, 1810–1877* (Tucson: University of Arizona Press, 1982), "[Jesuit] missions [were] integrated into an emerging larger network . . . and production went to stock and supply newly-established missions — in particular those in Baja, which had to be provisioned on a permanent basis, owing to acute climatic obstacles and the nomadic traditions of the tribes there" (5).

34 The idea of a self-supporting mission, of course, in reality means a site, controlled by the missionaries (and their military aides), which minimally produces what is necessary for the maintenance of the mission, and which is primarily obtained through the labor of the indigenous people.

35 Robert H. Jackson, *Indian Population Decline: The Missions of Northwestern New Spain, 1687–1840* (Albuquerque: University of New Mexico Press, 1994), argues that biological factors alone cannot address the significant decline in Indian population in this frontier. Rather, the "imposition of social control, coupled with the systematic effort to destroy the surviving elements of the Indian's culture caused . . . extreme stresses that contributed to high death rates" — and, I would add, to continued resistance to colonial dominance.

36 The mission was originally established in 1791, approximately thirty miles south of the present-day port city of Ensenada, Baja California, but was later moved from its original site in June of 1794 to a place above the Cañada of San Solano, where there was a more plentiful source of water, according to Hubert Howe Bancroft, *History of Texas*, 751, from Engelhardt, *Missions and Missionaries*, 574.

37 Magaña, utilizing Homer Aschmann's map of geographic distribution of indigenous groups in Baja California, however identifies the larger group residing
in a broad northwestern corner of the Frontera as *diegueños*, while José Luis
Aguilar Marco et al., *Misiones en la península de Baja California* (México, D.F.:
Colección, Científica, Serie Historia, Instituto Nacional de Antropología e Historia, 1991), using Ralph Michelsen's tribal group distribution in the northern
part of the Peninsula, proposes that the Santo Tomás region was inhabited by
Kwatl Indians of Pai-Pai lineage.

38 It should be noted that the creation of gender-specific sleeping quarters in the
missions was one of the missionaries' critical attempts at restructuring and gen-
dering social space. The Indians were taken from their parents at an early age
and made to sleep in the *monjerios* (for women) and the men's *dormitorios* or
sleeping quarters. This practice was further rooted in the Spanish patriarchal
normative concepts of honor and chastity, concepts that agreed with Catholic
beliefs and norms. In addition, Lisbeth Haas, in *Conquests and Historical Identities in California: 1769–1936* (Berkeley: University of California Press, 1995), has
clearly established that indigenous children were taken from their parents in a
concerted effort to sever them from the processes whereby they would learn
their traditional beliefs and way of life.

39 Lucila del C. León Velazco, "La presencia de la mujer Bajacaliforniana en la
época colonial," *Seminario de historia de Baja California, memoria 1992* (Ensenada, B.C.: Ciclo de Conferencias, Instituto de Investigaciones Históricas,
UABC, 1992).

40 Lucila León Velazco, "La administración político-militar de la frontera de Baja
California en la época misional," *Ensenada*, 79.

41 Jackson, *Indian Population Decline*, 79.

42 Haas, *Conquests and Historical Identities*, 28.

43 Manuel Clemente Rojo, *Apuntes historicos de la frontera de la Baja California*,
introduction and notes by Carlos Lazcano Sahagún and Arnulfo Estrada R.,
Colección de documentos sobre la historia y la geografía del municipio de Ensenada, Document no. 1 (Ensenada: Museo de Historia de Ensenada, Seminario de Historia de Ensenada, 2000). Sahagún's introduction to Rojo's *Apuntes
históricos* refers to Manuel Clemente Rojo as a recognized and true chronicler of
Baja California history. Rojo's *Apuntes históricos, corográficos y estadísticos del dis-
trito norte del territorio de la Baja California* was written in 1872 and published in
1958 by Enrique Aldrete, *Baja California heróica* (Baja California, México). In
addition, Sahagún reports that Rojo's *Apuntes históricos de la Baja California con
algunos relativos a la Alta California* was written in 1879 for the Bancroft project.
This collection was later published with an introduction by David Zárate Loperena, *Fuentes documentales para la historia de Baja California*, no. 5 (Tijuana:
Centro de Investigaciones Históricas, UNAM-UABC, 1987).

44 Lazcano Sahagún, introduction to Rojo, *Apuntes*, 16–19. Marysa Navarro and

Virginia Sánchez Korrol, *Women in Latin America and the Caribbean* (Bloomington: Indiana University Press, 1999), address the use of legend in reconstructing the stories of women of the past. They propose that "finding women in the histories of the non-Western world requires persistence due to the silence or obliqueness of 'traditional' historical sources." Thus, in order to realize a fuller understanding of women and their condition in Latin America, scholars must also use the entire spectrum of nonobvious sources such as oral testimonies, mythology, life histories, explorer accounts, oral and written literature, cultural lore, and fable.

45 Rojo's description of the Indian woman appears in *Apuntes históricos*, document 2, subheading "*La Bella Bárbara*," 85. According to Rojo, the old inhabitants of the area had praised Gandiaga so much so that he would have questioned the accuracy of their reminiscences if it were not for the sheer number of people who remembered her, who were compelled to tell her story even fifty-two years after her death, and for the "respectability" attributed to the storytellers.

46 The *conventos* or *monjeríos* were the mission dormitories, or sleeping quarters, where young, usually unmarried, indigenous maidens were held typically under lock and key. These young women were in some cases called *monjas*, and although they were Christianized, they were not nuns who were traditionally trained as catechistic instructors, or for the purpose of performing cloistered prayerful duties.

47 Rojo, *Apuntes históricos*, 85–86.

48 Ibid., 86–87.

49 Charles A. Hale, *Mexican Liberalism in the Age of Mora, 1821–1853* (New Haven: Yale University Press, 1968), 35.

50 Ramón E. Ruiz's *Triumphs and Tragedy: A History of the Mexican People* (New York: Norton, 1992), ch. 12, examines the Reforma, which he describes as a "cataclysmic triumph of the runt, provincial middle class." The Leyes de Reforma, assembled in the Constitution of 1857, attempted to abolish the Church's influence and privileges. The laws eliminated the Church's judicial authority, whereby it was "restricted to cases concerning canon law"; barred "ecclesiastical corporations from owning or administering lands," compelling the Church to sell its vast landholdings (with the exception of churches, monasteries, and convents) to private individuals; and "forbade the Church to charge exorbitant fees for administering the sacraments." The Reforma laws also promoted government sponsorship of secular public education to provide for schooling for Mexican urban and rural residents, including the Indian population.

51 According to David J. Weber, *The Spanish Frontier of North America* (New Haven: Yale University Press, 1992), Father Serra wrote to Viceroy Bucareli complaining of the soldiers' immorality, 247.

52 Sánchez, *Telling Identities*, 66.

53 José Luis Amao Rodríguez, *Mineros, misioneros y rancheros de la antigua California* (Mexico City: Instituto Nacional de Antropología e Historia, 1997), 32.

54 Nieser, *Las fundaciones misionales*, 248. It should be noted, however, that in Baja California the process to secularize the missions was delayed, since many considered the indigenous peoples unable to be self-supporting. Thus, instructions to secularize were reissued in the 1840s.

55 Aguilar Marco, Juan Luis et al., *Misiones en la península de Baja California* (Mexico City: Colección Científica, Serie Historia, Instituto Nacional de Antropología e Historia, 1991), 70.

56 It must be noted that Baja Californianos did not unilaterally benefit from Reforma policies. In fact the Juarez administration was responsible for what many consider a historic blow to Baja California's political and economic sovereignty known as the Leese Concession. Meant to open up the peninsula for foreign investment and economic development, the Concession allowed for fifteen Americans to hold massive tracts of open land comprising almost two-thirds of the peninsula. Finding the peninsular climate and labor resources wanting, the Americans were not extremely successful in making profits. In addition, Baja Californianos fiercely criticized the Juarez government for creating conditions that placed their territorial integrity and economic autonomy at serious risk.

57 Lazcano Sahagún, "Biographical Sketch of Don Manuel Clemente Rojo," in the introduction to Rojo, *Apuntes históricos*, 15–27.

58 Ibid., 28–32

59 Not to be confused with the Flores Magón, Praxedis Guerrero, and Librado Rivera–led movement. What may be commonly known as Liberal Party organization and politics, in Baja California, formally took place at the turn of the twentieth century with the creation of the Partido Liberal Mexicano, which sought to bring about a socialist government in Baja California. This essay simply addresses the notions promoted by Liberalists, their movement, and resulting legislation, which took place in Mexico, as described above, and whose discourse resonated with Baja Californians of that time. For more on the anarchist Liberal Party movement, see Gonzalo Aguirre Beltrán, *Ricardo Flores Magón* (México, D.F.: UNAM, 1972); Eduardo Blanquel, *El pensamiento politico de Ricardo Flores Magón, precursor de la revolucion mexicana* (México, D.F.: UNAM, 1963); Lawrence Douglas Taylor, *La campaña magonista de 1911 en Baja California* (Tijuana: Colegio de la Frontera Norte, 1992).

60 Lazcano Sahagún, "Biographical Sketch," 56.

61 Alessandro Portelli's *The Death of Luigi Trastulli and other Stories: Form and Meaning in Oral History* (Albany: State University of New York Press, 1991) is an insightful treatment of the use of oral testimonies in the reconstruction of historical events. Portelli posits that "the discrepancy between fact and memory ultimately enhances the value of the oral sources as historical documents. It is not caused by faulty recollections but actively and creatively generated by

memory and imagination in an effort to make sense of crucial events and of history in general." The legend of Bárbara Gandiaga as remembered by the old Baja Californianos, although possibly full of inaccuracies, gains meaning in their attempt to understand and represent that historical event. As Portelli states (from Walter Benjamin), "For an experienced event is finite—at any rate, confined to one sphere of experience; a remembered event is infinite, because it is only a key to everything that happened before and after it."

62 As David J. Weber points out, in California during the latter part of the colonial period, the Crown "relied on missionaries and small mission guards to establish dominion." See "Bourbons and Bárbaros: Center and Periphery in the Reshaping of Spanish Indian Policy," in *Negotiated Empires: Centers and Peripheries in the Americas, 1500–1820*, ed. Christine Daniels and Michael V. Kennedy (New York: Routledge, 2002), 91.

63 Antonia I. Castañeda, "Presidiarias y Pobladoras: Spanish-Mexican Women in Frontier Monterrey, Alta California, 1770–1821" (Ph.D. diss., Stanford University, 1990, UMI Dissertation Services, 82). This study primarily focuses on Alta California; however, the analysis holds when looking at the broader general area of the Californias. For another excellent essay on sexual violence as a tool of colonial domination in California, see Antonia I. Castañeda, "Sexual Violence in the Politics and Policies of Conquest: Amerindian Women and the Spanish Conquest of Alta California," in *Building with Our Hands: New Directions in Chicana Studies*, ed. Adela de la Torre and Beatriz M. Pesquera (Berkeley: University of California Press, 1993).

64 Castañeda, "Sexual Violence," 88–89.

65 The judgment against Bárbara Gandiaga, Lázaro Rosales, and Alexandro de la Cruz, AGN, vol. 18, exp. 13, IIH exp. 2.2, f. 57, dated 27 May 1806, clearly states that these cases, and the resulting convictions, were to "serve forever as an example to others of [their] class." AGN, IIH-UABC. My translation.

66 Note that, according to Albert B. Nieser, Mariano Carrillo, despite being found guilty of the murder of Father López, was only sentenced to six years hard labor, while Gandiaga, whose direct involvement in the murder was never corroborated or proven, was sentenced to die.

67 Jean Franco, *Plotting Women: Gender and Representation in Mexico* (New York: Columbia University Press, 1989), xxiii.

ANDRÉS RESÉNDEZ

An Expedition and Its Many Tales

D id the written word, the spread of literacy, and the rise of print capitalism have something to do with the rise of national identities along the United States–Mexico borderlands? Following Benedict Anderson's influential *Imagined Communities*, historians, sociologists, and literary critics have turned their attention to how the written word has shaped national/ethnic identities. The notion that the rise of print capitalism and its consequent codification of languages and reading publics somehow underpin the rise of nations has led to a protracted scholarly exchange that looms large in poststructural and postcolonial studies.[1] Some authors have underscored the homogenizing effect of print capitalism. As the nineteenth century unfolded, editors were better able to deliver standardized information in the form of newspapers, pamphlets, books, and other printed products across national domains.[2] Yet other scholars, writing against the grain of these stories of conformity and homogeneity, have turned their attention toward the writings of subordinate ethnic groups and nonelite members who hardly took part in this massproduced community of readers and writers. As a whole, such texts have shown the persistence of alternative pockets of opinion.[3] What follows here is a brief exploration of the literary cultures that coexisted in the U.S.-Mexico borderlands in the early nineteenth century. To make this topic manageable I specifically focus on the Anglo-American, Indian, and Mexican accounts arising out of a disastrous venture called the Texan Santa Fe Expedition.

In the summer of 1841 a party of 320 Texans started out from Austin, the capital of the Republic of Texas, with the intention of opening a direct line of communication with the Mexican settlements in neighboring New Mexico. Ostensibly they were undertaking a government-sponsored commercial enterprise meant to allow Lone Star merchants to tap into the lucrative Santa Fe Trail. Yet several expedition members knew the ulterior and far more important purpose: to claim more than half of New Mexico's territory as part of the expansive Texas Republic. The expedition turned into an unmitigated disaster. The party nearly perished from starvation even before reaching New Mexico. Along the way the trekkers suffered fatal encounters with Indian groups, especially with Kiowas. And once in New Mexico, the Texans—far from being welcomed with their wares—were regarded as pirates, invaders, and boorish interlopers. They were quickly subdued and sent in chains to Mexico City to be tried. Impressed by all these developments Anglo-Texans, Kiowas, and Nuevomexicanos generated several narratives of this episode that both reflected and shaped their collective identities on the eve of the Mexican-American War. My main purpose in this essay is to briefly sketch out the strikingly different literary cultures in which these different narratives were inscribed and explore how they served to promote notions of ethnic and national difference.[4]

Anglo-American Print Capitalism and the Telling of a Tale of Disaster

The press coverage and subsequent published narratives of the Texan Santa Fe Expedition leave no doubt that by the 1840s the "print revolution" that had transformed the northeastern United States had reached the southern frontier. Especially after the 1820s, newspapers started mushrooming in frontier towns like Louisville, Mobile, and Natchez. In 1837, New Orleans alone boasted no less than ten newspapers and eight more started up that year. Texas experienced a similar print rush during the Mexican and Republic periods, but along strict language lines. For all the active and critical Spanish-language journalism that would later flourish along the border area, no Spanish newspaper was published in Texas prior to the 1850s.[5] In contrast, Anglo-Texans enjoyed local papers beginning in 1829, including the *Texas Gazette* and the *Telegraph and Texas Register*.

The Texan Santa Fe Expedition added valuable substance to this flourishing print culture. Because of its colorful cast of characters and misfortunes, this venture would ultimately become something of a media phenomenon. Even before the expedition departed, the reading public seemed especially attracted by a venture that was headed into "uncharted territory," passing through Comanche lands and bound for exotic New Mexico. Not surprisingly, newsmen like George W. Bonnell, editor of the *Austin Sentinel*, and Commissioner Richard F. Brenham of the *Bulock's Logs* sheets readily joined the expedition, seeking fresh material. Most prominently, journalist and editor George Wilkins Kendall decided that the undertaking was so unprecedented that it would hold the interest of his readers of the New Orleans *Picayune*. He secured a place in the Texan Santa Fe Expedition expressly to write a chronicle that he intended to publish in weekly installments.[6] The adventures of the expedition and eventual imprisonment of its members dramatically increased public awareness. The tenor of a broadside published in Austin in 1842 is quite eloquent in this regard: "A Voice from the West!!! Fellow citizens, the piteous cries, and dying groans of our imprisoned and slaughtered countrymen, come to our ears in every breeze that sweeps over the western prairies."[7] The release of the expedition members paved the way for a second journalistic onslaught. Late in 1842, Thomas Falconer published an "Extended Account" in the New Orleans *Picayune* and Franklin Combs gave his "Narrative" to the *Niles' National Register* of Baltimore.[8] A far more significant editorial phenomenon was the publication in 1844 of Kendall's two-volume *Narrative of the Texan Santa Fe Expedition*.[9] Kendall's *Narrative* became an astounding commercial success. It went through seven editions in twelve years, selling more than forty thousand copies, which made it the most popular rendition of not only the Texan Santa Fe Expedition but of any (mis)adventures of Anglo-Americans in Mexico in the years leading up to the Mexican-American war.[10]

A clear sense of place and identity was evident in these Anglo-American publications. Most immediately, the coverage in newspapers in Missouri, Louisiana, and the Republic of Texas defined the parameters of a journalistic domain. Inside this domain—advertisements are especially revealing—one can see steam packets plying from port to port, cattle moving back and forth, and peoples doing business with each other on the basis of common assumptions. Beyond this domain news was sporadic and unreliable, landscapes became blurry and exotic, and peoples were dimly understood. Such journalistic domains did not necessarily overlap with formal national boundaries. For instance, the Anglo-American portion of Texas clearly fell under the purview of southern American newspapers and vice

NARRATIVE

OF THE

TEXAN SANTA FÉ EXPEDITION,

COMPRISING A DESCRIPTION OF

A TOUR THROUGH TEXAS,

AND

ACROSS THE GREAT SOUTHWESTERN PRAIRIES, THE CAMANCHE AND
CAYGÜA HUNTING-GROUNDS, WITH AN ACCOUNT OF THE
SUFFERINGS FROM WANT OF FOOD, LOSSES FROM
HOSTILE INDIANS, AND FINAL

CAPTURE OF THE TEXANS,

AND

THEIR MARCH, AS PRISONERS, TO THE CITY OF MEXICO.

WITH ILLUSTRATIONS AND A MAP.

BY GEO. WILKINS KENDALL.

IN TWO VOLUMES.

VOL. I.

NEW-YORK:
HARPER AND BROTHERS, 82 CLIFF-STREET.

1844.

Cover of George W. Kendall, *Narrative of the Texan Santa Fe Expedition*, 2 vols. (New York: Harper and Brothers, 1884).

versa. Journalistically speaking, the international border between Texan communities like Austin or Houston and American towns like Natchitoches or New Orleans did not exist. In order to speed the circulation of information, U.S. postal law allowed editors to exchange papers and copy freely from each other, a privilege that was extended to the Texas Republic.[11] At the same time, the Spanish-speaking section of Texas, the San Antonio–Goliad region, was for the most part excluded. The *Telegraph*, for instance, had a special section on news from "the West." Ethnically different, economically less developed, and immediately adjacent to Mexico and suspected of being mixed up in its rough-and-tumble politics, the San Antonio–Goliad region was treated almost as a foreign country:

> It must be peculiarly painful to every patriot to contemplate the condition of this unfortunate section of our Republic. For more than six years this once favored region has been desolated by a constant train of disasters . . . while every other portion of our Republic is enlivened with the cheering influences of industry and enterprise—here every thing languishes and a cheerless blighting torpor spreads its poisonous influence around. The farms are deserted, the villages are sinking under the ravages of decay, and the settlers seem rather as sojourners than possessors of their once happy homes.[12]

In addition to creating journalistic domains, newspapers like the *Picayune* or the *Telegraph* and accounts like Kendall's helped to forge a national/ethnic imagination by insisting on certain themes that appealed to the appetites of readers bent on establishing clear national and ethnic differences. The Anglo-Saxon character of the Santa Fe expedition was one of such themes that set imaginary boundaries while at the same time reinforcing the self-image of the intended readers. In newspaper articles and accounts of the expedition the varied human groups that inhabited the border region were classified according to shifting racial categories that placed Caucasians at the top. The venture was thus conceptualized as an attempt to introduce a measure of civilization among a whole spectrum of inferior races. A letter published in the *Columbia Patriot* expressed rather eloquently this point of view: "What field opens up before us for an adventure of the *Anglo-Saxon Nation*! What a wide door for the principles of republican government, of the arts and sciences of morality! . . . what opportunity at hand to raise the Cross and plant the holy institutions of Protestant Christianism! . . . the Bible will find its way to Santa Fe!"[13]

Journalists and chroniclers placed frontier Indians in a complicated and changing ranking system. Because Cherokees and Choctaws had frequent dealings with the United States, Kendall placed them high in the list; they had their eyes "somewhat opened to the plan of civil government . . . and had been made to know something of the system of the Christian religion by the pious zeal of missionaries." [14] In contrast, groups like Comanches and Wacos did not seem to exhibit any of the "fruits" of civilization in spite of some contacts; and certainly bellicose and roving tribes like Kiowas were at the bottom of the Indian hierarchy. [15]

Given the expedition's itinerary and purpose, it is not surprising that its chroniclers would devote a great deal of space to classifying Mexicans according to a changing racial categorization. All Anglo-American expedition accounts introduced a racial description of Mexico. The *Telegraph*, for instance, likened Mexico to the Hindustan, deeply divided into multiple and complicated sects and castes. In the editor's opinion, knowing and exploiting these cleavages was of the utmost importance for, as Great Britain had demonstrated, it was possible to conquer fifty million souls with only ten or twenty thousand soldiers and a few skillful operators like those of the East India Company. The *Telegraph* estimated that the population of northern Mexico—Nuevo León, Tamaulipas, Coahuila, Durango, Zacatecas, Chihuahua, New Mexico and the Californias—did not exceed two and a half million, and consisted of "infinitely the best portion of the Mexican nation . . . having more of the Castillian blood and having mixed less with the Indians." Even so the newspaper estimated that five-sixths of northern Mexicans were of Indian descent, leaving only 40,000 Hispanic whites. [16] The propagation of these racial categories applied to the heterogeneous border population constitutes one of the most critical ideological transformations facilitated by Anglo-American print culture in this era.

The uncharted, savage, and exotic nature of the country that was to be visited by the Texan trekkers was yet another recurrent theme that reified borders and emphasized ethnic difference. Anglo-American readers had shown a seemingly insatiable appetite for the exotic, pristine, and savage, whether along Egypt's Nile, in the Yucatan peninsula, or in the heart of the Congo. [17] The chroniclers of the Texan Santa Fe Expedition indulged such a taste by repeatedly (and mistakenly) stating that no white man had ever seen the Comanche wilderness and emphasizing its primeval character, a world unperturbed by civilization, living in its own time. For Kendall, for example, the Cross Timbers—a strip of wooded country flanked on the eastern side by clumps of woodland and on the west by an ocean of prairie—constituted a civilizational divide or an immense natural hedge dividing "the settled portions of the United States from the open prairies which have ever been the home and hunting-ground of the red man."[18]

Mexico was placed in a separate category in these narratives, neither as a pristine Indian world nor a civilized nation but rather disquietingly hybrid, although much closer to savagery than civilization. We get a first inkling of this perspective even before the expedition's departure when Kendall made a quick tour of San Antonio and its environs. Kendall was particularly impressed by the missions, silent and decaying testimonies of a high civilization. Yet he found it difficult to reconcile these imposing structures with the "primitive" character of the society that he saw.[19] By emphasizing the extent to which the indigenous element had persisted within the bounds of Mexico, chroniclers like Kendall articulated a deeply rooted nexus of beliefs among Anglo-American readers that revolved around the incapacity of Spain as a colonial power. Kendall's talent resided precisely in indulging and to some extent shaping shifting opinions toward Mexico.

In travelogues and memoirs set south of the border during the 1820s and early 1830s, Anglo-American writers still showed considerable sympathy—even when tinged by condescension—for a sister republic that had also managed to escape the clutches of European colonialism.[20] As of the late 1830s, however, Anglo-American authors portrayed the Mexican-Indian world as squarely antagonistic to the forces of civilization springing from both the Texas Republic and the United States. Undoubtedly, some of these notions had been molded in the crucible of the Texas Revolution and its legacy of bitter mistrust enshrined in the tales of the Alamo, Goliad, and San Jacinto.[21] Kendall's *Narrative* masterfully incorporated this anti-Mexican ferment of opinion that would later explode in the penny press and cheap literature of the wartime years.[22] Indeed, Mexico's transit from civilized to savage occurred progressively as these accounts unfolded. The dramatic fate of the expedition afforded a perfect backdrop. At the beginning of their narratives Falconer and Kendall portrayed Mexicans as inhabiting an intermediate stage in the scale of human development, potentially redeemable through association with more civilized nations but equally capable of slipping back into barbarism. But the expedition's first dealings with New Mexicans confirmed the worst. Even when these writers occasionally introduced nuance, their texts generally exoticized Mexicans, thereafter associating their character with treachery, cruelty, and servility. Kendall's hyperbolic description leaves no doubt: "we were now in the power of men who possessed all the vices of savage life without one of the virtues that civilization teaches."[23] Combs reduced New Mexican society to villainous leaders and mindless masses as he told how Mexican officers "excited the Peons to the highest degree of frenzy" and how the prisoners would have been slaughtered on the spot had they not been huddled together in a small yard enclosed by a mud wall and defended by the regular troops.[24]

From the perspective of the reading public of Texas, Louisiana, and Missouri, the Santa Fe expedition may have been a disastrous commercial and political experiment; yet editorially it was a resounding success. The expedition's newspaper coverage and the astounding commercial success enjoyed by writers like Falconer and above all Kendall reveal the intricate and powerful connections between imagination and market demand, between nationalism and profit making. However inaccurate, the texts of the Texan Santa Fe Expedition provided "depth" and "character" to a region about which precious little had been known in Texas and the United States, and in the process journalists and authors found a willing audience. New Mexico and the Comanche wilderness acquired concrete form and texture and became populated by frightful Mexican characters, honorable Waco warriors, and bloodthirsty Kiowas.

A Kiowa Tale of a Chance Encounter with the Enemy

The passage of the Texan Santa Fe Expedition was also recorded by the Kiowas. Initially this account did not circulate beyond the tribal realm. It would not be until 1892 that James Mooney, an ethnologist living in the Kiowa reservation, obtained four calendars or winter counts and subsequently published them. The oldest work chronicled yearly events beginning in 1833 and covering a period of sixty years.[25] This calendar had been kept for more than three decades by the family of Dohasan, head chief of the Kiowa, and thus the document became known as the Dohasan calendar. Sett'an (Little-Bear), a cousin of the great chief, kept a second calendar. The Sett'an was almost an exact copy of the Dohasan but made in greater detail and containing two additional pictographs. Both calendars were originally painted on hides and renewed from time to time as they wore out from age and handling, although the ones acquired by Mooney were already drawn in colored pencil on heavy manila paper. They con-

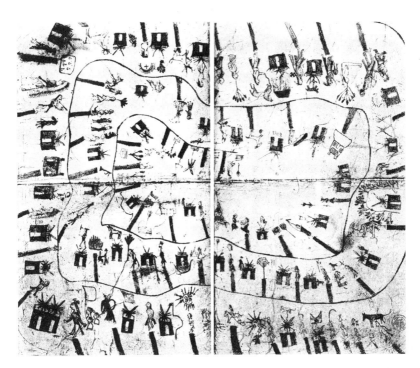

Se-Tan winter count. Taken from James Mooney, *Calendar History of the Kiowa Indians* (Washington, D.C.: Smithsonian Institution Press, [1898] reprinted 1979), plate 75.

sist of a series of pictographs arranged in a spiral beginning in the lower right-hand corner and ending near the center. An evolving oral tradition was associated with these drawings as it was customary for calendars to be brought out frequently during the long nights in the winter camp to be exhibited and discussed in the circle of warriors around a fire. At these gatherings, Mooney explained, "the pipe is filled and passed around, and each man in turn recites some mythic or historic tradition, or some noted deed on the warpath, which is then discussed by the circle. Thus the history of the tribe is formulated and handed down."[26]

Historians have tended to underutilize indigenous texts. Of course, archaeologists have long been fascinated with precontact writings; but oddly we know far less about the writings of historical—as opposed to archaeological—Indians of the eighteenth and nineteenth centuries.[27] In the nineteenth century, old forms of indigenous graphic representation coexisted alongside new methods. In the United States some Indians made their first incursions into the world of print by editing newspapers like the *Cherokee Phoenix and Indian Advocate* or becoming widely recognized authors like William Apess and Black Hawk, whose autobiographical accounts first appeared in 1829 and 1833 respectively. In Mexico, an Indian from Tixla, Ignacio Manuel Altamirano, became one of the preeminent literary figures of the 1860s and 1870s.[28] But even as indigenous peoples took advantage of modern print capitalism to further their collective and individual interests, old writing traditions continued to be practiced throughout the century. Among Plains Indians, winter counts persisted during this period of transition into modern print. A calendaric culture was evident throughout the plains from North Dakota—where the Sioux kept several chronologies including the famous Lone Dog's winter count—to the Texas–New Mexico border where the Kiowas and possibly the Apaches kept similar spirals of pictographs to symbolize memorable events.[29]

Just like any other historical accounts, winter counts derive their power from the particular selection of tales and detail. But while the written word allows for a certain latitude in the telling, pictographic writing requires concision in the extreme as pictographs function as mnemonic aids. Faced with the impossibility of graphically recording all battles, treaties, and other affairs of paramount importance, pictographic writers had to select one or two yearly events for depiction. The passage of time was represented by alternate black bars and sun-dance medicine lodge symbols representing winters and summers respectively. Pictographs placed close or on top of a black bar occurred during the cold period, while pictographs adjacent to the sun-dance medicine lodge symbol happened during the warm season. Here are some examples of Kiowa pictographs drawn from the Sett'an Calendar:

1833–34 "Winter that the stars fell." Meteoric display observed throughout North America on the morning of November 13, 1833.

1834–35 "Winter that Bull-Tail was killed." A war party was dispatched against the Mexicans of the waterless country—i.e., Chihuahua. One morning they were all surprised by Mexican troops and killed, including Bull-Tail.

1836–37 "Winter that K'inahiate was killed." K'inahiate (Man) was killed in an expedition against the Mexicans of the timber country—i.e., the lower Rio Grande valley.

1840   "Red-bluff sun dance." Summer when the confederation of Comanche, Apache, and Kiowa made peace with the Arapaho and Cheyenne.

1841–42 "Winter that A'dalhaba'k'ia was killed." A'dalhaba'k'ia (Sloping or One-sided Hair) was killed by a Texan detachment.

Calendars like the Sett'an include some events that outsiders would consider historically significant, such as the devastating smallpox epidemic of 1839 or the 1840 alliance of five nations, a peace that was never broken and single-handedly shaped the geopolitics of the area until the end of the century. But frequently the Sett'an depicts affairs of a personal or anecdotal nature, like the death of Sloping Hair. At the same time, there is no mention of events like the Texas Revolution or the Mexican-American war, events that unquestionably had tremendous repercussions for Kiowas and Comanches. These omissions do not imply that the Kiowas were disconnected from the Texas Republic, Mexico, and the United States. On the contrary, the Kiowa for a long time had become part and parcel of this fluid international space as their livelihood had come to depend on the ebb and flow of civil wars and international disputes in this area. The Kiowa regularly sent parties that operated in an enormous geographic area from California through Texas and sometimes ventured as far as Tamaulipas, Chihuahua, and Durango. In these forays Kiowas gathered a great deal of information from captives, allies, and other sources. Moreover, since the eighteenth century, Kiowas had established regular trade relations with New Mexican *comancheros* and Pueblo Indians and beginning in 1835 maintained periodic contacts with American trading houses.[30] Thus lack of information does not explain the absence of events like the Texas Revolution or the Mexican-American war in these chronologies.

Neither do these absences imply arbitrariness on the part of winter count keepers. Early ethnographers like Garrick Mallery ("discoverer" of the Lone Dog winter count) and Mooney were puzzled by the peculiar mix of historical and individual affairs depicted in these Indian chronologies. Mallery was persuaded that winter counts were not intended to be continuous histories but simply constituted sets of unusual or peculiar happenings well suited for depiction or particularly dear to the keeper. After careful consideration of pictographs covering more than sixty years, Mooney, too, concluded that the Kiowa calendars resembled the personal reminiscences of a garrulous old man rather than the full-fledged history of a nation.[31] This may have been the case. Yet, for all the seeming randomness, once chosen these events acquired great saliency as they served to fix all ordinary activities of the group. For instance, a person was said to have been born in the winter when the stars fell or a couple started living together in the winter when Sloping Hair was killed, and so forth.[32] While we know little about how winter counts were actually written, it seems likely that some discussion preceded the final choice of pictographs given their significance in the collective tribal memory.[33]

Having worked with only Kiowa calendars and informants, Mooney later realized that the pictograph for the winter of 1841–42 corresponded remarkably well with an Indian encounter narrated in Kendall's book of the Santa Fe expedition. The pictograph in question refers to the killing of war chief A'dalhaba'k'ia (Sloping or One-sided Hair) and shows a warrior with the right side of the head shaved and the left side with the hair at full length, a hairstyle that allowed the wearer to display ear pendants. A bird on top of the warrior's head represents a characteristic ornament of red woodpecker feathers. A stain on his body indicates that A'dalhaba'k'ia died of a bullet wound. According to oral tradition, the entire Kiowa tribe was camping on a small stream when it was discovered that a party of Texan soldiers was moving toward them. The Kiowa managed to surprise and kill five Texans who were ahead of the main body and captured their horses, but only after losing A'dalhaba'k'ia. The Kiowa then abandoned their camp but remained vigilant of the main body of intruders and, returning a few days later and finding a Texan who had strayed from the group, killed him.

This fateful encounter took place in the fall of 1841 on a small stream near the Llano Estacado that the Kiowa named Pabo P'a (American Horse River). Virtually all these details match other eyewitness accounts. On the basis of Anglo-American sources, we can identify the first five expedition members who were massacred as Lieutenant George R. Hull and his four companions. Anglo-American witnesses also agree that over the next few days parties of Kiowa scouts monitored the progress of the Texan party. They also state that another expedition member, a Mexican simply identified as Ramón, was murdered a few days later. Finally, Anglo-American sources justify the Kiowa usage of "American horse river," for, as Falconer and Gallagher explained, on the morning of September 4, 1841, Kiowa horsemen were able to stampede all the cattle and eighty-three horses of the expedition. Immediately pursued, the Kiowa were forced to leave the

Pictograph of Sloping or One-Sided Hair. Taken from James Mooney, *Calendar History of the Kiowa Indians* (Washington, D.C.: Smithsonian Institution Press, [1898] reprinted 1979), enlargement of a pictograph in plate 75.

cattle behind but took all the horses.[34] We know something more about what transpired in the Kiowa camp after the first violent encounter with the Texans. As it turned out, some New Mexican comancheros found themselves trading among the Kiowa when a group of warriors came dashing in with enemy scalps and entrails as well as the dead bodies of eleven fellow warriors, including a principal chief (presumably Sloping Hair). The comancheros reported that immediately all manner of ceremonies and performances were underway. Warriors danced around the Texan scalps and women smote and cut their breasts and ran naked through thorns and prickly pear-bushes to show their grief and affection toward the deceased.[35]

The Kiowa calendars in general and the depiction of the encounter with the Texans more specifically reveal a different way of seeing, interpreting, and writing about themselves and the people around them. Consider the notion of territory. Winter counts make it clear that the Kiowa understood the area where they lived as a homeland. Like many other prairie Indians, the Kiowa had originally migrated from the northern plains, driven out by the Dakota Sioux and Cheyenne. According to oral tradition, by the late eighteenth century the Kiowa ranged between the forks of the Platte River advancing along the base of the mountains and pushing the Comanche from the northern head streams of the Arkansas. Years of war ensued, but a settlement was reached sometime around 1790. It was a stunning feat of diplomacy. Instead of more years of uncertainty and violence, Kiowas and Comanches occupied together the territory along and south of the Arkansas, holding it in common for decades. In the course of these years of relative peace Kiowas and Comanches became even closer allies, often camping, hunting, trading, and conducting expeditions together, although the Kiowa tended to make their home camps toward the northwestern portion of the river while the Comanche kept near the *Llano Estacado* and along the Texas frontier.[36] From the early 1830s until reservation days in the late 1860s, the Kiowa homeland remained remarkably stable, although this did not preclude Kiowa bands from moving about within this large domain in patterns dictated by lifestyle, depletion of animals and plants, and military considerations. Still, the Kiowa developed strong emotional ties to specific locations to which they regularly returned. The Sett'an mentions that a place on the south bank of the North Canadian River at the Red Hills with great many cattail rushes was a favorite spot for holding sun dances. A nearby location was so frequently used for that purpose that it was given the name of Sun-Dance Creek. Others sites such as the American Horse River evoked events that were tragic but always meaningful to the collectivity. In 1867 Kiowa chief Satanta spoke eloquently of this sense of attachment: "All the land south of the Arkansas belongs to the Kiowas and Comanches, and I don't want to give away any of it. I love the land and the buffalo, and will not part with any."[37]

While it is clear that Kiowas developed a strong sense of territoriality in the early to mid-nineteenth century, it is also evident that they did not conceive boundaries as permanent demarcations guaranteed by formal treaties but merely as temporary expressions of relations of power. Thus the main narrative thrust of the Dohasan and Sett'an calendars revolves around the vital geopolitics of this fractious region. The Kiowa had been able to maintain control over one area by means first and foremost of skillful diplomacy. The smoking of the pipe with the Comanche had been a decisive event ending a period of internecine warfare and ushering in a new era of relative peace and stability. In 1840 the Kiowa helped to broker another momentous alliance joining five nations—Kiowa, Comanche, Kiowa-Apache, Arapaho, and Cheyenne—ensuring the Kiowa possession of the Arkansas basin and forming a veritable barrier to westward and southward-moving Indians (attracted by the prospects of trading horses with the Mexican settlements) as well as to encroaching whites from the northeast.[38] But sometimes negotiation was not enough. These calendaric accounts also underscore the enormous energy and determination on the part of the Kiowa to pursue, kill, and repel trespassers like the Osage, Pawnee, and Texans. The latter in particular emerged as a serious threat. In the late 1830s Texans conducted a war of extermination and removal in an area that the Comanche and Kiowa had long regarded as their own. The Kiowa-Comanche alliance was driven out of its best hunting grounds in violation of treaties and without compensation. In the spring of 1840 the Comanche suffered losses at the Council House Fight at San Antonio and along the edges of the white settlements at the hands of Texas Rangers. Kiowas and Comanches retaliated in the summer, raiding the Texas coast around Victoria and Linnville.[39] The Texan Santa Fe Expedition of 1841, the Kiowa victories over this advancing body of Texans, and the death of Sloping Hair have to be understood against the backdrop of this deep-seated enmity and quest to preserve a homeland free of encroachment.

Always pragmatic, the Kiowa regarded peoples around them neither as impossibly large nations nor as ethereal races, but as discrete human groupings. Breaking down these human aggregates into tribes served the Kiowa well, allowing them to cope effectively with changing configurations of Americans, Mexicans, and Texans. The Kiowa made a clear distinction between "Americans"—emigrants from the north or Kansas side and generally regarded as friendly—and "Texans" whom the Kiowa called *Tehaneko*, a word probably derived from the Spanish *tejano*. Indeed, the Kiowa continued to make this distinction long after Texas became annexed to the United States.[40] Large polities like the United States and Mexico were cut down to size according to their actual presence in the area. Revealingly, Kiowas called Americans *Hanpoko* or "trappers," given the primary occupation of Americans with whom they regularly came in contact. With regard to Mexicans, winter counts distinguish between various groups such as "Mexicans of the waterless country" (the people of Chihuahua) or "timber Mexicans" (those living in the lower Rio Grande valley). In fact, Kiowas not only wrote about but dealt with Mexico in subnational terms, making war on a half dozen Mexican states while keeping friendly relations with New Mexico, where they found a brisk market for war spoils.[41] The Kiowa were not disposed to judge nations by formal attributes and grandiose statements. Great chiefs and captains as far away as Mexico City and Washington may have claimed the allegiance of incredibly large numbers of people and sovereignty over vast territories, but what mattered most to the Kiowa were the actual conditions on the ground and the actions of flesh-and-blood human beings.

Kiowa calendars constitute fine-grained glimpses of human affairs, portraits made almost at a microscopic scale where individual gestures and chance encounters mattered greatly both for the consequences for the individuals involved and for their potential to disrupt delicate tangles of alliances and counteralliances that were so central to the well-being of human beings living in this contested space. The dragging of the head of an Arapaho warrior, the accidental encounter with a group of Texans, or the kidnapping of a young child acquire great significance when viewed in the context of a fluid human landscape where a faux pas can amount to the difference between peace and war. Dohasan and Sett'an did not depend on the vagaries of market fashions in the way Kendall, Falconer, and the other chroniclers of the Santa Fe expedition did. Yet these calendar keepers did seek a connection with their people striving to recreate the human, and sometimes the supernatural, universe in which the Kiowa operated and offering lessons ranging from the character of other groups to the wisdom and limits of negotiation and warfare. Finally, calendars served as conventional histories of a people, keeping a tally of how the Kiowa had managed the collective enterprise of survival. Already an old man in 1892, Sett'an took out the calendar he had kept for a long time and gave it to Mooney without asking for any payment in return. Complaining that the young men were already forgetting their own history, Sett'an asked Mooney to take the calendar to Washington so that the white people might always remember what the Kiowa had done.[42]

The Mexican State and Its Texts

Understandably, Mexicans produced a copious body of texts about the Texan Santa Fe Expedition. After 1838, when rumors of an invading expedition from Texas first reached Mexico, military and civil officials spilled liters of ink in patriotic *pronunciamientos* and correspondence denouncing the Lone Star interlopers. The Mexican press hailed the capture of the party of Texans as Mexico's most brilliant victory since the days of the Alamo and Goliad. In a letter that first appeared in *El Pigmeo* of Chihuahua and was later reproduced in *El Siglo Diecinueve* of Mexico City, editors marveled at how a determined but disorganized crowd of New Mexicans, barely armed with spears and slings, had been able to cow a well-armed force of invasion into surrender.[43] Carlos María de Bustamante, arguably the most influential historian of the time, joined in, writing a commentary of Governor Manuel Armijo's capture of the Santa Fe expeditioners and publishing an anonymous *memoria* from New Mexico.[44] While

Bustamante's account became the standard Mexican version of the fate of the Santa Fe expedition, it was not meant for the masses. Unlike Kendall's book, deliberately crafted as a bestseller, Bustamante's memoria and commentary targeted the influential few. His writing style was that of the consummate insider peppered with cryptic references and political lessons aimed at settling old scores and laying out fault lines emerging from the Texan Santa Fe Expedition.

Printing has a long and distinguished history in Mexico. It flourished in the course of the eighteenth century when periodical publications began to circulate throughout the kingdom, and it became decidedly political during the wars of independence as anticolonial rebels, critical literati, and imperial bureaucrats desirous of quelling dissention turned presses into propaganda tools.[45] Yet, it was in the tumultuous decades after emancipation that political printing reached a new plateau which would have been impossible to imagine just half a century earlier. Every army commander of importance, every bishopric and religious order, every state and local government of note, every self-respecting *caudillo* and regional strongman, and every revolutionary leader required the services of printing presses. Collectively, these opinion leaders issued a prodigious amount of loose sheets in the form of broadsides, pronunciamientos, open letters, accounts, satirical stories, sermons, *folletos*, and many other literary formats. These publications were so ubiquitous that Carlos María de Bustamante was convinced that the entire history of Mexico, from its famous episodes down to its most inconsequential details, could be pieced together from this torrent of paper. In fact, he made it his lifelong task to preserve these texts for posterity before they became irretrievably lost, as pharmacists and grocery store owners used these printed sheets for everything except reading. Firework makers were notorious for transmuting broadsides and folletos into smoke and dazzling pyrotechnics in the aftermath of every successful revolution.[46]

Mexicans were not only exposed to these printed sources but more commonly came in contact with handwritten texts copied and circulated by state and local governments. Such texts included addresses or regulations posted in prominent places in central plazas and often read aloud on Sundays and other special days. Owing to the dearth of printing equipment, New Mexicans learned about the "Texas question" and debated its implications in this fashion. For four years—as of 1838, when an invasion from Texas became a distinct possibility—New Mexicans heard various handwritten addresses and orders on the subject.[47] On each occasion the chain of events would start when Governor Armijo received confidential information about the possibility of an invasion and rumors began to spread. The governor would then convene a meeting in Santa Fe with the leading men of the territory. These conclaves ended with pledges of loyalty to the nation, a plan of defense, and written addresses—the governor's included—intended to stimulate the patriotic zeal of the people at large. In putting together his anti-Texas coalitions, Governor Armijo enlisted the help of key military and ecclesiastical leaders who, in turn, sent instructions and letters to their subordinates. In 1841, the governor pleaded in particular with the vicar of New Mexico, Juan Felipe Ortiz, to "display his influence over all classes" and by virtue of his dignity exhort all the faithful to help in the defense.[48] From Santa Fe many of these addresses, religious sermons, letters, and instructions were copied and sent to other communities, not only Hispanic towns but also Indian pueblos and Anglo-American ranches. What happened next depended on local authorities. Sometimes local authorities just affixed the document to a wooden beam of the municipal building, local church, or the most prominent structure. Other authorities, like Judge Miguel Mascareñas of Mora, a town in eastern New Mexico and likely stopover of the Texan party, went to greater lengths, gathering all residents in the central square to read aloud the governor's address. Judge Mascareñas reported that the people responded "in one voice" and with "Spartan will" to be united forever with the nation.[49] Sometimes the documents themselves—especially official communiqués or *bandos*—contained specific instructions about how they should be made known to the public: "to be read aloud on Sunday after being received" or, as in the case of Armijo's 1840 proclamation concerning the Texas invasion, "to be published as *bando* in this capital city for three consecutive Sundays, and displayed in public places, and thereafter every first Sunday of the month in all political districts."[50] Thus state-sponsored texts circulating in central plazas and supply stores reached ordinary New Mexicans, even those who were subliterate or downright illiterate.[51]

From this repertoire of harangues, addresses, and accounts of the Texan Santa Fe Expedition it is possible to isolate two recurrent themes that served both to repudiate the Texas Republic and to affirm elite views about what constituted Mexico's national identity. One had to do with the morality of Texans generally introduced with epithets like "criminal," "corrupted," "depraved," and "perfidious."[52] Catholic fervor constituted the

BANDO

MANUEL ARMIJO CORONEL DE CABALLERIA DEL EXERCITO PERMA-
NENTE DE LA REPUBLICA, GOBERNADOR Y COMANDANTE GENE-
RAL DEL DEPARTAMENTO A SUS HABITANTES.

Habiendose anunciado de mucho tiempo que los sublevados del Departamento de Te-
jas, tenian el atrevido proyecto de invadir este Departamento; con el fin de agregarlo á
su llamada Republica; désde entonces no he vasilado un momento para atender á la se-
guridad que debo proporcionar á la vida, intereses, y derechos sagrados de los Nuevo
Mejicanos; por esa gavilla de hombres desmoralisados, corrompidos y cargados de cri-
menes se pretende profanar el suelo sagrado de nuestra Cara Patria, nuestros derechos
y Religion, a esto atacan directamente ¿y vosotros Nuevo-Mejicanos vereis con indi-
ferencia que unos aventureros Extrangeros, vengan, y penetren hasta los senos de nuestros Pueblos á arrebatarnos nuestra apreciada Libertad, vida ó intereses, á corromper
vuestras innocentes costumbres, y en fin á hacer desaparecer nuestra verdadera, amable
y suave Religion, para que gravite sobre vuestros cuellos el Ilugo de fierro que siempre
el invasor descarga sobre el conquistado? como permitirnos de libres reducirnos á es-
clavos, y de semejante canalla? no, no es en nuestros intereses, ni propio del caracter de
Mejicanos; el hombre en sociedad esiste, mientras conserva su libertad, Independencia
Patria, y Religion, Derechos Sagrados que á toda costa debe mantener, pues la misma

Para que, llegado el caso, no se omita por teinor ó negligencia hacer la defensa
á que todo Ciudadano esta obligado, ni se cometan por ignorancia otros hechos crimi-
nales, y dañosos asi mismo, mando se observen las prevenciones siguientes-
1 ° Todo hombre de diez y seis años arriba, inmediatamente que tenga noticia
donde quiera que se halle, que alguno de los puntos fronterizos de este Departamento es
atacado por tejanos, tomará sus armas y se presentará inmediatamente á la autoridad po-
litica ó militar del lugar de su residencia.
2. ° Ningun individuo saldrá de Departamento al campo donde estubieren los ene-
migos, por ningun motivo, ni de ninguna manera se tendran relaciones con ellos.
3. ° Por ningun individuo se les ministrarán biveres y artículos de guerra, ni otro au-
silio. en donde quiera que estubieren acampados.
4. ° Los Ciudadanos extrangeros que se hallan naturalizados, tienen las mismas obliga-
ciones que los Mejicanos de nacimiento, y los que no lo estan y solo trafican observa-
ran una perfecta neutralidad.
5. ° Los individuos que faltaren á la óbservancia de estas prevenciones se declaran
fuera de la Ley y seran castigados irremisiblemente sin qué escusa ni pretesto alguno
les exonere de la pena.
Y para que llegue anoticia de todos, y nadie alegue iguorancias, mando sé publique
por Bandó en esta Capital, por tres Domingos consecutivos, se fije en los parajes publico; y despues el primer Domingo de cada mes se repita; circulandose á las Prefecturas
del Departamento para que asi se ejecute en todos los lugares de sus Distritos.
Santa Fé de Nuevo Mejico Julio 16 de 1840.

Manuel Armijo

Guadalupe Miranda
Secret. de Gob.

Imprenta del Sôr D. Antonio José Martinez á Cargo del Ciudadano Jesus Maria Baca.

Mexican *bando* of the Texas invasion of New Mexico. Taken from the microfilm edition of the Mexican Archives of New Mexico, reel 27, frame 1265.

second recurrent theme in these harangues, addresses, and instructions. Even before the Texas Revolution, Anglo-Texans had been viewed by many Mexicans as irreverent opportunists. Anglo Texans—just like Anglo Americans in New Mexico—were required to convert to Catholicism in order to obtain Mexican citizenship and be allowed to purchase land and conduct other transactions. Most complied out of necessity, but their degree of participation in Catholic ritual, with a few exceptions, remained notoriously low or nonexistent. Indeed, the extent of Anglo-Texans' repudiation of Catholicism became evident after Texas seceded from Mexico. Pious Nuevomexicanos learned with dismay that the parish priest of San Antonio, Refugio de la Garza, was suspended from his ministry, cheated out of his properties, and even chained and paraded through the streets of San Antonio like an ordinary criminal.[53] In New Mexico, Vicar Ortiz had already taken concrete steps to limit the number of foreign-born residents who acquired Mexican citizenship via marriage with Mexican women, by insisting on strict procedures to grant dispensations and by mandating a thirty-peso surcharge for the paperwork.[54] As New Mexicans grappled with real or imaginary invasions from Texas, Catholicism emerged as a cornerstone of resistance: "New Mexicans, will you look on with indifference as a handful of foreign adventurers march all the way to our communities to take away our freedom and interest, to pollute our innocent traditions, and to do away with our true and loved Religion?"[55]

Were ordinary New Mexicans receptive to these public texts? It is exceedingly difficult to tell. While the commercial success of Kendall's *Narrative* and the arduously discussed and evolving oral tradition that accompanied winter counts provide at least an inkling of how these texts played out in wider audiences, we have no comparable gauge for Mexican proclamations. Still, we have some tantalizing clues. In the summer of 1840, in the midst of an anti-Texas propaganda campaign, a conspiracy was discovered in the Rio Abajo district. A group of laborers and peons had secretly set out to burn all account books and traces of their indebtedness since the year of 1830. Captured before the plan went into effect, the leaders— all members of the "lower classes" according to Armijo's report—revealingly explained in their judiciary depositions that they welcomed a Texan takeover as it would result in their deliverance from debt. The insurgents somehow believed that Texans would favor a more equitable distribution of power and money.[56] Indeed, Governor Armijo, who so many times had stood in front of ordinary New Mexicans trying to rouse their patriotic zeal, privately worried that nonelite New Mexicans could easily be persuaded to support Texas if they saw the slightest advantage in such a course.[57] But at the same time, it is also evident that Governor Armijo was able to marshal a respectable and heterogeneous force of resistance consisting of a few wealthy individuals—who raised what amounted to private armies—ecclesiastics, political allies of the governor, less affluent civil and military officers, as well as an unspecified number of ordinary New Mexicans who enlisted in the army of resistance without receiving any compensation or salary.[58] It is possible that these latter citizens agreed at least with some of the ideas expressed in the many passionate addresses denouncing the Lone Star Republic that circulated in the territory or were concerned by real or imagined conspiracies like the one described in Bustamante's published memoria.

Perhaps the most convincing evidence of this concern comes from the extreme hostility evinced toward foreign-born residents by many Nuevomexicanos during and immediately after the capture of the Santa Fe expedition. The American consul in Santa Fe reported that once definite intelligence had reached the territory of the invading body of Texans, many New Mexicans insulted foreign-born residents on the streets and in public places.[59] Indeed, on the day that regular soldiers and the militia of Santa Fe departed for the frontier to face the Texans, a throng of people and a few soldiers burst into the house of the American consul and wounded him in the face with a knife.[60] After the Texans surrendered and in the midst of improvised celebrations, an angry mob cheered as the Texas constitution was burned in the main plaza of Las Vegas, and in Santa Fe groups of disgruntled Nuevomexicanos swept through the streets insulting foreign-born residents and plundering one of their stores.[61]

The capture of the Texan party gave temporary relief and confidence to a nation that had been badly shaken during its short existence as an independent nation. Bustamante, for one, felt confident that such glorious episodes would provide sufficient material to "poets, painters, and speakers who will communicate to future generations a fact worthy of celebration and ennobling of the New Mexican people." He followed the story of the Texan expeditioners until their final release in Mexico City on President Santa Anna's birthday and ended with a sigh: "God willing these acts of magnanimity on the part of the Mexican government won't be lost and forgotten by these men who are bound to pay us back mounting another charge as soon as they are able!"[62]

✳ ✳ ✳

The many tales surrounding the Santa Fe expedition show that as late as the 1840s Anglo Americans, New Mexicans, and Kiowas were immersed in strikingly different literary cultures in spite of their relative geographic proximity to one another. While it is clear that print capitalism had made significant inroads into the border region by the 1840s, the preceding discussion also emphasizes that alternative literary cultures that were not tied to market forces continued to thrive and shape peoples' understandings of collective identities. In the fragmented frontier world, independent and very particular mechanisms existed for the propagation of texts. Texts were produced within different landscapes of institutional structures in which different entities like the market, the state, or group leaders took the leading role in fashioning and disseminating such textual material. Clearly the narratives of Anglo-American journalists of the Texan Santa Fe Expedition appeared in the context of a fierce journalistic competition, a situation that compelled authors to face the market squarely and take into consideration readers' tastes and preconceptions of the area. In contrast, the Mexican state produced and disseminated texts about the Texan expedition to New Mexico using all the trappings of governmental power including public readings and exhortations to get its message across. Among Kiowas certain leaders became the keepers of crucial textual material. In this sense, the frontier was not different from what we find in other regions. As Richard H. Brodhead has observed more generally for the United States in the nineteenth century, writing was (and continues to be) inextricably linked to the particularized mechanisms that bring the text to public life.[63] It is precisely the cultural specificity of the settings in which texts occur that may explain the remarkable permanence of fragmented literary spaces along the United States–Mexican borderland long after the onset of print capitalism.

Perhaps the most salient feature of the different texts associated with the Texan Santa Fe Expedition is that they conveyed widely different notions of collective self. Anglo-American journalistic renditions and subsequent narratives of the expedition tended to blur the boundary between the United States and the Texas Republic while emphasizing the divide between *Anglo-America* on one side and the Mexican-Indian world on the other. It is a world organized around language, racial, and ethnic categorizations. In sharp contrast, Mexican texts, closely tied to the Mexican state, not surprisingly emphasized the *national* space and its citizens. The national domain and state-sponsored religion emerge as the most obvious organizing principles in these texts, as the Texan Santa Fe Expedition was construed as an attack on the territorial integrity of Mexico and an alarming assault on Catholicism. Finally, Kiowa calendars provided yet another understanding of the human landscape of the frontier. These texts privileged discrete local and regional groupings like the "people of New Mexico" or "the people of Chihuahua" over national constructs like *Mexico* or the *United States* or overarching racial categorizations like *Indians*. In spite of their relative proximity, Anglo-Americans, Mexicans, and Kiowas understood and wrote about their collective identities in strikingly different ways.

Print capitalism eventually displaced alternative literary cultures. We know that Kiowa calendars ceased to be written by the end of the nineteenth century, just as Elliott Young's essay in this volume suggests that by the turn of the century print capitalism was a primary vehicle of textual production in northeastern Mexico. In this sense, Benedict Anderson's elegant formulation linking nationalism with the rise of print capitalism does apply to the Mexico–United States border region. But such a shorthand description fails to explain why a variety of alternative literary cultures survived well after nations were first established in the region and glosses over the intricate ways in which these textual worlds propagated different notions of collective self.

Notes

1   In addition to Benedict Anderson's work, other classics in this debate include Homi K. Bhabha, ed., *Nation and Narration* (London: Routledge, 1990); Terence Ranger and Eric Hobsbawm, eds., *The Invention of Tradition* (Cambridge: Cambridge University Press, 1983); and Allen Carey-Webb, *Making Subject(s): Literature and the Emergence of National Identity* (New York: Garland, 1998).

2   For example, Larzer Ziff has argued that print culture in the United States functioned as an imperial project that imposed interpretations, views, and voices on subordinate peoples like Native Americans who, unable to represent themselves until the latter part of the nineteenth century, underwent a process of "literary annihilation." Larzer Ziff, *Writing in the New Nation: Prose, Print, and Politics in the Early United States* (New Haven: Yale University Press, 1991), 173. See also Richard Brown, *Knowledge Is Power: The Diffusion of Information in Early*

America (New York: Oxford University Press, 1989); and William Huntzicker, *The Popular Press, 1833–1865* (Westport, Conn.: Greenwood, 1999).

3 Partly reacting against Ziff's interpretation, Cheryl Walker investigated the writings of American Indians in the nineteenth century. See Cheryl Walker, *Indian Nation: Native American Literature and Nineteenth-Century Nationalism* (Durham: Duke University Press, 1997), 7–9. In a different context, Genaro Padilla has examined autobiographies of Californios, Tejanos, and Nuevo-mexicanos as a way of probing into their evolving national identities. Genaro Padilla, *My History, Not Yours: The Formation of Mexican American Autobiography* (Madison: University of Wisconsin Press, 1993).

4 Throughout this essay I use the word "nation" in two distinct ways. Generally by nation I actually mean the *nation-state*, that is, a political entity like Mexico or the United States that included many different ethnic groups within its confines. But following early-nineteenth-century usage, the word "nation"—especially in quotes—sometimes refers to an ethnic group as in *Anglo-Saxon nation* or *Cherokee nation*. Because many of my arguments apply to both nation-state and ethnic identities, I often couple the two terms, as in national/ethnic loyalties.

5 For a complete compilation of early Texas newspapers, see Thomas W. Streeter, *Bibliography of Texas, 1795–1845*, 2nd ed. (Woodbridge, Conn.: Research Publications, 1983), 189–213.

6 On Kendall's life, see Fayette Copeland, *Kendall of the Picayune*, 2nd ed. (Norman: University of Oklahoma Press, 1997).

7 Broadside, Austin, 1842, microfilm of Texas as a Province and Republic, 1795–1845, reel 9, no. 551. Copeland traces the newspaper coverage of the expedition; see *Kendall of the Picayune*, 83–84.

8 Thomas Falconer wrote no less than three accounts of his experiences in the expedition. All three versions and related documentation can be found in Thomas Falconer, *Letters and Notes on the Texan Santa Fe Expedition, 1841–1842*, ed. F. W. Hodge (Chicago: Rio Grande Press, 1963). Combs's "Narrative" appeared in the *Niles' National Register*, 5 March 1842. His account has been republished: Franklin Combs, "Narrative of the Santa Fe Expedition in 1841," *New Mexico Historical Review* 5:3 (1930): 306–7.

9 George W. Kendall, *Narrative of the Texan Santa Fe Expedition* (New York: Harper and Brothers, 1844), xxix.

10 For an insightful discussion of Kendall's popularity, see Carroll H. Bailey, *The Texan Santa Fe Trail* (Canyon, TX: Panhandle-Plains Historical Society, 1952), 2–16.

11 Marilyn McAdams Sibley, *Lone Stars and State Gazettes: Texas Newspapers before the Civil War* (College Station: Texas A&M University Press, 1983), 8.

12 *Telegraph and Texas Register*, 6 April 1842.

13 *Columbia Patriot*, 13 April 1839. Copied and translated by Guadalupe Miranda,

Santa Fe, 28 July 1839, Herbert E. Bolton Papers, box 41, file 688, Bancroft Library.

14 Kendall, *Narrative of the Texan Santa Fe Expedition*, 181–82. For another contemporary detailed effort to place the Kiowas vis-à-vis Comanche and other Indians, see George Catlin, *Letters and Notes on the Manners, Customs, and Conditions of North American Indians*, 2 vols. (New York: Dover, Inc., 1973 [1844]), 2, 73–74.

15 Kendall, *Narrative of the Texan Santa Fe Expedition*, 1, 281–82.

16 *Telegraph and Texas Register*, 10 April, 28 August 1839, and 19 October 1840.

17 See Janis P. Stout, *The Journey Narrative in American Literature: Patterns and Departures* (Westport, Conn.: Greenwood, 1983).

18 Kendall, *Narrative of the Texan Santa Fe Expedition* 1, 139.

19 Ibid., 1, 52–53.

20 For instance, see the decidedly statistical and generally positive works of the first ministers of the United States and Great Britain in Mexico, respectively: Joel R. Poinsett, *Notes on Mexico, Made in the Autumn of 1822* (New York: F. A. Prager, 1969 [1824]); and Henry George Ward, *Mexico in 1827* (London: H. Colburn, 1828). Other works tend toward the idyllic. See Mary Austin Holley, *Texas* (Austin: Texas State Historical Association, 1985 [1833]; and even Richard H. Dana, *Two Years Before the Mast* (New York: Random House, 1936 [1840]).

21 Other expeditions along the Texas-Mexican border spawned their own anti-Mexican accounts. See, for instance, *Interesting Account of the Life and Adventures of One of Those Unfortunate Men, who was Shot at Tampico* (New York, 1836); and Thomas Jefferson Green, *Journal of the Texian Expedition Against Mier* (New York: Harper Brothers, 1845).

22 For an excellent analysis of how Americans perceived the war with Mexico, see Robert W. Johannsen, *To the Halls of the Montezumas: The Mexican War in the American Imagination* (New York: Oxford University Press, 1985), esp. chapters 6 and 7.

23 Kendall, *Narrative of the Texan Santa Fe Expedition*, 391.

24 Combs, "Narrative 1841," 309.

25 James Mooney, *Calendar History of the Kiowa Indians* (Washington, D.C.: Smithsonian Institution Press, 1979), 143. Reprinted from the *Seventeenth Annual Report of the Bureau of American Ethnology* published in 1898.

26 Ibid., 144–45.

27 For a recent assessment of scholarly uses of indigenous texts in central Mexico, see James Lockhart, *The Nahuas after the Conquest: A Social and Cultural History of the Indians of Central Mexico, Sixteenth through Eighteenth Centuries* (Stanford: Stanford University Press, 1992), 5–9.

28 For an enlightening discussion of Altamirano's patriotism, see David A. Brading, "El patriotismo liberal y la reforma mexicana," in *El nacionalismo en Mexico*, ed. Cecilia Noriega Elio (Zamora: El Colegio de Michoacán, 1992), 179–204.

29 Apaches apparently had "picture books." Mooney, *Calendar History*, 142.

30 See Mildred P. Mayhall, *The Kiowas*, 2nd ed. (Norman: University of Oklahoma, 1971), 85–91.

31 Mooney, *Calendar History*, 146.

32 Ibid., 273.

33 Winter counts constitute invaluable historical sources, but one has to bear in mind that the original pictographs are then interpreted by the keepers, the translators, and ethnologists like Mooney. See Melburn D. Thurman, "Plains Indian Winter Counts and the New Ethnohistory," *Plains Anthropologist* 27:96 (1982): 173–75. For other winter counts among Plains Indians, see Garrick Mallery, "Picture-Writing of the American Indians," *Tenth Annual Report of the Bureau of American Ethnology, 1888–89* (Washington, D.C.: GPO, 1893); and N. A. Higginbotham, "The Wind-Roan Bear Winter Count," *Plains Anthropologist* 26 (1981): 1–42. There are more than 150 known Lacota winter counts. See Russell Thornton, "A Rosebud Reservation Winter Count, circa 1751–1752 to 1886–1887," *Ethnohistory* 49:4 (Fall 2002): 723–41.

34 Falconer, 38–41, Kendall, *Narrative of the Texan Sante Fe Expedition*, 257–85; Peter Gallagher, "Journal of the Santa Fe Expedition" reproduced in Carroll H. Bailey, *The Texan Santa Fe Trail*, 174–75; George W. Grover, "Minutes of Adventure From June, 1841," edited by Carroll H. Bailey in *The Panhandle-Plains Historical Review* 9 (1936), 35.

35 Kendall later met these comancheros; see *Narrative of the Texan Santa Fe Expedition*, 352.

36 Mooney, *Calendar History*, 164.

37 Satanta's speech at the Treaty of Medicine Lodge, Kansas, in 1867 as reported by journalist Henry M. Stanley. Quoted in Colin G. Calloway, *Our Hearts Fell to the Ground: Plains Indian Views of How the West Was Lost* (Boston: Bedford Books of St. Martin's Press, 1996), 114.

38 Mayhall, *The Kiowas*, 92–93.

39 Ibid., 93.

40 While Kiowa animosity toward Texans was deep-seated, distinguishing between Texans and Americans was difficult in practice. American merchant Josiah Gregg points out that in 1839 his party encountered a group of Comanches who immediately made preparations for war and pointedly refused to smoke the pipe. After some time it became clear that the Comanches had mistaken the Americans for their Texan enemies, as the caravan was traveling outside the limits of the United States and over a hundred miles from the trail normally used by American merchants bound for Santa Fe. Texans sometimes used this confusion to their own advantage, traveling through Indian territory with American flags to avoid difficulties. Josiah Gregg, *The Commerce of the Prairies* (Lincoln: University of Nebraska Press, 1967), 197–211.

41 Peace with the Comanches had been the cornerstone of New Mexico's sur-

vival for over seventy years. New Mexicans had kept peace with the powerful Comanche-Kiowa-Kiowa Apache confederation even though the latter was
periodically at war with Mexican Communities in the states of Tamaulipas, Chihuahua, Durango, and Zacatecas.

42 Mooney, *Calendar History*, 145.

43 *El Siglo Diecinueve*, 1 November 1841. See also *El Cosmopolita*, 2 March 1842 and
12 March 1842.

44 "Espedicion de los tejanos rendida a las fuerzas del general don Manuel Armijo,
el 5 de octubre de 1841," in Carlos María de Bustamante, *El Gabinete mexicano*
(Mexico City: Imprenta de José M. Lara, 1842), reprinted as *Cuadro histórico de
la Revolución mexicana de 1810*, 8 vols. (Mexico City: INEHRM, 1985), 8, 216–
25. Bustamante and Governor Armijo were close political allies. In fact, Bustamante dedicated the second volume of his *El Gabinete mexicano* to the embattled
governor.

45 For a brief appraisal of the critical role played by these publications in the eighteenth and early nineteenth centuries, see Jaime E. Rodríguez O., *The Independence of Spanish America* (Cambridge: Cambridge University Press, 1998),
36–44.

46 Bustamante, "Advertencia al que Leyere," in Bustamante, *Cuadro histórico de la
Revolución mexicana*.

47 In 1838 Santiago Kerker (James Kirker), an Irish trader and trapper who was
working as an Indian scalp hunter for the governor of Chihuahua, informed Armijo that two thousand Texan soldiers were headed for New Mexico to claim
the territory as stipulated in the treaty of Velasco which Santa Anna had signed
to save his life. See Manuel Armijo to Chihuhua's military commander, Santa
Fe, 29 November 1838, microfilmed edition of the Mexican Archives of New
Mexico, reel 24, frame 1279 (hereafter MANM); and Manuel Armijo to Ministro de Guerra y Marina, Santa Fe, 18 August 1839, Barker History Center,
box 2q175, page 339 (hereafter BHC 2q175, 339), University of Texas at Austin.
In 1839 New Mexican officials received newspaper clippings from the United
States about a military company being raised in Texas under governmental sanction for the purpose of exploring the route to New Mexico and forming friendly
alliances with the Comanche nation and other tribes along the way. See *Columbia Patriot*, 13 April 1839. Copied in Santa Fe by Guadalupe Miranda on 28 July
1839, Herbert E. Bolton Papers, box 41, folder 688, Bancroft Library, University
of California at Berkeley. In the spring of 1840 a New Orleans resident wrote
to the authorities in Chihuahua informing them that one hundred Texans had
gathered together and armed themselves with rifles, pistols, swords, and lances
and were headed for New Mexico. See John Tennyson to Parker and Kelly, New
Orleans, 20 April 1840, translated by Angel Farías in Chihuahua, 16 June 1840,
BHC 2q175, 339, 88–89.

48 Armijo to Almonte, Santa Fe, 4 August 1841, MANM 28, 1443–46. See accep-

tance in Vicar Juan Felipe Ortiz to Guadalupe Miranda, Peña Blanca, 2 August 1841, MANM 28, 1324–26.

49 Judge Miguel Mascareñas to Guadalupe Miranda, Mora, 31 August 1841, MANM 28, 1335–37.

50 Governor Armijo's 1840 proclamation to the people concerning the Texas invasion was issued as a bando.

51 E. P. Thompson still provides the most compelling case of how texts were used and appropriated by subliterate workers. See E. P. Thompson, *The Making of the English Working Class* (New York: Vintage, 1963), 724–49.

52 For instance, see Armijo's proclamation to the people of New Mexico, Santa Fe, 16 July 1840, MANM 27, 1265.

53 Report of Santiago Vidaurri, Lampazos, 11 May 1841, Herbert E. Bolton Papers, box 590, file 87, Bancroft Library.

54 This measure was protested by the U.S. Consul in Santa Fe. See Manuel Alvarez to Guadalupe Miranda, Secretary of Government of New Mexico, Santa Fe, 22 May 1841, MANM 28, 1291–93.

55 Armijo to the people of New Mexico, Santa Fe, 16 July 1840, MANM 27, 1265.

56 Armijo to Minitro de Guerra y Marina, Santa Fe, 12 July 1840, MANM 26, 396–98.

57 See Armijo to Ministro de Guerra y Marina, Santa Fe, 17 June 1840, MANM 26, 387–89; Armijo to Colonel Mariano Chávez, Santa Fe, 1 August 1841, BHC 2q175, 339, 40–41; Armijo to Almonte, Santa Fe, 24 August 1841, MANM 27, 1135–38; and Armijo to Francisco García Conde, Santa Fe, 4 June 1841, Herbert E. Bolton Papers, box 41, file 688, Bancroft Library.

58 The wealthy Nuevomexicanos included José Chavez, Mariano Chávez, and Antonio Sandoval. Other prominent New Mexicans had their own reasons to join the effort: Diego Archuleta was a protégé of the governor who had received military instruction in Durango, and Captain Pascual Martínez of Taos was a member of the powerful Martínez clan and had long resented the influence of foreigners. Less affluent civil and military officers like Juan Andrés Archuleta, Antonio Sena, and Captains Manuel Doroteo Pino, Teodocio Quintana, Diego Beytia, Miguel Antonio Lovato of Galisteo, and Damacio Salazar of San Miguel del Bado opted for resistance as well. All these men (and their followers) had cast their lot with Governor Armijo under the "liberating army" to pacify the territory after the violent Chimayo uprising. Indian fighters and scouts such as Captains Pedro León Luján and José Francisco Vigil of Abiquiú also joined the anti-Texan coalition. Their fighting experience made them natural candidates to lead the territorial defense. See Armijo to Colonel Mariano Chávez, Santa Fe, 1 August 1841, BHC 2q175, 339, 40–41; Armijo to Almonte, Santa Fe, 4 August 1841, MANM 28, 1443–46; and anonymous memoria, 219, 222.

59 For an account of the stir that the Texans caused in New Mexico, see Thomas

Esteban Chavez, "The Trouble with Texans: Manuel Alvarez and the 1841 'Invasion,'" *New Mexico Historical Review* 53 : 2 (1978): 133–44.

60 *Memorial* of Manuel Alvarez to Daniel Webster, Washington, 2 February 1842, Dispatches from United States Consuls in Santa Fe, 1830–1846, record group 59, no. 199, New Mexico State Records Center and Archives in Santa Fe, New Mexico.

61 Diary of Manuel Alvarez, U.S. Consul in Santa Fe, Santa Fe, 1840–41, Read Collection, series 2, New Mexico State Records Center and Archives.

62 Bustamante, *El Gabinete mexicano*, 223.

63 Richard H. Brodhead, *Cultures of Letters: Scenes of Reading and Writing in Nineteenth-Century America* (Chicago: University of Chicago Press, 1993), 4–10. See also Michael Warner, *The Letters of the Republic: Publication and the Public Sphere in Eighteenth-Century America* (Cambridge: Harvard University Press, 1990).

Imagining Alternative Modernities:

Ignacio Martínez's Travel Narratives

Como quiera que sea, las Colonias en el actual siglo, me parecen no sólo un anacronismo, sino un gran crimen social. ¿Con qué derecho las naciones europeas, que se llaman civilizados, vienen a sangre y fuego a dominar estos países que tienen iguales prerrogativas para gobernanarse solos, que los pueblos todos del mundo? — IGNACIO MARTÍNEZ, *Viaje universal* (1886)[1]

[However they are, colonies in the present century not only seem like an anachronism but a great social crime. With what right do the so-called civilized European nations come with blood and fire to dominate these countries that have as much prerogative as all people of the world to govern themselves?]

The nation-state is a dream of modernity. The idea of creating a coherent community out of multiple cultures and peoples, all neatly bounded by a clearly marked border, was a dream, however, that took hold, not only in the imaginations of the elite but also among subaltern classes. This process of territorialization, meaning political control over a bordered space, reached maturity on the U.S.-Mexico border in the late nineteenth century as railroads and telegraphs linked this frontier region to the central core of both nations. Marking, policing, and enforcing borders were central tasks of nation building. As Lord Curzon put it in 1907, "frontiers are indeed the razor's edge on which are suspended the modern issues of war and peace, of life or death to nations." One historian has recently declared "territoriality" the preeminent framework for understanding the entire twentieth century.[2] However, the ideal of modernity and of a coherent bounded space was, and still is, somewhat an illusion. Cultures and migrants spilled over these imaginary vessels, implicitly posing the question of whether the border really delimits the boundaries of the nation.[3] The large numbers of Mexicans living in South Texas and intimately connected to Mexican political life in the late nineteenth century suggest that the Mexican nation was not totally contained by the cartographers' neatly drawn lines.[4]

By maintaining political and cultural ties with Mexico, Mexicans in Texas, and elsewhere along the border, constructed an alternative geography for Mexico. This alternative mapping of the Mexican nation included the communities of Mexican descent that existed beyond the boundaries established by the Treaty of Guadalupe Hidalgo in 1848. If the bounded nation was the dominant geography of modernity, border reality required an alternative modernity. Late-nineteenth-century liberal border intellectuals subscribed to hegemonic notions of civilization versus barbarism and progress versus backwardness, yet they stood at a critical distance from the centers of national power and they understood well the deformations that modernization produced on the periphery. As Andrés Reséndez's essay in this volume shows, alternative literary cultures, some decidedly outside the nexus of print capitalism, existed simultaneously in the borderlands in the mid-nineteenth century. And even after print capitalism had become dominant by the end of the nineteenth century, literary cultures were far from monolithic.

This essay analyzes two travel narratives written by a border Mexican journalist and revolutionary, Ignacio Martínez, as a way to understand the alternative vision of modernity that was being constructed on the border at the end of the nineteenth century. While Martínez cannot be said to represent all border people, his books provide one example of a border perspective on the process of modernization. In the early 1880s, Martínez fell out of favor with the Díaz regime and went into a self-imposed exile in Brownsville, Texas. Martínez not only published an oppositionist newspaper but also fomented an armed rebellion against the Mexican government in 1886. He would continue to organize armed resistance and to publish his anti-Porfirian newspaper from the Texas border until his death in 1891. The fact that Martínez's armed rebellions against Díaz employed the rhetoric and language of Mexican nationalism and sought to replace Díaz with another national leader suggests the power of modernist tropes even for someone who was beginning to question modernization.

In the mid-1870s, Mexico was still recovering from half a century of turmoil. Governments had come and gone with astonishing speed, two foreign powers had invaded (the United States and France), civil wars had wracked the countryside, and more than half of Mexico's land was lost to the United States in 1848. Martínez was born in this chaotic period of Mexican history. He was raised in Mexico's northeastern state of Tamaulipas, attended school in Monterrey, and fought with Benito Júarez's liberal government against conservative monarchists during the French occupation of Mexico in the 1860s. In 1876 he joined Porfirio Díaz's rebellion to restore liberal ideals, including the sacrosanct no-reelection principle. Díaz ended up reneging on his pledge, and ruled dictatorially for thirty-five years until a revolution in 1911 sent the old general sailing off to Europe. In 1886, just a decade after Díaz came to power, Martínez turned on his former comrade and orchestrated a rebellion against Díaz from Brownsville, Texas.

Although Martínez and his co-conspirators pointed to Díaz's corruption and his violation of the no-reelection pledge in their manifestoes, their revolt implied a broader critique of Díaz's modernization program. Díaz succeeded in bringing relative political stability to the country, as well as unprecedented levels of foreign investment, and he oversaw the construction of an extensive rail network. By all accounts, Mexico was booming during the Porfiriato. But what was being lost in this mad rush to follow a European and Anglo-American model of development? And who were the losers in this new order? These were the questions that Martínez obliquely asked in his travel writings. More than just addressing particular political battles in Mexico, Martínez began to question the kind of modernization scheme that Mexico was following.[5] Although he was skeptical about the path Díaz had chosen for Mexico, he was also committed, as were all nineteenth-century Latin American liberals, to the general notion of progress and modernization. Unlike later Mexican revolutionaries like Emiliano Zapata and Pancho Villa, who directly confronted modernization, or Francisco Madero, who championed it, Martínez took a position somewhere in between. His travel accounts therefore reflect ambivalence toward rather than an outright rejection of modernity.

Martínez was an intellectual and political actor who reflected critically on the meaning of modernity for Mexico. He had a unique perspective, not merely that of a Mexican viewing metropolitan culture but of a border Mexican writing from the periphery of both nations. Like the world-renowned Cuban poet, journalist, and revolutionary José Martí, who was living and writing in exile in New York City during the same period (1880–95), Martínez provided Latin Americans with an alternative view of the United States and of modernization.[6] Different from Martí, who lived in Havana and then in New York City, Martínez was situated at the margins of both countries, residing first in Monterrey and then Brownsville and Laredo. Both men, however, found the necessary critical distance to reflect on their countries from exile.

Martínez's 1886 insurrection was quickly crushed, but he continued his anti-Díaz campaign from the relative safety of Texas border towns. He joined with fellow border journalist and revolutionary Catarino Garza in opposing the Porfirian regime and in defending the rights of Mexicans in Texas. In September 1891 Garza led a major insurrection against Díaz. The Garza revolt evolved from Martínez's earlier rebellion and was instigated by Martínez's assassination in Laredo in February 1891.[7] However, more than his military skills, it was Martínez's journalistic activity, as the editor and publisher of a small Spanish-language newspaper in Brownsville and Laredo, *El Mundo*, that helped to forge an opposition movement in the region. It is impossible, however, to adequately reconstruct his journalistic activity because only scattered articles from his newspaper remain in archives. Nonetheless, Martínez's travel books have survived, providing a unique view into the ideological foundation of this border journalist and revolutionary.

Martínez's travel narratives were first published while he was traveling, as shorter articles in newspapers throughout Latin America and the United States. He later compiled these articles into longer book-length narratives about his journeys. It is significant that Martínez's writings circulated in newspapers at this critical moment of nation building. Although there were other literary cultures coexisting and even competing with print capitalism, as Andrés Reséndez astutely shows, the mass circulation newspaper was one of the central mechanisms through which to imagine the nation as a community.[8] The newspaper was also a place where Latin Americans reflected on the dominant model of modernization and how it functioned in their own countries. Martínez's descriptions of European and North American cities and his analysis of the colonized world provided a critique of modernization and a screen onto which he could begin to project alternative modernities.

The first of Martínez's books, entitled *Recuerdos de un viaje en América, Europa y Africa* (Memories of a Voyage in America, Europe and Africa), was published in Paris in 1884. Written in the early 1880s, *Recuerdos* described his travels for eight months in 1875 through major U.S., Mexican, and European cities, including a brief visit to Morocco. The second book, *Viaje universal: Visita a las cinco partes del mundo* (Universal Voyage: Visit to the Five Parts of the World) was published in 1886 in New York as an advanced abbreviated version of what would later become a longer, day by day diary of his journey entitled *Alrededor del mundo* (Around the World).[9] On this three-year trip, from 1883 to 1885, Martínez strayed far from the well-worn tour of European metropolitan cities; he visited China, Japan, the Philippines, Indochina, Indonesia, Australia, India, and most of Central and South America. Both books were written after Díaz had assumed power, the first in 1882–83 and the second in 1886, but the second journey occurred after Martínez had already fallen out of favor with Díaz's government. Furthermore, the second book was written after Díaz had broken his no-reelection pledge and therefore it included a much stronger critique of the Porfirian regime. Martínez had been a committed liberal prior to his world travels, but these journeys allowed him to understand his liberalism in light of late-nineteenth-century imperialism and a broader project of modernization.

Martínez announced that the purpose of his travels around the world was to gain knowledge that could be used for the benefit of humanity and of his nation. Most European and Anglo-American travel accounts provided a utilitarian view of the world, documenting and cataloging natural resources and people in foreign lands in order to promote colonization and business investment. While Martínez, like his European and Anglo-American counterparts, took part in this descriptive enterprise, his cultural exchange had a different end. He was trying both to imagine possible futures for Mexico and to further his liberal, anti-imperialist struggle on the border. In employing the travel narrative as a lens through which to view the metropolis from the periphery, Martínez offered critical perspectives on European and Anglo-American imperialism and on the Mexican government's complicity with foreign capitalists.

In addition to the political and socioeconomic context of his travel writing, Martínez was one of an emerging breed of Latin American writers

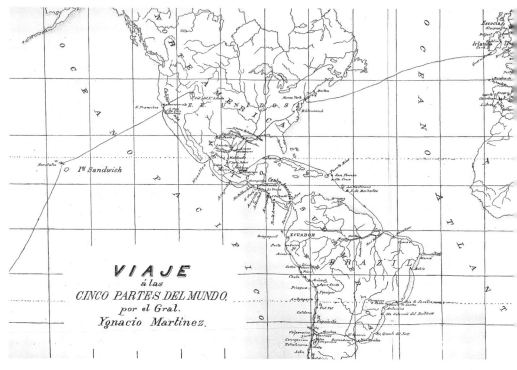

Doctor and General Ignacio Martínez's trajectory on his journey around the globe. From Ignacio Martínez, *Viaje universal* (1886).

who were experiencing a crisis of modernity. No longer were writers tied to the state as they had been in the mid-nineteenth century. When the Argentine educator and writer Domingo Sarmiento traveled to the United States and Europe between 1845 and 1848, for instance, he did so as a commissioner of the Chilean government.[10] By the end of the nineteenth century, writers were cast adrift and forced to compete in the marketplace, to justify their existence by producing a commercially viable product. While this made them subject to the vagaries of the market, it also gave writers a new degree of autonomy from the state, and a privileged position from which to critique both the state and society. Lacking legitimacy as part of the state or bureaucratic apparatus, writers had to claim their authority as autonomous purveyors of knowledge. Julio Ramos argues that the fragmentation of the republic of letters (*letrados*) in the late nineteenth century forced literature to legitimize itself in two ways: "as a defense of tradition, a tradition that it would at times invent; and as a critique of the moderniz-

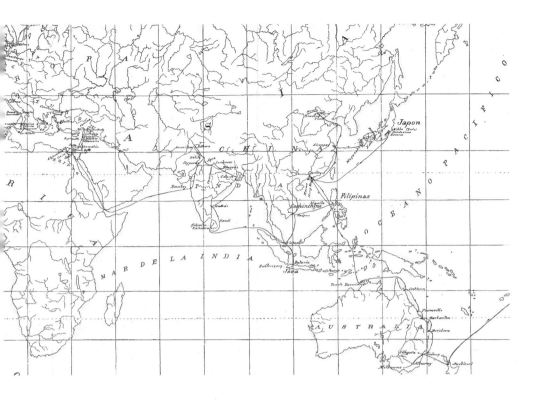

ing project."[11] Martínez declared his autonomy from the state by explaining that he earned all the money for his trip independently as a medical physician and was therefore not beholden to any patron, political party, or other group.[12] As with other modernist writers, the thrill and freedom of this independence was tempered by a deep ambivalence over the solitude, coldness, and fragmentation that modern industrial society offered. His critique of modernization was thus part of the modern discourse of Latin American literature.

In the prologue to Martínez's second book, *Viaje universal*, Vicente Riva Palacio, a well-known Mexican liberal intellectual, praised Martínez for his "frank," "truthful," and "impartial" observations and "straightforward but clear" descriptions. Riva Palacio approved of Martínez's writing because it seemed not to embellish the truth. "The stories of travels to distant and, for us, unknown countries are always interesting and fun, but are useful only on condition that truth guides the whole narration, without which fabulous reports or fantastic and imaginary descriptions begin to produce unsound ideas in the readers." Raising this issue was perhaps a subtle way for Riva Palacio to question the credibility of the many European and Anglo-American travel accounts of Latin America that seemed to be more influenced by fantasy and imagination than scientific observation. In contrast to these fantasies, Riva Palacio praised Martínez for writing the book just as he traveled, "with all of the *sang-froid* of a judicious and dispassionate observer."[13] However, more than a comparison with other fanciful tales of travel, Riva Palacio's preface bestowed a particularly modern form of authority on Martínez, that of the dispassionate and objective observer.

Martínez's travel writings were probably some of the first descriptions that Latin Americans received about Europe, the United States, and the colonial world. His dispatches were published in the Mexico City newspapers *La Patria* and *El Correo de las Doce*, and later reproduced in newspapers in San Francisco, Valparaiso (Chile), Buenos Aires (Argentina), and Montevideo (Uruguay).[14] As a free-lance writer, Martínez was tightly linked to the most important outlet for modern Latin American writers: the mass-produced newspaper. He thus translated and presented the outside world to Latin America, however, not in the objective manner that Riva Palacio suggested.

Martínez's prefatory remarks to the reader ironically undermined Riva Palacio's characterization of Martínez's observations as "cold blooded" and "dispassionate." Instead what we begin to see is the fragmentation that was so characteristic of the modern writer, a loss of identity in a chaotic and confusing world in which the old routines no longer made sense. Martínez suggested that the conditions and climate in which he traveled and wrote influenced his narrative to such a degree that he almost seemed overtaken by his surroundings. He wrote in noisy train stations, on ships while his stomach churned to the rhythm of the seesawing waves, under the "perturbing gaze of some beautiful woman," awaiting an attack of Bedouins, hanging in the basket of a hot-air balloon with his hands freezing from the "glacial cold of the pole," and suffocating "from the intense heat of the tropics, surrounded by a myriad of flying insects." He wrote "with the brain full of the world's realities; but forgetful of the rules and routines of school." In other words, he began to lose himself, or the training of his past, "the rules and routines of school," and discover a new language. His cognitive dissonance reached such proportions that not only did he not remember "the letters with which to write a word," but he could not affirm "whether the voice was Castillian, foreign or of those bastards which they call dialects."[15] He hung precariously at the brink of losing language, both written and spoken, yet he recorded his travels. The passion and feeling with which he described this immersion into foreign climates and languages stood in stark contrast to Riva Palacio's ode to objectivity on the preceding page. His was the fragmented language of the modernist writer confronting a new world.

Martínez prepared for this journey by saving money, learning English, consulting maps, and reading geographical travel accounts by Humboldt, Arago, Chateaubriand, Lamartine, Burton, and others. By the end of the nineteenth century, travel writing, especially to places distant from Western cities, had become a recognizable genre. Therefore, although Martínez set out to forge new paths and visit distant lands, he was in many ways retracing a well-worn path laid out for him by the explorers and geographers whose works he had read. Travel narratives usually focus on discovering and describing difference, the landscape, architecture, and customs of people and places visited, but the writer's job is also to translate that otherness to a vocabulary and language familiar to a domestic audience. Therefore, the travel narrative allows a view inside as well as outside, providing a glimpse into the author's *mentalités*, beliefs, prejudices, and cultural assumptions. The translation of cultural differences is an act of cultural exchange, rarely equal however, between the periphery and the center. As Mary Louise Pratt observes in *Imperial Eyes*, the very obsession of the metropolis "to present and re-present its peripheries and its others continually to itself" demonstrates the influence that the periphery has on European consciousness.[16] At the same time, those on the periphery were constantly re-presenting the metropolis and even other peripheries, but not in a strictly imitative manner. The production of knowledge about the metropolis and other peripheries can therefore be an act of appropriation and may have a subversive function.

Scholarly analyses of travelers' accounts have mostly focused on books by Westerners about their voyages to other countries, usually, though not exclusively, to "remote" and "exoticized" places. These stories about journeys from the center to the margins comprise the vast majority of published accounts, yet that alone does not explain or justify the lack of scholarly interest in the stories written from the margins about the center. While fewer in number, and symptomatically remaining unpublished or untranslated until recently, those on the periphery have written back to the center about their own countries or have traveled to Europe and the United States and written about the metropole.[17] In writing, they appropriated the conventions of the metropolitan genre, at the same time as they attempted to enter into a critical dialogue with them. The fact that not a single nineteenth-century Latin American traveler's account about a journey to the United States was translated into English until well into the twentieth century illustrates the U.S. blindness and lack of interest in Latin American views. Latin Americans spoke back to Anglo-Americans, but Anglo-Americans were neither listening nor responding. At the same time, North Americans were very interested in what Europeans had to say about their country. The continuing interest in French aristocrat Alexis de Toqueville's theories on American democracy, which have been translated, read, reprinted, and commented upon ad nauseum, exemplifies this long-standing obsession.[18]

Europe as Seen from the Periphery

In the late nineteenth century, Mexico underwent a period of rapid modernization, building railroads, encouraging foreign investment, and remaking its capital city in the image of Paris. Monterrey, a city in which Martínez had lived before going into exile, received a good portion of that foreign capital, and it was rapidly becoming the industrial capital of Mexico's North. As a liberal, Martínez advocated modernization and progress, but at the same time he was cautious about potential pitfalls of imitating a European model. The city was the symbol of modernity. As the Cuban educator and philosopher José de la Luz y Caballero put it, "Futuram, civitatem, inquirimos" (We are on a search for the future city).[19] In his own search for the future city, Martínez was favorably impressed by European cities' architecture and industrial technology, but he was pessimistic that such a model of modernization could be easily transferred to peripheral regions of the world.

Martínez sensed this dissonance between the ideal and the real on his visit to St. Petersburg, the showcase for the implantation of the model Western European city on the periphery. As Marshal Berman has argued, nineteenth-century St. Petersburg represents the "truncated and warped modernization [that] has spread throughout the third world." For Berman, "the modernism of underdevelopment is forced to build on fantasies and dreams of modernity, to nourish itself on an intimacy and a struggle with mirages and ghosts. In order to be true to the life from which it springs, it is forced to be shrill, uncouth and inchoate."[20] Martínez also found St. Petersburg "shrill, uncouth and inchoate," but more disturbing for him, he recognized the similarities between this city's warped striving to be like Paris and Mexico City's own desperate effort to remake itself as a European capital.[21]

It was in St. Petersburg that Martínez began to articulate his critical view of modern "civilization," especially its homogenizing influences and potential destructiveness. "Civilization," he observed, "does not seem to be anything other than a liquid that looks for its level in all parts: a level that the telegraphs signal and the railroad lines facilitate. In all of the great capitals there is the same service of hotels, the same vices of society and the same advantages of civilization."[22] It was the "advantages of civilization," the telegraph and the railroad, that caused the vices, including a loss of human communication. However, more than the vices, Martínez worried that the standardization that came with "civilization" would diminish humanity and erase cultural particularities. "The observant man seeing that human sentiment, good faith, the simplicity of customs, and the innate inclination that makes a man a friend of a man, diminishes and is almost extinguished in the towns where the telegraph and railroad arrive, cannot but ask whether civilization is good or bad for humanity."[23] Such a stark statement questioning the benefit of civilization indicates the profound doubts that lingered in the minds of even the most committed advocates of progress and modernization. Perhaps it was civilization itself, and not barbarism, that was antithetical to humanity.[24]

While he posed these questions in Europe, he was thinking of Mexico. In 1875, when Martínez departed on this journey, the rail system in Mexico had barely been born, with Veracruz–Mexico City as the only significant line. By the time his book was published in 1884, however, railroads spanned the length and breadth of the nation, with major lines tying Mexico's North to the U.S. rail system. In 1875, only 662 kilometers of railroad track had been laid in all of Mexico, whereas less than a decade later, in 1884, the total had increased nearly nine-fold to 5,744.[25] In this same period, South Texas saw its first railroads linking the border to San Antonio, Corpus Christi, and the major trunk line of the Mexican system. These rapid economic and social changes of the early 1880s inspired nostalgia for an earlier time when human contact took precedence over impersonal market relationships. In the past, Martínez contended, a traveler could arrive at any village in America or Europe and "in every house find hospitable lodging. . . . That family will be happy to supply you with a roof and food without the remotest idea of being repaid. If you become ill, you will be attended to with the same care and attention as to a brother; and upon departing you will leave memories in that home for a whole generation."[26] Familial relationships and kindness predominated in that romanticized past when a stranger would be treated like "a brother," and not a paying customer. This bucolic village life, Martínez surmised, would be destroyed the instant the railroad arrived, with vice and market-oriented relationships running roughshod over families and hospitality:

> If tomorrow this little town were crossed by the railroad, with the arrival of entrepreneurs, businessmen, soldiers and gentlemen of industry, its simplicity will become corrupt, its customs will become depraved, its hospitality and indifference to money will become sordid avarice; more than houses, there will be cantinas, inns and hotels; in each passenger they will see an enemy whose baggage can be robbed: if before they toasted the transient with free lodging and food, now whoever asks for a glass of water will be charged, and for however many means that can be imagined they will try to take your money.[27]

This dramatic conversion of the "humanitarian and simple inhabitants" into "impudent businessmen" provided a cultural critique of industrial capitalism. His analysis pointed to the emergence of a rising class of "company owners, businessmen, soldiers, and gentlemen of industry" as a corrupting influence that substituted "sordid avarice" for hospitality. Even for a modernizing liberal like Martínez, capitalism, or "civilization" as he preferred to call it, had its downside.

In his section on St. Petersburg, Martínez showed himself to be ambivalent and profoundly undecided about civilization. He was, as he put it, far from "condemning the immense advantages that bring with it a certain degree of civilization," but he was still not sure about how to reconcile the advantages and disadvantages. In an interesting gendered metaphor, one that would be repeated throughout his books, Martínez compared the degree of civilization of particular cities to the level of a woman's education. Rationality and intelligence combined with a lack of honor and sentiment could be found in the modern city and modern woman, he argued, while fanatical religious belief and ignorance marked village life and provincial women: "Between the great illustration of a Paris or a London, where the modesty, honor, and purity of the women is not very common, where the human sentiments in the man's heart are dimmed; and the lamentable backwardness of a village, in which a fanatic and indoctrinating priest is the director of consciences, and where the free thinker is exposed to be thrown to the flames for being a heretic or atheist, and where any swindler or charlatan can at a whim take advantage of the life and interests of an ignorant and simple people, I would not be sure which to choose."[28] Neither of these two options seemed attractive; either he ended up with an immoral and cold city like Paris or London or he had to suffer the repressive ignorance and superstitions of a country village. Moreover, as a self-declared freethinker and atheist, Martínez must have been particularly horrified by the thought of a "fanatic priest" burning "free-thinkers" and "atheists" at the stake. Martínez found himself in a kind of double exile. Not only was he politically cast out of Mexico but he felt at home in neither the traditional village nor the modern industrial city.

Martínez's concern about the "modesty, honor and purity" of Parisian women related directly to the anxieties of northern Mexico's middle class. As William French shows in *A Peaceful and Working People*, the middle-class reformers in Chihuahua, a border state in northern Mexico, advocated a new cult of female domesticity in response to modernization and the growing presence of industrial workers. Women were encouraged to become "guardian angels of the home," caring for their children and husbands and thereby ensuring the inculcation of morality and a proper work ethic. At the same time, middle-class Chihuahuans also emphasized the need to educate women so that they would be able to fulfill their civic duty of instilling values of work, thrift, and propriety.[29] Expressing this same ethic, Martínez stressed the importance of domesticity in the cold world of industry and commerce, and the need for women to be educated to better fulfill their roles in the home. Part of Martínez's crisis of identity had to do with his role as a man in modern society, which was no longer guaranteed by the virtue of being a man but depended on his ability to succeed in the marketplace. Women's entry into the market and the workforce threatened men's dominant role. Martínez expressed these anxieties clearly: "For a wife I would not want an uneducated little woman, who will embarrass me with her foolish talk and rustic manners each time that she would be presented in society, nor either an intellectual, poet or college graduate who in her dedication to her literary work would forget about me, or who in her moments of ill humor would reprove me for my lack of science, or not knowing by memory the classic authors."[30] He was caught between choosing a wife/village who would be an embarrassment to him in society and intellectually stunt his growth and a wife/city who would ignore him and expose his intellectual weaknesses. Gender relations had been altered with the growth of the modern city, leaving liberal men like Martínez to grapple with the contradictions between their emphasis on education and progress and their desire to keep women in a separate domestic realm. Modernization and the New Woman thus represented a potential threat to masculinity if it was not carefully controlled.

Martínez resolved this threat in his mind by imagining a middle ground, a wife/city that would have enough education to survive in the modern world, but not so much that she/it would lose a sense of tradition and sentimentality. The city, like the woman, served as a metaphor for the nation. As Mexicans searched for their national identity at the end of the nineteenth century, they worried both about not being modern and about being overwhelmed by foreign capital, ideas, and culture. Martínez laid out his model for the Mexican nation:

> I would look for a woman whose mediocre and regular education would be adorned with an innocent and pure heart, and with tender and candid sentiments that make an adorable being out of a baby; in the same way I would desire for the villages a degree of civilization that, giving them the necessary knowledge to live in society would conserve their moral sentiments; that with the whistle of the railroads, the inundation of books, and the telegraph networks, with the fever of commerce, would not lose their natural kindness nor relax their customs.[31]

Martínez was not alone in pointing out the deleterious effects of the "railroad's whistle, the inundation of books, and the telegraph networks," but he specifically blamed Western Europe and the United States for undermining the values and customs of less developed parts of the world. He therefore turned a generalized criticism of modernization into a more specific critique of colonialism and neocolonialism. Women, so often seen as the repositories and transmitters of culture, figured as the metaphoric symbol in his writing, through which the contradictions of the modernization of Western style were expressed and could be resolved. The educated yet sentimental and domesticated woman was a model for less developed countries to follow. Keeping the customs and purity of the woman/nation would temper the "fever of commerce," prevent the cultural colonization by the West, keep gender boundaries intact, and allow peripheral countries to modernize on their own terms.

Viaje Universal

An outbreak of a yellow fever epidemic in Matamoros in the middle of 1882 disrupted Martínez's plans for his second, more ambitious journey around the globe. After inventing a successful new treatment for yellow fever, he spent the following three months attending to patients in Matamoros and Mier, Mexico. As a result of his nonstop labors, Martínez had earned enough money for his ambitious voyage. His wealth, and therefore his independence, came from selling his medical services and being able to take advantage of an epidemic to make money. However, Martínez took great care to publicly deny materialistic motives in his medical practice. In 1888 he traveled to Jacksonville, Florida, to lend his hand treating yellow fever during an epidemic. In a letter to the New York *Herald*, he said he refused to accept compensation for his voluntary service in Florida. According to a hagiographic pamphlet written after his death, Martínez "had fulfilled his duty to help his brothers, he was a cosmopolitan on the subject of charity, and that he would help with the same tenacity as a black a white or yellow man."[32] Thus Martínez not only presented himself as a cosmopolitan, willing to lend charity regardless of nationality or race, but he also insisted that he was motivated by "duty to help his brothers." In a modern world ruled by commerce, Martínez stressed nonmarket values, but his survival, and ability to travel as an independent agent, depended on making a profit by selling his medical services.

As he waited for the train to begin his journey and his narrative, Martínez reflected on his national, racial, and political identity. Far from acknowledging the burden of his cultural baggage, he envisioned himself as a free agent, without ties to any government or job, a true citizen of the world setting out to record what he saw "for the benefit of humanity": "I count on absolute individual independence; without being subject, nor have any tie whatsoever with any government, company, sect, public or private society, and without the aid of one peso from anyone; with complete control of my faculties, without intentions to search for reasons to defend this or that principle or combat this or that doctrine; therefore my judgments will be as impartial and just as they can be for an honorable man." Whereas in a previous era travelers would have been writing for the king or commissioned by the government or the Church, he viewed himself as an independent agent. However, Martínez's self-conception of independence may be somewhat misleading. He was, after all, publishing his travel accounts in commercial mass-produced newspapers and writing travel books for sale to the public. While he had self-financed his journey through his medical practice, he had to be sensitive to the market in writing his travel narratives. His journey was thus, at least in part, a commercial product to be sold.

Nonetheless, despite these market pressures that must have subtly shaped his journey, Martínez insisted on his objectivity, and he promised to erase from his mind his nationality, political beliefs, and race. "I will not remember that I am Mexican, nor liberal, nor a descendant of any specific race," he wrote, "only a man who takes note of what he sees, in benefit of humanity, and, in an indirect way, of his own country."[33] This cosmopolitan and objectivist guise, however, did not prevent Martínez from remembering his Mexican nationality and his liberal politics. His pose as an objective and enlightened scientist, like Humboldt's, allowed him to garner the authorial legitimacy for the monumental task of describing the world. His first stop on this world tour was Texas, a place not so far from home and one in which his Mexicanness could not be so readily ignored. Having already visited most of the "civilized countries of the globe," Martínez stated his desire to travel through the rest, especially "the nations which they call semi-barbarous." On March 13, 1883, Martínez began his journey by crossing the Rio Grande to Brownsville, Texas, a highly appropriate place for a Mexican to begin his reflections on colonialism.[34]

The conditions of Mexicans living in Texas, a region that had been usurped from Mexico just fifty years earlier, demonstrated the effects of colonial rule. Martínez concluded that Mexicans in Central Texas faced discrimination, lived in segregated communities, and worked in the lowest-paid jobs. In San Antonio he found the situation for Mexicans "very humiliating: they have their separate barrio . . . comprised of old and ruined shacks; they do the most wretched work, and they are seen with more disdain than the blacks." To show the degree of "moral depression" among Mexicans in Texas, Martínez related an incident in which he asked a man in Spanish if he was Mexican and the man responded defensively in Spanish, "yes sir . . . why should I deny it." This defensiveness about identifying openly as a Mexican led Martínez to state that "these unfortunates believe . . . that before the Yankees it is a crime to be Mexicans."[35] Martínez implied that beyond economic deprivation and political disenfranchisement, colonialism produced internal psychological wounds that made Mexicans ashamed of their national origin.

On this second journey, Martínez confronted the question of colonialism and modern imperialism directly. The relationship between imperialism and modernity was fraught with contradictions and tensions. On the one hand, the discourse of civilization and progress justified imperialism by suggesting that the enlightened nations had a duty to spread their science, rationality, and prosperity to the backward nations. On the other hand, the idea of ruling over other people by force flew in the face of modern notions of free will and sovereignty.

While U.S. influence and control over Mexico differed juridically and qualitatively from Europe's direct colonization of Africa, Asia, and the Americas, Martínez pointed out the similarities between the two forms of dominance. As he arrived on train from Laredo to Monterrey, Martínez noticed that many of the signs announcing hotels and businesses were in English, whereas they had never been in French when the Austrian Emperor Maximillian ruled over Mexico a few decades earlier. The U.S. (and perhaps British) neocolonial commercial relationship with Mexico thus left a greater mark than the French military occupation of Monterrey. Beyond Texas, Martínez met colonial subjects who criticized empire and, in some cases, had engaged in their own struggles for national independence. It was this education in European imperialism that helped Martínez understand the predicament of Mexicans in Texas as part of a global process. Although the severity and manner of colonial rule varied from country to country, Martínez found an underlying hatred for the colonizers everywhere he went: "The English government in Egypt, the same as in Ireland and in Malta, is not liked, or better put, is hated and I doubt whether it can continue ruling in this country."[36] In the parts of India ruled by the British, Martínez described the natives as being "filled with venom," whereas in Jaipur, where they governed themselves, the Indians remained "kind and sincere."[37] Rather than stressing the geographical and psychological distance between Mexico and these "semi-barbarous" regions, Martínez found common ground in their anti-imperialist struggles.

In Ceylon (Sri Lanka), Martínez met with Arabi Pasha, a former Egyptian minister of war and leader of the nationalist struggle against British domination.[38] He was clearly impressed and identified with this "imprisoned General" who had to leave his country for "not wanting to bend his neck to the English yoke."[39] Explicitly making the comparison between Mexico and Egypt, Arabi had convinced him that "what [Mexicans] had suffered with the French invasion, they now suffer with the English."[40] Having fought against the French in Mexico, Martínez understood the differences between direct colonial rule and indirect neocolonial influence, but he chose to stress their similarities. Furthermore, although Martínez recognized differences between the manner of rule and mode of exploitation of French, British, and Dutch colonies, he penned an absolute and eloquent condemnation of all colonial projects. "No matter how they are, colonies in the current century seem to me not only to be an anachronism, but also a great social crime. With what right do the European nations, that they call civilized, come with blood and fire to dominate these countries who have equal prerogative to rule themselves on their own as all of the peoples of the world?"[41]

When he returned to the United States, Martínez noted many analogies between European colonies and the U.S. West. He mocked the republican pretenses of the United States. "The United States, reconciling their republican ideas with their great ambition, want countries, not with the name of colonies, how astute, but with the denomination of states, and close-by to keep a good watch over them, having them within sight."[42] Given that the United States took "its" West from indigenous inhabitants and from Mexico, Martínez's comparison between those states and European colonies makes sense.

Martínez also noted the similarities between how Europeans treated natives in their colonies and how Anglo-Americans treated Mexicans in the U.S. West. He commented on the rising tide of xenophobia and the miserable conditions for Mexicans in Texas, Nevada, and California, which he saw as equally "humiliating" as those for the Chinese and African Americans. "The Americans deprive [Mexicans] of their land with intrigue and fights. If they work in some mine, as soon as it bears fruit, they are denounced and it is taken from them on the pretext that they are not American citizens. They are pariahs in the United States. You see them as bellboys in hotels, as barmen, as maids, or in the lowest and most despicable professions."[43] Living in poverty, most Mexicans in San Francisco had only limited access to the legal system and had no protection from the Mexican consul, who did "nothing for them."[44]

At the same time, Anglo-Americans began looking south to Mexico with longing eyes, armed with their vision of Manifest Destiny and plenty of capital to buy what they could not take by force.[45] The patriotic Martínez seethed when he overheard Americans in California speak of taking over Mexico. "They brazenly say that they are doing it by [buying] lands and through debts against Mexico, and that this peaceful invasion is more effective than any other."[46] This was a new form of colonialism, one that ruled with dollars and debts instead of guns and soldiers. Even though salaries would be raised "if they come to conquer us," Martínez predicted that all Mexicans would sooner or later become "day laborers" and suffer the same "abject condition as the Chinese, blacks, and Mexicans now in California, Nevada and Texas." Unwilling to accept such servitude, Martínez exclaimed that "a thousand deaths would be preferable to being under the yoke of the Yankee."[47]

Empire, Race, and Sex

The border was a place where two different racial systems, one from Mexico and the other from the United States, met and collided. The Mexican and U.S. racial systems both privileged whiteness, but the high degree of *mestizaje* in Mexico and the discrimination Mexicans suffered in the United States made Mexicans critical of the stark racial lines in the United States. As a white border Mexican, Martínez condemned U.S. empire and racism at the same time as he claimed his own racial superiority in relation to Africans, Asians, and the indigenous. The contradictory nature of his racial arguments reflects the clashing racial hierarchies on the border. Therefore, although Martínez stridently condemned European intervention throughout the world, and racial discrimination in the United States, he did not challenge or reject the racial logic of empire. His views on racial difference, miscegenation, and gender reveal the extent to which he adopted colonialist paradigms, even as he turned them into weapons against empire. Following a mid-nineteenth-century strain in anthropology that held racial groups to be at different stages along a unilinear path of development, Martínez believed that trying to hurry the "civilization" process was at best futile, and at worst dangerous. He thus opposed colonial intervention because it jeopardized the coherence of each nation's race and culture.[48] "Each nation," Martínez proclaimed, "big or small, civilized or semi-barbarous has the right to govern itself. Who has given the great powers the prerogative to meddle in the internal affairs of other peoples, as weak and vulnerable as they may appear?"[49] The live-and-let-live tolerance of the statement did not, however, imply a fundamental equality of humans. In fact, Martínez firmly believed in the existence of a racial hierarchy in which indigenous and darker-complexioned people were at the very bottom. Echoing the dominant wisdom of his time, he stated confidently that "what everyone agrees upon is that the Cagats, Bushmen, Negritos, and Australianos, because of their small stature, deformed bodies, and their limited intelligence, form the last rung on the human ladder."[50]

Martínez believed that contact, especially sexual, between two groups at very different points on the linear scale of civilization would corrupt and destroy the less developed one. The degradation that he witnessed among the indigenous of the Amazon jungle proved this point. Although Martínez criticized "civilized" businessmen who took advantage of the "innocent" natives, he also denied any role for the indigenous, other than as passive victims. As in St. Petersburg, gender was the central metaphor through which he explained the relationship between the civilized and the primitive. Martínez had been informed while in Brazil "that in proportion to the degree that Indians civilize themselves and put them into contact with our people, they lose desire for their women and become perverted." Thus the emasculation of Indian men and loss of "their" women demonstrated both the dangers of racial mixing, especially that of a sexual nature, and the weakness of the indigenous. The introduction of alcohol, he explained, allowed businessmen to cheat Indians out of their wealth and to seduce their women. Contact between the two distinct worlds thus presented a sexual threat as it "perverted" the men and corrupted the women. "The closeness of the civilized peoples," he argued, "removes all of the innocence and virility from these primitive people."[51] The two concepts worked in tandem; the loss of an Indian woman's "innocence" to foreign men implied the loss of an Indian man's "virility." Just as Indians were losing control of the natural resources of the Amazon, so too were Indian men losing control of "their" women.

Martínez thus criticized colonialism, not only because it was an outside imposition on sovereign peoples but also because it led to unhealthy racial mixing. Europeans were "a race of animals, sister of the rest," opined Martínez, but their contact with other races had proved completely destructive. In particular, it was the European clergy and settlers who had biologically and educationally weakened indigenous races. The Darwinian understanding of plant and animal reproduction wherein hybrids ultimately lead to sterility and weakness corroborated this belief. While lengthy, this passage is worthwhile quoting, for it shows the close similarity between this type of anticolonial argument and the racial logic that justified imperialism:

> European civilization is a curse, a pestilence for these Orientals. The missions with their religious zeal, not accompanied by good judgment, and the settlers with their vicious and bad treatment extinguished the indigenous races with whom they made contact. The clergy, in educating these primitives, wanted to inculcate as much science as if they had European brains, accustomed for so many centuries to exercise memory and judgment on a grand scale; this excessive and imprudent education atrophied their organism, sterilized their race, or rather like the girls whose tender stomachs are disturbed by sausage and roasted meats: they are killed by indigestion. On the other side, the settlers come to these regions, they take, whether by force of arms or by astuteness, the best lands, or the rivers with the most fish, and the most favorable places in terms of climate, and they oblige the indigenous to wander through the villages like dogs without owners, and to work at tasks superior to their strength and habits, to earn food that is strange to them, and alcoholic drinks which poison them; exposed to contract diseases which decimate them for not knowing their gravity nor the means of curing them; better to remain savages in inhospitable and deserted terrain, where one year of drought kills them, like ice ended the lobster.[52]

The colonial project, described by Martínez in such vivid terms, was a nasty, short, and brutal affair. In *The Descent of Man*, Darwin had already voiced a similar concern in a section entitled "On the Extinction of the Race of Man," in which he explained that "extinction follows chiefly from the competition of tribe with tribe, and race with race. . . . When civilized nations come into contact with barbarians the struggle is short."[53] Or as one journalist summed up the imperialist equation to Martínez, referring to the rapid disappearance of the Maoris, "as soon as these people become civilized, they die."[54]

Although Martínez expressed great, if paternalistic, sympathy for the indigenous races, he also worried about how a civilized nation like Mexico would survive contact with "inferior" races like the Chinese. Along with paupers, convicts, and the mentally ill, Chinese immigrants became a favorite target of nativist sentiment in both the United States and Mexico in the late nineteenth century. In 1882, labor unions and political leaders joined forces in the United States to pass the Chinese Exclusion Act banning Chinese immigration. A similar debate in Mexico over the future of immigration policies for the Chinese led Martínez to discuss its effect on labor conditions and its implications for racial miscegenation. As Grace Delgado's essay in this volume shows, even though the Porfirian regime attempted to recruit white European immigrants, thousands of Chinese came to Mexico, especially northwestern Mexico. While many of the Chinese established themselves in small businesses and became successful, anti-Chinese sentiment in Mexico ran high.[55] Echoing the racist arguments of the day, Martínez concluded that because the Chinese worked very hard and ate little, they could easily undercut anyone in the labor market. However, for him the real dangers of Chinese immigration were not solely or even primarily labor competition but racial degeneracy. "Our race is not, as they say, very privileged. If in the moral part we have nothing to envy, physically we are a somewhat degenerated Spanish race. While our neighbors in the U.S. cross with Europeans, be they Germans, English or Spanish, will we do it with the Chinese?"[56] Although Martínez defended the moral stature of Mexico, he agreed that Mexicans suffered from a physical "degeneration." By "degenerated Spanish race," he may have meant the legacy of sexual mixing on the Iberian peninsula between the Moors, Jews, and other Spaniards, and/or the high degree of miscegenation with the indigenous in the Americas. In either case, Martínez saw a racial competition between the United States and Mexico, and he certainly did not want Mexico to be dragged down by Chinese blood while the United States enjoyed the genetic competitive edge by breeding with Europeans.

Martínez's comparison of U.S. and Mexican immigration policy regarding the Chinese was another way to assert the respectability and honorability of Mexico. While he opposed Chinese immigration to Mexico on racial grounds, Martínez also recognized the political importance of not totally prohibiting it. "I am opposed to [the Chinese] entrance in our country; [however] more liberal than the North American government, I would want that like the sons of other nations, they would be free to establish themselves in our land and live subject to our laws," but not by paying them to migrate. Therefore, even though he personally opposed

Chinese immigration and did not want the government to encourage it, he was against prohibitive measures.

Like his complex view of Chinese immigration, Martínez's perspective on European colonialism was shot through with contradictions. On the one hand, he criticized colonial rule in the most vociferous terms, calling it "not only an anachronism, but a great social crime."[57] On the other hand, Martínez adopted the European colonial racial logic that viewed the colonized as "inferior" and "primitive" races. Even though he condemned European imperialism, he still believed that Europeans were more "civilized" and racially superior than the colonized. Martínez's racist comment about the aborigines of Australia is instructive: "At first sight there is a greater difference between a wise European and a native Australian, than between this one and a gorilla or an orangutan. And say what you will, the indigenous of Australia look like recently civilized monkeys."[58] Having experienced Anglo domination in Texas and the growing presence of Anglos in northern Mexico, as well as having fought against the French invasion of Mexico in the 1860s, Martínez had an appreciation for the predicament of the colonized. However, his identification was based on liberal political convictions that every nation and every people had a right to govern itself, and not on a belief in the fundamental racial equality of all people. His concern about the sexual miscegenation between Europeans and the "natives" reflected an anxiety about his own racial status on the border. Whereas a fair-skinned person of Martínez's stature would certainly have been considered white in Mexico, his whiteness would have been questioned in the United States.[59] Although Martínez condemned U.S.-style racism, he was also trying to maintain his position on that same racial ladder.

*   *   *

Ignacio Martínez believed in civilization, individual freedom, and progress: that is, modernity. At the same time, just as the border began to undergo the cataclysmic changes of rapid modernization, Martínez stepped back and hesitated. He paused not because he rejected the principles of modernization but because he saw how those ideals, when applied in less developed parts of the world such as Mexico, and especially on the border, resulted in deformities. There was clearly something being lost in this rush to build telegraphs and railroads, and at his darkest moments he wondered whether this thing called civilization was good for humanity.

His was not a rejection of modernity per se but rather a proposal for an alternative modernity, one that would be fitted to the needs of the colonized and less developed parts of the globe.

Martínez was sensitive to the changes occurring around him because he was living them. He embraced his individual freedom, yet fretted over the loss of nationalist pride in Mexico. He wanted to be cosmopolitan, yet feared losing the customs and hospitality of the villages. He decried the homogenization and coldness of the market, yet it was this very market that provided the means of his own independence and enabled him to travel. These contradictions led to a fragmented sense of self-identity, one that Martínez tried to resolve in his travel narratives and dramatically in his revolutionary activities. While he posed as a cosmopolitan when he ministered to the ill in Florida or toured around the globe, he became an outright nationalist patriot when he led rebellions against Díaz. Although there was a tension between the two, Martínez found cosmopolitanism the best way to be a modern nationalist.

Martínez's travel narratives remind us that the border and border people were part of a bigger world at the end of the nineteenth century. While it is tempting to view the border as an isolated and remote region, in part because that is how it was constructed by outsiders who wanted to colonize and open the area to investment, the border was at the center of the imperial nation-building projects in both the United States and Mexico. Even though Ignacio Martínez was exceptional in many ways, his travel writings reflect a border perspective on modernization. Like many of his fellow border residents, he was searching for a way to enter the modern era on his own terms. While people throughout the industrializing world experienced the dislocation and fragmentation of modernity, the border was a place where one was doubly dislocated. Commercialization and commodification were generalized phenomena in all places touched by modern industry, but living on the border rendered identification with any one nation difficult.

Martínez came to understand this fragmentation of his identity on his journeys around the world. He tried to overcome his sense of dislocation and exile by organizing a nationalist revolution, but his efforts were abruptly stopped when Díaz agents assassinated him on the streets of Laredo, Texas, in 1891. Twenty years later, a nationalist revolution succeeded in toppling Díaz, but even today Mexico strives to reconcile its indigenous past and present with a foreign model of modernity. The increasingly complex realities on the border undermine the modernist dream of a culturally coherent nation. The border is the place where the nation continues to be made, but it is also the place where it is unmade.

Notes

1 Ignacio Martínez, *Viaje universal: Visita a las cinco partes del mundo* (New York: José S. Molina, 1886), 113–14. All translations are by the author.

2 George Lord Curzon of Kedleston, *Frontiers: The Romanes Lecture of 1907* (1908: rpt. Westport, Conn., n.p.: 1976), cited in Charles S. Maier, "Consigning the Twentieth Century to History: Alternative Narratives for the Modern Era," *American Historical Review* 105 (June 2000), paragraphs 22 and 2.

3 Victor Zuñiga argues that nation-states strive to erase their internal borders and differences "to territorialize history and transform mythical nations into earthly ones." Victor Zuñiga, "Nations and Borders: Romantic Nationalism and the Project of Modernity," in *The U.S.-Mexico Border: Transcending Divisions, Contesting Identities*, ed. David Spener and Kathleen Staudt (Boulder: Lynne Rienner, 1998), 35.

4 For an insightful article on how the Mexican nation was imagined by mid-nineteenth-century cartographers, see Raymond B. Craib, "A Nationalist Metaphysics: State Fixations, National Maps and the Geo-Historical Imagination in Nineteenth-Century Mexico," *Hispanic American Historical Review* 82 (February 2002): 33–68.

5 For an insightful analysis of Porfirian Mexico's vision of modernity, see Mauricio Tenorio-Trillo, *Mexico at the World's Fairs: Crafting a Modern Nation* (Berkeley: University of California Press, 1996).

6 See Julio Ramos, *Divergent Modernities: Culture and Politics in Nineteenth-Century Latin America* (Durham: Duke University Press, 2001), for an excellent analysis of Marti's critique of modernity.

7 For more on the connection between Garza and Martínez, see Elliott Young, *Catarino Garza's Revolution on the Texas-Mexico Border* (Durham: Duke University Press, 2004).

8 Benedict Anderson, *Imagined Communities* (London: Verso, 1991).

9 I have located several copies of *Recuerdos de un viaje*, both in Mexico and the United States. However, I have only located three copies of *Viaje universal*, one in Monterrey at the Acervo Cervantina of the Instituto Tecnologico de Estudios de Monterrey, another in the Fondo Reservado of the Biblioteca Nacional de México at the Universidad Nacional Autónoma de México (UNAM), and the third at the University of Pittsburgh. The Biblioteca Nacional also holds the final version of *Viaje universal*, published in two volumes as *Alrededor del mundo*

(Brownsville, Texas: Ignacio Martínez, 1880–1889?); it runs over 700 pages in length, much longer than the 278-page *Viaje universal*. Another copy of *Alrededor del mundo* can be found at the Amarillo Public Library.

10 Ramos, *Divergent Modernities*, 153.

11 Ibid., 42.

12 In the late nineteenth century, ethnologists, miners, and others continued to receive financing from various sources to conduct their explorations and publish their reports. However, even Adolph Bandelier, who received financing from the Catholic Church and the Archaeological Institute of America in the 1880s and 1890s to conduct his work in the U.S. Southwest, had trouble making ends meet. One of the ways he survived between his commissions was by selling articles to popular German and American publications. Carl Lumholtz, the Norwegian explorer who was supported in the 1890s by wealthy financiers including Andrew Carnegie, J. Pierpont Morgan, and Archer Huntington, and the American Geographical Society, did lecture tours and turned his scientific findings into a popular mass-circulating commodity: his book, *Unknown Mexico*. Don D. Fowler, *A Laboratory for Anthropology: Science and Romanticism in the American Southwest, 1846–1930* (Albuquerque: University of New Mexico Press, 2000), 176–77, 235.

13 Martínez, *Viaje universal*, v.

14 Although Martínez says that his stories were published in San Francisco, it is not clear whether it was an English or Spanish-language newspaper. Martínez, *Viaje universal*, vii–viii.

15 Ibid., vii.

16 Mary Louise Pratt, *Imperial Eyes: Travel Writing and Transculturation* (London: Routledge, 1991), 6.

17 The literature about Mexican travel writers is astonishingly limited. In part this dearth can be attributed to the relatively small number of travel accounts published in Mexico. For a lengthy list of Mexican travel writers, see Juan B. Iguiniz, "Bibliografía de obras de viajeros mexicanos en el extrangero," in *Memorias y revista de la sociedad científica "Antonio Alzate"* (México, D.F.: 1929–30), 17–72. For a bibliography of Latin American travelers' accounts of their journeys to the United States, see Esther Allen, "This Is Not America: Nineteenth-Century Accounts of Travel between the Americas" (Ph.D. diss., New York University, 1991, appendix A). For a general essay on Mexican liberal views about the United States in the nineteenth century, see Victoria Lerner, "Ensayo sobre la evolución de las ideas y actitudes de los liberales mexicanos hacía Estados Unidos durante el siglo XIX," in *Estados Unidos desde América Latina: Sociedad, política y cultura*, comps. Victor A. Arriaga et al. (México, D.F.: Instituto Mora, 1995), 58–75.

18 Allen, "This Is Not America," 104.

19 As cited in Ramos, *Divergent Modernities*, 41.

20 Marshall Berman, *All That Is Solid Melts to Air* (New York: Penguin, 1988), 232.

21 For an analysis of the remaking of Mexico City and particularly the redesigning of the Paseo de la Reforma, see Barbara A. Tenenbaum, "Streetwise History: The Paseo de la Reforma and the Porfirian State, 1876–1910," in *Rituals of Rule, Rituals of Resistance: Public Celebrations and Popular Culture in Mexico*, ed. William H. Beezley et al. (Wilmington: Scholarly Resources, 1994), 127–50. For an engaging look at how the 1910 centennial celebration of Mexico's independence attempted to project a vision of the ideal modern city onto Mexico's capital, see Mauricio Tenorio Trillo, "1910 Mexico City: Space and Nation in the City of the Centenario," *Journal of Latin American Studies* 28 (1996): 75–104.

22 Martínez, *Recuerdos*, 432.

23 Ibid., 432.

24 In a slightly different vein, Mexican anthropologist Guillermo Bonfil Batalla criticizes modernization in Mexico along Euro-American lines as being part of an "imaginary Mexico" that undermines Mesoamerican "civilization." Guillermo Bonfil Batalla, *México Profundo: Reclaiming a Civilization* (Austin: University of Texas Press, 1996).

25 John H. Coatsworth, *Growth against Development: The Economic Impact of Railroads in Porfirian Mexico* (DeKalb: Northern Illinois University Press, 1981), 36. Railroad construction continued apace throughout the Porfiriato, with total kilometers reaching 9,558 in 1890, 14,448 in 1900, and 19,205 in 1910 (36–37).

26 Martínez, *Recuerdos*, 432.

27 Ibid., 432.

28 Ibid., 432–33.

29 William French, *A Peaceful and Working People: Manner, Morals and Class Formation in Northern Mexico* (Albuquerque: University of New Mexico Press, 1996), 87–91.

30 Martínez, *Recuerdos*, 433.

31 Ibid.

32 Martínez, *Viaje universal*, 9–10. According to his own account, Martínez's new yellow fever treatment had a 92 percent success rate compared to the 30 to 35 percent rate of success of previous treatments (10). While in Jacksonsville, Martínez traveled for a couple of days to Havana under a false name, apparently to meet secret agents from Chihuahua. For more on Martínez's work in Florida and his trip to Cuba, see A. C. Vasquez, Mexican Consul in Havana, Cuba, to Rel. Ext., 20 October 1888, in Archivo Histórico de la Secretaría de Relaciones Exteriores de Mexico, leg. 11–10–16, f. 161–64. Several U.S. newspapers, including the *Jacksonville Times*, the *New Orleans Picayune*, and the New York *Herald*, praised Martínez's self-sacrificing efforts to cure victims of the epidemic. *Rasgos biograficos del general y doctor Ignacio Martínez. Asesinado alevosamente en esta poblacion el martes 3 de febrero del presente año entre 9 y 10 de la mañana* (Laredo: Tip. *El Mundo*, 1891), 27.

33 Martínez, *Viaje universal*, 11.

34 Ibid., 9–11.

35 Ibid., 18.

36 Ibid., 97.

37 Ibid., 100.

38 For more on Arabi Pasha's national movement, see A. M. Broadley, *How We Defended Arabi and His Friends* (Cairo: Arab Center, 1980 [1884]), and Arthur C. Dep, *The Egyptian Exiles in Ceylon–Sri-Lanka (1883–1901)* (Colombo, Sri Lanka: Aragi Pasha Centennary Celebrations Committee, 1983).

39 Martínez, *Viaje universal*, 105.

40 Ibid., 106.

41 Ibid., 113–14.

42 Ibid., 125.

43 Ibid., 165.

44 Ibid., 166.

45 For the most extensive account of U.S. investments in Mexico, see John Mason Hart, *Empire and Revolution: The Americans in Mexico since the Civil War* (Berkeley: University of California Press, 2002), 71–268.

46 Martínez, *Viaje universal*, 166.

47 Ibid., 166.

48 In an excellent book on the central role of sexual desire in imperialism, Robert Young argues that current culturalist notions and nineteenth-century scientific thinking on race are not that different, "for the racial was always cultural, the essential never unquivocal." Robert Young, *Colonial Desire: Hybridity in Theory, Culture and Race* (London: Routledge, 1995), 28.

49 Martínez, *Viaje universal*, 118.

50 Ibid., 119.

51 Ibid., 260.

52 Ibid., 150.

53 Charles Darwin, *The Descent of Man and Selection in Relation to Sex* [1871] (London: Murray, 1901), 282–83; as cited in Young, *Colonial Desire*, 13.

54 Martínez, *Viaje universal*, 153.

55 For a discussion of immigration policy under Díaz, see Mauricio Tenorio-Trillo, *Mexico at the World's Fairs* (Berkeley: University of California Press, 1996), 35–37. For anti-Chinese sentiment in Mexico, see Gerardo Rénique, "Race, Mestizaje and Nationalism: Sonora's Anti-Chinese Movement and State Formation in Post-Revolutionary Mexico," *Political Power and Social Theory* 14 (2000): 91–140; also, see Gerardo Rénique, "Race, Region and Nation: Sonora's Anti-Chinese Racism and Mexico's Post-Revolutionary Nationalism, 1920s–1930s," in Nancy Appelbaum et al., eds., *Race and Nation in Modern Latin America* (Chapel Hill: University of North Carolina Press, 2003).

56 Martínez, *Viaje universal*, 124.

57 Ibid., 113–14

58 Ibid., 146–47.

59 For an excellent discussion of how Mexican and Anglo-American views of whiteness clashed on the border, see Linda Gordon, *The Great Arizona Orphan Abduction* (Cambridge: Harvard University Press, 1999), 96–105.

✳ *Transnational Identities*

At Exclusion's Southern Gate:

Changing Categories of Race and

Class among Chinese *Fronterizos*,

1882–1904

Many images of the nineteenth-century overseas Chinese permeate the historical imagination: Cantonese men fleeing the war-torn province of Guangdong, sojourners searching for Gold Mountain, workers laying thousands of miles of track across the United States, and women working as prostitutes in California mining camps. The busy landscapes of American Chinatowns and the brimming detention barracks at the port of San Francisco also find their way into popular thought. Closer to their homeland, images of assiduous middlemen engaged in rubber and tin production in Malaysia and Thailand remind us that Chinese entrepreneurs met with frequent and open acceptance in these areas of the world. Multidirectional movements into Canada, Australia, and Cuba are also imprinted, although faintly, within collective historical memory.

These images exclude the complex social dynamics of Chinese living in the U.S.-Mexico borderlands.[1] While not as heavily populated with Chinese as other nations, Mexico was both host and home to several thousand Cantonese immigrants in the late nineteenth and early twentieth centuries. Chinese migration into Mexico coincided with an interest in populating and developing the Mexican North, but exclusion laws in the United States during the 1880s and 1890s also had a significant impact on the lives of Chinese immigrants in northern Mexico. Greeks, Syrians, Poles, Russians, Italians, Germans, and Hungarians settled in northern Mexico at the same time, but their movement between continents and countries did not raise the same types of questions about race and citizenship as that of the Chinese.

This essay brings together the stories of Chinese merchants and laborers at the U.S.-Mexico border in a time when racial ideologies profoundly determined their social marginalization and political exclusion in the United States. Racial ideologies did not, however, find uniform expression throughout the borderlands. As citizens or nationals of Mexico, the Chinese escaped ritualized practices barring their entry at the ports of San Francisco and New York when crossing at Mexico's northern border. The privileges enjoyed by Chinese merchants and laborers in Mexico prompted border officials to recognize, rather than deny, the ability of Chinese to assert Mexican claims of citizenship and nationality. In the late nineteenth century, when a racialized discourse of exclusion entered the legal domains of the United States, Mexican civil society, especially in the North, was uniquely poised to absorb Chinese émigrés into its fold.

La frontera norte, long a place plagued by ethnic hostilities, teetered toward capitalist expansion during the late nineteenth century, although amid many uncertainties. To foster progress, Mexico's president, Porfirio Díaz, lured foreign investors with the promise of profits and immigrants with the favorable circumstances of opportunity. Although Díaz's open economic policies were in direct contrast to those adopted in China and the United States, what yielded results for the Chinese was that Mexican civil law accorded them rights equal to those of Mexicans. This ran counter to policies in China and the United States. Mexico's northern neighbor barred the entry of Chinese laborers with the passage of the Chinese Exclusion Act of 1882. Although merchants, diplomats, teachers, travelers, and students were permitted entry, the hardening of exclusion laws ten years later curbed the admission of many exempt Chinese. Furthermore, U.S. state and federal courts no longer gave citizenship to Chinese. By 1890, Chinese living in the United States had few formal privileges and protections compared to those who held U.S. citizenship. China also practiced policies of exclusion. Until 1893, Qing dynasty (1644–1911) strictures forbade the reentry of émigrés returning from abroad. Repatriation occurred only when imperial authorities realized the value of remittances from overseas Chinese to their nearly bankrupt regime.[2]

The reception of Chinese tells us about more than just their treatment in places they came from and settled; it tells us about the historical circumstances that scripted their sojourning experiences in Mexico and the United States. In fact, what is significant is not exclusion or inclusion, but rather that immigration restrictionism as understood at the U.S.-Mexico border did not always assume racialized forms. Officials soon discovered that political rights and economic motivations of the Chinese were more tenacious than the bite of U.S. exclusion. Despite the appearances of a closed U.S. border, the Chinese, occupying a range of positions between citizen/national/foreigner and merchant/laborer, carved out a social space for themselves as border crossers and *fronterizos* in northern Mexico.

Class determined the most fundamental level of participation for Chinese merchants and laborers in northern Mexico, due in large part to the nature of Chinese exclusion laws in the U.S. during the last two decades of the nineteenth century. Merchants, enlisting the aid of Mexican and U.S. officials, petitioned for their entry north as Mexican citizens. This strategy suggests that the pliability of Mexican citizenship and nationality, at least for two decades, trumped the narrow confines of Chinese exclusion laws. Laborers, on the other hand, faced greater legal barriers to crossing the border, yet they also exercised more than nominal control over their deportation hearings. If they demonstrated Mexican citizenship or residency, they were deported to Mexico, not China. For both Chinese merchants and laborers, inclusion in the Mexican national community provided a means to contest exclusion laws and state-sponsored campaigns against them. How they used Mexican nationality and citizenship to defend their interests reveals much about the shifting notions of racial and national identity in the borderlands, while highlighting the legal and practical limits to exclusion and its enforcement in this continental crossroads.

Where East Meets West and South Meets North

As early as 1889, Chinese began traveling to Baja California Norte and Sonora to cross into the United States, thereby evading the barriers posed by the 1882 Chinese Exclusion Act. When, for example, a Chinese ship arrived in San Francisco in 1893, eighty-four Cantonese émigrés transferred to the *New Berne*, a U.S. steamship that frequented Mexican ports.[3] This roundabout course had practical advantages. By crossing the Mexican border, Chinese could avoid prolonged detentions at the port of San Francisco. Disembarking at Mexican port cities of Mazatlán, Guaymas, La Paz, San José, Cabo San Lucas, Ensenada, or Magdalena Bay, they traveled overland through Baja California or Sonora.[4] Their growing presence in Mexico indicated that many were crossing illegally through one of the last frontiers of the United States. Given its proximity to several hundred miles of coastline, it was no surprise that the borderlands would become a major Chinese thoroughfare into the United States.

In stark contrast to U.S. policies, Mexico encouraged Chinese immigration in the late nineteenth century. The 1886 *Ley de extranjería y naturalización*, passed under President Porfirio Díaz, lured foreign settlers to Mexico with liberal ideals of citizenship and nationality. The Mexican government was particularly interested in attracting immigrants from abroad to the sparsely populated borderlands, since the *científicos* believed the Mexican peasant was inherently incapable of building and participating in a modern, industrial society. They saw European immigrants, especially those practicing Roman Catholicism, as ideal. Yet there were few incentives for would-be immigrants: Apache, Yaqui, and Seri Indians continued to dominate the border region, there were few waterways for irrigation development, and access to arable land was limited. With the exception of colonies of Russians and European Jews in Baja California, greater opportunities pulled immigrants of European descent to the United States or elsewhere.[5]

The Chinese, nonetheless, participated in the new immigrant experiment in northern Mexico. Between 1890 and 1895, Mexican government officials reported that over 4,350 Chinese landed at the Pacific ports of Salina Cruz and Mazatlán and Gulf ports of Tampico and Veracruz.[6] Commercial and agricultural opportunities drew many to the territory of Baja California Norte and the states of Coahuila, Chihuahua, Sinaloa, and Sonora. Sonoran census records of 1890 reported 229 Chinese living and laboring in the state as hotel workers, cooks, launderers, ranchers, merchants, and skilled tradesmen. Chinese later gained a foothold in local manufacturing and sale of apparel, shoes, and men's furnishings, quickly dominating what little small-scale manufacturing existed in the state. In 1895 the census recorded 126 men and eleven women living in the port city of Guaymas, 84 in the mining camp of Minas Prietas, 46 in the capital of Hermosillo, and 16 in the border town of Magdalena.[7] By 1900 Sonora was home to the largest Chinese population in Mexico, with over 850.

Substantially fewer Chinese lived just west in Baja California.[8] San Diego customs officials enumerated more than a hundred Chinese in Baja California Norte during the late 1880s, many ostensibly working in the mining and fishing enterprises of the Chinese Six Companies.[9] Although the demand for labor may have lured more Chinese into the peninsula, these projects eventually collapsed.[10] Over the next decade, the lack of employment and investment opportunities stunted the growth of the Chinese population. By 1900 only 188 Chinese resided in Baja California Norte.[11] Despite the demographic and economic differences between Baja California Norte and Sonora, the Chinese in both areas found themselves in relatively flexible circumstances. Exclusion laws in the United States, along with the push for immigration and development in northern Mexico, placed several choices in the hands of the Chinese: the possibility of settlement, the opportunity to naturalize, or the challenge of crossing the U.S. border. The lives of Chinese merchants narrate this interlacing history.

In 1879, Lee Sing, an ambitious young merchant, established a dry goods business with his brother in Tucson, Arizona. The small store, stocked with items such as beef jerky, beans, and whiskey, was quite enterprising in the context of the burgeoning Tucson economy. Financial connections with prominent Jewish businessman Louis Zeckendorf made his business prospects bright.[12] Sing's own success inspired expansion into the production and sale of shoes in Nogales, Arizona. Over the next few years, Sing's second business enterprise flourished with the economy of this booming border town, but by 1889 the operation of his businesses took a back seat to his personal priorities. After some years of engagement to a Mexican woman, Sing decided to liquidate his assets and properties in Nogales and Tucson in order to marry, relocate to Sonora, and become a Mexican citizen.

After his wedding in Mexico, Sing established stores in the Sonoran towns of Imuris, La Cienega, and Santa Ana. Like many Chinese proprietors in northern Mexico, Sing lived in a transnational world. He established financial and familial ties in both the United States and Mexico, holding investments with his brother in Tucson while creating a home and family in Sonora. Yet his growing wealth and economic status did not necessarily guarantee trouble-free entry into the United States. During a routine trip north in 1893, Sing was detained by Arizona border inspectors and questioned about his status as a merchant. The thirty-two-year-old Sing was fortunate; he was able to call on Mexican and American officials for assistance. D. A. Moreno, president of the border city of Santa Ana, verified Sing's *ciudadania* (citizenship), his eleven years of residency in Mexico, his marriage to a Mexican woman (and the fact that he was father of three Mexican children), his annual income of eight to ten thousand pesos, and his ownership of a local general store. Also persuasive were the confirmation by the prefect of Magdalena, Ignacio Bonillas, of the merchant's real estate holdings, and Sing's affidavit to the American consul at Nogales, Sonora, Josiah E. Stone.[13]

This overwhelming record of settlement held sway, and officials permitted Sing to pass freely across the border over the next four years. No single aspect, be it merchant status, Mexican citizenship, or familial roots in Sonora, determined entry. All were important, and all would have an impact on local enforcement of Chinese exclusion laws. It is useful to compare Sing's situation to that of most Mexicans, who were relatively free to cross the border during the 1890s; they were stopped at the border only when customs officials suspected them of evading paying appropriate tariffs, or smuggling contraband whiskey, cigars, and opium.[14] Unlike the Chinese, Mexicans' proof of citizenship or nationality was not required to pass into the United States. A Mexican national simply declared his name to U.S. customs officials and paid whatever duty or fine was due. Chinese residents of Mexico, by contrast, were always stopped at the border with the assumption that they were "aliens" in the region.

Claims of Mexican citizenship and nationality yielded positive results when immigrant officials stopped and detained Chinese border crossers. In fact, most Chinese merchants who asserted such privileges benefited from the rights bestowed on Mexicans at the U.S. southern line: they gained legal entry north. Moreover, conscious assertions of *mexicanidad* on the part of Chinese border crossers indicate that membership in the Mexican polity had not yet assumed narrow and ethnically confining requisites associated with the postrevolutionary identity of *mestizaje*. While Mexican nationality, and its subsequent power at the U.S. southern border, continued to perplex immigrant and customs officials attempting to make sense of rather extraneous exclusion laws, Chinese merchants continued to cross, although their movements were not always effortless.

The 1897 murder of Lee Sing's brother in Tucson, Arizona, threw the orderly world of the shoe merchant into confusion. Unbeknown to Sing, trouble began almost immediately with his arrival in Tucson to settle his dead brother's estate. After an eight-year absence, no one recognized Sing. Immigration officials and residents assumed he was a laborer illegally in the country. Unaware of these suspicions, Sing began to take care of his brother's affairs, selling his dry goods store to a local Chinese merchant for three thousand dollars. Somewhere along the way, sentimentality took

Josiah E. Stone, Esq,
    Consul of the United States of America
        Nogales, Sonora, Mexico.
           Respected Sir:
                I am a resident and citizen
of Sonora, Mexico, and am conducting a
general merchandise business in the town
of Santa Ana. This business requires me to make
occasional visits to the United States for the
purchase of goods, &c. And as I was born in
China I do hereby make application for registra-
tion at the Consulate and the authentication of
my identification as a citizen and merchant
of Mexico, in order that I may secure the privilege
accorded me by Section 6 of the Act of Congress
of the United States, approved July 5, 1884 of
having the right of free and unmolested entrance
and exit through the port of Nogales, Arizona
    Herewith I present a certificate signed by
Mexican officials who have known me for years
and who attest to my status as a citizen
and merchant of Mexico.
        Respectfully Submitted.

                Lee Sing

A. B. Gibson,
    Witness

Lee Sing's petition to Josiah E. Stone, the American consul at Nogales, Sonora. Sing's testimony of citizenship and merchant status aided his entry north. Records of the District Court of the United States for the Territory of Arizona, First Judicial District, Criminal Case Files, 1882–1912, RG 21, case no. 823. Courtesy of the National Archives, Pacific Region, Laguna Niguel, California.

over, and Sing contemplated relocating his wife and their three young children to Tucson.[15] He returned to Imuris and persuaded his wife of the town's virtues, including the quality of its schools. Sing then left for Tucson to arrange for the move, leaving with his wife the money and documents related to the sale of his brother's property.

Sing passed without incident across the international border. Once in Tucson, he took up short-term residency at the Star Laundry, a downtown shop in the Old Pueblo owned by an elderly friend of Sing, Sam Lee. It was here that a local passerby, who had witnessed Sing ironing what were later determined to be his own clothes, mistook the merchant for a laborer. Not surprisingly, this type of manual activity threw Sing's status as merchant into question. In a matter of a day, Tucson immigration officials arrested Sing, believing he was a laborer illegally in the United States. As the merchant's lengthy testimony revealed, the exchange of money in the form of a wage never occurred between Sam Lee and Lee Sing. The proprietor of the laundry washed his guest's clothes free of charge, and if any ironing was to be done, Sing would have to do it himself.

Sing's experience was a common one among Chinese merchants in the United States. According to historian Lucy Salyer, merchants could be stopped at "every hamlet, village and town . . . on the charge of being a laborer who has failed to register."[16] A similar predicament held true for Mexican merchants Ah Suey, Hi Chung, Wong Nam, Wong Fong, and Mary Fong of southern Arizona.[17] All gained admission into the United States, albeit after a period of detention, questioning, and litigation. Declarations of citizenship and merchant status aided their disputes. The territorial court even recognized the dual residencies of merchants Mary and Wong Fong as Tombstone, Arizona, and San Pedro, Sonora, Mexico. The couple, as a result, operated stores on both sides of the border while maintaining their home in Tombstone.[18] Likewise, legal maneuverings and the assertion of Mexican citizenship eventually freed Sing from the grip of the territorial courts.[19]

Citizenship, family, and merchant status would remain the cornerstones of Mexico's Chinese business community over the next five decades. Their place in Mexican society allowed Chinese merchants to exert control and influence in their national lives while maintaining fluid relationships and identities across borders. As more Chinese from Sonora and Baja California insisted on traveling into the United States, customs officials stopped and detained Chinese merchants with growing frequency.[20] Patterns of transnational travel, social ties, and economic activity, however, were not so easily broken. U.S. customs officials wrestled with this social reality, as well as the ambiguities of enforcing exclusion laws. Some consular officials began to feel that temporary Chinese travel into the United States should be allowed within the framework of exclusion laws. Within this ambiguous and negotiable intersection between formal law and social reality, requests by Chinese merchants to enter the United States were, more often than not, resolved in their favor.

Sifting Through and Enforcing the Law

By the mid-1890s, the difficulties of determining admission or exclusion of Chinese overwhelmed U.S. immigration officials.[21] Understaffed and ill-equipped, customs collectors and immigrant inspectors vastly underestimated the force of this new diaspora seeking entry—legally and illegally—into the United States. To assist in this complex and challenging task, the Bureau of Immigration in 1895 created the Chinese Bureau, which shared with customs agents the responsibility of enforcing exclusion laws. Yet this new body hardly seemed in a position to enforce exclusion laws along the Mexican border. At the port of San Francisco, the Chinese Bureau was part of a vast administrative organization under the control of the customs collector. By contrast, only five permanent-status customs officials ran the entire San Diego customs station in 1891. Equally undermanned were the customs offices in Tucson and Nogales, Arizona. To guard the 300-mile border with Sonora, both stations shared two collectors, two Chinese inspectors, and one mounted inspector.[22]

These officials were keenly aware that the lack of sufficient personnel brought even more pressure to bear on their daily responsibilities. The duties incumbent on customs officers—searching all incoming vessels, determining the appropriate duties for taxable items, tracking and fining smugglers of cigars, mescal, sheep, and opium—were made more demanding when deciding whether to admit Chinese originating from Mexico. Exclusion laws, customs officials soon discovered, were not only wholly inadequate and too general, they were often irrelevant. Their misgivings about the law engendered a frequent reliance on Mexican officials, who reluctantly assisted U.S. customs officials. Enforcing Chinese exclusion laws also dramatized the often circumspect political relationship between the United States and its southern neighbor.

Frustrated by the ability of Chinese laborers to slip through the unguarded border, customs agents soon realized that effective patrolling of the border meant monitoring the activities of the Chinese from within Mexico. In 1890, when eighty Chinese landed in Mazatlán, Sinaloa, and Guaymas, Sonora, the fear of a Chinese invasion loomed in the mind of San Diego customs collector John R. Berry. "It looks as if the experiment had been tried of entering Chinamen in this round-about way and in small numbers," he reported, "and having proved successful an attempt is being made to operate the plan on a larger scale."[23] To his satisfaction (but also to his annoyance), Mexican constables, not U.S. customs officers, caught thirteen out of eighty Chinese south of Tijuana. Because U.S. customs agents could not cross into Mexico, informal arrangements with Mexican constables were necessary to capture those Chinese attempting to cross the line. Happenstance placed the constables, on duty for no more than thirty minutes, in the path of the border crossers.[24]

Berry now sought to formalize enforcement of exclusion laws, seeking among other things to expand the power of his inspectors south into Mexico. He began to negotiate with Mexican customs officials and the governor of Baja California Norte immediately following the capture of the Chinese laborers. He asked M. G. Montaño, collector of customs at Tia Juana, Baja California, to allow his men to pursue Chinese into Mexican territory. "It is the desire of the Government of the United States to scrupulously respect the desire of the Government of Mexico, and I have no doubt it is equally the desire of the Mexican Government to extend to the Government of the United States such international courtesies as may be practical and that may be necessary," he wrote. "If it is consistent with your wishes and within the scope of your official authority, I would respectfully request that you issue a permit for the Chinese inspectors . . . to cross."[25]

Governor Luís E. Torres responded by authorizing limited power to U.S. customs inspectors in Mexico to cross the border.[26] His hesitation to offer full border-crossing privileges was not so surprising considering that just two months earlier Baja California Norte had been subject to filibustering attempts by a marauding band of Americans.[27] Not wanting to disrupt economic relations with the United States, Torres sought a balance between maintaining friendly relations between the two republics and reasserting Mexican sovereignty.[28] Inspectors could enter as private citizens, he explained, but could "do nothing as a United States official" once in

Mexico.[29] Left neither with the capacity to detain nor the power to arrest, mounted inspectors decided to monitor the movements of Chinese from the ports of Ensenada and La Paz.

The ability of inspectors to warn agents at the border about potential Chinese movements from the coast yielded modest results yet did not solve the problem of what to do with the Chinese once they reached Arizona.[30] Chinese laborers stopped at the Arizona-Sonora border were not always subject to the same exclusionary practices as those entering elsewhere. Arizona's Territorial Commissioners did not automatically deport Chinese from Mexico to China. Instead, they recognized Chinese residency in Mexico and, by extension, valued Chinese community life there. These actions also indicate that Arizona officials acted outside the predominant racial ideology of the day when interpreting exclusion laws. With virtually no legal precedents to guide decision making, or political pressure to sway their judgment, the actions of Arizona Territorial officials reveal that customs officials found themselves in the position to interpret exclusion law based on their own understanding of Chinese life at the border.

Territorial Commissioners Louis C. Hughes, Allen R. English, and D. J. Cumming made distinctions between border crossers and border residents — those Chinese laborers sojourning through Mexico and those from Mexico. Until roughly 1900, Chinese laborers of Mexican citizenship or nationality crossing the border were simply deported to Mexico, the most favorable outcome possible for Chinese laborers at the time. Chinese with no claims to Mexican residency or citizenship continued to risk crossing into the United States from Mexico, even if it meant deportation to China.

In the hot summer months of 1890, twenty-two Chinese with names like Ta Ho, Ah Cheong, Hom Jung, Gwan Gong, and Ning Saung Hoe were captured and imprisoned in Nogales and Tucson.[31] They were not residents of Mexico and had no other intention except to cross into the United States. Without any legal representation, each of the laborers signed an affidavit, translated into Chinese by interpreter C. Richards, about the nature of the circuitous journeys that landed them in Arizona. The testimony of Ning Ah Goon was typical: "My name is Ning Ah Goon. I am 42 years old, was born in China. I am a laborer. I arrived in San Francisco from China Jan. 20 to Feb. 17–1890 on S. S. *City of Peking*. I then went to Guaymas Mexico where I arrived Feb 27–1890, I do not know from which vessel."[32] By the time these laborers completed their declarations there was no longer any question as to their status — they were

UNITED STATES OF AMERICA.

First Judicial District of Arizona,

D. J. Cumming ~~Commissioner.~~ Commissioner.

UNITED STATES OF AMERICA

vs.

Lin Gee

Charged with being a Chinese person
unlawfully within the United States
of America.

This case having been regularly brought on for hearing in ~~the Court Room~~ *Nogales*, Territory of Arizona, before ~~D. J. Cumming~~ Commissioner of the District Court of the First
Judicial District of the Territory of Arizona which District Court, has and excercises the
same jurisdiction in all cases arising under the constitution and laws of the United, States,
as is vested in the Circuit and District Court of the United States, and _____*Lin Gee*_____
_____being charged, upon oath, with having unlawfully come
into, and unlawfully being in, the United States of America, and upon the issue joined
herein, the United States Attorney for the Territory of Arizona, having appeared on behalf
of the United States and the accused having appeared in person and by attorney, and the
testimony having been heard, and the case having been duly submitted, and due consideration thereon had, It is ordered and adjudged by the Commissioner that _____*Lin Gee*_____
_____is a Chinese person ~~and a subject of the Emperor of China~~,
found unlawfully within the jurisdiction of the United States of America, in the First Judicial District of the Territory of Arizona, and that he is guilty of having unlawfully entered the United States of America from the ~~_____~~ in violation of the Acts of
Congress of the United States of America in such cases made and provided, and that he is
unlawfully in the United States of America, and that he is not lawfully entitled to be and
remain in the United States of America.

It is therefore ordered that the said_____ *Lin Gee*
be remanded to the custody of the United States Marshal for the Territory of Arizona, to be
by him taken to the City of San Francisco, in the State of California, in the United States
of America, and there delivered to the Collector of Customs at the Port of San Francisco,
to be by him returned, in accordance with law, to the ~~_____~~ from whence he
came.

And for the purpose of carrying this order into effect, It is further ordered that the
United States Marshal for the Territory of Arizona, shall take_____ *Lin Gee*
_____ into custody and him safely keep until this order shall be fully executed.

Entered this **23** day of *August* 189**0**

D. J. Cumming
Commissioner.

This is one of several hundred certificates documenting the court proceedings of Chinese exclusion cases in the Arizona Territory. Note the many modifications, especially
what previously read "and a subject of the Empire of China." Records of the District
Court of the United States for the Territory of Arizona, First Judicial District, Criminal Case Files, 1882–1912, RG 21, case no. 410. Courtesy of the National Archives,
Pacific Region, Laguna Niguel, California.

Chinese laborers and nationals illegally in the United States and had to return to China. A month after their arrest, they were officially deported.

However, the fact that many Chinese laborers crossed the border with no claims to Mexican residence or citizenship did not deter Territorial Commissioners English, Cumming, and Hughes from seeking to verify Mexican citizenship and residency when possible. That same summer, they held thirteen Chinese laborers for illegal entry into Arizona. Sam Hing, Chu Yun, Charley Quong, and Charley Ah Fong, without the assistance of attorneys, asked not to remain in the United States but to be deported to Mexico.[33] To return to China would mean returning to the homeland with a dream of a better life in Mexico unfulfilled—or at the least, a bit delayed. Each defendant, self-identified as a laborer, declared nationality or citizenship in Mexico. Support for Sam Hing was especially evident. Tombstone residents Wong Lung and James Reese posted a hundred-dollar bond on behalf of Sam Hing. They also testified to Hing's activities in Tombstone and provided important documentation, hoping that their friend would escape deportation to China. After the proceedings were completed, territorial marshal R. H. Paul escorted Sam Hing, Chu Yun, Charley Quong, and Charley Ah Fong to the border town of Nogales, Sonora.

The language of the territorial court suggested that deportation of laborers to Mexico was not as significant as the deportation of laborers to China. English, Cumming, and Hughes viewed sending laborers to Mexico as a mere discharge. The order of deportation by Commissioner English underscored this point: "I certify the order on the 26th day of June, AD 1890, by carrying the defendant, Chin Yan, to Nogales, State of Sonora, Republic of Mexico, and there discharging him."[34] That "deportation" meant returning to China and "discharge" meant a short escort to the border town further obscured the intent of the law to prohibit entry. In effect, Chinese attempting to enter the United States at its southern border prompted Territorial Commissioners to weigh the significance of Mexican citizenship or nationality against exclusion laws that targeted Chinese originating from China. The largely informal category of "discharge" emerged from Chinese residents and citizens of Mexico who fell outside the official purview of exclusion laws. This discursive practice also allowed officials to maintain a guise of enforcing the law.

Not all appreciated the consequences of these distinctions. Exclusionists had good reason to fear a "Chinese invasion" from the southern border, because, in fact, several hundred Chinese began to pour into the Mexican

Sam Hing at Fly's Gallery in Tombstone, Arizona. This photograph was part of the evidence submitted on behalf of Hing. Records of the District Court of the United States for the Territory of Arizona, First Judicial Court, Criminal Case Files, 1882–1912, RG 21, case no. 413. Courtesy of the National Archives, Pacific Region, Laguna Niguel, California.

port cities of Guaymas and Mazatlán intent on crossing into the United States by way of San Diego and Nogales.[35] Customs officials in San Diego echoed these concerns and were impatient with the Arizona practice of discharging Chinese. This practice, they felt, made a mockery of their exclusion efforts. "To take them to the line and turn them loose below it, does no good whatsoever, as they simply take the first opportunity to cross again," remarked collector Berry. "The farce enacted [occurs] when officials backs are turned [and] the opportunity is created for their returning again."[36]

For a while, conflicting perceptions about Chinese laborers from Mexico widened the divide between San Diego and southern Arizona officials. However, after 1900, mounting political pressure forced the hand of American immigration officials at the border. The actions that had once ensured deportation of laborers to Mexico and the travel of merchants to the United States became relics of the past. Rather than maintain immigration procedures based on the preservation of the transnational lives of Chinese laborers and merchants, American officials mimicked the restrictionist practices of the ports of San Francisco and New York. This meant that laborers were routinely deported to China while merchants' petitions to travel into the United States were received with intense circumspection.[37] Curiously, neither law nor statute mandated these changes.

By the early 1900s, the importance of Mexican nationality and citizenship lessened significantly. In 1902, exclusionists, responding somewhat to the high numbers of Chinese entering the United States through its southern border, suspended the immigration of Chinese laborers for another ten years. These laws made it nearly impossible for any Chinese person originating from Mexico to enter the United States. Even extraordinary diplomatic efforts by Mexican and American officials who advocated admission for Chinese Mexicans were no match for the enforcement of exclusion laws. The bureaucratic machinery also increased at the border when, in 1903, the Bureau of Immigration was placed under the authority of the Department of Commerce and Labor to strengthen controls at the Mexican border. At the beginning of the twentieth century, race, in effect, cast a wide net over Chinese Mexican merchants and many hundreds of laborers caught at the U.S. southern border and crossing into the United States from Mexico assumed greater organization. No longer were Chinese traversing through the border without the assistance of vast smuggling operations. *Coyotes* (smugglers) were but one link in a transnational network of human trafficking responsible for substantially increasing illegal entries from Mexico. Their activities, a direct response to the grip of Chinese exclusion laws, would continue to plague the U.S.-Mexico border over the next few decades.

A Nest of Corruption: Smuggling Chinese through the Underground Railroad

At the turn of the twentieth century, the sparsely populated border region around the twin border cities of Nogales, Arizona, and Nogales, Sonora, became the principal thoroughfare by which smugglers channeled Chinese from Mexican port cities of Salina Cruz, Manzanillo, Mazatlán, and Guaymas. Once across the international boundary, smugglers moved "contraband" Chinese to Los Angeles and San Francisco via southern Arizona. For those seeking to profit from the geographic convenience and economic demand of smuggling Chinese into the United States from the Arizona-Sonora corridor, the clandestine activity proved lucrative and reasonably easy to facilitate. With the exception of an occasional Southern Pacific train route or patrol by customs line riders on horseback, the barren Sonoran desert seemed an open field for Chinese traversing north.

The systematic practice of trafficking Chinese into the United States from Mexico began in the early 1900s along the Arizona-Sonora corridor. When a plot to smuggle 20,000 Chinese "coolies" from Guaymas was discovered in 1903, Arizona immigration authorities were already in the midst of exposing the so-called underground railroad. The stealthy movements of smugglers and their clients brought in thousands of Chinese by way of covert transportation on stagecoaches, boxcars, and burros. This method allowed for both the evasion of exclusion and the avoidance of deportation. Jim Bennett, the mastermind of this elaborate smuggling scheme that began in 1901, had controlled operations so meticulously that it took immigration officials over three years to uncover the plot. The clandestine route, originating in the Sonoran port city of Guaymas, meandered through Hermosillo, Cananea, Magdalena, and Naco. In Arizona the underground route twisted through the Santa Cruz and Santa Rita mountain ranges where border crossers took a respite in the railroad town of Fairbank, Arizona. Making Fairbank the main terminal of activity, Bennett was able to maintain a constant flow of Chinese border crossers from Sonora into southern Arizona.

Bennett's operation proved remarkably resilient even in the face of vigilant Chinese inspectors who were well aware of the existence of smuggling rings in the area. Rather than err on the side of haste, the success of the operation depended on time-tested relationships forged between the ringleader and his assistants. Relying entirely on his own careful discernment of character and temperament, Bennett hired men to generate business in Sonora, monitor the routines of immigrant agents, and harbor Chinese border crossers. Bennett's approach proved quite successful. His shrewd manner of selecting smugglers engendered such a high degree of confidence among fellow guides that the Fairbank gang was reputed to have netted thousands of dollars a month from their efforts. Without fear of detection, Bennett and his crew escorted Chinese laborers into the United States for a fee that ranged from $50 to $200.[38] Usually the collection of the full fare for passage occurred in the city of final destination. In other instances, the smugglers required a good-faith payment at Fairbank. As a long-standing rule, Chinese border crossers needed to prove to the smugglers that they possessed the full fee for passage before proceeding to California.[39]

The illicit activity that facilitated the passage of hundreds of Chinese into the United States relied on clever techniques of forgery and deception. Bennett's ring seemed heavily dependent on the efforts of three men, Lee Quong, Louis Greenwaldt, and B. C. Springstein.[40] While Quong escorted Chinese through the underground route, Greenwaldt and Springstein forged certificates of residence to ensure the safe passage of border crossers once in the United States. Greenwaldt, a former San Quentin convict who served a term of six years for Chinese smuggling in 1892, joined Springstein in Cananea, Sonora, to complete the forgery ring.[41] Armed with a metal plate for imprinting documents, rubber stamps, and a seal maker that impressed "O.M. Welburn Internal Revenue Collector, First District of California," the Fairbank gang produced replicas of certificates of residence.[42] The team of Springstein and Greenwaldt duplicated over 300 certificates, and for $100 filled in the appropriate information for passage.[43]

As soon as Chinese nationals secured a certificate, they sojourned north with Lee Quong and one of his assistants. Quong, nicknamed "The Jew" and "Sheeney John" because he allegedly resembled someone of the "Hebrew race," employed Wonk Tunk and Charley Lee to aid him in the efforts to escort and harbor Chinese.[44] Fluent in English, Quong was also a part-time truck farmer in the area who, at times, sold his produce in nearby Bisbee and Tombstone. However, Quong's principal occupation was that of Chinese smuggler. Taking advantage of the long-distance patrolling techniques of immigrant inspectors, Quong and Tunk loaded Chinese posing as Mexicans into boxcars destined for northern Sonora. To blur the line between Chinese and Mexican, Quong and Tuck had their Chinese patrons "cut off their queues and dressed as Mexicans" to escape detection.[45] Once they were safely inside boxcars, Quong quickly refastened the door seal as if it had not been broken. In northern Sonora, the Chinese would travel to the final destination of Fairbank on a road not recently patrolled by inspectors. By closely monitoring the routines of Chinese inspectors, Quong could fairly easily determine the routes he and his clients could take into Fairbank. Bennett's guides and their patrons traveled without fear of detection and were relatively successful in gaining passage without incident.

Chinese inspector Charles Connell cracked the smuggling ring after months of trailing the Fairbanks gang. Appointed as inspector only eighteen months before the bust, Connell was no stranger to politically controversial activity. Born in Mount Vernon, Iowa, and educated on the East Coast, Connell arrived in Arizona during its pioneering days. At the age of twenty-one, in 1880, he administered the first census of the Apache Indians at the San Carlos Reservation.[46] Considered a foremost authority on the tribe, Connell served as a "diplomatic agent" to the Apache on behalf of the federal government.[47] Only a few years later, when the Spanish-American War broke out, Captain Connell continued his government duties as a secret service agent along the U.S.-Mexican border. From this experience, Connell reportedly carried a mental map of the entire Mexican border between El Paso and San Diego and "knew every trail, road, pass, canyon, mountain and water hole."[48] His experience as an Apache agent and wartime officer proved quite appropriate in Connell's future duties for the federal government, especially in his duties as Chinese inspector that began early in 1903.[49]

On a visit to Naco, Sonora with special immigrant agent V. M. Clark, Inspector Connell encountered two Chinese men who had in their possession blank certificates of residence. The two border crossers stated that they had secured their documents from Springstein. Connell, in an attempt to confirm their account, queried federal immigration authorities who had supposedly issued the official certificates of residence. Numbers located at the upper left corner of the documents in question seemingly confirmed their authenticity. As it turned out, Connell's watchful eye caught an inconsistency not found in official certificates of residence: an additional letter "m."[50] Even though Connell and Clark were acting outside their jurisdiction, they pursued the case into Sonora, arrested Springstein, and confiscated mounds of evidence against the ringleader.[51] Springstein confessed to his illegal activity soon after agents interrogated the smuggler in their "sweat box."[52] Among those implicated were Quong, Greenwaldt, and Bennett. Moreover, written evidence recounting the particulars of smuggling cast doubt on Quong's innocence. Connell came upon a letter written by Quong to his friend, Ho Kwong:

> Yesterday I received a letter from you acknowledging the receipt of $25 sent for urgent use and speaking of your having five pieces of merchandise [sic] there are white men who would take a hand if there should be customers to be smuggled over right along. . . . A few days ago they got Wong Shai In, Wong Chun Yick, Yee Tuk Wai, and several others . . . you cannot smuggle anybody out by the fast trains. . . . There are boats now coming from China to Guaymas, which will no doubt bring over a great many customers. Just as soon as you receive any let me know immediately without fail.[53]

With the arrests of Quong and Springstein, inspectors concentrated their efforts on apprehending the elusive Greenwaldt and Bennett. Greenwaldt, who possessed the original metal plate used to manufacture fraudulent certificates, managed to evade Connell. Before his escape to Vancouver, British Columbia, Greenwaldt left Springstein holding six hundred unused certificates of residence. Once Greenwaldt arrived in Canada, he immediately established a regular line of ships of Chinese nationals headed for the port of Guaymas.[54] Bennett, the founder of the line, also escaped the grips of Connell and lived in "princely fashion as an American capitalist in Mexico." With the conviction and deportation of Quong in June 1904, Arizona and Sonora's underground railroad ceased operation.[55]

Before his deportation, Quong revealed several poignant aspects of the smuggling ring. He testified that he witnessed Chinese being routinely packed into boxcars and provided with food and water in their trek toward San Francisco, the principal destination of most crossers. In one unfortunate incident, Quong described the capture of five Chinese crossers traveling in a Southern Pacific boxcar on their way to San Francisco. One crosser died of thirst along the way, and others suffered severe dehydration. Despite his detailed description of incidents of Chinese smuggling, Quong denied all participation in the ring and tried to preserve his status in the United States by producing a seemingly authentic certificate of residence issued out of San Francisco.[56] After hearing the testimony of Arizona residents Frank Meyer, Gus Klein, and George McDonald, authorities deported Quong to China.[57]

Exclusion's Southern Gate

From the early 1880s to the late 1890s, the lives of Chinese merchants and laborers at the U.S.-Mexico border were not always sharply constrained by social class, nationality, or race. Family ties, the search for work, and the maintenance of transnational economic exchange between Chinese merchants in northern Mexico and those in the United States softened exclusionists' calls for the closure of the American southern border. Merchant fronterizos continued to travel to Chinatowns in San Francisco, Tucson, San Diego, Los Angeles, and El Paso to supply their stores and cultivate economic and social relationships. At the same time, their dealings with border officials demonstrate that they could not completely escape the forces of U.S. immigration restrictionism. In a similar fashion, the power of exclusion did not completely overtake Chinese laborers as they engaged in extraordinary measures to avoid deportation to China when caught at the border. Nonetheless, after 1900, the re-entrenchment of exclusion laws marked the Chinese of Mexico racially. Mexican nationality or citizenship no longer facilitated Chinese admission into the United States or deportations to Mexico, while smuggling emerged concomitantly with the intensification of exclusion, especially after the U.S. Congress extended the laws indefinitely in 1904.[58] The resonance of Chinese border life has modern-day reverberations for Mexicans crossing north. Chinese fronterizos and Mexican immigrants traversed the same routes and aspired to maintain similar transnational ties while facing comparable challenges at the border. Then and now, racialized borders remain constant expressions of immigration restrictionism, and the most poignant and enduring reminders of the immigrant experience.

Notes

I am grateful for the assistance of my colleagues and friends in this endeavor. Luís Leobardo Arroyo, Xiaolan Bao, Maria E. Ramas, Jessica Wang, and

K. Scott Wong provided incisive and meaningful comment. Without the urgings of these individuals, this project would certainly have fallen quite short of the mark. Special thanks are due Julie Rivera for her timely assistance. Paul Worsmer, Director of Archival Operations at the National Archives and Records Administration, Pacific Region (Laguna Niguel), proves once again that the work of historians would be much more arduous if not for the genius of archivists.

1 This essay is part of a larger research project on the history of Chinese along the U.S.-Mexico border. See Grace Delgado, "In the Age of Exclusion: Race, Region, and Chinese Identity in the Making of the Arizona-Sonora Borderlands, 1863–1943" (Ph.D. diss., University of California, Los Angeles, 2000). My goal here, if only partially, is to uncover a history that shows Chinese life as simultaneously local and transnational. I draw on the seminal work of Charles Cumberland, Leo Michael Dambourges Jacques, and Evelyn Hu-DeHart. Building on some central experiences scholars have established as common ground, my work here advances our understanding of the Chinese in Mexico that reaches across national borders. See Charles C. Cumberland, "The Sonoran Chinese and the Mexican Revolution," *Hispanic American Historical Review* 40:2 (1960): 191–211; and the following essays by Evelyn Hu-DeHart: "Immigrants to a Developing Society: The Chinese in Northern Mexico, 1875–1932," *Journal of Arizona History* 21 (1980): 49–86; "Racism and Anti-Chinese Persecution in Sonora, Mexico, 1876–1932," *Amerasia* 9 (1982): 1–28; and "Coolies, Shopkeepers, Pioneers: The Chinese of Mexico and Peru," *Amerasia* 15 (1989): 91–116. The most comprehensive work on the Chinese in Sonora remains Leo Michael Dambourges Jacques, "The Anti-Chinese Campaigns in Sonora, 1900–1931" (Ph.D. diss., University of Arizona, 1974).

2 The Qing dynasty perceived overseas Chinese as deserters, traitors, rebels, and conspirators who rejected their filial duties. Despite the possibility of harsh punishment upon their return, over 125,000 Chinese emigrated to the Americas by 1880. See Lynn Pan, ed., *The Encyclopedia of the Chinese Overseas* (Cambridge: Harvard University Press 1999), 98.

3 John R. Berry to J. G. Carlisle, Secretary of the Treasury, 1 April 1893. Record Group 36, San Diego Collection District, Letters Sent to the Secretary of the Treasury, 1892–1908 (9L-39) National Archives and Record Administration/ Pacific Region at Laguna Niguel (hereafter referred to as NARA/LN). San Diego Collection referred to hereafter as SDCD-LSST.

4 By 1890, the frequency of illegal border crossings prompted U.S. congressional members to form a subcommittee to inspect immigration issues at the San Diego–Mexico border. See San Diego Customs District-Special Agents, Letters Sent (SDCD-SALS), John R. Berry to Anthony Godbe, 8 December 1890.

5 Robert H. Duncan, "The Chinese and the Economic Development of Northern Baja California," *Hispanic American Historical Review* 74:4 (1994): 616.

6 Mexico, Ministero de Fomento, *Boletín semestral de la dirección general de estadística de la República Mexicana, año de 1892.* Número X (México, D.F.: n.p., 1892), 418–19; and Mexico, *Anuario estadístico de la República Mexicana*, vol. 15 (México: n.p., 1893–1899).

7 Miguel Tinker Salas, *In the Shadow of the Eagles: Sonora and the Transformation of the Border during the Porfiriato* (Berkeley: University of California Press, 1997), 225.

8 I use the contemporary term, "Baja," rather than the anachronistic "Lower California" when referring to both Baja California Norte and Baja California Sur.

9 Thomas Arnold to the Secretary of the Treasury, 25 February 1890. Record Group 36, San Diego Collection District, Outgoing General Correspondence (9L-38) 1885–1909, NARA/LN. Hereafter referred to as SDCD-OGC.

10 Duncan, "Chinese and Economic Development," 618.

11 Evelyn Hu-DeHart, "The Chinese of Baja California Norte, 1910–1934," *Proceedings of the Pacific Coast Council on Latin American Studies* 12 (1985–86): 15.

12 *United States v. Lee Sing*, 1412 AZ-CCF [Records of the District Court of the United States for the Territory of Arizona, First Judicial District, Criminal Case Files, 1882–1912]. A database of these records is in the possession of the author.

13 *United States vs. Lee Sing [alias Gee Sing]*, 823 AZ-CCF.

14 Letters received from the Treasury Department, 1880–1909, box 3. Record group 36, San Diego Collection District, (9L-44), NARA/LN. Hereafter referred to as SDCD-LRTD.

15 *United States v. Lee Sing*, 1412 AZ-CCF.

16 Lucy E. Salyer, *Laws Harsh as Tigers: Chinese Immigrants and the Shaping of Modern Immigration Law* (Chapel Hill: University of North Carolina Press, 1995), 46.

17 *United States v. Ah Chung*, 1099; *United States v. Hi Chung*, 1100; *United States v. Ah Suey*, 1101; *United States v. Mary Fong and Wong Fong*, 1291 AZ-CCF.

18 *United States v. Mary Fong and Wong Fong*, 1291 AZ-CCF.

19 *United States v. Lee Sing*, 1422.

20 William Wallace Bowers to the Commissioner General of Immigration, 20 May 1902, SDCD-OGC.

21 In 1891 the Secretary of the Treasury supervised immigration and a year later established twenty-four customs inspection stations including those border districts in San Diego and Nogales. The primary focus of these districts in terms of immigration was to enforce Chinese exclusion laws. The Collector of Customs also received applications for return certificates from Chinese individuals wishing to travel abroad.

22 This statistic derives from a database of over six hundred Chinese exclusion and criminal case files from the Arizona Territory and Southern District Court of California. Compiled by the author, the database highlights twenty-three fields of information such as place of arrest, Chinese interpreter, deportation

destination, and commissioner. The database draws from the following files of record group 21: Records of the District Court of the United States for the Territory of Arizona, First Judicial District, Chinese Criminal Case Files, 1882–1912 [AZ-CCF]; Chinese Exclusion Cases, 1886–1906 [AZ-CEC]; Commissioners' Early Case Files [AZ-CECF]; Commissioners' Dockets [AZ--CD]; and Commissioners' Case Files, 1882–1912, [AZ-CMCF]; NARA/LN. The database from hereafter is referred to as CEDAZCA (the Chinese Exclusion Case File Database for Southern Arizona and Southern California).

23 John R. Berry to L. S. Irvin, 3 April 1890, SDCD-OGC; John R. Berry to William Windom, 7 April 1890, SDCD-OGC.

24 John R. Berry to William Windom, 7 April 1890, SDCD-OGC.

25 John R. Berry to M. G. Montaño, 17 June 1890, SDCD-SALR [Special Agents Letters Received].

26 General Luís E. Torres to John R. Berry, 19 June 1890, SDCD-SALS.

27 *San Diego Union*, 21 May 1890.

28 *San Diego Union*, 23, 25 and 27 May 1890.

29 John R. Berry to T. J. Monahau, 18 November 1890, SDCD-SALS.

30 A. E. Higgins to William Windom, 12 July 1890, SDCD-OGC.

31 CEDAZCA, 378, 388, 390–410.

32 *United States v. Ah Hoon [alias Ning Hoon and Ning Ah Goon]*, 398 AZ-CCF.

33 *United States v. Chu Yun [alias Chin Yan]*, 387; *United States v. Sam Hing*, 413; *United States v. Charley Quong*, 416; *United States v. Charley Ah Fong*, 417 AZ-CCF.

34 *United States v. Chu Yun [alias Chin Yan]*, 387 AZ-CCF.

35 W. W. Bowers to the Commissioner General of Immigration, 5 April 1902, SDCD-OGC.

36 John R. Berry to William Windom, 3 April 1890, SDCD-OGC.

37 The four exceptional cases are: *United States v. Fong Soon*, 568; *United States v. Ah Loo*, 944; *United States v. Hop Sam*, 1585; and *United States v. Yee Kim*, 1588 CEDAZCA.

38 *The Border Vidette*, 21 August 1901.

39 *The Bulletin: Sunday Magazine*, 21 August 1904.

40 Lee Quong was also known as Lee Quan. See *Bisbee Daily Review*, 18 August 1903.

41 *San Francisco Examiner*, 13 June 1904.

42 The Charles Connell Collection, Manuscript 188, Scrapbook of Charles Connell, newspaper article entitled "Chinese Ring Broken Up: Agent of Smugglers' Chief, Who Is a San Franciscan, Arrested and Outfit for Making Bogus Certificates Seized," Arizona Historical Society. Hereafter referred to as CCC-AHS.

43 *San Francisco Examiner*, 13 June 1904. Greenwaldt and Springstein sold blank certificates of residence for $50. See edition of 18 June 1904.

44 CCC-AHS, Scrapbook of John Murphy, folder 3, newspaper article entitled "Im-

portant Arrest of Chinese Smuggler: Inspector Connell Captures Lee Quan [*sic*] on the San Pedro River," not dated.

45   *San Francisco Bulletin*, 21 August 1904.

46   *Los Angeles Times*, 27 January 1931. Also see the *Los Angeles Examiner*, 26 December 1928 and *The Gazette and Republican*, 15 March 1931.

47   *Arizona Republican*, 12 April 1934. See CCC-AHS, box 2, folder 11, paper entitled "Excerpt from McClintock's History of Arizona."

48   *Los Angeles Examiner*, 26 December 1928.

49   *Los Angeles Times*, 27 January 1931.

50   *Los Angeles Examiner*, 13 June 1904.

51   *San Francisco Examiner*, 13 June 1904. Part of the evidence included a camera and several fountain pens. Inspector Clark made Springstein demonstrate how he filled out the certificates, placed the seal on the document, and took the photographs.

52   *Los Angeles Examiner*, 13 June 1904. See also Charles Connell Collection, Scrapbook, newspaper article entitled "Chinese Ring Broke Up: Agent of Smugglers' Chief, Who Is a San Franciscan, Arrested and Outfit for Making Bogus Certificates Seized." AHS. The *San Francisco Bulletin* reports quite a different story about the breakup of the ring. The newspaper attributed the breakup to the daring persistence of Charles Connell. One day Connell pulled a lone Chinaman off a boxcar at Naco, Sonora, and was en route to Fairbank. In his possession was a paper, which bore the name of Lee Quong. Connell, pursing his suspicions, discovered that Quong had also been harboring Chinese nationals at Crance Ranch. See 21 August 1904. See newspaper articles entitled "Connell Meets a Wily Chink" and "An Elusive Chink Caught" for the type of chivalrous portrayal of the inspector's exploits. The use of "chink" was quite common when referring to Chinese border crossers in Arizona newspapers. For those Chinese established in Tucson as legal residents, Arizona newspapers did not use these racial epithets. See the Scrapbook of Charles Connell, and box 2, folder 2, CCC-AHS. The American newspapers, *Harper's Weekly*, and *Harper's Weekly Illustrated Magazine* also use similar racist language. Similarly, Sonora educator and politician José María Arana espoused vitriol when referring to the Chinese as dogs, pestilence, and as "having the venom of serpents."

53   Scrapbook of Charles Connell, newspaper article entitled "Lee Quong Deported: Three Americans Testify Positively to His Identity." The letter written by Quong to Kwong is dated 23 April 1903. CCC-AHS. The *Bisbee Review* reported that only three hundred certificates were confiscated during the raid. See edition of 10 June 1904.

54   *Los Angeles Examiner*, 25 June 1904.

55   *The Bulletin*, 21 August 1904.

56   Connell Scrapbook, newspaper article, "Lee Quong to be Deported: Three Americans Testify Positively to His Identity," undated. Yet, another account re-

veals that the Chinese were smuggled into the United States embarking in El Paso via Yuma to San Francisco—the final point of destination. Connell has reported several incidents where Chinese who were loaded into boxcars died of thirst very quickly. See Connell Scrapbook, "How Chinks Were Smuggled." CCC-AHS.

57 Connell Scrapbook, newspaper article, "One Less Chink: Lee Quong Ordered Deported by Commissioner Pirtle," undated. For an account about the smuggling of Chinese into the United States, see W. W. Husband to Henry L. Stimson, Secretary of State, 6 June 1929. CCC-AHS. The Chinese Six Companies remained complicit in the smuggling rings that were expanded into underground routes of passage into Lower California.

58 The U.S. Congress passed this act on 29 April 1904. This new bill regulated Chinese immigration on the expiration of the 1894 treaty between China and the United States. In effect, the bill separated domestic legislation on Chinese immigration from treaty obligations with China. As a result, exclusion laws grew even more stringent while the Chinese were restricted from U.S. shores indefinitely.

Between North and South:

The Alternative Borderlands of

William H. Ellis and the African

American Colony of 1895

Borders not only divide; they also unite. Although one of the defining concepts of the modern nation-state is territoriality—a bounded geographical space over which the state exercises exclusive control—in the real world such control is always partial. Through pathways licit and illicit, peoples and goods, plants and animals, waters and wastes continually breach the orderly lines nation-states draw around themselves. Borderland regions are thus by their very nature undergirded by the countervailing impulses of separation and linkage, of political division and the myriad continuities—ecological, economic, familial, and other—that persist across national boundaries.[1]

In North America, the peculiar character of border regions emerged with particular clarity during the late nineteenth century, when Mexico and the United States each sought, for distinct yet mutually reinforcing purposes, to integrate the remote buffer zone between them into its constituent nation-state. The Mexican and American governments deployed their militaries along the border to eliminate the threat indigenous groups such as the Yaqui and Apache posed to national sovereignty and heightened their mapping and surveying of the border region. In concert with these state-building efforts, the railroad expanded into the area from both the American and Mexican sides, piercing the border at several locations in the 1880s. Ironically, the coming of the railroad, presented by its Mexican and American advocates alike as uniting the recently pacified border region more securely with its home country, also created new transnational linkages, facilitating the spread of American capital southward and the flow of peoples and natural resources from Mexico north into the United States.[2]

As a result of this rapid yet uneven transformation from a frontier zone to the border between modern nation-states, the turn-of-the-century borderlands was an unstable setting that could be reconfigured in multiple and unexpected ways. While many of those who attempted to direct these transformations were powerful elites—American capitalists and Porfirio Díaz's *científicos*—subaltern figures on both sides of the international boundary also saw in the unresolved character of the region the opportunity to articulate their own, alternative vision of the borderlands. Among the most dramatic, yet forgotten, of these efforts began in the late 1880s, when a little-known figure from Texas, William H. Ellis, undertook a project that articulated the novel possibilities that the late-nineteenth-century borderlands possessed. Capitalizing on the region's new rail links, which brought northern Mexico and the southern United States into more direct contact than ever before, as well as the ongoing tension between the borderland's economic integration and its legal separation, Ellis imagined a place for a group that, until now, has remained virtually invisible in historical studies of the border region: African Americans. In so doing, Ellis underscored not only the structural changes that had transformed the borderlands by the late nineteenth century but also the region's growing import in shaping notions of race and nation in Mexico and the United States alike.[3]

Reconstructing and Deconstructing Race in the Borderlands

Although Ellis's early years are cloaked with uncertainty—much of it of his own creation—they nonetheless reveal Ellis's precocious abilities at navigating the physical and cultural spaces that divided and united Mexico and the United States in the latter half of the nineteenth century. Ellis was born in 1864 in Victoria, a town in southern Texas. Despite its location some 200 miles from the international boundary, Ellis later recalled his birthplace as "near [the] Mexican frontier," no doubt in recognition of Victoria's Hispanic heritage (it was originally founded by Mexican settlers in 1824) and its significant Mexican American population. As a youth, Ellis found rather typical employment for a young man from Texas, working first as ranch hand and then as an assistant to a leather dealer. Reportedly, it was during a trip to Mexico for this latter employer that Ellis discovered that cotton sold for almost twice as much south of the international boundary, the result of Texans' frequent unease at doing business in Mexico. Fluent in Spanish and comfortable with Mexican culture from his early experiences in Victoria, Ellis saw untapped opportunities in the reluctance of other Texans to market goods to their southern neighbors. He began dealing cotton across the border, as well as wool, hides, horses, and cattle, and soon "in that way laid aside a tidy little sum of several thousand dollars."[4]

Other aspects of Ellis's history receded to the background, if not out of sight altogether, during this period as Ellis reinvented himself as the archetypical self-made American man. Ellis's ancestry, for example, remained cloaked in mystery. Although most of the available evidence suggests that he was born to recently freed slaves on one of the cotton plantations outside Victoria, nineteenth-century observers rarely classified Ellis as "negro." To some he appeared a "light-colored mulatto," but many others concluded that he had "the looks and dash of a Spaniard"—so much so, in fact, that by the turn of the century the national press repeatedly described him as a Spaniard, a Mexican, or "an enterprising Cuban."[5]

Building on his ability to speak Spanish and his business success south of the border, Ellis encouraged such interpretations of himself as a wealthy Hispanic rather than the child of African American field hands. In later years, for example, he gave his parents' names, ethnicities, and birthplaces not as they appear in the 1880 United States census—Charles Ellis and Margaret Nelson Ellis, "mulattoes" born in Kentucky in the 1840s—but instead as Carlos Ellis and Margarita Nelsonia, and insisted he was "the son of a Cuban father and a Mexican mother." On occasion, Ellis even went by the name "Guillermo Enrique Eliseo," a Hispanic identity he crafted for himself by translating his full name, William Henry Ellis, into Spanish. Such subterfuges offered tangible rewards. Being able to pass, not as an Anglo-Saxon white but as a well-to-do Mexican or Cuban, allowed Guillermo Enrique Eliseo, the Hispanic, entry to hotels, railroad cars, and business settings that would have been closed to William Henry Ellis, the African American.[6]

As ambivalent as Ellis's connections to his African American ancestry may have been, he never severed them completely. The complex mix of emotions Ellis possessed about his background emerged perhaps most powerfully when a newspaper reporter challenged the authenticity of his Hispanic identity in the early 1900s. Ellis at first conceded that "I . . . have some African blood in my veins." With the next breath, however, he added that "I am of mixed Cuban and Mexican blood" and warned that he would sue any newspaper that claimed he was "a damned nigger." In spite of the tensions involved in this position—acknowledging his "African blood" yet denying that he was "a damned nigger"—Ellis never sought to pass entirely into Hispanic society. He regularly involved himself in African American politics, particularly in his home state, where his early financial success gave him a certain prominence in the black community. Ellis's apparent preference for expediency over ideology manifested itself in his diverse set of allies, who varied from powerful insiders in the political establishment to the forerunners of black separatism. For much of the 1880s and early 1890s, Ellis aligned himself with Wright Cuney, the Texas national committeeman of the Republican Party from 1886 to 1896. As the holder of one of the most important political positions of any African American in the nineteenth century, Cuney was an outspoken opponent of efforts to colonize American blacks outside the United States. Nonetheless, at the same time he cultivated Cuney, Ellis also became a leading follower of Bishop Henry Turner, the chief proponent of the back-to-Africa movement in the post-Reconstruction era, and played an important role in the Committee on Emigration at the national convention Turner called in 1893.[7]

Despite the presence of these prominent mentors, the course that Ellis ultimately charted was uniquely his own. After the mid-1890s, Ellis evinced little further interest in following Cuney into mainstream politics. But he had also reached a position that distanced him from Turner as well. Whereas Turner advocated emigration to Africa as the only plausible solution to the problems blacks faced in a thoroughly racist United States, Ellis's experiences in the borderlands led him to embrace Latin America as the ideal home for African Americans. Thus, in place of Turner's proposed diaspora linking African Americans to their past in Africa, Ellis imagined instead a diaspora connecting African Americans to their future in rapidly modernizing northern Mexico.

To Ellis, the U.S.-Mexico borderlands' status as a politically divided yet economically unified region offered several advantages to African Americans. Not only was Mexico far closer than Africa; since the international border demarcated distinct legal and political systems, crossing the boundary between Mexico and the United States allowed American blacks to liberate themselves from the discriminatory racial codes that were eroding their progress in the post-Reconstruction South. Unlike its northern neighbor, "the laws of Mexico are fair and impartial," enthused Ellis. "[As long] as the negro is suppressed as he is in the United States, the better class of them will seek new fields, and Mexico, standing at the very doors of the United States, offering inducements to all, will prove a welcome home to the negro."[8]

Furthermore, it had not escaped Ellis's attention that for all the legal differences between the two nations, the growing commercial ties between Mexico and the United States meant that they shared many familiar economic features. Like the American South, the Mexican North produced cotton and corn for the international market. In Ellis's eyes, the prominence of the American South in this endeavor was directly attributable to the agricultural skill of African American farmers. "The American negro [is] as a cotton grower and in agricultural pursuits unexcelled in the world," he explained proudly. "He has proven this by producing in the United States one fourth of the entire cotton crop of the world." If black farmers frequently courted violence when they tried to purchase agricultural land in the United States, Mexico had "millions of acres" of uncultivated lands that the country was willing to offer to whoever might develop them. It was in Mexico, in other words, that African Americans might finally achieve the independence and self-sufficiency so long celebrated in American agricultural ideology—yet so long denied them north of the border.[9]

With these goals in mind, Ellis visited Mexico City in 1888, where he persuaded President Porfirio Díaz to grant him a permit to establish a colony of 20,000 African Americans in Mexico. In addition to advancing Ellis's own plans, this unusual agreement knit together two strands of colonizationist thinking that had heretofore existed in isolation from one another across the international border. For members of the Porfirian elite, the colonization of skilled foreigners had become by the late nineteenth century a key component of their campaign to transform Mexico into a modern nation-state with a capitalist, export-oriented economy. As early as 1877, Díaz had declared that attracting immigrants who could unlock Mexico's natural wealth was one of the "imperious necessities of the republic." Ideally, the Mexican government hoped to tap the streams of European immigrants flowing across the Atlantic, which had already contributed so much to the prosperity of the United States as well as to Latin American countries such as Argentina and Uruguay. According to Porfirian reformers, such immigrants would both bring needed skills and help Mexico address its own racial "problem"—its large and unassimilated Indian population—by intermarrying with indigenous Mexicans, thus "improving" the country's racial stock—a scenario that neatly captures the linkage of race and modernization so central to the thinking of the científicos.[10]

For African Americans, of course, colonization sprung from very different roots. For Ellis and Turner, colonization involved not the project of improving the Mexican nation but rather an incipient black nationalism that saw the construction of African American communities outside the United States as providing both a refuge for oppressed blacks in the United States and a way to demonstrate American blacks' capacity for self-improvement when freed from white prejudice. Nonetheless, in spite of these divergent sources, a number of elements united the Mexican and African American visions of colonization. Advocates on both sides of the border believed that through a combination of preexisting skills, hard work, and access to natural resources, colonists would uplift not only themselves but their host countries as well. In addition, African American and Mexican backers of colonization shared a distrust of white Americans. For African Americans, it was the refusal of white Americans to accept blacks' full legal and social equality that necessitated colonization in the first place; for many Mexicans, the repeated losses of national territory to the United States and the frequent infiltrations of Anglo filibusters underscored the ongoing risks these expansionist people posed to their republic. Given these common fears, as well as the fact that Mexico had so far had little success in attracting its ideal immigrants, European Catholics, when Ellis proposed to colonize African Americans—the labor force that had proven so vital to the American South's plantation economy—Díaz and his followers proved willing to permit Ellis's extraordinary experiment.[11]

Although colonization was an explosive topic in the African American community—like Cuney, Frederick Douglass and many others saw it as undermining efforts to achieve equality within the United States—Ellis's ambitious project soon commanded favorable notice in much of the African American press. In the words of the *Cleveland Gazette*, "as Mexico is an importer of cotton and comparatively free from the prejudice which is such a barrier to our progress . . . in the South, it would not be a bad idea to make successful this colonization scheme because both would benefit by it." But Ellis's plans languished for several years as he struggled to raise the necessary funds to finance his colony. Not until 1894 did his luck change when he learned of a Mexican hacienda, incorporated under the name "Compañía Agrícola Limitada del Tlahualilo," that faced a pressing difficulty. Solving the hacienda's problem, Ellis soon realized, might solve his problem as well.[12]

Established in 1887 by a group of Spanish investors, the hacienda that caught Ellis's eye exemplified the foreign-owned, capital-intensive investments reshaping the Mexican North during the Porfiriato. In the early 1890s, the hacienda's engineers had constructed a dam on the Nazas River and diverted the river's water through an extensive network of irrigation canals, bringing under cultivation hundreds of thousands of acres of fertile land in the Laguna region of Durango. The new enterprise also imported modern industrial farming procedures from the United States: a steam cotton gin, an oil mill to process the cottonseeds, a factory to make soap out of the cottonseed oil, and an electric generator. Despite these sizable investments, however, the hacienda's managers had so far found it difficult to locate sufficient labor to work their new lands. As was often the case in northern Mexico, the area surrounding their property in Tlahualilo was sparsely inhabited, with few of the Indian communities that served as the principle reservoirs of labor during the Porfiriato.[13]

In 1894, Ellis visited the head of the Tlahualilo corporation, Juan Llamedo, at his office in Mexico City with a startling proposal. If the company would advance him funding, Ellis promised to bring experienced black field hands from the American South to settle the hacienda's lands. This unusual offer struck an immediate chord with Llamedo, who may well have reasoned, like those in Porfirio Díaz's government, that if one truly wanted to emulate the success of the American cotton plantation, one might as well draw on the same work force as planters in the United States. Llamedo and Ellis thus signed a contract to bring five thousand African American workers to the hacienda. Ellis returned to the United States in late 1894 and hired a long-time African American labor agent named "Peg" Williams (so named for his loss of a leg in the Civil War) to recruit potential colonists.[14]

Williams's efforts first manifested themselves north of the border on January 25, 1895, when flabbergasted whites in the Cotton Belt town of Tuscaloosa, Alabama, discovered hundreds of African Americans crowding the community's railroad depot, all eager to board the "paradise train" to Mexico. For the preceding month, Williams had spread the word among Alabama's African Americans that the Mexicans, "need[ing] labor badly, and prefer[ing] the colored people," were willing to offer "unequaled inducements for agricultural laborers in the growth of cotton and corn." Moreover, added Williams, in a none-too-subtle allusion to the segregationist code erected in the American South after Reconstruction, "the great Republic of Mexico extends to all of its citizens the same treatment— equal rights to all, special privileges to none."[15] Such promises found fertile ground in Tuscaloosa, which contributed close to six hundred colonists to Ellis's plan. Smaller groups from such nearby towns as Eutaw (162 colonists), Gadsden (58), Williams (24), Birmingham (24), Johns (15), and Carter (9) joined the train as it made its way west across Alabama and toward Mexico. But news of Ellis's plan apparently spread by word of mouth to even more distant locations as well, for a group of twelve colonists traveled all the way from Griffin, Georgia, almost two hundred miles to the east, to take part in the exodus.[16]

Although a few whites expressed hope that this unexpected departure of so many African Americans meant that the newly accessible borderlands might now function as an escape valve for discontented blacks, most fretted that the Mexican colonization movement would soon strip the region of its workforce. Anxious whites in Eutaw, for example, reported that "the Mexico emigration fever" had already disrupted agriculture there. "Much excitement exists here amongst land owners over the negro exodus," wrote one. "Renters are leaving plantations they have leased for this year. . . . This means much loss to the land owners and to the railroads, as the corn and cotton will not be grown to freight away."[17]

Given how the departure of a few hundred black sharecroppers could throw local agriculture into turmoil, it took little imagination for Southern whites to picture the devastation that the departure of an even larger number of African Americans for Mexico might create. "If accounts from that country prove satisfactory to them, hundreds [of African Americans] will yet go," warned one newspaper. Ellis's and "Peg" Williams's comments to the Southern press, in which they proposed to "solve the race problem" by conducting thousands of the South's "surplus colored population" to Mexico, did little to calm such fears. Wild predictions began to be heard from some quarters—that within a few years, hundreds of thousands of African Americans would abandon the South for Mexico.[18]

These rumors acquired extra potency from long-standing white fantasies of blacks as naturally preferring "the tropics" and, if allowed, of eagerly searching out a more "tropical" nation such as Mexico. In the words of the nineteenth-century journalist John Van Evrie, "the negro is as much a product of the tropics as the orange or the banana . . . and the instinct of his nature prompts, as well as urges, him onward to his original and final home." [19] During the Civil War, several members of Lincoln's cabinet resorted to such logic to argue for the colonization of freed slaves in Mexico. "It is a law of nature," declared Postmaster General Montgomery Blair, "that Negroes live in hot climates. Mexico has these hot climates. It would be as advantageous for the Mexicans as for the Negroes that the latter should be established on those lands." [20] Other Southerners doubtless recalled that the quintessential African American crop—cotton—was itself a "native of the tropics" and that its establishment in the United States had been aided in the early decades of the nineteenth century by the importation of hardier, larger-bolled cotton plants from Mexico. This linkage of Mexico, cotton, and climate had already propelled American filibusters into Mexico in the 1850s and disgruntled Confederates south of the border following the Civil War. Faced with such precedents, many white Southerners in the 1890s had little difficulty envisioning the same set of factors leading most African Americans to "find their way to Mexico." [21]

Although they rejected the racist assumptions behind such thinking, African Americans had reasons of their own to believe Mexico might prove a welcoming home. Ever since the peculiar institution first reached the Texas border region in the early nineteenth century, Mexico had served as a refuge for fugitive African Americans. By the 1850s, outraged American planters estimated that more than four thousand slaves had fled to Mexico in recent years. For its part, seeing support of runaways as a way to undermine slavery in Texas and reduce the American desire for further territorial expansion, Mexico rejected all efforts to negotiate a treaty permitting the extradition of escaped slaves back to the United States. As a result, small communities of escaped African Americans developed on the Mexican side of the Rio Grande during the mid-nineteenth century. When Frederick Law Olmsted visited the Mexican village of Piedras Negras, just across the Rio Grande from Eagle Pass, Texas, in 1856, for example, he encountered several fugitive slaves. One of the runaways told Olmsted that "the Mexican government was very just to them, they could always have their rights as fully protected as if they were Mexicans born" and described how "several negroes . . . in different parts of the country . . . had acquired wealth . . . positions of honor. . . . [and] had connected themselves by marriage, with rich old Spanish families." According to Olmsted, runaway slaves, drawn by such conditions, "were *constantly* arriving" in Piedras Negras and other towns in northern Mexico.[22]

Such incidents left an enduring imprint on African American popular culture. For many American blacks, Mexico had once represented a sanctuary from racist exploitation, the border a gateway from oppression to freedom. As one former slave later remembered, "In Mexico you could be free. . . . Hundreds of slaves did go to Mexico and got on all right. We would hear about 'em and how they was goin' to be Mexicans." It took little effort to imagine that Mexico and the border might fill these same roles yet again. Although Ellis had undertaken what was at the time the most ambitious project to capitalize on this impulse, he was by no means the first. There had been smaller African American colonization efforts in Mexico since at least the middle of the nineteenth century. In 1857, for example, Luis N. Fouché, a free African American from Florida, established a colony named "Eureka" near Tampico, and that same year some forty-odd African Americans from New Orleans settled on land granted them by the Mexican government near Veracruz.[23] Following the collapse of Reconstruction, such efforts multiplied. Plans were floated for "The American Colored Men's Mexican Colonization Company" to found a colony of farmers in Sonora. African Americans in New Jersey and Indiana attempted to organize a sugar- and coffee-growing colony in Mexico. During the 1890s, blacks in California incorporated "The Colored Mexican Colonization Company," the "Afro-American Colonization Company of Mexico," and similar associations for the purposes of "owning, selling, colonizing, and farming lands, [and] raising, buying, and selling stock . . . in the Republic of Mexico."[24]

Apparently having concluded along with these other would-be colonists that Mexico represented the new promised land, few of those who joined Ellis's enterprise planned to return to the United States. Many reportedly sold off whatever belongings they could not take with them, and some, as they waited to board the "paradise train" to Mexico, finally felt free to voice what they had long thought of the oppression meted out by their white neighbors. In the words of one white observer: "While they were at the depot waiting for the train to take them to Mexico they indulged in the most open and insulting abuse of the white men of the community. . . . Had it not been that they were on the eve of what was sincerely hoped to be their permanent departure they would have been roughly

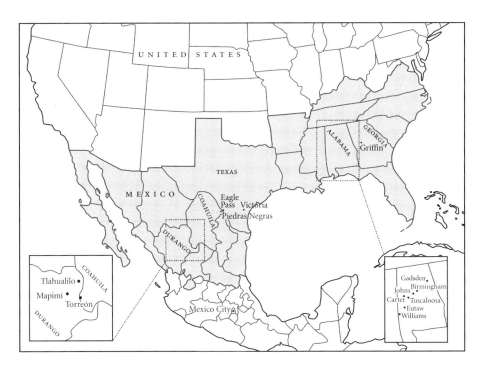

The borderlands of the African American Colony of 1895.

handled." To Ellis and the colonists who joined his project, emigrating to Mexico must surely have seemed like their long-hoped-for opportunity to leave such threats behind them forever.[25]

From Plantation to Hacienda

Traveling first by one of the new railroad lines connecting Mexico with the United States and then in horse-drawn wagons emblazoned with the slogan "God and Liberty," Ellis and his colonists reached Tlahualilo in early February. The hacienda owners had prepared a township for the colonists to settle in, to which Ellis apparently gave the name "Razas," Spanish for "peoples" or "races." In typical Mexican fashion, the village contained an open square at its center, surrounded by abutting adobe homes. Ellis appointed three policemen and one justice of the peace from among the colonists and soon established himself in a large house that served not only as his residence but as a store and warehouse as well. As Ellis later recalled, it was "the completest negro town ever started. . . . The preachers began to perform marriages—some intermarriages. Seven children were born and the dream of my life was being realized. I had lived to see the Afro-American in 'the Country of God and Liberty.' " In a few more years, Ellis predicted, his colonists would own much of northern Mexico and "be as prosperous as Americans."[26]

Yet despite this promising start and the familiar American-manufactured plows, harrows, and harnesses that the hacienda's managers bought for their new workers, many features of life in Mexico proved unsettling for the colonists. Among the first to profess dissatisfaction with conditions in Tlahualilo was "Peg" Williams. After only two weeks at the colony, Williams hastened for Texas, where he issued a circular disassociating himself from Ellis's colony. Williams's complaints highlight the myriad distinctions that existed between the American cotton plantation and the Mexican hacienda in the 1890s, despite their similar economic function of producing cotton and corn for the international market. A substantial number of these differences had to do with cultural matters such as food and language. Williams classified the unfamiliar food provided to the newly arrived colonists as "such slops as the Mexicans use" and he described the manager of the hacienda as "a Spaniard who has never had any experience in handling colored people and can speak very little English." But Williams also expressed concern at the forms of labor control used in northern Mexico, particularly the use of armed and mounted supervisors, which struck him as deeply troubling.[27]

The extent to which the other colonists shared Williams's critique of conditions in Tlahualilo is harder to fathom. One contingent, finding life in Mexico less appealing than imagined, abandoned the colony at the first opportunity, despite Tlahualilo's daunting isolation. In interviews with white newspapermen, the returning colonists echoed many of Williams's criticisms about the food and living conditions. Although similar manufactured goods, for instance, could be found on both sides of the border, prices were much higher in Mexico: "a common jeans which sells [in Alabama] at thirty cents a yard, sells [in Mexico] for $2.25 and common red canton flannel, worth here 12 1/2 or 15 cents a yard, sells there for $1.25."[28] Tlahualilo's unfamiliar and arid landscape also provoked concern. Despite the hacienda's extensive irrigation works, many colonists became alarmed by Tlahualilo's long dry season, during which it might not rain for months at a time. Such parched conditions, some feared, would destroy their cotton plants and, along with them, any hopes of making a living in their new home. To prevent such an outcome, large numbers of colonists began shortly after their arrival in Mexico to organize fervent prayer meetings to implore rain.[29]

Seemingly most alarming of all, however, for those colonists who abandoned the colony was their sense that while the laws of the Republic of Mexico did not incorporate the racist measures of the Jim Crow South, they did little to protect agricultural laborers from economic exploitation. Debt peonage, for example, was not uncommon on Mexican haciendas during the Porfiriato. Furthermore, the physical layout of the colony—a hollow square of adobe buildings, with a gated entrance at each of its four corners—although typical for northern Mexico, where haciendas often had to withstand attacks by Indian raiders, soon led to rumors among the colonists that they were being kept in a "prison," a conclusion that the presence of armed Mexican overseers did little to assuage. Many of the returning colonists declared that such conditions led them to fear being reduced to forced servitude in Tlahualilo—no doubt a palpable anxiety for a group so recently freed from bondage in the United States, whose rights in Mexico as disaffected American citizens and not yet legalized Mexican citizens remained unclear. To those colonists who fled, in short, the problem with the Mexican hacienda was that it was too foreign in its food, housing, language, dependence on irrigation, and the like—yet all too familiar in regard to its labor controls and to the economically dispossessed status of its farmworkers.[30]

These signs of discontent underscore a fundamental tension in Ellis's colonization plans. While Ellis's followers had come to Mexico out of a desire for personal liberty and economic advancement, the owners of the Tlahualilo hacienda possessed the far less lofty goal of securing a reliable workforce. Moreover, while Ellis and his followers envisioned agriculture as the first step to black self-sufficiency, the hacienda owners sought a permanent pool of laborers, not temporary sojourners who would soon move on to other pursuits. These differing perspectives often placed the two groups at cross-purposes. Before arriving in Mexico, the colonists had signed with Ellis a sharecropping contract similar to those in the American South. In exchange for being furnished with sixty acres of land and "farming implements, such as are used in the United States," each family would give 50 percent of their cotton and corn crop to the hacienda. In an effort to achieve greater productivity, however, the hacienda owners soon tried to organize the colonists in large gangs working under the direction of hacienda supervisors, as they often did with their Mexican workers. The colonists bristled at this change, seeing it an assault on each family's freedom to direct its labor as it saw best—a liberty that was, for African Americans, among the most significant advances achieved during their recent transition from slavery.[31]

Other aspects of unrest at the colony can be attributed to Ellis himself. To be sure, by many measures, Ellis's colonization scheme was already a remarkable success. After two decades of effort, Ellis's much-heralded mentor, Bishop Turner, had only managed to transport about one thousand American blacks to Africa. In contrast, Ellis had settled a nearly equal number of African Americans in Mexico in just a few months. Yet, as much as the colonists may have shared Ellis's larger goal of founding a black homeland in Mexico, it is also worth noting that they possessed no deep investment in Ellis as a leader. Most had not even met him prior to their departure from Alabama, as it was "Peg" Williams who had done the actual recruiting of participants. All had at least some reason to be suspicious of Ellis. After all, the colony in Tlahualilo functioned not only as a nascent black homeland but also as a money-making scheme: according to his contract with the hacienda, Ellis was to receive a percentage of the crop, and he ran the store on the hacienda from which the colonists bought their supplies. In addition, while Ellis was a creature of the borderlands—a well-to-do businessman comfortable conversing in Spanish with government officials and investors in Mexico City—his followers had grown up hundreds of miles from the border region, in the cotton plantations and coal camps of Alabama and Georgia. They found the language, food, and cultural norms of northern Mexico disorienting, and they found themselves treated more like Mexican *peones* than as valued newcomers. Ironically, the very qualities that had made Ellis so successful in the borderlands—his entrepreneurial skills, his chameleonlike ability to shift racial identities, his facility with languages, and his general ease at crossing political, linguistic, and cultural boundaries—rendered him to the colonists an uncertain leader, whose commitment to their cause seemed questionable.[32]

Still, the colony might have been able to weather these obstacles had it not encountered a difficulty that Ellis and his Mexican backers had failed to predict. Despite moving to the unfamiliar disease environment of northern Mexico, the colonists had not received any vaccinations or other medical precautions prior to leaving Alabama. In July 1895, just a few months after their arrival, a mysterious malady broke out among them. When several died despite the efforts of a local Mexican doctor, the desperate hacienda managers hired an American doctor named Trolitnger from San Antonio, Texas, to care for the colonists. Unfortunately, Trolitnger had little more success combating the disease than his Mexican counterpart, for, as he confessed, "nothing in its nature has heretofore come under my observation." The rapid spread of this mysterious illness confirmed in many colonists' minds the dangers of a seemingly very foreign Mexico. Before long, the colony was, in Trolitnger's words, "panic stricken. . . . The victims are afraid to go to bed, for they say that no one has ever arisen who has done so."[33]

The situation fast flared into crisis. When perhaps as many as seventy colonists died of disease at Tlahualilo, most of the survivors fled the colony on July 20 (although sixty or so remained behind to harvest what observers termed an excellent crop of cotton and corn). After abandoning Tlahualilo, many colonists headed for the mining town of Mapimí, the nearest railway stop. But few had any money to purchase return tickets, and their food soon began to run out, reducing them to eating the seeds from mesquite trees. Other colonists headed for the city of Torreón, some fifty miles away, where most were intercepted on the city's outskirts by Mexican police. Somehow, though, several members of the group eluded their would-be captors. Making their way to the U.S. consulate in Torreón, they reasserted their status as American citizens and insisted that the consuls help them.[34]

Initially, the startled consuls, unwilling to bear the cost of transporting the colonists back to a United States they had abandoned so readily a few months earlier, tried to place the colonists among the American enterprises expanding into northern Mexico. But despite the promise of the more familiar setting of an American corporation, the colonists refused such offers. Rather than scattering to these potential sources of employment, they opted instead to remain together. While this effort only drew complaints from the U.S. consuls, it offers a clue to the bonds that may have united the colonists. One of the colonists' first acts upon reaching the hacienda in Mexico had been to raise a church, and several of the leaders who emerged during the flight from Tlahualilo were ministers.[35] Given such evidence, it seems probable that at least some of the groups that joined Ellis's colony were, in fact, church congregations that decided communally to move en masse to Mexico. Doing so would not only make sense on a social level (it is far easier to contemplate moving to a strange new country if one does so as part of an already established community), it may well have resonated with African American religious traditions, particularly African Americans' close identification with the book of Exodus and its story of an oppressed people migrating out of bondage.[36]

As the consuls debated what to do with the colonists, attention throughout the United States focused on the latest developments in Mexico. With great relief, many white commentators, noting the colonists' unhappy experiences south of the border, concluded that the risk of a mass migration of African Americans to Mexico had been overstated and that conditions for African Americans in the South were not as bad as many blacks asserted. "This is the home of the negro," declared the *Alabama Courier*. "He should better accept the Southern sun and the cotton fields and make of himself a more useful citizen."[37] Responding to such sentiments, John H. Bankhead, the congressional representative from the sixth district, which included both Tuscaloosa and Greene counties, urged the State Department to aid these "poor, deluded ignorant colored people [who] were my constituents." Amid growing public concern, President Grover Cleveland authorized the War Department on July 26, 1895, to send rations to the colonists and instructed the consuls to contract with the Mexican Central Railway Company to transport the colonists back to the United States.[38]

Upon hearing this news, the colonists may have thought that their ordeal was drawing to a close. But a final tragedy awaited. Following their flight from the Tlahualilo hacienda, a significant number of the colonists had developed smallpox. Texas authorities responded to the potential passage of these sick colonists across their territory with what was to become an increasingly common tactic: recasting the United States–Mexico border as a medical boundary. As the colonists crossed the international border into the Texas village of Eagle Pass, they were quarantined at a camp outside town limits, a condition that would last for almost two months, during which time close to sixty colonists died. Not until late September, when the Marine Hospital Service certified them as free of smallpox, were the colonists allowed to return to Alabama.[39]

Between the Mexican North and the American South

The voyage of the remaining colonists back to their homes in Alabama marked the end of Ellis's experiment to colonize African Americans in northern Mexico. For a while, Ellis maintained that his project remained feasible, given the greater political freedoms and economic opportunities available to African Americans south of the border. But the owners of the hacienda in Tlahualilo retained little enthusiasm for the project. Having lost money on Ellis's scheme, they reported they were seeking Mexican workers for their properties and would make no further attempts to "import negroes."[40] Mexican authorities manifested a similar lack of interest in new efforts to colonize African Americans in Mexico. In his message to the state congress, the governor of Durango, Juan Manuel Flores, summed up the prevailing official view: the Tlahualilo experiment had failed because of the unreasonable complaints of the colonists, who had revealed themselves to be less hard-working than native Mexican labor. "The colonists," Flores maintained, "were treated perfectly; they had no reason for complaint. . . . The company fulfilled its obligations and even exceeded them, and treated the colonists better than its other workers." Juan Llamedo of "la Compañía Agrícola Limitada del Tlahualilo" concurred. The colony's failures, he wrote American authorities, could be attributed to "the laziness of the Negroes" rather than to any shortcomings of the hacienda system.[41] Mexico's government and business leaders thus echoed the conclusions reached across the border by many Southern whites: the collapse of Ellis's colony demonstrated the essential correctness of prevailing labor arrangements and the folly of any attempt at change.

Within this conclusion lurked a hardening of racial barriers for African Americans in Mexico. Ellis may have presented Mexico as the "land of God and liberty," a new land unmarked by prejudice toward blacks, but peoples of African descent in fact possessed a long and complicated history in Mexico. During the colonial period, New Spain had been an active participant in the Atlantic slave trade — so much so, that during Mexico's early years, Africans had outnumbered Europeans in the colony. Between the beginning of the slave trade in 1519 and its end in 1827, some 200,000 slaves were imported into New Spain to compensate for the indigenous laborers lost to disease and conquest and as an ironic outcome of the policies of the Spanish crown, which outlawed Indian slavery in 1542 and enacted other measures during this period to protect Mexico's native population from overexploitation. These Africans and their Mexican-born children were exposed to grueling labor in Mexican mines, plantations, and households and subjected to a colonial caste system that divided them into a number of different categories — *bozal* (African born), *pardo* (of African-Indian ancestry), *mulatto* (of African-European ancestry), and *negro* (of African ancestry)—while keeping them at the bottom of a complex hierarchy of gradations between light- and dark-skinned peoples.[42]

Following independence in the early nineteenth century, Mexico eliminated slavery and the racial caste system, and Afro-Mexicans as a category disappeared from the census and other official documents. Although there continued to be clusters of Mexicans of African descent in certain regions of Mexico—most notably in the plantation zone near Veracruz and in the Pacific coast states of Guerrero and Oaxaca—most Afro-Mexicans intermarried into Mexico's mestizo majority. This seeming disappearance of Afro-Mexicans from the newly independent Mexican republic was facilitated by the limited arrival of additional persons of African ancestry in the years following emancipation in 1827. The few that did immigrate were almost exclusively refugees from the United States (discontented freedmen, escaped slaves, or Seminole Indians and others of mixed Native American/African ancestry). These newcomers clustered along Mexico's lightly inhabited northern border, where, as suggested by the runaway slave whom Olmsted interviewed in Piedras Negras, they were welcomed as valuable allies in developing the frontier and securing it against Anglo and Indian raiders.[43]

The often hostile response that greeted Ellis's colonists in 1895, however, brought to the surface the altered racial landscape that existed within Mexico by the turn of the century. A series of interlocking changes, as well as lingering prejudices against peoples of African descent dating from the colonial period, had made African Americans—even skilled cotton growers such as Ellis's colonists—less appealing to many Mexicans. There was no longer a pressing need to protect the nation's northern borderlands, which had been transformed by the late nineteenth century from a vulnerable frontier to a relatively stable international boundary. At the same time, in an effort to modernize Mexico, Porfirio Díaz's científicos had begun to import the latest scientific racism, with its highly negative views of peoples of African descent, from the United States and Europe. Finally, the construction of a new Mexican national type, the mestizo, obscured the once prominent place of Afro-Mexicans in New Spain by defining mestizaje as forged solely through the mixture of white and Indian races in Mexico.[44]

As a result of these shifts, African Americans who made their way south of the border in the 1890s experienced for the first time Mexican efforts to emulate customs north of the border and segregate African Americans. In Tampico, for example, African Americans hired to work on one of Mexico's railroads found themselves refused service at the local hospital, as Mexicans followed the example of the white Americans employed on the Tampico railway, who refused to work alongside the black newcomers. Similarly, in 1895 three African Americans were refused service at the dining room of the Hotel Iturbide in Mexico City, much to the approval of several white Americans at the same establishment.[45]

Once news of Ellis's colony spread, the tension that the Mexican supporters of the project had initially papered over—that between Mexico's desire for skilled colonists and its prejudice toward peoples of African descent—exploded into public debate. Many in the Mexican press brooded about the risk of Mexico becoming a dumping ground for hundreds of thousands of unwanted blacks from a United States anxious to export its "race problem" to its southern neighbor. While almost no Mexican commentator opposed the idea of colonization per se, many, adopting a line of reasoning that echoed contemporary debate in the southern United States, insisted that African Americans were not the proper sort of colonists for the republic. Blacks were inherently lazy and uncivilized. The "corrupt, effeminate, and vicious inhabitants of the [American] South" would therefore not uplift Mexico. They would only spread bad habits and pollute the "pure race of our Indians," complicating Mexico's efforts to solve its own racial problems.[46]

Yet, for all the distress that many in Mexico expressed at the possibility of large-scale black immigration, individual African Americans, especially educated and economically successful ones such as Ellis, continued to find Mexico a welcoming home. Henry O. Flipper, the first African American graduate of West Point, for example, spent most of his postmilitary career south of the border because of the greater tolerance he experienced in Porfirian Mexico. Such opportunities persisted because Mexico shared with the rest of Latin America a system of race relations that embraced class as well as complexion. Wealthy, accomplished individuals would not be treated simply on the basis of their color but according to their status as well—a situation that helps to explain why an entrepreneur like Ellis found his reception in Mexico so cordial, while the colonists at Tlahualilo, who discovered themselves occupying essentially the same class position as Mexican peones, received far different treatment.[47]

As a result of the greater tolerance he experienced south of the border,

Ellis remained involved in Mexican affairs throughout his life. Immediately following the colony's collapse, Ellis had disappeared from sight, fearing that legal action might arise out of the failed venture. He re-emerged a few years later in New York as a prominent businessman with substantial interests in the estate of Benjamin Hotchkiss, an inventor of the machine gun, and in the New York Westchester Water Company. Although he experimented in the early 1900s with posing as Hawaiian rather than Hispanic and temporarily acquired the nickname "the Duke of Abyssinia" for his efforts to found a colony of American blacks in that African kingdom in 1904, Ellis never abandoned his interest in Mexico. He named one of his children Porfirio Díaz Ellis after the Mexican dictator and supported Victoriano Huerta and then Venustiano Carranza during the Mexican Revolution. By the time of his death in 1923, Ellis was president of companies with interests south of the border — the "Mexican Securities and Construction Company" and the "Mexican & Toluca Light & Power Company" — and had been living in Mexico City for almost a year, negotiating a series of business deals with the Mexican government.[48]

Whatever bitterness Ellis may have harbored towards the Mexican government or the owners of the Tlahualilo hacienda for their failure to support a sequel to his 1895 colony, it was doubtless tempered by an awareness of the individual benefits that remained available to African Americans in Mexico. Indeed, if the great problem of the twentieth century was, as W. E. B. Du Bois famously observed in 1903, the color line, Ellis had found at least a partial solution: the border line. This interconnection between racial boundaries and political boundaries emerged most clearly for Ellis in 1909, when during a journey from Mexico City to New York City, he crossed the border at Eagle Pass, the same town where many of his former colonists had been quarantined fourteen years earlier. Although he had been traveling in a first-class Pullman railroad coach all the way from the Mexican capital, once Ellis crossed the border into Texas he was forced, over his protests, to move to the Jim Crow car.[49]

While individual African Americans such as Ellis continued to find Mexico a refuge from American racism well into the twentieth century, never again after the collapse of the colony of 1895 would commentators on either side of the border prophesy the imminent migration of thousands of American blacks into Mexico. One may ponder the apparent fragility of Ellis's alternative borderlands or wonder at what might have happened if disease had not broken out when it did or if Ellis had proven to be a more charismatic leader, able to rally the colonists at a time of crisis. But any consideration of such contingencies must also take into account Ellis's prescience as to the structural changes that had by the late nineteenth century brought the Mexican North and the American South into an intimate embrace with one another. It was an insight that received one of its greatest confirmations just as Ellis's experiment collapsed. Beginning in the early 1890s, the boll weevil (an "enemy [that] came from Mexico, and is sometimes known as the Mexican weevil") spread via the newly developed networks between Mexico and the United States into the southern United States. Crossing from Mexico's cotton fields into Texas sometime around 1892, the boll weevil had by 1911 migrated to the cotton-growing regions of Alabama that contributed so many colonists to Ellis's project little more than a decade earlier, devastating the local economy. Just a few years later, the pink bollworm, another cotton pest, spread across the border via Mexican cotton sold in the United States, wreaking havoc on cotton growing in Arkansas, Louisiana, Mississippi, Florida, and other Southern states.[50]

Humans would join this flow of goods and animals through the new borderlands between the Mexican North and the American South, albeit not always in forms imagined by Ellis. As early as 1904, American cotton growers in Mississippi were experimenting with hiring Mexicans as temporary laborers, a development that prefigured the thousands of agricultural workers who were to come to the United States under the *bracero* program of the 1940s–60s. Ironically, among the braceros during these decades were many Mexicans from the Tlahualilo region, the descendents of workers for the "Compañía Agrícola Limitada del Tlahualilo." By the 1980s, increasing numbers of Mexicans had discovered that for them *el Norte* was, in fact, the American South. Mexican *colonias* sprouted in Southern cities and rural villages alike, adding a new layer of complexity to the South's long-standing black/white system of race relations. Mexican immigrants found ready employment in Southern chicken-packing plants, hotels, restaurants, landscaping services, and carpet factories, and picked the tobacco, tomatoes, and other Southern crops that had once been harvested by African Americans like Ellis's colonists. During the same period, as the 1994 North American Free Trade Agreement attempted, with only limited success, to bridge the legal and economic divisions still fissuring the borderlands, the textile mills and assembly lines of the American South began a migration of their own, moving to the low-wage cities of the Mexican North.[51]

These flows of parasites, peoples, and industries across the U.S.-Mexico border highlight the variety of registers on which the borderlands that took shape in the closing decades of the nineteenth century need to be interpreted. Most immediately, of course, the demarcation of the U.S.-Mexico border involved the *national* project of consolidating the bounded territory of the nation-state. The resulting border region, however, often functioned *transnationally*. The newly defined borders of the late-nineteenth-century nation-state did not simply represent limits; they also represented opportunities for those, like Ellis and countless others after him, who knew how to move across them. Not only could one seek a more favorable legal climate on one side of the line or discover a new source of income by managing the passage of goods and migrants across the border; one could even assign new meanings to as seemingly national an issue as citizenship, as Ellis cleverly did by claiming to be Mexican north of the international boundary and American south of it.

And yet, if they were national and transnational, the turn-of-the-century borderlands were also *transregional*. Within two large, heterogeneous nations like Mexico and the United States there existed substantial regional variations, which Ellis's colonization effort cast in sharp relief. The colony at Tlahualilo was not just an outgrowth of increased contact between Mexico and the United States. Rather, it was profoundly influenced by a variety of regional factors: labor conditions in the Mexican North; race relations in the American South (the dwelling place of the vast majority of African Americans in the nineteenth century); the shared status of the Mexican North and the American South as formerly isolated and economically backward regions of their home countries, dominated by plantation agriculture and dependent on the industrialized North of the United States for markets and goods.

Three decades after C. Vann Woodward first questioned the uniqueness of Southern history and called for scholarship comparing the American South with other regions of the globe, it has, oddly enough, fallen to Latin American fiction writers to offer some of the most compelling observations on the complex and contradictory relationship between the U.S. South and its Spanish-American neighbors. Mario Vargas Llosa, for example, noted in 1991 that for all the obvious differences between them, common historical traditions confronted authors in both regions, creating an intellectual kinship between Latin American authors and such Southern writers as William Faulkner:

The world out of which [Faulkner] created his own world is quite similar to a Latin American world. In the Deep South, as in Latin America, two different cultures coexist, two different historical traditions, two different races—all forming a difficult coexistence full of prejudice and violence. There also exists the extraordinary importance of the past, which is always present in contemporary life. In Latin America we have the same thing. The world of Faulkner is preindustrial, or, at least, resisting industrialization, modernization, urbanization, exactly like many Latin American societies.

Indeed, the "two souths," the Mexican novelist Carlos Fuentes has written, share an "image of defeat, of separation, of doubt[,] of tragedy" that links them to one another while simultaneously distinguishing them from the northern United States. For his part, Jorge Luis Borges has commented that like Latin America, the American South is "creole," part of a "peculiar world" composed of "rivers of brown water, disorderly villas, black slaves, equestrian, lazy, and cruel wars."[52]

Although historians have only begun to explore the expansive new vistas these observations suggest, the landscape they point toward was already familiar to Ellis over a century ago. As his colonization plan reveals, he had recognized that the border did not simply divide Mexico and the United States. Rather, it created a transregional borderlands where the Mexican North and the American South collided, conflicted, fused, confused, and—for a moment at least—offered a glimpse of new alternatives.[53]

Notes

1 The concept of the territoriality is explored by Charles S. Maier, "Consigning the Twentieth Century to History: Alternative Narratives for the Modern Era," *American Historical Review* 105 (June 2000): 816–25; Victor Zúñiga, "Nations and Borders: Romantic Nationalism and the Project of Modernity," in David Spener and Kathleen Staudt, eds., *The U.S.-Mexico Border: Transcending Divisions, Contesting Identities* (Boulder: Lynne Rienner, 1998); Raymond B. Craib, "A Nationalist Metaphysics: State Fixations, National Maps, and the Geo-Historical Imagination in Nineteenth-Century Mexico," *Hispanic American Historical Review* 82 (February 2002): 33–68; and Michel Foucher, *Fronts et frontières: un tour du monde géopolitique* (Paris: Librairie Arthème Fayard, 1988). The growing circulation of labor and capital between Mexico and the United

States at the turn of the century has been surveyed by a number of scholars. See Ramón Eduardo Ruiz, *The People of Sonora and Yankee Capitalists* (Tucson: University of Arizona Press, 1988); Miguel Tinker Salas, *In the Shadow of the Eagles: Sonora and the Transformation of the Border during the Porfiriato* (Berkeley: University of California Press, 1997); Emilio Zamora, *The World of the Mexican Worker in Texas* (College Station: Texas A&M University Press, 1993); David M. Pletcher, *The Diplomacy of Trade and Investment: American Economic Expansion in the Hemisphere, 1865–1900* (Columbia: University of Missouri Press, 1998), 77–113; and Roberto R. Calderón, *Mexican Coal Mining Labor in Texas and Coahuila, 1880–1930* (College Station: Texas A&M University Press, 2000).

2   For a fuller description of the progression from frontier to border in northern Mexico, see Friedrich Katz, *The Secret War in Mexico: Europe, the United States, and the Mexican Revolution* (Chicago: University of Chicago Press, 1981), 7–21.

3   Ellis awaits a proper biography. For preliminary studies of his career, consult J. Fred Rippy, "A Negro Colonization Project in Mexico, 1895," *Journal of Negro History* 6 (January 1921): 66–73; Alfred W. Reynolds, "The Alabama Negro Colony in Mexico, 1894–1896," *Alabama Review* 5 (October 1952): 243–68, and *Alabama Review* 6 (January 1953): 31–58; Karl Jacoby, "From Plantation to Hacienda: The Mexican Colonization Movement in Alabama," *Alabama Heritage* (Winter 1995): 34–43; and William R. Scott, "A Study of Afro-American and Ethiopian Relations, 1896–1941" (Ph.D. diss., Princeton University, 1971). Note that a recent, otherwise exhaustive study of Americans in Mexico by a major American scholar makes no reference to Ellis and includes only four passing mentions of African Americans in 677 pages. See John Mason Hart, *Empire and Revolution: The Americans in Mexico since the Civil War* (Berkeley: University of California Press, 2002).

4   For accounts of Ellis's early years, see "An American Promoter in Abyssinia," *The World's Work* 7 (March 1904): 4601–2 and *Who's Who in New York, 1918*, 336.

5   Physical descriptions of Ellis can be found in the *New York Tribune* and the *New York Sun* as quoted in Richard Pankhurst, "William H. Ellis/Guillaume Enriques Ellesio: The First Black American Ethiopianist?" *Ethiopia Observer* 15 (1972): 89, 105. See also the *New York Herald*, 26 and 30 June 1904; *New York Tribune*, 25 June 1904; and the *New York Times*, 28 June and 19 July 1904. For a contrasting account from a boyhood friend, who describes Ellis as "the son of a slave," see *Washington Post*, 28 June 1904.

6   Ellis and his family appear in the 1880 federal population census, Victoria, Texas. Film T9-1330, p. 172C, record group 29, National Archives. For an example of Ellis's creation of Guillermo Enrique Eliseo, see the *Chicago Tribune*, 28 June 1904, and *Trow's General Directory of the Boroughs of Manhattan and the Bronx, 1900* (New York: Trow Directory, Printing and Bookbinding, 1900), which lists "Eliseo, Guillermo" and "Ellis, Wm H" as separate individuals, despite giving

the same home address. Ellis signed his marriage certificate (which lists his color as "brown") as both "Guillermo E. Eliseo" and "W. H. Ellis." Marriage Certificate #10242, 27 May 1903, New York City Department of Records and Information Services. For examples of Ellis using his non–African American persona to gain entry into hotels, see the *New York Herald*, 30 June 1904 and the *Washington Post*, 30 June 1904. It was not an uncommon tactic for light-complexioned African Americans to present themselves as Spanish at the turn of the century. The son-in-law and daughter of Norris Wright Cuney, one of Ellis's political allies in Texas, successfully passed as "Spanish-American" for several years. Maud Cuney-Hare, *Norris Wright Cuney: A Tribune of the Black People* (New York: G. K. Hall, 1995 [1913]), xvii–xviii, 154.

7 Cuney's opposition to colonization is discussed by his daughter in Cuney-Hare, *Norris Wright Cuney*, 31. For more on Ellis's relationship with Turner, see Edwin S. Redkey, *Black Exodus: Black Nationalist and Back-to-Africa Movements, 1890–1910* (New Haven: Yale University Press, 1969), 176, 188, 193. Ellis's description of his African yet Cuban/Mexican ancestry comes from an interview in the *New York Sun* reprinted in Pankhurst, "William H. Ellis," 105.

8 Quotes from Ellis come from an interview with him printed in the *San Antonio Express*, 14 October 1895. A clipping of this interview can be found in entry 95, Despatches from United States Consuls in Piedras Negras, 1868–1905, microcopy 299, record group 59, National Archives.

9 *San Antonio Express*, 14 October 1895.

10 For more on colonization in Mexico, see Chester Lloyd Jones, *Mexico and its Reconstruction* (New York: D. Appleton, 1922), 220–38 (quote from Díaz on 229, n.12), and Moisés González Navarro, *La colonización en Mexico, 1877–1910* (México, D.F.: Talleres de Impresión de Estampillas y Valores, 1960). For more on ideas of race in Porfirian Mexico, see Alan Knight, "Racism, Revolution, and *Indigenismo*: Mexico, 1910–1940," in Richard Graham, ed., *The Idea of Race in Latin America, 1870–1940* (Austin: University of Texas Press, 1990), 78–81.

11 For a discussion of colonization in general and Mexican fears of white American colonists in particular, see Moisés González Navarro, *Los extranjeros en México y los mexicanos en el extranjero, 1821–1970* (México, D.F.: El Colegio de México, 1994), 2: 151–63.

12 *Cleveland Gazette*, 6 July 1889. Other coverage of Ellis in the African American press can be found in the *Cleveland Gazette*, 29 June and 13 July 1889; the *Kansas Blackman*, 8 June 1894; and the St. Paul and Minneapolis *Appeal*, 1 March 1890. Note the wide geographic dispersal. Even the *Las Vegas Optic*, 28 October 1889, makes reference to a Mexican colonization project.

13 For more on the Tlahualilo company and region, see *Escritura y estatutos de la Compañía Agrícola Limitada del Tlahaulilo* (México, D.F.: Imprenta de Francisco Diaz de Leon, 1889); C. P. MacKie, "Canal Irrigation in Modern Mexico," *Engineering Magazine* 13 (May 1897): 197; *New York Evening Post*, 25 July 1895;

Diccionario Porrúa de historia, biografía y geografía de México (México: Editorial Porrúa, 1986), 2936–37; Juan Ballestros Porta, *Explotación individual o colectiva?: El caso de los ejidos de Tlahualilo* (México, D.F.: Instituto Mexicano de Investigaciones Económicas, 1964), 21–25. Foreign involvement in the Tlahualilo region is explored in depth by William K. Meyers in *Forge of Progress, Crucible of Revolt: The Origins of the Mexican Revolution in La Comarca Lagunera, 1880–1911* (Albuqerque: University of New Mexico Press, 1994). The Tlahualilo region's postrevolutionary history is examined in Jocelyn Olcott, "Las Hijas de La Malinche: Women's Organizing and State Formation in Postrevolutionary Mexico" (Ph.D. diss., Yale University, 2000). For an overview of hacienda conditions during the Porfiriato, see Friedrich Katz, "Labor Conditions on Haciendas in Porfirian Mexico: Some Trends and Tendencies," *Hispanic American Historical Review* 54 (February 1974): 1–47.

14 The number of colonists specified in Ellis's contract varies in the sources. Southern newspapers and "Peg" Williams cited five thousand; a reporter for the *New York Evening Post* gave the number as a thousand. See Mobile *Daily Register*, 3 January 1895; and the *New York Evening Post*, Thursday, 25 July 1895. For a copy of the contract signed by the colonists, see House of Representatives, 54th Cong., 1st sess., Document No. 169 (hereafter HD), 4–5.

15 HD, 59. For more on Williams, see William F. Holmes, "Labor Agents and the Georgia Exodus," *South Atlantic Quarterly* 69 (Autumn 1980): 436–49.

16 These numbers come from the list of names featured in HD, 47–56. It is not entirely clear who compiled this list or whether it is complete. But it does seem to be useful as a rough guide to the makeup of the colony, and the total number is in keeping with estimates printed in newspaper articles at the time.

17 Quoted in Mobile *Daily Register*, 10 March 1895.

18 Mobile *Daily Register*, 3 January 1895; Eutaw *Whig and Observer*, 7 March 1895.

19 Van Evrie quoted in George M. Fredrickson, *The Black Image in the White Mind: The Debate on Afro-American Character and Destiny, 1817–1914* (Middletown: Wesleyan University Press, 1987 [1971]), 138.

20 Thomas D. Schoonover, ed., *Mexican Lobby: Matias Romero in Washington, 1861–1867* (Lexington: University Press of Kentucky, 1986), 5. The Mexican ambassador, Matias Romero, was not opposed to the idea of freed slaves emigrating to Mexico, but only if they were willing to become Mexican citizens. For more on Lincoln and colonization, see Michael Vorenberg, "Abraham Lincoln and the Politics of Black Colonization," in Thomas F. Schwartz, ed., *"For a Vast Future Also": Essays from the Journal of the Abraham Lincoln Association* (New York: Fordham University Press, 1999), 35–56.

21 For more on the importation of Mexican cotton into the United States, see Eugene Clyde Brooks, *The Story of Cotton and the Development of the Cotton States* (Chicago: Rand McNally, 1911), 329, and James L. Watkins, *King Cotton: A*

Historical and Statistical Review, 1790–1908 (New York: James L. Watkins, 1908), 15, 126, 162, 164, 172, 193. The phrase about the supposed emigration of African Americans to Mexico comes from Edward L. Ayers, *The Promise of the New South: Life after Reconstruction* (New York: Oxford University Press, 1992), 150. For accounts of white Southerners moving to Mexico after the Civil War, see Andrew F. Rolle, *The Lost Cause: The Confederate Exodus to Mexico* (Norman: University of Oklahoma Press, 1965) and W. C. Nunn, *Escape from Reconstruction* (Westport, Conn.: Greenwood, 1974 [1956]).

22 Quoted in Randolph B. Campbell, *An Empire for Slavery: The Peculiar Institution in Texas, 1821–1865* (Baton Rouge: Louisiana State University Press, 1989), 64; and Frederick Law Olmsted, *A Journey Through Texas: Or, a Saddle-Trip on the Southwestern Frontier* (New York: Dix, Edwards, 1857), 323–25 (emphasis in the original). See also Ronnie C. Tyler, "Fugitive Slaves in Mexico," *Journal of Negro History* 57 (January 1972): 1–12; Alwyn Barr, *Black Texans: A History of Negroes in Texas, 1528–1971* (Austin: Jenkins, 1973), 28–32; Mrs. William Cazneau [Cora Montgomery], *Eagle Pass: Or, Life on the Border* (Austin: Pemberton Press, 1966 [1852]), 139–40; Kenneth Wiggins Porter, *The Negro on the American Frontier* (New York: Arno, 1971), 424–35, 463–65; and Quintard Taylor, *In Search of the Racial Frontier: African Americans in the American West, 1528–1990* (New York: Norton, 1998), 60–61.

23 Quote from Felix Haywood in George P. Rawick, ed., *The American Slave: A Composite Autobiography, Texas Narratives* (Westport, Conn.: Greenwood, 1972), IV: part 2, 132. Rosalie Schwartz, *Across the Rio Grande to Freedom: U.S. Negroes in Mexico.* Southwestern Studies, Monograph no. 44 (El Paso: Texas Western Press, 1975), 23–33, 40–41. See also Martin Robison Delany, *The Condition, Elevation, Emigration, and Destiny of the Colored People of the United States, Politically Considered* (Philadelphia: [self-published], 1852), 178–88, which advocates African American migration to Mexico and Central America.

24 Bureau of the American Republics, *Commercial Information Concerning the American Republics and Colonies, 1891,* bulletin no. 41 (Washington, D.C.: GPO, 1892); *New York Times,* 6 August 1890; Lawrence D. Rice, *The Negro in Texas, 1874–1900* (Baton Rouge: Louisiana State University Press, 1971), 204; and articles of incorporation of the Afro-American Colonization Company of Mexico, Colored Colonization Company, The Colored Mexican Colonization Company, and the Colored Colonization Association of Fresno County, California State Archives, Sacramento.

25 *Montgomery Daily Advertiser,* 10 March 1895; *Birmingham Age-Herald,* 21 September 1895.

26 The description of wagons bearing "God and Liberty" can be found in Moisés González Navarro, *Historia moderna de México: El Porfiriato: La vida social* (México. D.F.: Editorial Hermes, 1957), 176. Ellis's descriptions of the colony come from the *New York Times,* 17 August 1891 and the *San Antonio Express,*

14 October 1895. The name of the colony was recorded as "Rasas" and "Razes" in English-language sources. See HD, 26.

27 Mobile *Daily Register*, 9, 12 March 1895; Montgomery *Daily Advertiser*, 10 March 1895.

28 See *Montgomery Daily Advertiser*, 29 March 1895 and *Mobile Register*, 21 March 1895.

29 *New York Evening Post*, 25 July 1895. This article is one of the few eyewitness accounts of the colony.

30 *Mobile Daily Register*, 6 March 1895. For more on debt peonage, see Katz, "Labor Conditions on Haciendas in Porfirian Mexico."

31 Copies of the contract signed by the colonists can be found in HD, 4–5. For more on the rise of Southern sharecropping, see Eric Foner, *Reconstruction: America's Unfinished Revolution, 1863–1877* (New York: Harper and Row, 1988), 404–9.

32 My statistics for Turner's colonization program come from Ayers, *The Promise of the New South*, 428.

33 Dispatches from United States Consuls in Piedras Negras (Ciudad Porfirio Díaz), 1868–1906, record group 59, reel 4, entry 84, National Archives.

34 It appears as though these colonists remained in Tlahualilo until 1896. See record group 59, Department of State, M 97, roll 122, entry 129, National Archives.

35 For an account of the church raising, see HD, 59. For a listing of leaders that indicates the presence of several ministers, see the clipping from the *Eagle Pass Guide News*, 2 November 1895, included in entry 95, Dispatches from United States Consuls in Piedras Negras, 1868–1906, reel 4 (record group 59, microcopy 299), National Archives. In addition, a reporter for the New York *Evening Post* remarked upon visiting the colonists in Mexico that "there are four preachers in the colony, men of more than average intelligence and force of character." New York *Evening Post*, 29 July 1895.

36 An extended discussion of the attractions of the book of Exodus can be found in Michael Walzer, *Exodus and Revolution* (New York: Basic Books, 1985). For materials linking Exodus to the colonization movement, see Delany, *Destiny of the Colored People*, 159; Turner's speech in *The Possibilities of the Negro in Symposium: A Solution of the Negro Problem Psychologically Considered* (Atlanta: Franklin Printing, 1904), 92; and Nell Irvin Painter, *Exodusters: Black Migration to Kansas after Reconstruction* (New York: Knopf, 1977).

37 Alabama *Courier*, 8 August 1895; Tuskegee *News*, 26 September 1895. Both quoted in Reynolds, "Alabama Negro Colony" (1953), 50.

38 HD, 10. See also Birmingham *Age-Herald*, 12 September 1895.

39 For a description of the quarantine process and location, see Reynolds, "Alabama Negro Colony" (1953), 38–41.

40 *New York Times*, 12 August 1895, 8.

41 HD, 26; *Memoria presentada al H. congreso del estado por el gobernador constitu-cional de Durango C. General Juan Manuel Flores* (Durango, México: Impresa de la Mariposa, 1896), 4 (translation by author). Flores refers in his memorial to an investigation into the colony by the "juez de la primera instancia de Mapimí" done at the request of the "Secretario del Despacho de Relaciones," but I have so far been unable to locate a copy of this report.

42 Colin A. Palmer, *Slaves of the White God: Blacks in Mexico, 1570–1650* (Cambridge: Harvard University Press, 1976), 3–4; Patrick J. Carroll, *Blacks in Colonial Vera-cruz: Race, Ethnicity, and Regional Development* (Austin: University of Texas Press, rev. ed. 2001), 80–87; Gonzalo Aguirre Beltrán, *La Poblacíon negra de México* (México: Fondo de Cultura Economica, 1972), 341, show how compli-cated racial categories became over time in New Spain.

43 For examples of Mexican acceptance of African American immigrants into northern Mexico, see Schwartz, *Across the Rio Grande*, 22–24 and Schoonover, ed., *Mexican Lobby*, 5. Immigration during the Porfiriato is discussed in Bureau of the American Republics, *Laws of the American Republics Relating to Immigra-tion and the Sale of Public Lands*, Bulletin No. 53 (Washington, D.C.: GPO, n.d. [1892?]), 98–113. For a discussion of the fate of Afro-Mexicans after indepen-dence, see Beltrán, *La población*, 277–92.

44 The rise of a mestizo national identity in Mexico is discussed by Agustín F. Basave Benítez, *México mestizo: Análisis del nacionalismo mexicano en torno a la mestizofilia de Andrés Molina Enríquez* (México: Fondo de Cultura Econó-mica, 1992).

45 González, *Los Extranjeros en México*, 185, 189.

46 Ibid., 186–88 (quotes on 186 and 188; translation by author). See also the letter written by Francisco Pimental in 1879 in opposition to black colonization in Mexico, which adopts many of the racist tropes that prevailed in the American South during Reconstruction. Francisco Pimental, *Obras completas* (México: Tipografía Económica, 1904), 5:509–13.

47 For a description of Flipper's career in Mexico, see Theodore D. Harris, ed., *Black Frontiersman: The Memoirs of Henry O. Flipper* (Fort Worth: Texas Chris-tian University Press, 1997). For a useful description of Mexican ideas of race, especially along the northern frontier, see Taylor, *In Search of the Racial Frontier*, 32–36. For another account of an individual African American finding personal liberation in northern Mexico, see Maya Angelou's account of her father's visits to Baja California in *I Know Why the Caged Bird Sings* (New York: Random House, 1969), 223–30.

48 Redkey, *Black Exodus*, 278. A description of Ellis presenting himself as Hawai-ian can be found in the *Washington Post*, 30 June 1904. For a reference to Ellis as the "Duke of Abyssinia," see Anderson to Washington, 3 October 1912, in Louis R. Harlan and Raymond W. Smock, *The Booker T. Washington Papers* (Urbana: University of Illinois Press, 1982), 12: 31. For materials on Ellis's later

involvement in Mexico, see *Trow's General Directory of New York City, 1920–21* (New York: R. L. Polk, 1920), 1269; *New York Herald*, 23 November 1904; the *New York Times*, 28 June, 9 July, 17 July, 4 September, 22 and 23 November 1904, 24 March 1914; 25 April 1914; 4 and 6 July 1920; and 30 September 1923; and *Who's Who in New York, 1918*, 336.

49 The W. E. B. Du Bois quote is from *The Souls of Black Folks* (New York: Signet, 1969 [1903]), 54. Ellis's experience on the railroad in 1909 is recounted in the *New York Times*, 15 March 1909 and the *New York Tribune*, 30 September 1923. In later years, Ellis tried to avoid such situations by traveling in his own private railroad car.

50 Quote from Brooks, *Story of Cotton*, 325–27. See also Arvarh E. Strickland, "The Strange Affair of the Boll Weevil: The Pest as Liberator," *Agricultural History* 68 (Spring 1994): 157–68; and W. Eustace Hubbard, *Cotton and the Cotton Market* (New York: D. Appleton, 1923), 39–40, 47, 121. A fascinating example of perhaps the only effort to colonize African Americans in Mexico after 1895 can be found in Ted Vincent, "Black Hopes in Baja California: Black American and Mexican Cooperation, 1917–1926," *Western Journal of Black Studies* 21 (1997): 204–13.

51 Watkins, *King Cotton*, 186; Ballestros, *Explotación*, 75. For more on the new presence of Mexicans (and Latino immigrants in general) in the American South, see Daniel Rothenberg, *With These Hands: The Hidden World of Migrant Farmworkers Today* (Berkeley: University of California Press, 2000); Arthur D. Murphy, Colleen Blanchard, and Jennifer A. Hill, eds., *Latino Workers in the Contemporary South* (Athens: University of Georgia Press, 2001); and Carole E. Hill and Patricia D. Beaver, eds., *Cultural Diversity in the U.S. South: Anthropological Contributions to a Region in Transition* (Athens: University of Georgia Press, 1998).

52 Some of Woodward's thoughts on Southern uniqueness and comparative history can be found in "The Irony of Southern History," in *The Burden of Southern History* (Baton Rouge: Louisiana State University Press, rev. ed., 1968), 187–211 and in "Comparisons in History," in *The Future of the Past* (New York: Oxford University Press, 1989), 129–200. Vargas Llosa, Fuentes, and Borges quoted in Deborah N. Cohn, *History and Memory in the Two Souths: Recent Southern and Spanish American Fiction* (Nashville: Vanderbilt University Press, 1999), 35, 36, 43.

53 For recent, thought-provoking studies of the cultural links between northern Mexico and the U.S. South, see José E. Limón, *American Encounters: Greater Mexico, the United States, and the Erotics of Culture* (Boston: Beacon, 1998); and Frederick B. Pike, *The United States and Latin America: Myths and Stereotypes of Civilization and Nature* (Austin: University of Texas Press, 1992), 55–85. A useful overview of regional difference in Mexico at the turn of the century can be found in Thomas Benjamin and William McNellie, eds., *Other Mexicos: Essays on Regional Mexican History, 1876–1911* (Albuquerque: University of New Mexico

Press, 1984). Borderlands historians are just beginning to explore the borderlands as a meeting ground for African Americans, Mexicans, and Anglos and for Western and Southern systems of race relations. Promising first steps in this direction are Taylor, *In Search of the Racial Frontier*; James N. Leiker, *Racial Borders: Black Soldiers along the Rio Grande* (College Station: Texas A&M University Press, 2002); and Neil Foley, *The White Scourge: Mexicans, Blacks, and Poor Whites in Texas Cotton Culture* (Berkeley: University of California Press, 1997), which is limited by its national rather than transnational approach to race. Similar liabilities exist in David Montejano's otherwise excellent *Anglos and Mexicans in the Making of Texas, 1836–1986* (Austin: University of Texas Press, 1987).

Transnational Warrior:

Emilio Kosterlitzky and the

Transformation of the U.S.-Mexico

Borderlands, 1873–1928

On March 12, 1913, residents of the border town of Nogales, Sonora, prepared for battle. Sonora was in revolt against President Victoriano C. Huerta, who had assumed control of Mexico after a violent military coup, and Colonel Álvaro Obregón was marching an army north from the state capital to Nogales to eject the last federal troops loyal to Huerta from Sonora. As federal soldiers and customs guards under Colonel Emilio Kosterlitzky dug trenches and threw up earthworks in the nearby hills, local residents and merchants began carting valuables across the border into the neighboring town of Nogales, Arizona. North of the border, U.S. troops reinforced the small patrol that policed the line between the two towns. That afternoon, consular and military officials made last-minute trips into Sonora to ask Obregón and Kosterlitzky to keep their bullets and men in Mexico. Only a street divided the Mexican town of Nogales from its U.S. counterpart, and with battle looming, this thin line on the map of nations seemed tenuous indeed.[1]

Any hope of containing the battle in Sonora vanished after fighting broke out at dawn. Unfamiliar with local geography, some of the attackers stumbled across the border into the hands of U.S. troops. Meanwhile, a "rain of bullets" fell on Arizona. One killed a Mexican customs officer watching from the U.S. side, another wounded a Mexican boy near his Arizona home, and countless others riddled walls and shattered windows.[2] "I am convinced that both of the belligerents were anxious and as careful as they could be not to endanger the lives of Americans," wrote Vice Consul Thomas Bowman, "but as the two towns are practically one and are separated only by a street, it was impossible to conduct belligerent operations against one without endangering the other."[3] When a bullet struck an American soldier, the U.S. commanding officer demanded that the federal troops and customs guards cease firing. Facing state reinforcements from the south, and U.S. troops to the north, "who had begun to point their rifles at our trenches, hoping perhaps to effect the cease-fire," Kosterlitzky found he had few options. Under "vigorous protest," he later wrote, he and his men crossed the border, stacked their rifles near the customs house, and surrendered to U.S. military authorities.[4]

Local residents may have viewed the defeat of this Russian-Mexican officer as an ominous sign. For years, Emilio Kosterlitzky had been a heroic icon of Sonora's passage into the modern age. He had battled "indios bárbaros" in the late nineteenth century, and as an officer in the *Gendarmería Fiscal*, or customs guard, he had helped border elites fight banditry and "disorder." Although he was an agent of a "modernizing" Mexican state and a patriotic Mexican, Kosterlitzky's fame was transnational. This "D'Artagnan of Mexico," as one Arizona resident called him, led efforts on both sides of the border to criminalize and control striking workers, Yaqui Indians, political dissidents, and other such "outlaws" in the early twentieth century.[5] Working for corporate and state elites, he facilitated what Friedrich Katz calls the transformation of the frontier into the border — the incorporation of a former periphery into the modernizing circuits of neighboring nations.[6] Yet with the onset of the Mexican Revolution, this "progressive" process seemed inverted, as border elites fit revolutionaries into a conceptual space once reserved for "barbarous" Indians and bandits. The surrender of former Apache fighter and lawman Emilio Kosterlitzky to U.S. troops in 1913 may have simply reinforced local suspicions that this modern transnational landscape had fallen into the abyss of its "savage" past.

For Kosterlitzky, however, the borderlands had never been clearly fixed to begin with. Because he was an immigrant, his acceptance as a border citizen was contingent not only on his work as a formal agent of the Mexican nation but also on his ability to navigate informal networks of custom and kinship rooted in the frontier past. His efforts to transform this world were thus selective; he attacked some of its "frontierish" qualities while preserving others. Local and national desires to encourage transnational development further limited the state's ability to transform the border as it saw fit. Kosterlitzky's reputation lay in his ability to balance the concerns of a modernizing state, entrepreneurial border elites who sought to maintain autonomy from the center, and U.S. corporate interests with their own financial motivations. Historians Jeremy Adelman and Stephen Aron argue that after the Apache Wars, formerly fluid "borderlands" between nations became "bordered" lands marked by state-imposed hegemony and nationally and ethnically bounded cultural relations.[7] Yet for Kosterlitzky, who began his border life as an Apache fighter, this was a world where state power and national and ethnic boundaries remained unsettled. Only at the end of his life, in exile in the United States, would he find his world "bordered" in the ways that Adelman and Aron propose—and even then, his proper place would remain unresolved and subject to constant negotiation.

On the Frontier between Nations

From the outset, Emilio Kosterlitzky was the child of a transnational world. Born in Moscow as Emil Kosterlitzky in 1853, he was the son of Russian army officer Ernst Kosterlitzky and his German wife, Emily Lenbert. Little is known about his youth except that he was raised in Russia and Germany and educated at the Military College at St. Petersburg. Some later claimed his father was a Cossack cavalryman, and at least one contemporary insisted that young Emil Kosterlitzky hoped to defend Mother Russia from the saddle like his father but was pressured by his family to join the navy. We know that he sailed from Russia in 1872, at the age of eighteen, as a midshipman aboard a naval training vessel. We also know that when his ship reached port at Puerto Cabello, Venezuela, that December, Kosterlitzky deserted. "Still clinging to his love for horses and his boyhood ambition to become a leader of cavalry," one writer later embellished, "the youthful naval officer slipped away from his naval comrades."[8]

From Puerto Cabello, Kosterlitzky sailed to New York and then boarded another ship for San Francisco. When his ship briefly set anchor at the port of Guaymas, Sonora, on its passage north along Mexico's west coast, he cut his journey short. Two days later, on May 1, 1873, he enlisted as a private of cavalry in the Mexican Army and began a new life as Russian immigrant Emilio Kosterlitzky. Drawing on his military training, he rose rapidly through the ranks. In a little over a year he had attained the rank of sergeant and major general of Sonora's military colonies, settlements that had been established in the late Spanish and early Mexican periods to help defend the state against Apache Indians to the north. In 1880 he was promoted to first lieutenant and three years later he became a captain. By the mid-1880s he was working mostly for the Mexican customs guard but continued to rise through the ranks of the Mexican army. In 1890 he earned the rank of lieutenant colonel, and in 1906, after thirty-three years of Mexican residency, he became Colonel Emilio Kosterlitzky, one of the highest-ranking officers in Sonora.[9]

These details, a matter of official military record, are most of what we know about Kosterlitzky's life in Sonora before the mid-1880s. These early years of service took him across much of the state, offering him an intimate knowledge of his adopted land and its people. U.S. mining entrepreneur Frank Saunders recalled meeting Kosterlitzky in 1878 in Fronteras, Sonora—across the border from what would soon become the boomtown of Tombstone—and Tombstone residents in 1882 found him in pursuit of Apaches in nearby Bacoachi, Sonora.[10] These sightings say as much about the early U.S. presence in Sonora as they do about Kosterlitzky. In the 1880s, new railroads to Arizona and the conquest of the Apaches opened the floodgates to eastern capital and immigrants. The rise of mining boomtowns along the border and extension of rail ties into Sonora in 1882 inspired many entrepreneurs to factor northern Mexico into their visions of resource extraction. Mining and ranching elites from Tombstone and the nearby copper camp of Bisbee forged a wide range of economic ties to Sonora during the late nineteenth century, and it was within this emerging transnational context that Kosterlitzky became a public figure.[11]

Americans seemed irresistibly drawn to this immigrant officer. Perhaps it was the juxtaposition of a Russian horseman with the equally romanticized Mexican countryside. The idea of the Cossack as a free and "wild" hero had currency among nineteenth-century audiences who equated this Old World horseman with the American cowboy. Visitors to Sonora may have read the 1877 edition of Jules Verne's popular *Michael Strogoff*, which featured a rugged "courier to the Czar" who, though Siberian, could still be assimilated to the romantic image of the Cossack.[12] The fascination with Kosterlitzky appears also to have been racialized. Even though U.S. photographs show him with his Mexican military garb or sombrero, his white skin and white horse often set him apart from his colleagues, whose brown skins made them—at least to many U.S. observers—more bandit than hero. Kosterlitzky was a "picturesque" leader with a "pronounced military air," argued one; his men, by contrast, "were a rough set of characters."[13]

If Kosterlitzky's origins and skin color marked him as a hero on the moral frontier between nations, he also attracted attention for more practical reasons. He had a gift with languages, allegedly speaking Russian, German, Spanish, French, Polish, Italian, Danish, Swedish, and English.[14] Such claims were not far-fetched. He probably learned Russian, German, French, and Polish as a student in Russia and Germany, where he also may have received training in English and Spanish. Swedes and Danes were common in sea-bound professions, and if Kosterlitzky did not study Swedish or Danish, he might have picked up working phrases on the Russian training vessel.[15] And after decades in Mexico, he would have become fluent in Spanish. Yet what probably mattered most for Americans was his ability to speak English. His correspondence shows a clear mastery of the language, and some claimed he spoke it without an accent. This would have been of enormous utility to Americans at a loss for words in Mexico. What Kosterlitzky lacked in rank in these early years, he made up for with his ability to "translate" Sonora for U.S. entrepreneurs.

These U.S. encounters with Emilio Kosterlitzky point to the fluid nature of ethnic and national categories in the early Arizona-Sonora borderlands. The fact that Americans considered him exotic—a romantically "un-Mexican" Mexican—suggests that these categories were hardening, but their embrace of Kosterlitzky as a "native" guide indicates that this fixing of social boundaries was far from complete. And indeed, Kosterlitzky's passage from European to Mexican was anything but unique for the time. After Mexican independence, the rise of ocean-based trade through the port of Guaymas opened Sonora to immigrants from nations such as France, Spain, Germany, and the United States, many of which married into local families and assimilated into a Mexican majority. When Kosterlitzky arrived, families such as the Camous from France, the Sterns from Germany, the Ortizes from Spain, and the Robinsons from the United States had already forged cosmopolitan identities in Sonora, and Anglo entrepreneurs from Arizona—not unlike their counterparts from the same era whom Louise Pubols and Benjamin Johnson, in their essays in this volume, describe for the Texas and California borderlands—were finding it practical (and often acceptable) to increase their fortunes by marrying into elite Sonoran families.[16]

Yet Kosterlitzky's ability to become Mexican was also shaped, paradoxically, by the construction and policing of other ethnic and racial boundaries that were anything but permeable. In northeastern Sonora, where

Kosterlitzky spent most of his Mexican career, elite families had generated status and wealth since colonial times as leaders of a military fraternity of "Indian fighters" who policed the border between Mexicans and Apaches. In the 1880s, Kosterlitzky battled Apaches under Colonel Angel Elías, scion of a prominent Indian-fighting family, and gained local fame for campaigns against "los indios barbaros" in the violent borderlands between Mexican Sonora and the Apache-controlled Sierra Madres.[17] These were christening ceremonies; through them Kosterlitzky earned a right to call himself not only a Mexican patriot but also a "frontiersman." Ana María Alonso and Daniel Nugent have discussed the significance of this frontier self-fashioning among *Chihuahuenses*, who claimed rights to power and land as former Indian fighters, and Raúl Ramos, in his essay in this collection, analyzes how war (and peace) with Indians shaped *Norteño* identity in Texas and Coahuila. Elites of northeastern Sonora made much of their Indian-fighting pedigrees, and Kosterlitzky's ability to claim a military kinship with these elites gave him privileged access to local networks of power and authority.[18]

Kosterlitzky's Indian-fighting background also tied him to networks of power and influence in Arizona. In the 1880s the United States and Mexico negotiated "reciprocal crossing" treaties so troops could pursue Apaches across the border. Within this legal framework, Kosterlitzky helped U.S. soldiers capture Geronimo and his fellow Apaches in 1886, and when some Apache prisoners escaped back to Mexico he led efforts to track them down. He was "a favorite with all the boys in blue," one American noted.[19] Kosterlitzky's own memory of these days was likely tempered: in 1885 he was called to defend the village of Huásabas against the U.S. Army's Apache scouts, who were harassing their traditional enemies.[20] If this put Kosterlitzky at odds with the U.S. military establishment, it drew him closer to many Anglo-Arizonans, who also distrusted the Apache scouts and felt that the U.S. Army had put their communities in danger by using them. Kosterlitzky would later agree with his Arizona friends that General George Crook, head of the military campaign against the Apaches, was "unfitted" to "deal with savages," having coddled Indians rather than avenging the deaths of Arizona and Sonora "pioneers."[21]

Fighting Indians and distrusting central authority were just two things that Anglo-Americans and Mexicans in the Arizona-Sonora borderlands found they had in common. Both put great stock in "pioneer" rhetoric and identities. Even though Anglo pioneering was also based on hating

Photograph of Lieutenant Colonel Emilio Kosterlitzky taken in 1896 in Nogales, Sonora, and given as a gift to Tombstone "pioneer" John Slaughter and his family. This photograph was taken at the time that Kosterlitzky and Slaughter collaborated—using Slaughter's border ranch as a base of operations—in the unsuccessful hunt for the Apache Kid. AHS Photograph #9429. Courtesy of the Arizona Historical Society/Tucson.

and taking land from Mexicans, these processes of frontier self-fashioning nevertheless helped anchor early transnational alliances. As in Sonora, these alliances were often resolved within a kinship of Indian fighting. Many of Kosterlitzky's close U.S. acquaintances, including local entrepreneurs John Slaughter, Burdett Packard, Allen C. Bernard, James Kirk, and William Cornell Greene, claimed to be veterans of the Apache wars. The fact that they fought as frontier "citizens," and not as federal soldiers, resonated in Sonora, where militias had long compensated for a weak federal military.[22] When William Cornell Greene, for instance, later graduated from frontier entrepreneur to copper king of Cananea, Sonora, his allies in Sonora supported his claim to Mexican land by pointing to his Indian-fighting pedigree.[23]

In this way, frontier rhetoric would inflect entrepreneurial connections to map out a new border geography that reconciled transnational ties with older regional and national identities. Kosterlitzky secured a more visible place within this transnational landscape in 1885, when he moved laterally from the Mexican Army into the Gendarmería Fiscal.[24] Created that March from a patchwork of previous state customs guards, fiscal police, and military colony squadrons, the Gendarmería Fiscal was the border police of the Mexican Treasury Department, with a mandate to patrol the line for smugglers and contraband.[25] Kosterlitzky was assigned a position under Colonel Juan Fenochio of the Third Zone of the Gendarmería, which was headquartered in Magdalena, Sonora.[26] As a local leader of the gendarmes, he further developed his complex and ambivalent relationship to national and transnational space. He patrolled the border between Mexico and the United States, but he also managed the flow of people, goods, and capital between nations. As an agent of the state, he sought to formalize these ties, but as an adopted frontier citizen, he would continue to rely on local, largely informal relationships that complicated efforts to control this continental crossroads from the center.

Kosterlitzky and the Copper Borderlands

No factor more clearly shaped transnational connections in the Arizona-Sonora borderlands at the turn of the century than the rise of copper mining. By the late 1880s, Tombstone's glory years had ended, and investors began to shift their gaze more fully to the copper boomtown of Bisbee, Arizona. Phelps, Dodge, and Company, the chief mining company at Bisbee, bought the Pilares Mine near Nacozari, a Mexican town seventy-five miles to the south, in 1896. That same year, William Cornell Greene joined with local Arizona and Sonora entrepreneurs to work copper claims near Cananea, Sonora, forty miles below Bisbee. Both enterprises paid off handsomely. By 1904 Nacozari and Cananea were the most important hubs of economic development in Sonora. Four border towns—Douglas and Naco, Arizona, and Agua Prieta and Naco, Sonora—emerged where copper railroads crossed the line. Geographer Donald Meinig has dubbed this transnational landscape the "copper borderlands," a label that nicely captures the relationships that tied these towns and their rural hinterlands to the global fortunes of copper mining.[27]

"The home of the Apache is the site of a prosperity not often witnessed," reported mining geologist Robert T. Hill of this transnational landscape in 1902. "From the top of Huachuca Mountain, whence Geronimo sent up his signal smokes, you can see three of the most profitable mining camps in the Southwest [Bisbee, Globe, and Cananea], and where he hid in Bisbee Canyon you can sit in a club, read the latest literature, and eat and drink all that the world affords."[28] Such descriptions resonated with frontier mythologies, but things were not so simple. Frontier "disorder" persisted, often adapting to the modern age. In the 1890s, the Apache Kid raided this increasingly productive landscape from his hideout in the Sierra Madres, eluding capture by the U.S. Army and Mexican gendarmes under Kosterlitzky. He was followed by white "bandits" such as Billy Stiles, a lawman-turned-train robber who terrorized the region for years.[29] The industrial borderlands, with its growing wealth, attracted these new "outlaws." Even though state and corporate elites could use claims of vanquished frontier barbarism to preface their progressive tales, they were unable to dispel the mounting fear that border banditry, rather than fading before the modern age, had begun to develop new profitable relationships to it.

"What we need," insisted Arizona Governor Nathan Murphy in 1901, "is a hard riding, sure shooting outfit something like the Texas Rangers or the Mexican *Rurales*." Responding to his plea, the territorial legislature created the Arizona Rangers, a force that the governor could call on when he felt Arizona to be in a state of "public emergency."[30] Border entrepreneurs embraced the Rangers, since they could manipulate governors more easily than distant bureaucrats or military officers to improve investor confidence in the region. The Phelps Dodge mining interests made the new force feel particularly at home. They were initially headquartered at Bisbee, and their first captain, Burt Mossman, was a Bisbee entrepreneur selected for his post by "poker-playing cronies," including William Cornell Greene of Cananea and Epes Randolph of the Cananea, Yaqui River, and Pacific Railroad, which linked Cananea to Bisbee. During their brief existence (1901–09), the Rangers remained in the copper borderlands, moving to the Phelps Dodge border town of Douglas in 1902 and then to Naco, the border gateway to Cananea, in 1907. From these bases, Rangers policed the countryside for bandits and "outlaws," at times helping copper companies battle labor strikes and other such "public emergencies."[31]

Emilio Kosterlitzky worked closely with the Arizona Rangers. As diplomats had in the Apache Wars, Rangers and gendarmes negotiated reciprocal crossing agreements. Yet unlike the previous treaties, these were simply informal arrangements. They were notably absent from the official record; locally, however, they were common knowledge. Ranger Lieutenant John Foster told a reporter in 1903 how the Rangers often crossed into Sonora to help Kosterlitzky catch horse thieves. "In the past much time has been lost on account of our having to stop at the boundary line when we were close on the trail of men wanted for crimes in Arizona," he explained. "We can now go into Mexico whenever necessary." In 1904, Arizona Ranger John Brooks captured an escapee from a Sonoran jail, and rather than formally arranging his extradition, told Kosterlitzky where he could pick the man up on the border. When Brooks crossed the line with a "posse" in 1907 to recover stolen horses, they turned their prisoners over to the local Mexican authorities—without a second thought for the illegality of the maneuver. Kosterlitzky later told Brooks that the men "had been disposed of."[32]

How could these men cross the border with such disregard for international law? Historian Bill O'Neal claims that Rangers would simply request a leave of absence from the force in order that "technicalities of Mexican law would be satisfied."[33] There is also evidence that these relationships were grounded in local tradition. Kosterlitzky helped military and local civilian officers—all close friends—"subdue Bandits & outlaws" in Sonora as early as the 1880s. Informal ties of friendship and trust continued to anchor these crossings after 1900; this was the case, for instance, with Kosterlitzky and Ranger Captain Thomas Rynning. These transnational relations of law and order also gave rise to new forms of "outlawry." Ranger Joe H. Pearce recalled that Kosterlitzky's men wore .44 Winchesters and Colt .45s, the fruit of covert trade. "For after the monthly confiscation of guns in the tough joints or the tough towns," he wrote, "Rangers were not averse to making a not too dishonest dollar, even though of Mexican coinage."[34] That Pearce saw this commerce as "not too dishonest" speaks to the enduring moral authority that border residents—even those who served as formal agents of the state—assigned to informal relations of law and order. And yet it also suggests that the state itself condoned a degree of informality, even criminality, among its own agents as a pragmatic compromise in a region where its power to enforce the law remained tenuous and uneven.[35]

If the "modern" age of transnational capitalism spawned relations of disorder and informality reminiscent of earlier "frontiers," it also inherited unresolved ethnic conflicts from these frontiers. Although the Apache Indians had presumably been ejected from Sonora in the 1880s, the "Apache Kid" aroused suspicion that Apache "renegades" continued to live in the Sierra Madres of eastern Sonora. Well into the twentieth century, Mexican villages continued to live in fear of these refugee Apache enclaves and mounted expeditions against them as late as the 1930s.[36] Even more significant was the enduring battle between Sonorans and Yaquis, a conflict that increased in intensity as modernizing elites sought to open Yaqui land to development.[37] Emilio Kosterlitzky had led efforts to subdue the Yaquis as early as the 1880s, but his later campaigns would be complicated by the fact that Yaquis were becoming progressively more valuable as mine workers on one hand—gaining widespread support from U.S. employers, in particular—and increasingly resistant to the "modernizing" state on the other. This conflict of interests was made even more complicated because many "tame" Yaquis who worked so well in the mines used their wages to buy arms and ammunition for their "wild" relatives.[38] Capitalists and state elites therefore increasingly turned to men such as Kosterlitzky to sort out the blurry distinctions between productive and dangerous Indians.

As in his collaboration with the Rangers against "banditry," this was a profoundly transnational task. Kosterlitzky regularly met with journalists at the border, since it was in embroidered news stories, rather than in the Mexican countryside, that Mexicans and Yaquis waged their most heated battles. In Bisbee and Cananea, he regularly assuaged fears that violence would spill over into the copper borderlands (most fighting took place farther south). Most rumors of violence were "fakes manufactured out of whole cloth," he noted in 1905. At times he became exasperated at having to constantly defend against "fantastic stories." Risk was not unique to Sonora, he grumbled to one reporter—weren't holdups and murders also common in U.S. cities?[39] His defensive tone reflected the thin line he walked between national and transnational concerns. He countered tales of Yaqui violence to promote confidence in Sonora, both as an agent of a modernizing state and as an individual who often took part in transnational ventures.[40] Yet his retort that violence just as often occurred north of the border indicates frustration with how easily Americans associated Mexico with disorder, a habit that seemed to offend his patriotic sensibilities. Kosterlitzky patrolled the border to promote a thriving transnational economy, but he also did so with his adopted nation centrally in mind.

Moral Economies of Power

The careful line that Kosterlitzky maintained between national and transnational interests on one hand, and formal law and informal custom on the other, was brought into sharp relief in 1906, when Mexican miners went on strike in Cananea. The strike began peacefully enough; Mexican workers demanded to be paid and promoted like their Anglo counterparts and called for an eight-hour workday.[41] As worker representatives met with company and municipal officials, the strikers began marching through the streets of town, calling on other workers to join them. It was when they reached the company lumberyard on the mesa above town that events took an unfortunate turn. Corporate manager George Metcalf—perhaps reacting to wild rumors that the workers were conspiring to dynamite company property and kill all Americans—shut the gate to the lumberyard and opened a high-pressure fire hose on the crowd.[42] As outraged strikers threw themselves at the gate, gunfire filled the afternoon air, and within minutes several men on both sides lay dead or wounded on the ground.

According to Mexican reports, the Americans fired first. Most pointed the finger at George Metcalf, who was said to have killed two Mexicans before they could open the gate. Metcalf then took refuge with his brother William in the lumberyard office, from which he continued to fire on the workers through an open window. The Metcalfs were eventually forced out after strikers set fire to the office and surrounding lumber and grain warehouses. They tried to escape, but were caught by the crowd, disarmed, and killed.[43] Not surprisingly, U.S. eyewitnesses claimed Mexicans had shot first, and in most cases portrayed the Metcalf brothers as innocent victims. George Metcalf met the strikers with his gun in hand but was struck down before he could fire it, one witness claimed. "The mob was upon him in an instant," and before Metcalf could get back on his feet, "a dozen knives and candlesticks had pierced his lungs and heart."[44]

With men lying dead in the street, and the lumberyard in flames, the population of Cananea began to panic. Once they heard about the violence at the lumberyard, company officials began arming their U.S. employees as deputies, according to an informal agreement with Cananea's desperate chief of police.[45] William Cornell Greene reported to company officials that the strikers were beginning to migrate toward the center of town, with the expressed goal of destroying and looting the bank and company store. Armed managers and employees moved toward the mesa to intercept them, Greene and fellow Cananea "pioneer" James Kirk driving their "modern" new automobiles "50 miles an hour through the thick crowds, scattering them in all directions."[46] Near Greene's imposing mansion, strikers and American employees clashed again, with the better-armed Americans taking the upper hand. When the air cleared, half a dozen more Mexicans lay dead in the streets. Meanwhile in the center of town, police engaged panicked strikers who had begun to loot pawnshops for guns and ammunition to defend themselves against equally panicked local authorities and their armed corporate "deputies."[47]

Corporate and municipal officials sent a barrage of alarming messages to officials on both sides of the border. Greene wired Governor Rafael Izábal to come as quickly as possible with troops. U.S. consular agent W. J. Galbraith sent a similar telegram to the U.S. State Department, claiming Mexicans were murdering U.S. citizens and dynamiting property. For their part, municipal officials generated images of unrestrained "cowboy" capitalists roaming the streets of Cananea. In his own telegram to Izábal, Judge F. López Linares said Greene and corporate manager Arthur S. Dwight were riding around town, ordering Americans to shoot at Mexicans.[48] Arizona residents could see the smoke from the lumberyard from the border, and rumors spread that Cananea was burning, and that Mexican workers were dynamiting houses and killing Americans. In the border town of Douglas, "crowds thronged both telegraph offices," and "the telephone office was in a continuous furor," a reporter wrote: "Men with rifles, revolvers and ammunition congregated on the streets, waiting for word that their services were required."[49]

After receiving news of the strike, Governor Izábal boarded a train for the border, with a guard of twenty *rurales*. In Magdalena he ordered Kosterlitzky to ride east to Cananea with his gendarmes, and in nearby Imuris he disembarked his rurales and told them to do the same, to avoid any complications that might arise from crossing them into Arizona. He reached Nogales after midnight. From here, the quickest route to Cananea was east to the border town of Naco, and then south by train to Cananea. Izábal made the next leg of the journey with Vice Consul Albert J. Brickwood, who had been receiving frantic news from Cananea all day, and the two no doubt fed each other's fears along the way. They arrived around six o'clock that morning at Naco and found waiting for them a large group of Americans armed with rifles and shotguns, led by Arizona Ranger Thomas Rynning.[50] Rynning and Phelps Dodge elites in Bisbee had assembled the body of "volunteers" the previous night, at the request of William Cornell Greene, but they had been denied entry into Mexico. When Izábal arrived, Rynning approached him and asked if he and his men could ride with him to Cananea.[51]

Izábal initially refused, but after making a telephone call to Greene he changed his mind. Greene told Izábal that conditions were serious—that strikers "intended to blow up the company with dynamite," and that he should ride south with an armed escort. When Izábal asked for help in Naco, Sonora, he later claimed, he "was presented with only four ancient insomniacs." Yet there were risks in letting U.S. volunteers make up the deficit. Izábal claimed the men were doctors, lawyers, and other professionals, but Rynning was closer to the truth. They were "cowpunchers, miners who'd seen service in Cuba and the Philippines, some of my rangers, and the usual scattering of outlaws," he wrote.[52] Many linked the "liberation" of Cananea to a hybrid of older frontier models—where "posses" took things into their own hands—and new imperial models tied to a rough-riding image of U.S. militarism abroad.[53] This volatile mixture no doubt concerned Izábal. There was also another issue; just as Izábal could not cross rurales into Arizona, Rynning could not lead armed men to Sonora. And perhaps with this scenario in mind, Territorial Governor Joseph H. Kibbey had wired him to remain in Arizona.[54]

The two men then made a choice that would forever haunt the copper borderlands. Rynning told the men to "break ranks and string across the line as civilians," and as they did, Izábal made them Mexican "volunteers." "I told them that they had to be exclusively under my orders and therefore under the authority of the laws of Mexico," Izábal wrote in his most candid report of the incident.[55] They then entered the train "amid cries of 'Viva el Gobiernor!' 'Viva la Cananea!' 'Viva Yzabal!'," noted a participant. "The Bisbee boys had already learned the language and were doing the thing up brown." When the train reached Cananea at ten o'clock that morning, the volunteers disembarked and marched around the concentrators and smelters. The Americans "overawed the rioters, for they very soon dispersed," Rynning recalled. They then stood by as Izábal and Greene made speeches to the workers.[56]

Perhaps because corporate and state officials made such a radical break with their own prescriptions of "order" and "progress" by letting disorderly and unofficial outsiders invade Cananea, these performances seemed to hold little sway. Such breaches of proper official behavior, writes James C. Scott, "disrupt or desacralize the ceremonial reverence" of performances of power—and so it seemed at Cananea.[57] Greene himself noted that the miners seemed to pay no attention to Izábal, and some even threatened to kill him. "The situation was very much strained a number of times," he wrote, "and it was only by the exercise of the greatest forbearance on the part of our boys that another collision was averted." The governor was "frequently interrupted by young men," confirmed another witness, who claimed that Greene was ridiculed as well. The arrival of Izábal's rurales only made things worse; that afternoon, following a "drinking spree," locals again traded gunfire in the street, generating fresh casualties on both sides. Izábal and his men could do nothing, one official later insisted, "since between the Mexicans and Americans, there were more than 3,000 men, many of them armed."[58]

According to most accounts, it was Kosterlitzky's arrival just before sundown that resolved this awkward situation. "Kosterlitzky's name was on everybody's lips and there was a feeling of security that had not existed since the hostilities commenced," wrote one participant.[59] If Americans expected Kosterlitzky to champion their view of transnational order, however, they were only partly satisfied. To undo Izábal's damage, Kosterlitzky had to reassert the official performance of power, which meant removing from the public stage all informal "arrangements" that might be seen as circumventing the state's claims to national authority.[60] Kosterlitzky drew on informal relationships to police the copper borderlands all the time, but he knew what Izábal had forgotten—that one had to disguise such relationships. They needed to remain offstage for performances of formal,

Photograph of Emilio Kosterlitzky and two gendarmes, and Thomas Rynning and two Rangers, at the 1906 strike of Cananea. This image was probably taken just before Rynning and his "volunteers" returned to Arizona. The backside of the image reads: "Rangers & Rurale leaders suppressing Cananea War, 1906." AHS Photograph #4362. Courtesy of the Arizona Historical Society/Tucson.

national power to be convincing. Not surprisingly, he began by publicly reproaching the invading army that had instigated the trouble. "I have known you . . . for a long time, and we have always settled our little affairs peacefully," he said to Rynning. "I wish you would order your men to immediately board your train and return to the border."[61]

Rynning played his part as well. Not only did he back down but the "scolding" became part of the public record in Arizona. He ordered the volunteers to board the train, which left Cananea without incident.[62] Soon after this public performance, Kosterlitzky and Rynning posed offstage for a photograph. The photo depicts three Rangers on horseback facing three mounted gendarmes on a desolate plain. A yucca in the middle divides warriors with cowboy hats from those wearing sombreros. Whether the yucca is meant to symbolize wild nature or the border itself, it is an ambivalent focal point. In one reading it might represent the problems bringing the horsemen together, but in another it is a prickly dividing line between them. The back of the photograph reads: "Rangers & Rurale [*sic*] leaders suppressing Cananea War, 1906." Interpreted in light of the inscription, the photo is less ambivalent; it shows a transnational gathering of heroes, commemorating the official triumph of the state over frontier disorder. And indeed, Kosterlitzky quickly restored the official veneer of order. "No one was allowed on the streets, under penalty of death," one reporter later claimed, "and wherever any one refused to go indoors he was shot down." The strike leaders were "stood against an adobe wall the next morning and shot," recalled the wife of one participant; whereas another recalled that authorities buried Mexicans "all night one night to keep the people from knowing how many were killed."[63]

Whether or not Kosterlitzky shot untold dozens to restore order, the belief that he could have done so only amplified his military mystique. Many saw his ejection of the volunteers (and in some stories, of Izábal himself) as an extension of his earlier work as a warrior for "civilization," even if Cananea's strikers, unlike Apache and Yaqui Indians, also became heroes.[64] And yet the strike was also a turning point, for despite Kosterlitzky's attempt to defend sovereign borders, the event transformed him more than ever into a transnational warrior. The Department of War placed a permanent garrison at Cananea, and American residents successfully rallied to have Kosterlitzky stay as its commander. The copper company also hired gendarmes through Kosterlitzky—who served as a *patron*, or labor broker—to extend its police power into the rural countryside. Not only did Kosterlitzky disburse wages for these men but he also used personal connections to corporate elites to secure other jobs for them as well, drawing in this way on informal transnational linkages that had served him for decades.[65]

Kosterlitzky's long history as a twin agent of the Mexican state and transnational corporate power also continued to serve those in power. After the Cananea strike, which had been influenced by anti-Díaz liberals, the Mexican government became increasingly nervous about "revolutionary" activity in the copper borderlands. For his part, William Cornell Greene blamed the strike on the U.S. Western Federation of Miners, whose local activities he now patrolled with a vengeance. Both used Kosterlitzky to help police this transnational landscape of radicalism. Kosterlitzky kept watch on the local dissemination of radical literature—such as the WFM's *Miners Magazine*—and helped contain Mexican radicals who increasingly used Arizona as their operational headquarters. In September 1906, Kosterlitzky worked with the Arizona Rangers to track down and arrest *revoltosos* in Douglas and mining towns near Nogales.[66]

In 1907, using informal arrangements they traditionally applied to border thieves, Kosterlitzky and Ranger Sam Hayhurst kidnapped and deported Flores Magón associate Juan Sarabia from Douglas to the neighboring town of Agua Prieta, and from there to jail in Cananea.[67]

Perhaps most valuable to mining elites in the months leading up to the Mexican Revolution was Kosterlitzky's ability to "read" native space. "For several days past, my men have informed me that things look quite serious at your camp," he wrote copper elite Joe Bordwell in 1910. While there were no "outward signs" that most Americans would recognize, he noted, "still there seems to be trouble breeding."[68] These local networks of knowledge were a culmination of years of work on the frontier between nations—and yet things had changed since Apache "renegades" and European American "outlaws" eluded border police. Whether tracking criminals in the countryside or assessing revolutionary sentiments in mining towns, Kosterlitzky had more official resources at his disposal. As always, he had to keep a foot firmly planted in informal terrain—drawing on decades of local experience to decipher social transcripts that remained hidden to outsiders—but he worked within increasingly formal, official, and modern networks of power and authority to bring the borderlands in line with corporate and state visions of progress.

Transnational Divides

The Mexican Revolution came to Sonora in the winter of 1910, as small guerrilla bands began to spill west across the Sierra Madres from Chihuahua. By early 1911, fears that rebels were planning to take Sonora were enough to push fainter-hearted U.S. mining interests north across the border.[69] From that point forward, waning investor confidence and disruptions in labor and transportation networks—not to mention the threat posed by local battles—motivated a general flight of U.S. capital. Until 1913, when Sonora would revolt against Huerta, revolutionary activities tended to be local, often taking the form of invasions from neighboring Chihuahua. Many of these outsiders raided from the Sierra Madres and took refuge in isolated mountains near Cananea, as Apache "renegades" and "bandits" once had.[70] This no doubt reinforced a habit among Arizonans and Sonorans to equate these outsiders with frontier enemies of the state. Americans called them outlaws and made comparisons between the Mexican Revolution and earlier Apache "invasions," whereas Sonorans drew on their Indian-fighting rhetoric, assimilating the defense of their state to a longer tradition of defending "civilization" against "barbarism."[71]

As refugees of Pascual Orozco's Chihuahuan army began to spill across the Sierra Madres in 1912, Emilio Kosterlitzky—retired after almost forty years of military service—decided to return to the saddle. In late August he went to Mexico City to lobby President Madero for the creation of a special body of gendarmes. He was particularly interested in organizing veterans of the Yaqui wars, "who are willing to follow him into the jaws of death if he led them," explained a reporter. "Let them come," Kosterlitzky said. "I want nothing more to complete my career [than] to drive this invading horde from the state."[72] Ironically, this "invading horde" included Chihuahuenses, who also prided themselves as "frontier" defenders of civilization, and who now employed "frontier" models of warfare and masculinity against the Mexican state. Although Sonorans tended to convert their Indian-fighting past into rhetoric of modernization and state making, like their neighbors they saw the revolution as an event replete with symbolic ties to earlier frontiers.

Frontier rhetoric, of course, often poorly reflected border reality. One found few "grizzled warriors" like Kosterlitzky on the battlefield who had actually fought Apaches. More men could claim to be Yaqui fighters, since that conquest was ongoing, but for that matter many Sonoran revolutionaries *were* Yaqui Indians.[73] And although Kosterlitzky saw battle against revolutionary "hordes" as a crowning event in his venerable career as frontier warrior, he lived in a fundamentally transformed world. In the 1880s he chased Apaches across a space that was still worlds apart from the national cores of the United States and Mexico. It seemed coherently bounded on state-generated maps, but one required a local guide to keep from getting lost between nations.[74] The world beyond state and corporate control was, in a real sense, spacious. Yet by the early twentieth century, Mexico and the United States were not only growing rapidly, they had grown closer together. The metropolis had moved more formally and completely to the frontier, with real consequences. It is telling that when Kosterlitzky bid farewell to his adopted land in 1913, he simply walked across a line and surrendered to military agents of a foreign state. The frontier had become the borderlands—a profoundly transnational space anchored in local knowledge and power—but had also become something else. It had become the border.

This modern world of formal transnational divides was at least partly a product of Kosterlitzky's previous efforts to make the border region safe, legible, and available for consumption. And his later flight across the line revealed just how profoundly the state had come to mark out, consume, and control space. After surrendering, Kosterlitzky and his men were shipped to Fort Rosecrans in San Diego, California, where they joined more than 400 other Mexican refugees from border battles.[75] Just as the frontier—a space that required transnational law-keeping alliances to track elusive "renegades" and "outlaws" through regions of refuge— had shrunk to a line patrolled by soldiers (and, increasingly, their Immigration and Justice Department counterparts), so too were these refugee spaces bounded and controlled. Single Mexicans were packed by eight into conical tents, and families were assigned to tents and shacks. Mexican Fort Rosecrans, a reporter noted, "is surrounded by a 10-foot, 3-inch mesh barb wire fence and a patrol of U.S. soldiers around that, night and day."[76]

If the refugee camp echoed the larger collapse and control of border space, it also reproduced other border relationships. Not unlike corporate elites and lawmen in Sonora and Arizona, military officers at Fort Rosecrans developed informal relationships of trust with Kosterlitzky, granting him a range of special privileges. He served as an auxiliary law-keeper at the camp, a role that diminished the grip of the state on his daily life, while preserving his authority over the other internees.[77] In 1913, responding to a complaint from internee Major A. Duhagon, military officer William Davis investigated conditions in the camp. He learned that among Kosterlitzky's special "duties," he controlled passes for temporary parole in nearby San Diego and Wonderland Park—and that he had refused passes to Duhagon, a one-time labor "agitator" and "bandit" at Cananea. "He is not a regular soldier, and knows nothing about discipline," Kosterlitzky claimed. Responding to Duhagon's claim that he told officials to confine some men to the guardhouse on a diet of water and bread, Kosterlitzky explained that there was no other way to maintain "order and discipline." He had also encouraged army officers to search the men's tents for guns and knives, another invasion of personal liberties that Duhagon protested. "Such search is customary in Mexico," Kosterlitzky retorted.[78]

Kosterlitzky was the ranking officer in camp, but he was no longer in Mexico. He was ultimately able to convert hypothetical authority into actual power through the same kinds of transnational ties that empowered him in Sonora. His power, moreover, was not limited to the constrained refugee and parolee spaces of Fort Rosecrans and Wonderland Park; in 1914 he helped officers track down refugees who had escaped through a tunnel into the nearby countryside.[79] He also preserved earlier patron-client relationships with his gendarmes, periodically lobbying U.S. Consul Frederick Simpich in Nogales, Sonora, on their behalf. "It is now more than a year that we are held as internes and it is now five months that we have not received any pay whatsoever," he wrote Simpich in 1914. If he could not help them all, maybe he could secure the release of Leonardo Manzaneda, one of Kosterlitzky's most loyal men: "His family is suffering want at Nogales, Arizona and his is well deserving." Although Simpich could do nothing for Manzaneda, he did convince military authorities in Washington, D.C., to release another gendarme, Anselmo Bustamante, a feat that only reaffirmed the enduring reach and strength of Kosterlitzky's transnational connections.[80]

The Fort Rosecrans internees were finally released on September 14, 1914. Most returned to Mexico, but Kosterlitzky remained in California, moving with his family to a new home in Los Angeles. The move was not surprising; many Porfirian elites in Sonora (including Kosterlitzky and his family) had vacationed in Los Angeles, and some moved there permanently after 1910.[81] Weeks before his release, Kosterlitzky had started work with the Bureau of Investigation (a precursor to the FBI), who asked him to send parolees undercover to mingle with Mexicans in San Diego and learn about their sympathies with revolutionary factions in Mexico. Soon afterward, Kosterlitzky accepted a permanent job as special agent with the Department of Justice, which he held until 1927. According to some sources, the government was drawn to Kosterlitzky's knowledge of Mexican and German affairs and his fluency in multiple languages. His native German was especially useful in World War I. "Scores of enemy Germans who would 'hoch the kaiser' with him at secret banquets and meetings," noted one writer, "the next day found themselves under arrest or bound for an internment camp."[82]

As a Department of Justice agent, Kosterlitzky also focused on Mexican affairs. His intimate knowledge of Mexico and its leaders, "coupled with his ability to 'read' the minds of Mexicans and Mexico," as one reporter put it, was useful not only to U.S. spies but also to other government officials. For years he corresponded with old friend and military colleague General Leonard Wood about the strengths and weaknesses of various revolutionary and postrevolutionary regimes. When he retired in 1927, at the age of seventy-three, he was investigating a plot to overthrow the government of Baja California.[83] One might assume that in his new job as border spy Kosterlitzky had once again jumped ship, abandoning Mexico for a new U.S. identity. But as always, his national and transnational ties were more complex than this. In 1927 the "Mexican exile" newspaper in Los Angeles, *La Opinión*, claimed Kosterlitzky had renounced Mexican nationality when he joined the Department of Justice. Kosterlitzky fired back, declaring that he had been a Mexican patriot for forty years and had never renounced his Mexican citizenship.[84] "We consider Kosterlitzky as a soldier of the Republic," agreed friends at his 1928 funeral, "consecrated as such by his service during the best years of his life." An onlooker added that this citizenship had also been consecrated by marriage to a Mexican woman, Francisca López.[85]

If efforts by Kosterlitzky and his friends to preserve his Mexican identity pointed to enduring transnational connections, they also echoed the larger bounding of space by U.S. and Mexican states. Nowhere was Kosterlitzky's proper national place more clearly articulated than at his death in 1928: a former border crosser became, in exile, a patriotic Mexican. For their part, Americans would increasingly claim Kosterlitzky as one of their own. Reports that Kosterlitzky was born in Maine, later becoming a soldier of fortune in Mexico, circulated well before his death, and another story that he had been a U.S. officer at Fort Apache before deserting and going to Mexico was told in Arizona as late as 1947.[86] Even Kosterlitzky's own daughter, Mary Louise, weighed into the creative "bounding" of her father's identity in the 1950s, when she saw him depicted on an episode of *Twenty-Six Men*, a TV series on the Arizona Rangers. He "appeared very Spanish, good looking, but with a marked accent," she wrote her brother. "This of course was out of character, because as you know Dad spoke completely without accent." Her complaint, legitimate as it may have been, reflected concerns of a new generation of ethnic Mexicans seeking to establish a new "American" identity. As a Mexican American employee of a congressional office in the nation's center, Mary Louise Kosterlitzky seemed to care deeply about how others remembered her father.[87] Whether Russian, Mexican, or American, Emilio Kosterlitzky found his final place in a rapidly shifting transnational world that seemed more concerned than ever with mapping proper boundaries.

Notes

1 Álvaro Obregón to Interim Governor Ignacio Pesqueira, 15 March 1913, in Álvaro Obregón, *Ocho mil kilómetros en campaña* (México: Fondo de Cultura Económica, 1959), 36–39; Emilio Kosterlitzky to Mexican Secretary of War, 19 March 1913, in Cornelius C. Smith Jr., *Emilio Kosterlitzky: Eagle of Sonora and the Southwest Border* (Glendale, Cal.: Arthur H. Clark, 1970), 197–203; *Douglas Daily International*, 11 and 12 March 1913; *Nogales Oasis*, 15 March 1913; and Thomas D. Bowman to U.S. Secretary of State, 16 March 1913, *Records of the Department of State Relating to Internal Affairs of Mexico, 1910–29* (hereafter DS-RIAM), roll 24, vol. 29, 812.00/6792. For the larger context, see Héctor Aguilar Camín, *La frontera nómada: Sonora y la Revolución Mexicana* (México: Cal y arena, 1997), 351–407.

2 Kosterlitzy to Mexican Secretary of War, 19 March 1913; *Douglas Daily International*, 13 and 14 March 1913; and *Nogales Oasis*, 15 March 1913.

3 Bowman to Secretary of State, 16 March 1913, DS-RIAM, roll 24, vol. 29, 812.00/6792.

4 *Nogales Oasis*, 15 March 1913; *Douglas Daily International*, 14 March 1913; Kosterlitzky to Mexican Secretary of War, 19 March 1913; and L. W. Mix, undated report, filed 16 August 1913, DS-RIAM, roll 24, vol. 29, 812.00/9585.

5 *Douglas Daily International*, 1 January 1907.

6 Friedrich Katz, *The Secret War in Mexico: Europe, the United States, and the Mexican Revolution* (Chicago: University of Chicago Press, 1981), 7.

7 Jeremy Adelman and Stephen Aron, "From Borderlands to Borders: Empires, Nation-States, and the Peoples in between in North American History," *American Historical Review* 104:3 (June 1999): 814–41, but for other borderland histories that similarly view the fixing of power and ethnic relations, see Juan Mora-Torres, *The Making of the Mexican Border: The State, Capitalism, and Society in Nuevo León, 1848–1910* (Austin: University of Texas Press, 2001), and James F. Brooks, *Captives and Cousins: Slavery, Kinship, and Community in the Southwest Borderlands* (Chapel Hill: University of North Carolina Press, 2002).

8 1928 résumé of Kosterlitzky, and "Kosterlitzky Retires as U.S. Agent" (unidentified newspaper clipping), Emilio Kosterlitzky Papers, University of Arizona, Tucson, Arizona, and Smith, *Eagle of Sonora*, 29–37.

9 Kosterlitzky résumé, "Emilio Kosterlitzky, Figura Histórica del Noroeste" (unidentified newspaper clipping), and undated document from the Secretaría de Estado y del Despacho de Guerra y Marina, Kosterlitzky Papers.

10 *Douglas Daily International*, 28 May 1909, and *Tombstone Epitaph*, 5 February 1882.

11 For this larger transnational context, see Samuel Truett, *Transnational Dreams: Transforming the U.S.-Mexico Borderlands* (New Haven: Yale University Press, forthcoming).

12 Judith Deutsch Kornblatt, *The Cossack Hero in Russian Literature: A Study in Cultural Mythology* (Madison: University of Wisconsin Press, 1992), 4. The cover of the U.S. edition of Jules Verne, *Michael Strogoff, The Courier of the Czar* (New York: Scribner, Armstrong, 1877), showed a man on horseback, conflating this courier to the czar, an agent of the state, with the "free" Cossack.

13 *Bisbee Daily Review*, 2 September 1903.

14 "Kosterlitzky Retires as U.S. Agent."

15 I thank Richard Robbins, Russian historian at the University of New Mexico, for help in sorting out the likely origins of Kosterlitzky's multilingualism.

16 See the discussion of Europeans in post-independence Sonora (and the families I mention here) in Stuart F. Voss, *On the Periphery of Nineteenth-Century Mexico: Sonora and Sinaloa, 1810–1877* (Tucson: University of Arizona Press, 1982), 139–40; Miguel Tinker Salas, *In the Shadow of the Eagles: Sonora and the Transformation of the Border during the Porfiriato* (Berkeley: University of California Press, 1997), 24–26; and Gregorio Mora Torres, "Los comerciantes de Guaymas y el desarrollo económico de Sonora, 1825–1910," in *VIII Simposio de historia de Sonora* (Hermosillo: Instituto de Investigaciones Históricas, 1984), 210–39. Also see Ernesto de la Torre Villar, ed., *Las notas sobre Sonora, del Capitán Guillet (1864–1866)* (México, D.F.: 1953).

17 27 September 1902 certificate, and 2 September 1893 certificate, Kosterlitzky Papers.

18 Ana María Alonso, *Thread of Blood: Colonialism, Revolution, and Gender on Mexico's Northern Frontier* (Tucson: University of Arizona Press, 1995), and Daniel Nugent, *Spent Cartridges of Revolution: An Anthropological History of Namiquipa, Chihuahua* (Chicago: University of Chicago Press, 1993). For Sonora's "Apache fighting" families, see James E. Officer, *Hispanic Arizona, 1536–1856* (Tucson: University of Arizona Press, 1987), 126–33, and Voss, *On the Periphery*, 82–110. As Ramos notes for Texas, these leaders were pragmatic, often negotiating peace as well as war. See Edwin R. Sweeney, " 'One of Heaven's Heroes': A Mexican General Pays Tribute to the Honor and Courage of a Chiricahua Apache," *Journal of Arizona History* 36:3 (Autumn 1995): 209–32, but also see José Luis Mirafuentes Galván, "Los dos mundos de José Reyes Pozo y el alzamiento de los apaches chiricahuis (Bacoachi, Sonora, 1790)," *Estudios de Historia Novohispana* 21 (2000): 67–105.

19 Joe Wise to Ernest Kosterlitzky, n.d., Kosterlitzky Papers; Britton Davis, *The Truth about Geronimo*, ed. M. M. Quaife (New Haven: Yale University Press, 1929), 231; *Cananea Herald*, 14 December 1902.

20 Shelley Bowen Hatfield, *Chasing Shadows: Indians along the United States–Mexico Border, 1876–1911* (Albuquerque: University of New Mexico Press, 1998), 98.

21 *Tombstone Epitaph*, 15 February 1890. See also John A. Turcheneske, "The Ari-

zona Press and Geronimo's Surrender," *Journal of Arizona History* 14:2 (Summer 1973): 133–48.

22 Allan A. Erwin, *The Southwest of John H. Slaughter, 1841–1922* (Glendale, Cal.: Arthur H. Clark, 1965), 167–267; *Tombstone Epitaph*, 15 October 1929; *Tucson Citizen*, 5 August 1911; "Allen C. Bernard," in *Arizona: Prehistoric-Aboriginal-Pioneer-Modern*, vol. 3, *Biographical* (Chicago: S. J. Clarke, 1916), 871; Mildred Young Wallace, *We Three: Papa's Ladies* (San Antonio: Naylor, 1957), 60. For militias in Sonora, see Officer, *Hispanic Arizona*, 123–29.

23 Federico García y Alva, *"México y sus progresos": Albúm-directorio del estado de Sonora* (Hermosillo: Imprenta Oficial, 1905–07), n.p.

24 Undated document from Secretaría de Estado y del Despacho de Guerra y Marina.

25 Carlos J. Sierra and Rogelio Martínez Vera, *El resguardo aduanal y la Gendarmería Fiscal, 1850–1925* (México, D.F.: Secretaría de Hacienda y Crédito Público, 1971), 51–52.

26 Résumé of Kosterlitzky; "Figura Histórica del Noroeste"; and Vera, *Resguardo aduanal*, 56.

27 D. W. Meinig, *The Shaping of America: A Geographical Perspective on Five Hundred Years of History*, vol. 3, *Transcontinental America, 1850–1915* (New Haven: Yale University Press, 1998), 152–57, but see Truett, *Transnational Dreams*, for more in-depth treatment of this regional history.

28 Robert T. Hill, "The Wonders of the American Desert," *World's Work* 3:5 (March 1902): 1830.

29 *Tombstone Epitaph*, 2 August 1896, and *Bisbee Daily Review*, 13 May 1904.

30 Frazier Hunt, *Cap Mossman: Last of the Great Cowmen* (New York: Hastings House, 1951), 143–45; Bill O'Neal, *The Arizona Rangers* (Austin: Eakin, 1987); and Jay J. Wagoner, *Arizona Territory, 1863–1912: A Political History* (Tucson: University of Arizona Press, 1970), 373–95.

31 O'Neal, *Arizona Rangers*, 2–7, 34, 48–55, 118, 161–62, and Philip J. Mellinger, *Race and Labor in Western Copper: The Fight for Equality, 1896–1918* (Tucson: University of Arizona Press, 1995), 52–53.

32 *Bisbee Daily Review*, 4 March 1903; *Douglas Daily International*, 22 November 1904; and *Bisbee Daily Review*, 6 July 1907.

33 O'Neal, *Arizona Rangers*, 64.

34 Wise to Kosterlitzky, Kosterlitzky Papers, and Joe H. Pearce, "Line Rider," typewritten reminiscence in J. H. Pearce Papers, Arizona Historical Society, Tucson, Arizona, 111, 114.

35 For insightful discussion of these sorts of compromises in the borderlands, see Peter Andreas, *Border Games: Policing the U.S.-Mexico Divide* (Ithaca: Cornell University Press, 2000), but also see essays on state power and the tolerance of illegal practices in Josiah McC. Heyman, ed., *States and Illegal Practices* (Oxford: Berg, 1999).

36 Howard Carroll Groton, "Riding the Flying Tortilla: Recollections of a Gringo Storekeeper in Mexico," *Journal of Arizona History* 31:2 (Summer 1990): 213–14, and Grenville Goodwin and Neil Goodwin, *The Apache Diaries: A Father-Son Journey* (Lincoln: University of Nebraska Press, 2000).

37 See the larger discussions in Edward H. Spicer, *The Yaquis: A Cultural History* (Tucson: University of Arizona Press, 1980), and Evelyn Hu-DeHart, *Yaqui Resistance and Survival: The Struggle for Land and Autonomy, 1821–1910* (Madison: University of Wisconsin Press, 1984).

38 Hu-DeHart, *Yaqui Resistance*, 119–54, 163–65, and Spicer, *The Yaquis*, 149–50; Kosterlitzky's diploma for service in the Yaqui-Mayo wars of 1885–1886, appendix of Smith, *Eagle of Sonora*, 316.

39 *Bisbee Daily Review*, 7 June 1902, 21 January 1904, 26 May 1903, and 1 March 1905.

40 He was involved with William Cornell Greene in the Greene Consolidated Gold Company. See Emilio Kosterlitzky to William C. Greene, 17 January 1901, Documentación Procedente de la Compañía Minera de Cananea (hereafter referred to as CMC), microfilm 71/147, folder 16, Centro Regional del Noroeste del Instituto Nacional de Antropología y Historia, Hermosillo, Sonora. He also owned (with Americans) the Queatica Mining Company near Cananea. *Cananea Herald*, 12 July 1906. Kosterlitzky and Fenochio had also been awarded lands by Díaz for their campaigns against "bandits" and Indians, which they sold to Mormon colonists in 1892. Thomas H. Naylor, "The Mormons Colonize Sonora: Early Trials at Colonia Oaxaca," *Arizona and the West* 20:4 (Winter 1978): 329.

41 The 1906 strike at Cananea has generated significant scholarly attention on both sides of the border. The best documentary source on the strike is Manuel González Ramírez, *La huelga de Cananea*, vol. 3, *Fuentes para la historia de la Revolución Mexicana* (México, D.F.: Fondo de Cultura Económica, 1956), but see Eugenia Meyer et al., *La lucha obrera en Cananea, 1906* (México, D.F.: INAH, 1980); Dirk Raat, *Revoltosos: Mexico's Rebels in the United States, 1903–1923* (College Station: Texas A&M Press, 1981), 65–91; Rodney D. Anderson, *Outcasts in their Own Land: Mexican Industrial Workers, 1906–1911* (DeKalb: Northern Illinois University Press, 1976), 110–17; Michael J. Gonzales, "United States Copper Companies, the State, and Labour Conflict in Mexico, 1900–1910," *Journal of Latin American Studies* 26 (October 1994): 651–81; and C. L. Sonnichsen, "Colonel William C. Greene and the Strike at Cananea, Sonora, 1906," *Arizona and the West* 13:4 (Winter 1971): 343–68.

42 On rumors, see Municipal President Filiberto Barroso to the Second Judge of the First Instance, 1 June 1906, in González Ramírez, *Huelga de Cananea*, 32–33; William C. Greene, "Brief Resume of the Recent Disorders in Cananea," 11 June 1906 and Statement by Cananea Consolidated Copper Company Manager Arthur S. Dwight, June 8, 1906, CMC, microfilm 72/147, folder 19.

43 Governor Rafael Izábal and Secretary of State Alberto Cubillas, Hermosillo, to Secretary of Government, México, 19 June 1906, published in *El Correo de Sonora*, 9, 10, and 11 July 1906, in González Ramírez, *Huelga de Cananea*, 95–96, and Esteban Baca Calderón, *Juicio sobre la guerra del yaqui y genesis de la huelga de Cananea* (Hermosillo: Contrapunto 14, 1997), 74–75.

44 *Douglas Daily International*, 4 June 1906. The story that the miners killed the Metcalfs with candlesticks played up the "savage" aspects of the "riot" and can be found in some histories, e.g., Sonnichsen, "Strike at Cananea," 350. In his reports on their death Vice Consul Brickwood claimed they died from gunshot wounds and, in George's case, "blows from stones." 13 June 1906 reports on the death of William and George Metcalf, *Despatches from United States Consuls in Nogales, 1889–1906*, microfilm T-323, roll 4, vol. 4 (Washington, D.C.: National Archives, 1961). Some Americans did assign blame to the Metcalfs; see I. Kemperman to David Cole, 24 July 1906, CMC, microfilm 69/147, folder 7, and Thomas Rynning, *Gun Notches: A Saga of Frontier Lawman Captain Thomas H. Rynning as Told to Al Cohn and Joe Chisholm* (San Diego: Frontier Heritage Press, 1971), 306.

45 Statement by Arthur S. Dwight, CMC, microfilm 72/147, folder 19.

46 Former Apache fighter Greene saw the automobile as the latest gadget in his imperial toolkit; only this time "backwards" Mexicans were the "savages" to be conquered. "The automobiles were a new feature to the mob; anything that could get from one end of the camp to the other in a few minutes was something they did not know anything about, and, although at one time they fired about 100 shots at the autos they all went wild," he reported. "The men who did the firing were evidently too badly rattled for fear the things would jump at them, to take aim." Greene, "Brief Resume," CMC, microfilm 72/147, folder 19.

47 Barroso to Second Judge, 1 June 1906, and Izábal and Cubillas to Secretary of Government, 19 June 1906; and Testimony of Plácido Ríos, in González Ramírez, *Huelga de Cananea*, 31–33, 96, and 138–40; Greene, "Brief Resume"; Statement by Arthur S. Dwight, CMC, microfilm 72/147, folder 19; and Report of Vice Consul Albert W. Brickwood Jr., Nogales, to Assistant Secretary of State Robert Bacon, 22 June 1906, *Despatches from Nogales*.

48 U.S. Consular Agent W. J. Galbraith, Cananea, to the U.S. Department of State, 1 June 1906, *Despatches from Nogales*; William C. Greene to Rafael Izábal, 1 June 1906, and F. López Linares to Rafael Izábal, 1 June 1906, in González Ramírez, *Huelga de Cananea*, 27–28.

49 Calderón, *Juicio*, 76; *Douglas Daily International*, 2 June 1906; Luis E. Torres to Vice President Ramón Corral, 5 June 1906, in González Ramírez, *Huelga de Cananea*, 75–76; and Rynning, *Gun Notches*, 291–92.

50 Izábal and Cubillas to Secretary of Government, 19 June 1906, in González Ramírez, *Huelga de Cananea*, 97; Brickwood to Bacon, 22 June 1906, *Despatches*

from Nogales; and Izábal's testimony in Torres to Izábal, 5 June 1906, in González Ramírez, *Huelga de Cananea*, 75.

51 Rynning, *Gun Notches*, 291–92, Comisario Adrián M. Cubillas, Naco, to Vice President Ramón Corral, México, 5 June 1906, in González Ramírez, *Huelga de Cananea*, 29–30; C. I. McReynolds to William C. Greene, 6 June 1906, CMC, microfilm 69/147, folder 7; and Izábal's testimony in Torres to Izábal, 5 June 1906, in González Ramírez, *Huelga de Cananea*, 75–76.

52 Izábal's testimony in Torres to Izábal, 5 June 1906, in González Ramírez, *Huelga de Cananea*, 75–76, and Rynning, *Gun Notches*, 292–93.

53 Rynning was himself a former rough rider. O'Neal, *Arizona Rangers*, 32–33.

54 Rynning, *Gun Notches*, 297–99.

55 Rynning, *Gun Notches*, 298–99, Brickwood to Bacon, 22 June 1906, *Despatches from Nogales*; Izábal's testimony in Torres to Izábal, 5 June 1906, in González Ramírez, *Huelga de Cananea*, 76–77; *Douglas Daily International*, 3 June 1906 and 7 June 1906. I say "most candid report" because soon afterward the governor modified his story. According to this official report, the Americans just happened to take the same train as Izábal. Vice President Ramón Corral to Rafael Izábal, 8 June 1906, in González Ramírez, *Huelga de Cananea*, 85–86.

56 *Douglas Daily International*, 3 June 1906 and 7 June 1906.

57 James C. Scott, *Domination and the Arts of Resistance: Hidden Transcripts* (New Haven: Yale University Press, 1990), 105.

58 Greene, "Brief Resume," 11 June 1906, CMC, microfilm 72/147, folder 19; *Douglas Daily International*, 3 June 1906; Municipal President Filiberto Barroso, Cananea, to the Second Judge of the First Instance, Cananea, 2 June 1906, Luis E. Torres to Municipal President of Guaymas, 4 June 1906, and Governor Rafael Izábal to Vice President Ramón Corral, 3 June 1906, in González Ramírez, *Huelga de Cananea*, 42–43, 68, and 72.

59 *Douglas Daily International*, 2 June 1906.

60 See the discussion of these dynamics in Scott, *Hidden Transcripts*, 105. "A ruling stratum whose claim to authority rests on the provision of institutionalized justice under law with honest judges," notes Scott, "will have to go to exceptional lengths to hide its thugs, its hired assassins, its secret police, and its use of intimidation."

61 *Douglas Daily International*, 2 June 1906. See also Rynning, *Gun Notches*, 307.

62 *Douglas Daily International*, 2 June 1906.

63 *Douglas Daily International*, 2 June 1906; Mrs. I. L. Burgess to Ernest Kosterlitzky, 19 September 1947, Kosterlitzky Papers; and *Douglas Daily International*, 13 August 1906. The official count of the dead was twenty-three, but some estimated that well over a hundred were killed. For the official count, see Izábal and Cubillas to Secretary of Government, 19 June 1906, in González Ramírez, *Huelga de Cananea*, 97.

64 The Mexican newspaper *El Imparcial* remembered Kosterlitzky as a hero who

compensated for Izábal's transgression. According to its later story, when Izábal opposed him, he ejected him with his protectors. *El Imparcial*, 23 January 1914, Kosterlitzky Papers. For a similar historical assessment, see "Emilio Kosterlitzky," in Francisco R. Almada, *Diccionario de historia, geografía y biografía sonorenses* (Hermosillo: Instituto Sonorense de Cultura, 1990), 371.

65 *Douglas Daily International*, 13 July 1906 and 13 August 1906, and Emilio Kosterlitzky to George Young, 10 April 1907, and 31 July 1907, CMC, microfilm 71/147, folder 16.

66 See discussion of these collaborative efforts in Raat, *Revoltosos*. Kosterlitzky reportedly drew on a spy network led by a shadowy figure called *El Zorro* (the Fox). Clark A. Cubley and Joseph A. Steiner, "Emilio Kosterlitzky," *Arizoniana* 1 (Winter 1960): 13.

67 Raat, *Revoltosos*, 142–43.

68 Emilio Kosterlitzky to George Young, 1 June 1910, CMC, microfilm 71/147, folder 16. Kosterlitzky continued to use these networks during the first months of the revolution. Emilio Kosterlitzky to Porfirio Díaz, 26 November 1910, Kosterlitzky Papers; and Emilio Kosterlitzky to William H. Brophy, 23 November 1910, Frank Cullen Brophy Papers, box 31, folder 952, Arizona Historical Society, Tucson, Arizona.

69 Louis Hostetter to U.S. Secretary of State, 30 December 1910, RDS-RIAM, roll 10, vol. 1, 812.00/620, and Alexander V. Dye to U.S. Secretary of State, 4 February 1911, RDS-RIAM, roll 11, vol. 3, 812.00/767.

70 See, for instance, Alexander V. Dye to U.S. Secretary of State, 28 February 1911, RDS-RIAM, roll 11, vol. 3, 812.00/892, but also see Alexander V. Dye to U.S. Secretary of State, 31 July 1912, RDS-RIAM, roll 19, vol. 20, 812.00/4566.

71 Louis Hostetter to U.S. Secretary of State, 30 December 1910, RDS-RIAM, roll 10, vol. 1, 812.00/620, and "The Situation in Mexico," *Engineering and Mining Journal* 94:14 (5 October 1912): 626.

72 *El Paso Herald*, 28 August 1912, Kosterlitzky Papers.

73 Spicer, *The Yaquis*, 227–35, and Hu-DeHart, *Yaqui Resistance*, 206–10.

74 See similar discussion of local knowledge in James C. Scott, *Seeing Like a State: How Certain Schemes to Improve the Human Condition Have Failed* (New Haven: Yale University Press, 1998), 54.

75 Kosterlitzky résumé. For a general history of Fort Rosecrans, see George Ruhlen, "Fort Rosecrans, California," *Journal of San Diego History* 5:4 (October 1959).

76 "Costing U.S. $1,800 a Day to Feed and Shelter Mexican Soldiers in Two 'Parole Camps,'" unidentified January 1914 clipping in Kosterlitzky Papers.

77 Letter of reference for Emilio Kosterlitzky from F.W. Benteen, 16 October 1914, Kosterlitzky Papers.

78 Major A. Duhagon to President Woodrow Wilson, 29 October 1913, and 12 November 1913 Report by Major William C. Davis, Coast Artillery Corps, RDS-

RIAM, roll 30, 812.00/9984. See Alexander V. Dye to U.S. Secretary of State, 29 February 1912, RDS-RIAM, roll 16, vol. 14, 812.00/3074, and George Young to Cirilo Ramírez, 14 February 1912, CMC, microfilm 69/147, folder 12, for Dugahon at Cananea.

79 Letter of reference for Emilio Kosterlitzky from F. W. Benteen.

80 Emilio Kosterlitzky to Frederick Simpich, 13 April 1914, and Wilbur J. Carr to Frederick Simpich, 4 May 1914, RDS-RIAM, roll 36, 812.00/11617.

81 Smith, *Eagle of Sonora*, 232. Another Porfirian elite who took vacations in Los Angeles before the Mexican Revolution was Rafael Izábal; see *Douglas Daily International*, 22 July 1904.

82 F. P. Webster to Bureau of Investigation, 24 September 1914, RDS-RIAM, roll 41, 812.00/13388, and "Kosterlitzky Retires as U.S. Agent." It is worth noting that at the same time Kosterlitzky was chasing down German "enemies" in Los Angeles, former Arizona Ranger Harry Wheeler was leading a deportation of "foreign" workers in Bisbee, owing to fears of a German-Mexican conspiracy to take over the copper borderlands. Bill O'Neal, "Captain Harry Wheeler, Arizona Lawman," *Journal of Arizona History* 27:3 (Autumn 1986), 297–314.

83 "Kosterlitzky Retires as U.S. Agent"; Emilio Kosterlitzky to General Leonard Wood, 13 January 1917, and Emilio Kosterlitzky to General Leonard Wood, 12 February 1919, Kosterlitzky Papers.

84 *La Opinión*, 18 July 1927, Kosterlitzky Papers. One has to keep in mind that this "Mexican exile" newspaper was hardly neutral on the issue of national allegiance and Kosterlitzky's statement was pitched for a pro-Mexican readership. For a discussion of *La Opinión*, see Francine Medeiros, "*La Opinión*, A Mexican Exile Newspaper: A Content Analysis of Its First Years, 1926–1929," *Aztlán* 11:1 (Spring 1980): 65–87.

85 "Soldier of Mexico Is Buried Here," 1928 newspaper clipping in Kosterlitzky Papers. The López family was prominent in Magdalena, Sonora; Francisca was Kosterlitzky's third wife. Smith, *Eagle of Sonora*, 291.

86 *Bisbee Daily Review*, 26 May 1903, denial in *Bisbee Daily Review*, 21 January 1904, and *Arizona Republic*, 27 April 1947, Kosterlitzky Papers.

87 Mary Louise Kosterlitzky to Ernest Kosterlitzky, 12 February 1959, Kosterlitzky Papers. For Mary Louise Kosterlitzky's career, see Smith, *Eagle of Sonora*, 291. See, for treatment of the rise of a "Mexican American" identity between the 1930s and 1950s, Mario T. García, *Mexican Americans: Leadership, Ideology, and Identity, 1930–1960* (New Haven: Yale University Press, 1989), but also see George J. Sánchez, *Becoming Mexican American: Ethnicity, Culture, and Identity in Chicano Los Angeles, 1900–1945* (Oxford: Oxford University Press, 1995).

✳ *Body Politics*

The Plan de San Diego Uprising

and the Making of the Modern

Texas-Mexican Borderlands

One of the most prolonged episodes of racial violence in United States history occurred at the southern tip of Texas from 1915 to 1919. It began in the summer of 1915 as a series of raids on ranches, irrigation works, and railroads by ethnic Mexicans and quickly developed into a full-blown rebellion.[1] Groups of armed men—some from across the Rio Grande, others seemingly from out of nowhere—stole livestock, burned railroad bridges, tore up tracks, killed farmers, attacked post offices, robbed stores, and repeatedly battled local posses, Texas Rangers, and the thousands of federal soldiers dispatched to quell the violence. The groups ranged from two or three assailants who quickly vanished into the brush to scores of well-organized and disciplined mounted men.

The rebels, who came to be called "Sediciosos" or "Seditionists," killed dozens of Anglo farmers. Many Anglo residents fled the region. "As soon as the bandit raids started the more timid ones commenced to move out at once, and inside of three months," remembered one local dairy farmer, "all the tenant farmers had left and a good many people there left their own farms, and others went up north or came to town and stayed until the bandit troubles were over."[2] Hundreds, perhaps several thousand, clustered in urban areas.

The raids appeared to be the fulfillment of a manifesto entitled the "Plan de San Diego." This document came to light early in 1915 but remained largely ignored until the outbreak of violence. It called for a "liberating army for races and peoples" composed of Mexicans, blacks, and Indians to kill all white males over the age of sixteen and overthrow United States rule in Texas, Colorado, New Mexico, Arizona, and California. The freed territory would form an independent nation, perhaps to rejoin Mexico at a future date.[3] Modeled after other proclamations of the ongoing Mexican Revolution, the Plan seemed to promise—or threaten, depending on where one stood—that a revolution would erupt north of the Rio Grande.

The reprisals that followed the insurrectionary violence were even worse. Texas Rangers and local vigilantes led a brutal counterinsurgency that included indiscriminate harassment of ethnic Mexicans, forcible relocation of rural Tejanos, and mass executions. A San Antonio reporter observed that "finding of dead bodies of Mexicans, suspected for various reasons of being connected with the troubles, has reached a point where it creates little or no interest. It is only when a raid is reported or an American is killed that the ire of the people is aroused." On a single day in late 1915, for example, "near Edinburg . . . the bodies of two more Mexicans were found. They had been slain during the night. During the morning the decapitated body of another Mexican roped to a large log floated down the Rio Grande." Respectable citizens openly made statements of near-genocidal racism: "The recent happenings in Brownsville country indicate that there is a serious surplus population there that needs eliminating," argued the editor of the *Laredo Times*.[4]

*   *   *

At first glance these events seem sadly characteristic of the Southwest in the decades after its conquest by the United States. Ostensibly endowed with the full rights of citizenship by the 1848 Treaty of Guadalupe Hidalgo, many ethnic Mexicans remained north of the border. Those who stayed, and their descendents, saw the victorious Anglos seize political and economic power. Even many formerly proud landowners ended up doing field work on land that had once belonged to them. In some places—most notably, South Texas and northern New Mexico, but for several decades also southern California—ethnic Mexicans remained a majority. In these enclaves, as Louise Pubols's essay in this volume discusses, Anglos generally inserted themselves into the preexisting social hierarchy, often marrying into elite Mexican families and relying on their paternalist social relations to wield power without constantly resorting to force.[5]

In South Texas, although a political "machine" run by Anglos and their elite ethnic Mexican compatriots ruled for nearly seventy years, popular resentment of marginalization and racism led to instances of open and even concerted rebellion. The region witnessed repeated clashes between defiant Tejanos and Rangers and other security forces. Two major uprisings, one led by Juan Cortina in 1859 and the other by Catarino Garza in 1891, were only defeated after intervention by the U.S. Army.

Such defiance was often articulated in the lingo of Mexican nationalism. Where their Anglo oppressors denigrated Mexican culture, rebels proclaimed their pride. Where Anglos celebrated the "manifest destiny" epitomized by their defeat of the Mexican nation, rebels often linked the protection of Mexicans in the United States to the redemption of the Mexican state. Indeed, both Juan Cortina and Catarino Garza were active partisans in internal political struggles within Mexico. The borderlands, it thus seems, were the physical site of the clash between two distinct and irreconcilable national (cum racial) projects: the United States and "American civilization" represented Anglo dominance, and Mexican nationalism the hope that ethnic Mexicans could escape or overthrow their oppressors.

A closer look at the tumult of the Plan de San Diego undermines this dualistic notion. The uprising not only became the occasion for massive and horrific racial violence but also precipitated protracted conflict among Tejanos. Its crushing defeat weakened the appeal of irredentist and Mexican nationalist politics, strengthening the position of those willing to use U.S. institutions and citizenship rights to advance the interests of ethnic Mexicans. Even as the Plan's failure solidified Anglo dominance and racial segregation in South Texas, it also helped push some Tejanos to embrace identities as Mexican Americans. Instead of continuing the contest of which nation would rule what territory, they aimed to change what United States rule would mean for those not of Anglo descent.

This essay examines the conflict between different Tejano factions during the Plan de San Diego uprising. In the decade before the uprising, ethnic Mexicans responded in divergent ways to an agricultural boom and consequent influx of Anglos. As their socioeconomic and political position became ever more tenuous, some continued to cooperate with the region's Anglo-dominated political machine. Others, inspired by the Mexican Revolution, advocated a violent redistribution of land. A third group, the "Tejano Progressives," embraced many of the region's economic changes even as it called for a revitalized Tejano community to combat discrimination and oppression. The revolt and backlash pit these groups against one another. The Texas-Mexico borderlands would continue to be influenced by the governments, capital, culture, and citizens of both Mexico and the United States. But the Plan de San Diego uprising transformed the pattern of future resistance to Anglo domination.

The World Comes Rushing In

Cattle ranching, dominant since colonization by the Spanish empire in the mid-eighteenth century, lay at the heart of South Texas's social structure, politics, and identity. Though the U.S. conquest in 1848 did change the region, in many ways the Anglo newcomers assimilated themselves to Tejano social mores and institutions. Cattle ranching became more tightly linked to the U.S. market but remained the region's dominant economic institution. Anglos married into elite ranching families. The machine that controlled South Texas electoral politics, much like southern California's political system in the decades after conquest, depended on the patron-client relations that these elites created. Ethnic Mexicans were thus subordinated but not entirely dispossessed. They retained a measure of land, independence, and political power into the early twentieth century.

For the daily lives of Tejanos, 1904 was more of a turning point than 1848. On July 4, 1904, the first passenger train from the rest of the nation's railroad system arrived in Brownsville. The connection that it represented fatally undermined the social and political accommodation that Anglos and Tejanos had maintained for the previous six decades. By providing rapid and easy connection to major market centers, the railroad unleashed an agricultural boom. Real estate developers aggressively marketed the Lower Rio Grande Valley to farmers in Midwestern states, who soon flooded the area, founding dozens of new towns and nearly doubling the Valley's population in the years 1905–1910. As the number of acres under the plow and irrigation ditch inexorably grew, the value of farm property in South Texas quintupled from 1900 to 1920. In 1924 Hidalgo County became the nation's highest-producing agricultural county.[6]

The agricultural boom subjected the ranching economy to a new set of pressures. Before the railroad, unimproved pastureland sold from fifty cents to two dollars per acre. By 1912, undeveloped land cost between one hundred and three hundred dollars an acre, and property that was easily irrigated or had particularly rich soil was sold for five hundred dollars or more per acre. These rapid increases strained the operations of *rancheros* who were not interested in or sufficiently capitalized to do well in this new

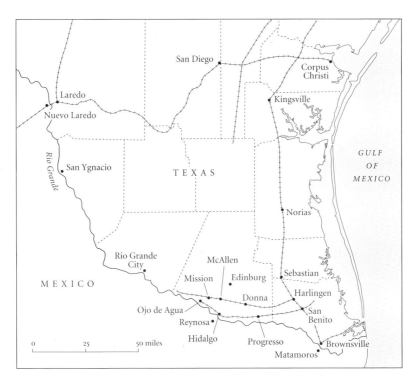

Major towns and railroads of South Texas, early twentieth century.

market. Inability to pay property taxes led to a dramatic increase in the number of sheriff's sales of tax-delinquent lands in Hidalgo County, sales that almost always transferred land from Tejanos to Anglos. The rise in land values also intensified conflict over land ownership. Land became too valuable to remain unoccupied or lightly used. "Clarification" of property ownership could be done by legal mechanisms, such as forcing the partition of an undivided tract by purchasing the interest of one of the heirs, or it could be done by the simple expedient of occupying a desired tract and violently dislodging previous occupants.[7]

The combination of economic pressure, title challenges, and outright violent appropriation led to significant Tejano land loss shortly after the railroad's construction. From 1900 to 1910 Hispanic-surnamed individuals lost a total of more than 187,000 acres in Cameron and Hidalgo counties. In Hidalgo County during this decade, the percentage of rural land in Tejano hands declined from 28.6 percent to 16.8 percent. The corresponding drop in Cameron County was from 20 percent to 16.4 percent.[8]

If the new agricultural economy strained the position of Tejanos, changing political dynamics in South Texas were even more hostile. Whereas Tejanos played an indispensable part in South Texas's political machine, the farmers' politics threatened to leave them with no political power at all. The newcomer farmers were fiercely antimachine, wanting little to do with what they perceived as a hopelessly corrupt political system that made the terrible mistake of enfranchising their racial inferiors. The solution to this problem, from their perspective, was simple: eliminate Tejano political power by disenfranchising those of Mexican descent. The tools for this strategy were readily at hand, for by 1910, Texas, like most of the South, had created the system of poll taxes, white primaries, and vigilante violence that all but stripped African Americans of the vote.[9]

Tejano Politics at the Crossroads

The new agricultural order affected Tejanos in different ways. Many became semimigrant laborers, working in towns like Brownsville or McAllen for part of the year, serving on land-grubbing crews, or picking crops from South Texas all the way to Oklahoma or Arkansas. A few prospered as merchants and land developers, carving out niches for themselves in sectors dominated by Anglo newcomers. And yet others continued as ranchers, whether as large market-driven businesses or small, subsistence-oriented family operations.

Tejano politics was similarly diverse. Some families continued to play an indispensable role in the machine as vote-deliverers and candidates for low to midlevel offices. The machine's defense of ethnic Mexican voting in the face of calls of disenfranchisement gave it a new semipopulist tinge. Nevertheless, this political system had little place for nationalism, or indeed for any other ideology. Ties of kinship and economic dependency, not notions of citizenship or ethnic solidarity, made the machine work. In contrast, two more ideological factions of Tejano politics arose in the early twentieth century in response to the agricultural boom and influx of Anglos. Radicals, inspired by the Mexican Revolution, believed that violence was required to restore ethnic Mexican power in South Texas, a project which would in turn depend on the overall revitalization of Mexico vis-à-vis the United States. Others, whom I have termed "Tejano Progressives," saw hope in many of the political and ethnic developments of the Progressive Era United States. They encouraged ethnic Mexicans to combat their marginalization through economic success, education, and political power. They pointed to useful traditions and examples from both Mexico and the United States. These two currents fed both the Plan de San Diego and Mexican American politics.[10]

Merchants and small businessmen of cities like Brownsville and Laredo, joined by elements of landed wealth, dominated Tejano progressivism. Progressives adapted many of the tenets of Mexican liberalism to the circumstances of life in the United States. The ideal liberal society was one dominated by autonomous individuals equal before the law, unrestrained by such corporate entities as an established church or Indian communities. A central government with powers authorized by a written constitution and private property rights were the foundational institutions for such a society. Liberal elites and intellectuals were vehemently anticlerical and opposed to village commons and other collective lands. As the industrial revolution lifted western Europe and the United States to new heights of economic wealth and global power, Mexican liberals struggled to modernize their own country by preparing and even forcing its citizens to compete in a market economy. A sort of folk liberalism, however, also enjoyed wide support among the Mexican populace for much of the nineteenth century. This tradition emphasized local self-rule and constitutional checks on central government more than the need to transform ordinary Mexicans into acquisitive and rational citizens of a modern state.[11] Steeped in this liberal tradition, the Progressives argued that Tejanos needed education and economic success to overcome the racism and political corruption confronting them. They aimed inward, seeking to remold Tejanos as a modern people, and outward, to secure their rights in an increasingly racist society.

South Texas's agricultural boom stimulated Progressives with the hope that economic development would both make Tejanos more industrious and give them a much-needed base of economic security. Laredo's Idar family, writers and publishers of the influential newspaper *La Crónica*, were so impressed with the Valley's transformation that they called for ethnic Mexican landholders farther upstream to construct their own rail system. "The stream of immigrants that would invade this region upon the line's construction," they argued, "would be immense and the land would rise in price to 10 or 15 times its current value" and a large number of crops could be grown profitably. The Idars' compatriot in Brownsville, lawyer and politician José Tomás Canales, described the arrival of the railroad as "the beginning of a new era in the Valley: the Era of Progress."[12]

An awareness of Tejano land loss and the rise of segregationist politics tempered this enthusiasm. "The shepherd and cowboy are gradually disappearing," Progressives wrote in 1910, "and agriculture has replaced the ranch. The lands which mainly belonged to Mexicans pass to the hands of Americans . . . [and] the old proprietors work as laborers on the same lands that used to belong to them." The ascendant farmers, moreover, were not content with just economic dominance but also failed to respect the established social and political position of ethnic Mexicans in South Texas. "The rapid industrial and agricultural development of the lower Rio Grande daily brings to our land . . . numerous elements unfamiliar with our prior rights as old inhabitants of the border," *La Crónica* noted in an article on Brownsville politics. Given "our lack of political foresight," the paper warned that "the newcomers," with their "new ideas, resources and lofty ambitions, will not hesitate to fleece us . . . of the representation that we have collectively exercised for many years in banking, commerce, society, and politics."[13]

The rising tide of racial segregation elsewhere in Texas particularly alarmed Progressives. Tejanos who witnessed Jim Crow in the rest of Texas or other parts of the South often feared that they saw their own future in whites-only train cars, restaurants, and waiting rooms. If this was what deepening the border's ties with the rest of the country meant, then they wanted none of it. Octavio García's memories prove a telling example. Born into a secure if not rich ranching family in South Texas in the 1890s, he moved to San Antonio to further his education. Here García had his first direct experience with Jim Crow. More than seventy years later, he still recalled how surprised he was to see a sign for a "Negro" waiting room once he had left the ranching zone of South Texas. Although fairly isolated from the white and black parts of San Antonio while at the school, García was so stunned by Jim Crow restrictions that he immediately wondered if Mexicans in South Texas were not headed for the same fate.[14]

Fears like García's haunted Progressives, who watched as Jim Crow subsumed more and more areas where Mexicans previously enjoyed a measure of political power and social respectability: "In San Antonio, Corpus Christi, Seguin, Goliad and other currently important cities, founded by Mexicans," lamented the Idars, "there is no public place for Mexicans except for the inferior and poorly-paid jobs allowed them."[15]

Avoiding this fate, according to the Progressives, required Texas Mexicans to increase their power through individual education, ethnic unity, and economic success. Although the Progressive position obviously demanded changes from Anglos—an end to lynchings, an undoing of segregation, respect for Mexican culture and traditions—it also insisted that Tejanos transform themselves, collectively and individually. "The time has come," *La Crónica* editorialized in 1910, "for the Mexican element to adopt a strategy to achieve the dignity and position that it deserves, leaving the shadow of ignorance that humiliates it, and this strategy is education." The paper lauded those who followed such a strategy, featuring glowing accounts of Tejano success in the midst of increasing adversity.[16]

Weakening patriarchal family patterns, as in the writings of Ignacio Martínez, a borderlands journalist and liberal revolutionary, became an important part of this project of racial uplift. On the one hand, Progressive rhetoric consistently associated the accomplishments of leaders with masculine virtue, thereby seeming to reaffirm the dominant position of men. On the other hand, it called for the "moral and physical education" of women and girls and sharply criticized the "false love" that discouraged women from learning gainful trades. Indeed, the Idars pointed to the fact that many American women worked outside the home as excellent proof of the advanced nature of the United States. They similarly endorsed women's suffrage, and published and highly praised the poems, essays, and stories of women writers.[17]

Success in electoral politics was one way to preserve and restore Tejano power. Most Progressives saw the South Texas political machine as an obstacle to their plans for unification and uplift. Indeed, they could be as antimachine as the most rabid of newcomer Anglo racists. Like these Anglos, Progressives thought that the personal ties that the machine relied on to deliver its votes reflected a weak-willed and dependent attitude. In 1910, for example, J. T. Canales declared, "From now on, let us give our support not to those candidates recommended by corrupt politics, but rather to those persons who share our ideas . . . who are just, honorable and virtuous, and who protect the rights of the people." For some Progressives, racial solidarity was a critical part of this political strategy. The Idars went so far as to call for the replacement of ethnic Mexican support for the machine with a "party of Mexican-Americans."[18]

The Progressives held ambivalent and sometimes contradictory notions about their own national identity. They kept one foot planted in the soil of Mexican liberalism, frequently condemning Catholicism and other "superstitious" beliefs, while lauding such Mexican heroes as Benito

Juárez. At the same time, they looked beyond Mexico to other ethnic and racial groups as examples of the successful implementation of their strategy. Clemente Idar called for "la Raza Mexicana" in Texas to follow the model of numerous ethnic groups within the United States. He hoped that Texas Mexicans would wield the same sort of political power that European ethnics exercised in the areas where they were numerically superior. Citing the Swedes in Minnesota as the preeminent example of such a group, Idar argued that "in this country, from its founding, even when all lived loyally under the national flag and as American citizens, its inhabitants have always divided themselves into peaceful factions along lines of racial origin." There were similar models of success on an international level. Japan, for example, had quickly risen to the status of a powerful and respected country after it opened itself up to Europe and the United States and sent its brightest children to Western universities. Mexico, on the other hand, had made no intellectual progress and ceded most economic development to foreigners.[19]

Despite an important sense of kinship, Tejanos were for the Progressives different from Mexico-born Mexicans. "They have their own ways of living in their own country," Emeterio Flores said of Mexican nationals, "and it is absolutely different from ours. We people who were born in this country feel for them because they are our own race, although we were born and educated here in this country; we feel for those poor unfortunates, and we would not like to see them come here any more unless conditions changed a great deal."[20]

Tejano Progressives harbored a similarly ambivalent attitude about the United States. Like the Latin American liberalism in which much of their own politics was steeped, they had deep admiration for some U.S. political traditions. In opposing the poll tax, for example, *La Crónica* referred to the "glorious and sublime principles of individual liberty and civil rights embodied by the Declaration of Independence and the Federal Constitution of the American Republic." The Idars encouraged Mexicans and Texas Mexicans to invoke such freedoms to protect themselves from discrimination and violence. They demanded protection for Texas Mexicans from lynchings and believed that such protection was more likely to come from federal power than from either Texas or the Mexican government. Given their harsh criticism of segregation and racial violence, their praise for the openness of U.S. life was high indeed. "In this country," they argued, "there are neither *lords, nor nobles*; here there are no tyrants who can survive; here exists the most exalted democracy practiced in the civilized world . . . the doors are open."[21]

The Idars even demonstrated at least a strategic interest in adopting some aspects of U.S. culture. They admired the business sense of Americans—even that of the farmers whose racism so offended them. As part of their education campaign, they wanted Texas Mexicans to learn "the language of the country in which they live." When he was elected the superintendent of Cameron County's school system, J. T. Canales implemented such a plan, instructing teachers that "the English language should be spoken both in the school-room as well as during recess; and, also, that school children should be taught to sing, in English, either sacred or patriotic songs."[22]

Despite the Progressives' attachment to aspects of United States politics and culture, the currents of Mexican nationalism tugged at them. While some American traditions were admirable, Tejanos risked losing their Mexicanness. Houston resident J. J. Mercado, for example, argued that Anglicisms corrupted the Spanish spoken by Texas Mexicans. For Mercado the use of terms like "bordeando" for the English "boarding" demonstrated that the isolated social life of Mexicans in Texas stunted their culture and even their mental faculties.[23] Whatever their resentment of Mexican politics—or even of many of the Mexicans in Texas—and whatever the attraction of aspects of U.S. politics and culture, many Progressives hoped for the redemption of the Mexican national project.

The 1911 toppling of Porfirio Díaz and subsequent election of liberal Francisco Madero to the presidency of Mexico bolstered this hope. The Idars speculated that Mexicans might be able to leave the increasingly inhospitable Texas and return to "the sacred native ground of our ancestors." Indeed, the increasing likelihood of such a return was all the more reason "that before our relocation, we should study some lessons in democracy." Later that year, on Mexico's Independence Day, Tejano Progressives from Laredo and beyond hosted the "Primer Congreso Mexicanista," which drew delegates from dozens of Texas and Tamaulipas towns in an effort to defend the beleaguered rights of Mexicans in Texas. The largest ethnic Mexican civil rights meeting ever held up to that point, the conference hewed to the Progressive position on many ideological and pragmatic issues. At the same time, Mexican nationalism clearly dominated the attendees' political consciousness. Where the Idars and other Progressives were conflicted in their national consciousness, speaker after speaker at the conference emphasized that Texas Mexicans' future lay within the institutions and culture of Mexico. The "absent children" of Mexico, one delegate typically stated, "who have been obliged to seek their living outside the *patria*, have regathered today . . . to seek ways to make their exile less sad."[24]

Borderlands Radicalism

If the advent of the Mexican Revolution seemed to turn Tejano Progressives away from their experimentation with U.S. citizenship rights, then in another sense it also energized Texas-Mexican politics. The plethora of Mexican politicians, military leaders, and intellectuals who found refuge in Texas brought with them a wide spectrum of political philosophies and visions of the future of Mexico.

Ricardo and Enrique Flores Magón were some of the earliest and most influential exiles. First fleeing to Texas, then St. Louis, and ultimately to Los Angeles, they achieved remarkable success in spreading their newspaper, *Regeneración*, across the Mexican community in the United States and into Mexico itself. By 1906 nearly 20,000 people in both nations paid for subscriptions and avidly read the brothers' calls for formal political reforms such as a four-year presidential term with no reelection, classical liberal proposals such as taxing church property, and social reforms such as an eight-hour workday and an end to child labor. Their manifesto circulated across Mexico, gaining the support of many local liberal organizations, including groups involved in major industrial strikes, and helped to spark numerous small and unsuccessful uprisings in Mexico's North over the next several years.[25]

Enrique and Ricardo, relocated in Los Angeles, became both more explicitly radical and less influential by the time that Francisco Madero became president in October 1911. Whereas liberals like Madero thought that private property allowed individuals to function as autonomous members of society, the Flores Magón brothers came to embrace the anarchist idea that property needed to be redistributed so that the direct and decentralized control of the means of production could create an egalitarian and just society. They denounced Madero as a "traitor to the cause of liberty" and called for an armed struggle to redistribute land and wealth and destroy the power of the church, foreigners, and the rich. This stance cost them the support of Tejano Progressives, many of whom enthusiastically supported

Madero. Although Nicasio Idar had briefly been an associate of the Flores Magóns after their arrival in Laredo, by 1911 *La Crónica* ridiculed their utopian plans and referred to them as "traitor[s]" who were "enriching some American tramps." Similarly, Emeterio Flores told a federal commission that "how the United States has ever consented to [*Regeneración*] to go through our mails is something we can not understand. . . . Several copies of this filthy paper have reached our offices and we think it very disgraceful to let such a thing be transmitted."[26]

In the teens, the Flores Magóns had trouble enough paying their bills and staying out of U.S. prison, let alone leading a successful revolution. Nevertheless, *Regeneración* continued to be an influential publication for Mexicans. Indeed, it may have influenced Mexicans residing in the United States, and especially in Texas, more than those in Mexico. By 1915 fully 42 percent of its papers circulated in Texas, as compared with 13 percent each in California and Mexico.[27]

In South Texas, Aniceto Pizaña, a rancher who lived near Brownsville, appears to have been the single most active Partido Liberal Mexicano (PLM) partisan. Pizaña not only faithfully contributed his own money to the legal defense of jailed PLM partisans; he also raised money and sold PLM literature in the Brownsville area. The *ranchero* was introduced to *Regeneración* by a friend in 1908 and soon distributed, as he put it, "the propaganda of Land and Liberty for all." Pizaña founded a South Texas PLM *grupo* named "Perpetual Solidarity." The anarchist condemnation of wage labor as a form of servitude would have had enormous resonance with rancheros like Pizaña, who found such labor (which was almost always in agriculture) exploitive and humiliating. Pizaña himself had gone on a long cotton-picking excursion into central Texas in the 1890s, in his mid-teens.[28] One account indicates that he became a devoted follower of the Flores Magón brothers after meeting them in Laredo in 1904. Pizaña supported PLM efforts in Tamaulipas, where extremely concentrated land ownership patterns along the border helped build support for land reform across a wide range of the political spectrum. At one point he even contemplated joining a PLM border raid against a prominent Tamaulipan hacienda.[29]

The Plan de San Diego and Its Hidden Tejano Civil War

Soon enough Texas itself became the site of a rebellion. In 1915, rancheros' anger at their displacement boiled over into a sustained uprising. Aniceto

Pizaña, attacked at his own ranch by Anglo vigilantes, joined the rebellion along with several of his PLM compatriots. Receiving some aid from a revolutionary commander based in Matamoros, the Sediciosos mounted an impressive series of raids in the fall of 1915. They attacked irrigation pump houses, derailed a passenger railroad car leaving Brownsville, terrorized and killed Anglo farmers against whom they bore grudges, and attacked a branch of the enormous King Ranch. Vigilantes, in response, began killing ethnic Mexicans—in some cases engaging in mass executions—and driving many rancheros off their lands. In the midst of this clearly racial violence, Tejanos were also set against one another. The three pre-uprising political factions—machine lieutenants, PLM-inspired radicals, and the Progressives—found themselves at odds and sometimes even at arms.

The first apparent killing of a Tejano by the rebels occurred on July 12, about a week after the first sustained flurry of raids on Anglo farmers. Ignacio and Adelair Cantú shot and killed Brownsville deputy constable Pablo Falcón while he was on duty at a dance. The Cantús, according to witnesses, called out to Falcón and Cameron County deputy marshal Encarnación Cuellar and then shot both men from behind. The *Brownsville Herald* portrayed this shooting as another instance of the senseless violence that plagued Mexican dance grounds. "The magnolia baile ground is a notorious resort, and has been the scene of many shootings and several killings in late years," its article stated.[30]

Perhaps most of its readers took this explanation at face value. But Harbert Davenport, a Brownsville lawyer and sometimes legal partner of J.T. Canales, later described Falcón as "the raiders' first victim" and expressed his confidence that if he had the chance, Falcón "would have undoubtedly, warned me of the trouble brought about by the 'Plan of San Diego.'" Another Cameron County deputy sheriff, Carlos Esparza, who "allegedly had a reputation of mistreating local residents," was killed some two weeks before Falcón. Esparza's family had a long-standing dispute with the nearby Escamillas, some of whom soon joined the uprising. Two weeks after Falcón's shooting, one of the bands active in Cameron County killed a local Tejano, José María Benavides, during a raid on the Los Indios Ranch.[31]

Low-level office holders such as Falcón were not the only Tejanos affiliated with the machine to be targeted by the Sediciosos. Pizaña and his comrades resented the complicity of many machine figures in the agricultural boom. The political establishment's willingness to resort to violence to crush the uprising only exacerbated this resentment. Indeed, the estate of a key Hidalgo County *jefe político* became the rebels' favorite target. The small town of Progreso, right along the river in the portion of eastern Hidalgo County known as Ojo de Agua, was a virtual private kingdom for Don Florencio Saenz. Saenz's prosperous store, his integrated farming and ranching operation (more than 40,000 acres, complete with its own private irrigation system), and the post office set up to cater to his community's needs reflected his success in navigating the currents of the Valley's new commercial order. Like most ranchers who benefited from the agricultural boom, Saenz relied on a nexus of economic and political power. He served as Hidalgo County commissioner from 1852 to 1905, delivering the numerous votes of his tenants, retainers, and kin to the Hidalgo County machine. According to one neighbor, "he practically controlled the votes of the eastern part of Hidalgo County for years and years."[32]

Saenz's store had been robbed in May of 1914, more than a year before the wider-scale uprising began. Saenz named two local Tejano residents as participants in the robbery. They became some of the earliest lynching victims in 1915. The Sediciosos struck back hard, attacking Progreso four times in August and September of 1915. Soldiers and raiders exchanged gunfire on August 17 and 25, a four day-battle raged in the area from September 2 to 5, and another sustained and bloody fight took place on September 24. "Progreso was, for some unknown reason, down in the raiders' books for punishment. They seemed to have an especial grudge against the little town and centered their activities in that vicinity," recalled one puzzled local law enforcement officer. Those who knew the area were not so puzzled. They could name the local Tejanos who had turned on Saenz.[33]

If the rebels wanted to punish Saenz, they certainly succeeded. The September attacks forced him to shut down his store and transfer his goods to Mercedes. Although he hired a private security force to defend his vast estate, the frequent raids forced most of his tenants and nearby population out of the area for the better part of three years. "Consequently," as his heirs later wrote, Saenz "was unable to operate his fields and ranch properties at Toluca, as it was impossible to get employees to live near the river and operate these properties . . . the fields were abandoned, grew up in brush and will . . . have to be opened up and cleared at a large expense." Indeed, so many fled the Progreso area that Saenz judged it unwise to reopen his store even after the "bandit troubles" ended.[34]

Other Tejanos became victims of raiders with less clear motives. On

September 9, for example, a small party of four or five raiders, if not all locals, at least led by one, killed a Texas-Mexican resident near Lyford. Nearby soldiers gave pursuit but quickly lost the band in the chaparral. The next day, a band of about twelve raiders attacked a nearby ranch but were fought off by a few Anglos and their Tejano ranch hands. On September 11 the Lyford area saw its third consecutive day of combat. "Near Lyford two Mexican-Texans, one known and the other thought to be pro-American, have been killed by bandits, our troops near hunting the bandits and making them scatter or take to the dense brush and disappear," reported a nearby army officer the same week. Four or five men fired on a Tejano mail carrier as he made his normal Edinburg–Del Fino run in Hidalgo County.[35] No doubt many other similar instances with unclear motives occurred but went unnoticed by authorities.

The political differences between radicals, Progressives, and machine participants did not cause all Tejano clashes, of course. The advent of the uprising and its brutal suppression created openings for the use of force to solve a variety of conflicts, some having nothing to do with the uprising or politics at all. It is difficult to tell, for example, if political differences or family resentment induced Sostenes Saldaña and his illegitimate son, Sostenes Jr., to take different paths during the uprising. The elder Saldaña served for many years as Cameron County deputy and worked actively in 1915 and 1916 to stop the raids. His son apparently bragged "that he was a big man among the bandits . . . [and] urged all the Mexicans to join in the movement." The younger Saldaña was killed in October or November of 1915.[36]

*   *   *

The reprisals and vigilantism launched by the newly unified Anglo newcomers exacerbated the divisions among Tejanos. Rancheros opposed to the uprising found themselves in a very difficult position, fearing both vigilante posses, often led by Texas Rangers, and attacks by the Sediciosos. As the raids and vigilantism continued into the fall of 1915, the Sediciosos seemed to prompt something of a backlash. Some Tejanos began cooperating with the army and local law enforcement officers to put an end to the raids. L. H. Bates wrote to the Texas adjutant general, the commander of the Texas Rangers, that "most all Mexican ranchmen in this section [near Brownsville] are ready to cooperate and do all they can to aid militia with aid of scouts and Mexican-Texas ranchmen who know the country."[37]

Key Tejano Progressives joined the backlash. The Progressives found themselves in an awkward and in-between position. On the one hand, they wanted little to do with any violent upheaval or radical overthrow of established economic power. The Sediciosos' attacks on the railroad and the farmers affronted the Progressive support of economic development in general, and of South Texas' agricultural boom in particular. On the other hand, the Progressives abhorred the growing vigilantism. The events of 1915 and 1916 must have confirmed their fear that a loss of Tejano economic power subjected them to marginalization and social violence. The machine's inability or unwillingness to limit such violence reflected the Progressive judgment that it held little promise for the betterment of Tejano lives.

Because no early raids occurred near Laredo, the Idars did not have to confront these tensions directly in the fall of 1915. J. T. Canales, on the other hand, was caught in the middle of them. His family's land (which included five different ranches at the time) and his own enthusiasm for agricultural development made Canales a staunch opponent of the uprising. He proved to be an active opponent as well. Although not part of a large meeting held in late October to coordinate a response to the raids, Canales chose his own method of action, organizing a regular patrol of like-minded Tejanos who assisted the army's efforts to turn back all raids at the river. A Brownsville resident suggested the potential usefulness of such a patrol at least as early as August, and by fall such a system was in place. As the army commander at Los Indios wrote in late October, "a system of patrolling along the River bank with Mexicans has been in operation for two days. If properly supplemented with observation posts along the River, it is thought this would practically prohibit the bandits from crossing or operating in this sector." Canales's efforts bore fruit. Soon, cavalry officers were reporting that the scouts he recruited had allowed them to detect and halt raids that otherwise would have slipped past their own patrols.[38]

At the same time, Canales also made efforts to stop the vigilantism. Convinced that Aniceto Pizaña had been the victim of a neighbor who coveted his land, Canales did what he could to help the ranchero's family. When Aniceto's brother Ramón was charged with attempted murder for defending his ranch, Canales served as his legal counsel, ultimately winning his acquittal on the grounds of self-defense in an appeals court. On at least one occasion Canales secured the release of Tejanos detained for suspicion of involvement with the uprising. When the vigilantism grew more extreme in the fall of 1915, he spoke out publicly against the Texas Rangers' brutality. In 1919, again a member of the state legislature, Canales launched an investigation into the conduct of the Rangers that would document their worst crimes.[39]

If Canales was in a difficult position, a split between the army and the Texas officials and citizens responsible for the vigilantism made it more tenable than it otherwise would have been. While local Anglos set aside their differences to face a shared threat, federal and state authorities found themselves increasingly at odds. Federal officers and the U.S. Army took a dim view of vigilantism. Because it generated support for the uprising among both the local Tejano population and some of the revolutionary forces across the river, such violence made the government's goal of restoring order more difficult. Consequently, army officers did not engage in arbitrary executions, killings, or removals. Some even made some efforts to prevent Rangers and civilians from doing so. Tejanos showed themselves to be very aware of the differences between state and local officers, sometimes asking for army units to be assigned for their protection. The deployment of federal soldiers could offer protection from Sedicioso reprisals and Ranger vigilantism alike. An army officer stationed near Los Indios told his superiors that the "Mexican population seems to be considerably exercised over rumors current to the effect that a withdrawal of the troops was being contemplated. They fear that, if the troops are suddenly withdrawn, former conditions of outlawry will be resumed, vengeance being meted out against those Mexicans who have been friendly to, or have been employed as scouts or spies by, the Americans; that the Rangers will return, killing innocent as well as guilty; and that the Mexicans' only recourse will be an exodus en masse to Mexico."[40]

The experiences of Laredo's Tejano Progressives indicate how the suppression of the South Texas uprising also silenced a wide range of political dissent. Although the Idars, living in Laredo, were removed from the majority of the raids and reprisals in 1915, the shock waves of the Plan de San Diego soon reached them. Like J. T. Canales, they showed little sympathy for the Plan or its adherents. In the early stages of the Mexican Revolution, the Idars sided with Francisco Madero, even as the Flores Magón brothers denounced him as a sellout, and would have had little sympathy for calls for a violent revolution on the north side of the Rio Grande.[41] Clemente Idar actively opposed the Plan when the opportunity presented itself. After the June 1916 clashes in the Laredo area, local and federal authorities needed a reliable Spanish-speaking witness and translator to deal with the captured raiders. Court documents name a "C. N. Idar" as a witness to the statements of three men captured after the Webb Station raid on June 12. Idar copied and translated the letter from one of the prisoners to Mexican general Álvaro Obregón. Moreover, when it looked as though the Sediciosos would extend their campaign to the Laredo area in May and June of 1916, Clemente also served as an agent of the U.S. Department of Justice, passing along information about a raid nearby.[42]

*   *   *

By 1919, when the end of World War I finally led to the withdrawal of the armed forces sent to quell the uprising, South Texas was in important respects a different place than it had been before. The defeat of the Plan de San Diego in 1916, high commodity prices, and vigorous marketing prompted a resumption of the region's agricultural boom. The balance of political and economic power shifted decisively to newcomer farmers. The machine and its Tejano lieutenants lost much of their power. Soon the Jim Crow–style segregation and disfranchisement that the Progressives had feared became a reality for all too many Tejanos. The land that produced Juan Cortina, Catarino Garza, and the Plan de San Diego would never again witness another sustained uprising. Seventy years after the Treaty of Guadalupe Hidalgo, the South Texas borderlands were politically and economically integrated into the United States, with dire results for ethnic Mexicans. Conquest, it seemed, was finally complete.

But it was not so simple, as subsequent events would demonstrate. Tejanos did not stop struggling for political rights and economic security in the modern borderlands. What distinguished their protests from those of their ancestors was their use of the language of U.S. nationalism to articulate their grievances. The 1920s saw the emergence of a Mexican American civil rights movement, with the embrace of American citizenship and the struggle for political and social freedoms under its rubric. Tejano Progressives, pitted against Mexican revolutionaries and Anglo segregationists during the uprising, shed their previous ambivalence about United States citizenship and played a key role in shaping the political platform and institutions of the first generation of Mexican Americans. At the founding convention of the League of United Latin American Citizens (LULAC), the principal organization of this new political impulse, J. T.

Canales and Clemente Idar wrote much of the constitution and sponsored the controversial motion limiting membership to United States citizens.[43]

Most of LULAC's platform and techniques had been anticipated by the Tejano Progressives in the decade before the Plan de San Diego. The Progressives were as intent on the modernization of their own people, the fitting of them with the skills and attitudes necessary to compete in twentieth-century United States, as they were on confronting Anglo racism. So was LULAC. Earlier in the century, Canales, the Idars, and J. Luz Saenz pinned many of their highest hopes on the transformative potential of education, thereby singling out educational inequality and segregation as particularly offensive. So did LULAC. The Progressive current included politically engaged women and men who welcomed such activity. So did LULAC. The Progressives hoped that Mexican Americans would seek and gain political power on their own terms, rather than the machine's. So did LULAC. "One generation visualizes that which another brings into practice," wrote Clemente Idar shortly after the new organization's founding. "In the history of all peoples, that is exactly what human progress has brought about."[44]

There was one critical difference, however, between LULAC and the Tejano Progressives. Where the Progressives had been able to pick and choose between U.S. and Mexican nationalism, LULACers were now enthusiastic American citizens. This was not because they had turned their backs on Mexican culture or customs, but rather because what they had endured during the Plan de San Diego convinced them of the dangers of statelessness: that they risked becoming a people belonging to no nation at all. Mexican Americans had fallen through the crack between the two nations. "We are becoming a new people on the margin of two great and powerful nations," editorialized *El Paladín* in its announcement of the founding of LULAC, "and continue being Americans to religiously fulfill all of our obligations, and Mexicans when it comes to sharing rights, especially in the South of Texas." "Mexican-Americans," emphasized Castulo Gutiérrez, "as long as we do not elevate ourselves to the level of citizens, will be nothing more than the conquered."[45]

LULAC and its ideology of U.S. citizenship still competed with the machine and the nationalist politics of exile for Tejano loyalties. The remnants of South Texas's once mighty machine, which still ruled portions of the region's ranching areas, condemned the new organization. At times they even called in the Texas Rangers to harass and arrest LULAC organizers. Although vehemently opposed to the radicalism of the Flores Magón brothers and Aniceto Pizaña, the Mexican government created by the revolution called upon the loyalties of those of Mexican descent, insisting that their true home was south of the river. Angered by LULAC's American citizenship politics, Mexico's consul general in San Antonio warned those of Mexican descent "that they should always remember that they live in a foreign nation, that they came by their own choice to the United States and that they have no right to disturb the existing social conditions here." If "luck is bad in one place," he concluded, "they should seek their fortune in another or return to their country."[46]

Such appeals fell on deaf ears. The Plan de San Diego uprising, intended to cast off United States rule, had instead helped to create the category of Mexican American. A critical mass of Tejanos had come to believe that the borderlands could be the site not merely of clashing sovereignties but also of multiracial democracy.

Notes

1　There is no graceful racial or ethnic nomenclature for describing South Texas. For purposes of consistency I have chosen to use "Mexican" to refer to Mexican nationals with no deep roots in the United States, "Tejano" or "Texas-Mexican" to refer to Texas residents of Mexican descent, and "ethnic Mexicans" to subsume both groups. The label "Mexican American" is reserved for those of Mexican descent who considered themselves U.S. citizens.

2　U.S. Congress, Senate, *Investigation of Mexican Affairs*, 2 vols. S Doc 285, 66th Cong., 2nd sess., 1920, 1182.

3　For accounts of the Plan de San Diego, see James A. Sandos, *Rebellion in the Borderlands: Anarchism and the Plan de San Diego, 1904–1923* (Norman: University of Oklahoma Press, 1992); James A. Sandos, "The Plan of San Diego: War and Diplomacy on the Texas Border, 1915–1916," *Arizona and the West* 14 (Spring 1972): 5–24; Juan Gómez-Quiñones, "Plan de San Diego Reviewed," *Aztlán* 1:1 (Spring 1970): 124–32; Charles C. Cumberland, "Border Raids in the Lower Rio Grande Valley—1915," *Southwestern Historical Quarterly* 57:3 (January 1954): 285–311; Mario D. Longoria, "Revolution, Visionary Plan, and Marketplace: A San Antonio Incident," *Aztlán* 12:2 (Fall 1981): 211–26; Charles H. Harris III and Louis R. Sadler, "The Plan of San Diego and the Mexican–United States War Crisis of 1916: A Reexamination," *Hispanic American Historical Review* 58:3 (August 1978): 381–408; William M. Hagar, "The

Plan of San Diego: Unrest on the Texas Border in 1915," *Arizona and the West* 5 (Winter 1963): 327–36; and Douglas W. Richmond, "La Guerra de Texas se renova: Mexican Insurrection and Carrancista Ambitions, 1900–1920," *Aztlán* 11:1 (Spring 1980): 1–32.

4   *San Antonio Express*, 11 September 1915, cited in Sandos, *Rebellion in the Borderlands*, 98; "Exclusion Act Put in Force along Border," *New York Sun*, 15 September 1915, from clippings file in Secretaría de Relaciones Exteriores (SRE), Archivo de la Embajada Mexicana en los Estados Unidos (AEMEUA), legajo 685, expediente 3; quoted in James Sandos, "The Mexican Revolution and the United States, 1915–17: The Impact of Conflict in the Texas-Tamaulipas Frontier upon the Emergence of Revolutionary Government in Mexico" (Ph.D. diss., University of California at Berkeley, 1978), 164.

5   For examinations of the different ways that ethnic Mexicans navigated United States rule after conquest, see Albert Camarillo, *Chicanos in a Changing Society: From Mexican Pueblos to American Barrios in Santa Barbara and Southern California, 1848–1930* (Cambridge: Harvard University Press, 1979); Robert J. Rosenbaum, *Mexicano Resistance in the Southwest: "The Sacred Right of Self-Preservation"* (Austin: University of Texas Press, 1981); Sarah Deutsch, *No Separate Refuge: Culture, Class, and Gender on an Anglo-Hispanic Frontier in the American Southwest, 1880–1920* (New York: Oxford University Press, 1987); Deena J. González, *Refusing the Favor: The Spanish-Mexican Women of Santa Fe, 1820–1880* (New York: Oxford University Press, 1999); David Montejano, *Anglos and Mexicans in the Making of Texas, 1836–1986* (Austin: University of Texas Press, 1987); and María E. Montoya, *Translating Property: The Maxwell Land Grant and the Conflict over Land in the American West, 1840–1940* (Berkeley: University of California Press, 2002).

6   James Sandos, "The Mexican Revolution and the United States," 115, 119, 166; Armando Alonzo, "A History of the Mexicans in the Lower Rio Grande Valley of Texas: Their Role in Land Development and Commercial Agriculture, 1900–1930" (M.A. thesis, University of Texas Pan American, 1983), 44.

7   Emilio Zamora, *The World of the Mexican Worker in Texas* (College Station: Texas A&M Press, 1993), 33; Evan Anders, *Boss Rule in South Texas: The Progressive Era* (Austin: University of Texas Press, 1982), 139; *Pilar Villareal v. A.A. Browne, et al.* No. 2935 in the District Court, 28th Judicial District, Cameron County, Texas, transcript in Center for American History, University of Texas at Austin, 1205, 1317 (hereafter, *Villareal v. Browne*); Hidalgo County Deed Records, Hidalgo County Courthouse, Edinburg, Texas.

8   Tax rolls, Hidalgo and Cameron counties, Texas State Archives, Austin, Texas.

9   Anders, *Boss Rule*, 277–79; Montejano, *Anglos and Mexicans*, 143.

10   I have chosen the term "Tejano Progressive" to describe these Tejanos in order to emphasize the connections between their political program and the Progressive Era ferment of the United States. George Sánchez points to a similar

connection in California in "The 'New Nationalism,' Mexican Style: Race and Progressivism in Chicano Political Development during the 1920s," in William Deverell and Tom Sitton, eds., *California Progressivism Revisited* (Berkeley: University of California Press, 1994). Many historians view Progressives quite skeptically, emphasizing their fondness for social control and their unwillingness to confront the economic forces behind so many of the social problems they did address. Others, however, stress the enormous diversity of Progressives and the extremely democratic nature of many of their proposals. See Robert D. Johnston, "Re-Democratizing the Progressive Era: The Politics of Progressive Era Political Historiography," *Journal of the Gilded Age and Progressive Era* 1 (January 2002): 68–92; and Robert D. Johnston, *The Radical Middle Class: Populist Democracy and the Question of Capitalism in Progressive Era Portland, Oregon* (Princeton: Princeton University Press, 2003). Although most historians have treated U.S. Progressives as only part of the trajectory of U.S. history, Daniel Rodgers's recent study shows just how much they were in dialogue with European reformers as well. The term "Tejano Progressivism" therefore can help us see the ways in which American politics during this period was bound up in international developments. See Daniel T. Rodgers, *Atlantic Crossings: Social Politics in a Progressive Age* (Cambridge: Harvard University Press, 1998).

11 For discussions of liberalism, see Alicia Hernández Chávez, *La tradición republicana del buen gobierno* (México, D.F.: El Colegio de México y Fondo de Cultura Económica, 1993); Guy P. C. Thomson with David LaFranca, *Patriotism, Politics and Popular Liberalism in Nineteenth-Century Mexico* (Wilmington, Del.: Scholarly Resources, 1999); Guy Thomson, "Popular Aspects of Liberalism in Mexico, 1848–1888," *Bulletin of Latin American Research* 10:3 (1991): 265–91; Alan Knight, "El liberalismo mexicano desde la Reforma hasta la Revolución (una interpretación)," *Historia Mexicana* 35 (1985): 59–85; Charles Hale, *The Transformation of Liberalism in Late Nineteenth-Century Mexico* (Princeton: Princeton University Press, 1989); Jennie Purnell, *Popular Movements and State Formation in Revolutionary Mexico* (Durham: Duke University Press, 1999); Florencia Mallon, *Peasant and Nation* (Berkeley: University of California Press, 1995); and Peter Guardino, *Peasants, Politics, and the Formation of Mexico's National State: Guerrero, 1800–1857* (Stanford: Stanford University Press, 1996).

12 *La Crónica*, 5 March 1910, 1; "Personal recollections of J. T. Canales written at the request of and for use by the Honorable Harbert Davenport in preparing a historical sketch of the lower Rio Grande Valley for the Soil Conservation District, recently organized, in Cameron County, Texas" (Brownsville, Texas: 28 April 1945), 17, 15; Anders, *Boss Rule*, 89.

13 *La Crónica*, 7 May 1910, 3 December 1910.

14 Octavio García Interview [1975], Lower Rio Grande Valley Historical Collection, University of Texas Pan American.

15 *La Crónica*, 6 August 1910, 3.

16 Ibid., 7 May 1910.

17 Ibid., 1 October 1910, 1; 21 September 1911, 4; 26 October 1911.

18 Ibid., 16 July 1910, 5; 16 March 1911; 26 January 1911, 3.

19 Ibid., 26 January 1911; 15 October 1910; 12 January 1911, 2.

20 Commission on Industrial Relations, *Final Report and Testimony* (Washington, D.C.: GPO, 1916), S. Doc 415, testimony of Emeterio Flores, 9204.

21 *La Crónica*, 15 October 1910

22 Ibid., 7 May 1911; "Personal Recollections of J. T. Canales," 18.

23 *La Crónica*, 14 September 1911, 2.9

24 Ibid., 18 May 1911; "Primer Congreso Mexicanista, verificado en Laredo, Texas, EE. UU. de la A. Los Días 14 al 22 de Septiembre de 1911. Discurso y Conferencias. Por la Raza y Para la Raza" (Laredo: N. Idar, 1912), 8.

25 Sandos, *Rebellion in the Borderlands*, 1–12. Sandos's emphasis is on the Flores Magóns' experiences in the United States and the connection of their anarchism to the Plan de San Diego. For analyses of their political thought, see Salvador Hernández Padilla, *El Magonismo: Historia de una pasión libertaria, 1900–1920* (México, D.F.: Ediciones Era, 1984); Diego Abad de Santillan, *Ricardo Flores Magón: El apostol de la revolución social mexicana* (México, D.F.: Grupo Cultural Ricardo Flores Magón, 1925); and Hilario Tapete Lara, *Ideas en movimiento* (México, D.F.: Sociedad Cooperativa de Producción Taller Abierto, 1998).

26 Sandos, *Rebellion in the Borderlands* 29; Zamora, *World of the Mexican Worker*, 61; *La Crónica*, 15 June 1911; Commission on Industrial Relations, *Final Report and Testimony*, 9201.

27 Sandos, *Rebellion in the Borderlands*, 59.

28 Aniceto Pizaña, "Apuntes biográficos de un revolucionario del año de 1915," (n.p. [1933]), 21.

29 Ibid., 12 July 1912; 7 September 1912; and 21 September 1912; Pizaña, "Apuntes biográficos," 39, 21; Sandos, *Rebellion in the Borderlands*, 9; Carlos González Salas, *Acercamiento a la historia del movimiento obrero en Tampico (1887–1983)* (Victoria, Tamaulipas: Instituto de Investigaciones Históricas, 1987), 65–67.

30 "Two Officers Fatally Shot at a 'Baile'; One is Dead," *Brownsville Herald*, 12 July 1915, 1.

31 Harbert Davenport to Walter P. Webb, 13 November 1935, Webb Papers, box 2M260; "Records of the Department of State Relating to Internal Affairs of Mexico, 1910–1929," 812.00/16890; Rodolfo Rocha, "The Influence of the Mexican Revolution on the Mexico-Texas Border, 1910–1916" (Ph.D. diss., Texas Tech University, 1981), 262; Frank C. Pierce, *A Brief History of the Lower Rio Grande Valley* (Menasha, Wis.: George Banta, 1917), 90; John Peavey, "Day by Day Stories and History of Our Rio Grande Valley from 1906 till 1941," ms., 31 July 1915 entry.

32 United States Claim, Mexican Claims Commission, docket #850; *Texas Family*

Land Heritage Registry, Vol. 6 (Austin: Texas Department of Agriculture, 1980), 40–41; Jeffords affidavit, Mexican Claims Commission, docket #850.

33 U.S. Affidavit, Mexican Claims Commission, docket #850; Lott mss, 51; Report of R. L. Barnes, 1 February 1916, *Bureau of Investigation*.

34 Mexican Claims Commission, docket #798, 850.

35 "Records of the Department of State Relating to Internal Affairs of Mexico, 1910–1929," 812.00/16256; Pierce, *Brief History*, 94, Lott mss., 61; Peavey ms., 11 September entry; "Records of the Department of State Relating to Internal Affairs of Mexico, 1910–1929," 812.00/16256 and 16159.

36 4 November 1915 report of Agent Barnes, *Bureau of Investigation*; Mexican Claims Commission, docket #2667.

37 L. H. Bates to Adjutant General, 4 August 1915 (AG Correspondence, 550–18); Samuel Spears to Department of Justice, 6 August 1915, "Records of the Department of State Relating to Internal Affairs of Mexico, 1910–1929," 812.00/15814.

38 Testimony of J. T. Canales, *Proceedings of the Joint Committee*, 922; "Records of the Department of State Relating to Internal Affairs of Mexico, 1910–1929," 812.00/16752; L. H. Bates to Adjutant General, 4 August 1915, AG Correspondence, 550–18; *Proceedings of the Joint Committee*, 548–49.

39 *Proceedings of the Joint Committee*, 564, 375, 197–98.

40 30 October 1915 telegram from Robert Lansing, Mexican Claims Commission, docket #2745; 16 September 1915, Frederick Funston to James Ferguson, "Records of the Department of State Relating to Internal Affairs of Mexico, 1910–1929," 812.00/16198; Sandos, *Rebellion in the Borderlands*, 97; 16 November 1915, AG Correspondence, 552–13; "U.S. Soldiers Shoot Mexicans in Hot Fights," *New York Tribune*, 18 September 1915, in clippings file SRE, AEMEUA, leg. 685, exp. 3; "Records of the Department of State Relating to Internal Affairs of Mexico, 1910–1929," 812.00/16600 and 17030; *Proceedings of the Joint Committee*, 950–51.

41 Nicasio Idar died in 1914, but his children remained active in politics and cultural affairs. Because any issues of *La Crónica* published during the uprising are no longer extant, we do not know what this influential family said of the Plan de San Diego and the vigilantism.

42 "Confessions of Simon Solis, Antonio Cuevas, and Nolberto Pezzot," contained in typescript entitled "Webb Station Raids," in "Gray-Lane Files," Records of International Conferences, Commissions, and Expositions. Records of the United States Commissioners of the American and Mexican Joint Commission, 1916, record group 43, United States Nation Archives (USNA), Memo #11. 1 September 1916 letter from Seb. S Wilcox, Official Shorthand Reporter, 49th District of Texas, Laredo, Texas, to Gray-Lane Commission, ibid; James Sandos, *Rebellion in the Borderlands*, 199, n. 30.

43 See Benjamin Heber Johnson, *Revolution in Texas: How a Forgotten Rebellion and Its Bloody Suppression Turned Mexicans into Americans* (New Haven: Yale University Press, 2003).

44 C. N. Idar, "Nuestra liga: Motivos de meditacion," n.d. [1929], newspaper clipping in Album 2, Ben Garza Collection, LULAC Papers; Orozco, 229.

45 "Nuestra actitud ante la historia," *El Popular* n.d. [14 May 1929], Album 2, Ben Garza Collection, LULAC Papers; Castulo Gutiérrez, "Para los que no conocen nuestra inst."

46 *La Prensa*, 24 April 1930, fondo 4, legajo 74, expediente 14, Secretaría de Relaciones Exteriores.

ALEXANDRA MINNA STERN

Nationalism on the Line:

Masculinity, Race, and the Creation

of the U.S. Border Patrol, 1910–1940

Dedicated to Lionel Cantú, whose brilliant life was cut all too short.

In 1934, ten years after the creation of the United States Border Patrol, I. F. Wixon, deputy commissioner general of the Immigration and Naturalization Service (INS), took stock of this young governmental agency. Foremost on his mind were the desired skills of patrolmen, which were both myriad and in high demand. As Wixon wrote, "it is not an exaggeration to say that the ideal Patrol inspector must combine the attributes of an expert woodsman or plainsman, a veteran soldier, an accomplished diplomat, and an astute secret service operator," adding, "such men, naturally, are hard to find."[1] Indeed, during the first decade of its existence, the Border Patrol was plagued with personnel problems that included insubordination, despondency, and a turnover rate peaking at 30 percent. It was not until the late 1930s that the agency achieved any degree of coordination and routinization. By that time the Border Patrol, at least along the U.S.-Mexico border, was on the path to consolidating its role as the nation's gatekeeper, as it sought to monitor movement over and across an increasingly hardened boundary line. In doing so, the Border Patrol helped to orchestrate the criminalization of Mexicans and Mexican Americans, many of whom had circulated for years in a multiracial binational region and were now being gradually converted into "aliens" deemed admissible for temporary agricultural and industrial labor but not for full-fledged American citizenship.

The jagged development of the Border Patrol is connected to several historical processes that converged and collided in the U.S.-Mexico borderlands from the late nineteenth century to the mid-twentieth. First, the establishment of the Border Patrol coincided with, and intensified, a mounting focus on the southern border as a site of national anxiety and a concomitant rise in the perception that persons of Mexican origin were undesirables threatening to contaminate the body politic.[2] The establishment of the Border Patrol occurred in tandem with the aftermath of World War I, the passage of stringent immigration laws, and new regulations requiring visas and passports. Taken together, these shifts encouraged a reorientation of the gaze along the U.S.-Mexico border away from the Chinese, Syrians, and Germans to the ever less transparent Mexicans, whose familial and cultural connections to the region were not doubted by immigrant inspectors, although their racial fitness and economic autonomy certainly were. Second, the creation of the Border Patrol in 1924 intensified the jurisdictional struggle over boundary maintenance in Texas and the Southwest that had been playing out between federal agencies tied to the Immigration and Naturalization Service and local and state entities such as the Texas Rangers or the Arizona Rangers. An integral component of the creation of the Border Patrol was an attempt to subsume and domesticate provincial organizations into a centralized police unit. Finally, the Border Patrol took shape fractiously because, as a fraternal organization dedicated to protecting the national body and the American family from unwanted intrusion, it became a testing ground for differing conceptions of manhood. As Wixon made clear in his assessment, patrolmen were expected to embody protean masculinities, to agilely traverse the continuum from primitive hunter to civilized statesman, from cerebral cryptographer to regimented military officer, all in the name of boundary control.

The Border Patrol offers a compelling window onto the complicated intersections of gender systems, racialization, state formation, and nationalism in the United States in the first half of the twentieth century. As many scholars have argued, national spaces and imaginaries are intensely gendered, perhaps no more so than at their outer limits, where territorial perimeters are topographically inscribed, juridically codified, and physically and forcibly maintained through quotidian interactions and rituals of inclusion and exclusion.[3] At the extremities of the nation, border zones are often sexually charged arenas of both gender confusion and clarity, where definitions and enactments of femininity and masculinity can be fluid like mercury or as hard as steel.[4] Defined by its status as threshold, the U.S.-Mexico border has long served as a stage for the articulation of hypermasculinity, in the form of incursions, revolts, and gun-smuggling by Mexicans, Americans, and Indians.[5] Simultaneously, the border has also represented a flashpoint for dread and desire of female sexuality and sybaritic excess, most strikingly seen in persistent preoccupations with un-regulated vice and rampant prostitution.[6] Ontologically liminal, borders can also enable the plasticity of sexual identities and serve as conduits for the elaboration of transgendered modes of crossing and performativity.[7]

Regional and national borders that demarcate fixed and iconographi-cally reproducible cartographies are part and parcel of Western rationaliza-tion and the Cartesian logic of linearity that seek to erase but can only sub-merge.[8] Temporally and geographically layered, a border zone is, as Victor Zúñiga argues, "both diatopic and diachronic; yet as a space of adjacen-cies, it is a syntopic and synchronic space as well. A border is a diachronic and diatopic space in the sense that in it diverse times and diverse spaces converge."[9] Borderlands, thus, are replete with imbricated histories and numerous coordinates. The pasts and presents of the U.S.-Mexico border-lands encompass, quite kaleidoscopically, the scattered presidios and reli-gious settlement efforts of the Spanish empire, the brief interlude of Mexi-can nationhood, and, since 1848, the entrenchment of the United States as the region's military and economic motor and social and legal arbiter.

When it was formed in 1924, the Border Patrol became another facet of the polysemous history of militarization, nation building, cultural con-flict, and hybridization in the U.S.-Mexico borderlands. In this essay, I expand on the arguments about nationalism, race, masculinity, and milita-rization offered by Grace Delgado, Elliott Young, Benjamin Johnson, and Samuel Truett in this volume, by exploring the Border Patrol, primarily in Texas and Arizona, as a gendered and racialized project of state formation that irrevocably transformed the Southwest as it built upon the complexity of the region's pasts. Unraveling the making of the Border Patrol sheds light not only on the sui generis character of the U.S.-Mexico borderlands but also on the politics of gender, sexuality, and race in the United States during an era of xenophobia, immigration restriction, and demographic reconfiguration.

The Racialization of the U.S.-Mexico Border

The borderlands have long been an exceedingly militarized space, ever since the erection of presidios and forts by the Spanish empire in the seventeenth and eighteenth centuries. This arrangement, which came to be known as the "line of defense" (*línea de defensa*), was part of Spanish attempts to control raids by "hostile" Indians along its frontier and, especially during the late eighteenth century, to offset the increasing encroachment of the French, Anglo-American, and Russian empires into the area's embryonic trading economies.[10] After Mexico gained its independence in 1821, the area was beset by Anglo colonizers responding to Mexico's enticements of land in return for conversion to Catholicism. Militarism intensified with the Mexican-American War (1846–1848) and during the late nineteenth century as the U.S. cavalry and army regulars, stationed at a scattering of forts, began to carry out guerrilla warfare against Indians. Magnifying this environment were the Mexican *rurales* who hunted down Indians and defended the property of rich northern *hacendados*.[11] Just on the other side of the line, the Texas Rangers and Arizona Rangers mimicked their tactics, chasing southwestern Indians and shielding Anglo ranchers, and by the close of the nineteenth century, targeting Mexican laborers.[12] When immigrant inspectors arrived at the border zone at the dawn of the twentieth century, they added another layer to this much longer history of militarization in a turbulent postcolonial space.[13]

Initially, the U.S. government's presence on the U.S.-Mexico border was minimal. Customs Service "line-riders" were the sole federal agents, entrusted with curtailing smuggling of anything illegal, above all, livestock. In 1904, as federal immigration laws were expanding, the Bureau of Immigration (the INS's precursor) assigned a small cadre of "mounted watchmen" to the Mexican and Canadian lines.[14] By 1911 there were at least sixty such "mounted guards" along the southern border.[15]

Until the second decade of the twentieth century, immigration inspectors focused principally on apprehending Chinese immigrants violating the 1882 Chinese Exclusion Act.[16] The Immigration Service was also preoccupied with immigrants carrying "loathsome and contagious diseases" and those that were "likely to become a public charge." Unlike Asians, who were subjected to the most exclusionary laws of any ethnic group, Mexicans were continually waived from the requirements of many restrictions. When the 1917 Immigration Act was passed, for example, growers and industrialists were able to convince President Wilson to exempt Mexicans from the newly mandated literacy test, head tax, and contract labor clause.[17]

Despite these measures, passage across the boundary line for Mexicans and Mexican Americans was relatively lax in the early twentieth century as a fluid, though not harmonious, economy of peoples, industries, and cultures distinguished the region. Indeed, during this period, immigration and public health officials were not fixated on Mexicans but on the Chinese, Syrians, and Greeks who circumvented Ellis Island and then navigated the Southwestern desert into the United States.[18]

The outbreak of the Mexican Revolution in 1910 caused U.S. immigration and health officials to become uncomfortably aware of the openness of the border and the swelling circulation of insurgents, refugees, and temporary laborers in the twin cities of El Paso–Juárez and Laredo–Nuevo Laredo. Beyond being cast as transient and uprooted, Mexicans also began to be categorized as diseased and dirty. News of a typhus epidemic in Mexico's interior in 1915 and the discovery of several cases of the fever in El Paso in late 1916 led the Public Health Service (PHS) to launch a full-scale quarantine against Mexico and Mexicans in January 1917. Several months after the quarantine had been in effect, officials reported that the threat of typhus had all but disappeared. Nevertheless, medical inspections remained in force until the late 1930s; a public health response to a short-lived epidemic metamorphosed into a protracted quarantine along the entirety of the U.S.-Mexico border.[19] Although over time a sizable number of Mexicans, especially those who were well-dressed, traveled first-class on the train, or were recognized commuters, were exempt from the disinfection drill, the harsh reality and length of the quarantine helped to generate and underscore racialized stereotypes of Mexicans as germ-infested.

Thus shortly before 1920, facing the prospect of the quarantine procedures, many Mexicans began to avoid crossing into the United States at designated points of entry. In South Texas, this stirred enough alarm for the PHS to create a Mounted Quarantine Guard, which, starting in 1921 monitored fifty-to-one-hundred mile-long sections of the Rio Grande, hauling working-class Mexicans into quarantine stations for delousing and sterilization, vaccinating immigrants with no signs of scarification for smallpox, and searching out cases of trachoma and other bodily ailments. Although the Mounted Quarantine Guard was only in existence for three years, phased out after the formation of the Border Patrol in 1924, its approach served as a model for the first generation of patrolmen.[20]

It was over the course of the 1920s that the concept of illegal entry and the construct of the illegal alien became central to U.S. immigration policy.[21] The 1920s was a decade of xenophobia and purity campaigns, when eugenics was exceedingly popular, Prohibition the law of the land, and extremist groups like the Ku Klux Klan attracted thousands of zealous adherents. Immigration laws responded to the tenor of the times. Most strikingly, in 1924, the U.S. Congress passed the unyielding National Origins Act. This legislation stipulated a quota of 2 percent of all immigrant groups coming to the United States according to the 1890 census, thus radically restricting the entry of Mediterraneans and Eastern Europeans. The National Origins Act decreased the total amount of admissible immigrants to 150,000 per year, less than 15 percent of the pre–World War I annual average.[22] The formulation of the quota based on the 1890 census was a calculated choice that deliberately shut out so-called new immigrants, such as Italians and Poles, who had begun to disembark on Ellis Island in rising numbers after the turn of the century. Similarly determined to be biologically and morally undesirable, all Asians (except for Filipino colonial nationals) were debarred by the 1917 Immigration Act. In addition, after 1918, the Immigration Service began to require passports and visas to come into the country.

Now facing new financial and administrative requirements, as well as an exacting quota, many European immigrants began to enter the United States via land borders. With this shift, deportations—which hitherto had been few and far between—began to increase rapidly in the 1920s, from less than 3,000 annually to over 40,000 annually by the close of the decade.[23] In this context of tightened ports and borders, the focus shifted to Mexicans, who—unaffected by the National Origin Act quotas—were immigrating to the United States in greater numbers than ever before. From an average of 50,000 per year in the years before 1920, over 150,000 Mexicans of varying legal status entered the United States annually in the 1920s, increasing the Mexican-born population from 486,418 in 1920 to 1,422,533 in 1930.[24] While these statistics on Mexican immigration, mainly gathered from census data, are notoriously problematic, they do capture the dramatic growth of the Mexican origin population from 1920 to 1930.

The entrenched quarantine, harsh immigration laws, and a noticeable rise of Mexicans crossing the border, whether for day labor, seasonal work, or a long-term stay, set the stage for a battle between nativists, who were busy advocating a quota for Mexicans, and powerful agriculturalists in the Southwest and California, especially beet and citrus growers, who denounced any measure that might deter a steady supply of cheap labor. It was from this contradiction that the Border Patrol emerged as a compromise: a federal agency that would screen immigrants from the Western Hemisphere, above all, Mexico, to ascertain if they were economically, physically, and morally worthy to enter the United States. Added to a congressional appropriations bill that constituted part of the National Origins Act, the Border Patrol was officially established on May 28, 1924, and granted a seed budget of one million dollars.[25] Its job was to defend the "long wide-open stretches of unguarded border" between designated points of entry, serving as the "first line of defense" against an "army of aliens."[26] Thus, the Border Patrol developed into a gate-keeping organization that sometimes followed the prerogatives of capitalist interests to allow Mexicans in, and, in times of crisis, deported scores of Mexican nationals and Mexican Americans.

Mexicans, above all other immigrants, felt the punitive effects of a series of laws passed in the latter half of the 1920s. In 1924, for example, Congress passed legislation calling for the deportation of anyone entering the United States after July 1, 1924, without a valid visa. Five years later, unlawful entry was made a misdemeanor, and a repeat offense a felony.[27] By the late 1920s, more Mexicans were being deported than all Europeans combined, from 1,751 in 1925, to 5,407 in 1929, to 8,335 in 1931; these figures do not include the 8,000 to 10,000 Mexicans expelled voluntarily each year after 1927.[28] Mexicans' vague legal status made them especially vulnerable: they could be categorized as nonresident aliens (usually migrating across the border for seasonal labor with the intent of returning), commuters recognizable to immigration inspectors or carrying documentation, or American citizens certified by a passport or identification. These slippery categories meant that many Mexicans, if they were undocumented or looked "suspicious," could easily be classified as "aliens" subject to removal by the Border Patrol.

By the late 1920s, Mexicans had become the emblematic illegal aliens, and given that "illegal entry" was defined as an act that did not end until the immigrant arrived at his or her destination, Mexicans became synonymous with illicit movement into the interior of the nation.[29] Building on the "line-riders" and custom agents of yesteryear, the Mounted Quarantine Guard, and emboldened by the harsh dictates of immigration laws and visa regulations, the Border Patrol stood at the forefront of the reconceptualization of Mexicans into foreigners, aliens, and presumed criminals.

Domesticating the Frontier

The functioning of the Border Patrol as an agency entrusted with upholding immigration laws and protecting the perimeters of the nation-state was predicated on its constitution as a streamlined federal entity that successfully coordinated between Washington, D.C., and more than a dozen district headquarters. Federalizing boundary maintenance, however, was a trying task, particularly in the "untamed" borderlands, where the Texas Rangers and Arizona Rangers had long concerned themselves with running Indians and poor Mexicans across the line. During its first decade, the head administrators in the Border Patrol confronted insubordination, despondency, and a staggering rate of attrition, all the while fighting provincialism among the recruits. These problems certainly made the Border Patrol ineffectual in many regards, and its haphazard qualities meant that its interactions with immigrants were quite unpredictable. This, in conjunction with the nebulous legal status of Mexicans, promoted an environment of suspicion and uncertainty between Mexicans and Anglos in which patrolmen arbitrarily used their authority.

One year after its creation, the Border Patrol was granted the right to arrest, without warrant, any "alien" suspected of entering the country illegally or violating federal law, and to board and search vessels used to transport "aliens" or material contraband.[30] From the outset, although technically charged only with enforcing civil laws, the mandate of the Border Patrol was extensive and quasi-military: patrolmen were armed agents of the state, commissioned with guarding the nation as a whole from undesired persons and things. As Albert Johnson, coauthor of the National Origins Act, stated in a congressional hearing: "our border patrolmen arrests when he sees a violation of the law exactly like the policeman. He also has the right to serve any warrant that has been issued, exactly as a police officer may do, or as a marshal or deputy."[31] The fashioning of the Border Patrol into a homogeneous federal body was symbolized by its standardized military uniforms and distinct badge, markers that were not regularized among previous "line-riders" or the Texas Rangers.

Who were the personnel for this new "scouting and pursuit" organization? Primarily men whose pasts had either brought them "West" for reasons of health or adventure or whose careers had led them from civilian or military domains to the nation's edges. Many in the first cohort of patrolmen were mounted guards transferred from the Immigration Service or selected from the railway mail eligible registers. Clifford Perkins, for example, lured by a climate that assured a cure for a "suspected case of tuberculosis," moved from Wisconsin to Texas in 1908.[32] After working in El Paso's post office, he decided to transfer to the Immigration Bureau; in 1910 he became one of several dozen "Chinese Inspectors" charged with enforcing the Chinese Exclusion Act. In 1924 he became part of the Border Patrol's inaugural generation and helped to formulate the agency's policies, regulations, and district divisions. Commander Alvin Edward Moore, a naval officer, joined the Border Patrol in 1926. For two years he was stationed along the Arizona-Mexico border with approximately forty other men, most of whom were ex-cowpunchers or World War I naval and army veterans.[33] Edwin Reeves, who joined the Patrol in 1925, had seen duty as a naval aviator in France and Belgium during World War I and worked periodically for the Southwestern and Pacific Railroad. A self-described lover of the outdoors, Reeves met "a few fellows who were pretty good scouts" on route between Texas towns who encouraged him to join the Border Patrol.[34] Murphy Steen, born in 1895 in rural Louisiana, was a regular in the army during World War I. Working for the Missouri Pacific Railroad Company after an honorable discharge, Steen passed the civil service examination. Soon after being hired by the Border Patrol, he was ordered to Jacksonville, Florida, where he spent much of his career.[35]

Immigration officials were quick to emphasize that many patrolmen had served in the military.[36] However, through consulting census materials, family histories, newspapers, local sources, and city directories, Kelly Lytle has found that only 16 percent of patrolmen actually served in law enforcement or the military, including the Texas Rangers, before joining the Border Patrol. Instead, the majority held positions as common and skilled laborers.[37] From the perspective of district directors and patrol administrators—many of whom did have a military provenance and relocated to the borderlands from the East and Midwest—rank-and-file recruits were essential to the agency because of their willingness to work for comparatively meager salaries and their parochial knowledge of borderlands towns and topography. However, these young local recruits also posed the greatest danger to creating a genuinely professional and well-regarded national agency. Not only did the Border Patrol appeal to them because they wanted to engage in macho exploits, many were too fast on the trigger, could often be found in corner bars, or even milked their neighborhood contacts to set up smuggling rings. Thus, officials like Clifford

Perkins spent much of the late 1920s struggling to domesticate and federalize the Border Patrol, purging unruly upstarts of their uncouth ways. The tensions between Washington, D.C., and the Southwest, and the need for young local recruits who could navigate, without incident, what was frequently a bewildering and fascinating terra incognita for patrol directors, helped to make the Border Patrol ripe for conflict and confrontation in the 1920s and 1930s.

Largely in response to mounting denunciations that hot-headed patrolmen were randomly arresting Mexican American citizens and entering homes unlawfully, Perkins launched an investigation of the Laredo and San Antonio branches. According to his memoir, these districts contained a sizable percentage of ex-vigilantes. Entering San Antonio in 1926, he encountered a group of men inspired by the Texas Rangers and the corrupt state police, many of whom were in collusion with liquor runners.[38] Perkins was dismayed and spent over a year attempting to tame the San Antonio branch, explaining that professionalization of such men was a taxing and sometimes futile endeavor: "It took considerable indoctrinating to convince some of the inspectors they were not chasing outlaws, and we never did get it out of the heads of all of them, for we had to discharge several for being too rough."[39] Perkins encountered a similar situation in Laredo. Surveying the "strictly Mexican town," he was disturbed to find the patrolmen in the office "smoking, swapping yarns, and laughing."[40] In his eyes, these men, who ran an elaborate smuggling operation out of district headquarters, were sullying the reputation of the agency.[41]

In other districts, immigration officials intent on improving the prestige of the agency reported to their Washington, D.C., superiors numerous instances in which patrolmen shot or assaulted Mexicans with no provocation. Such indiscriminate use of force is illustrated by the case of Manuel Nájera, a young Mexican American who was assailed by patrolmen. Born in Alamogordo, New Mexico, Nájera had lived in the U.S. Southwest all his life and was working as a mailing clamp operator at the El Paso Sash and Door Factory. On the evening of March 14, 1927, he and several friends were sitting on a street corner in El Paso not far from the borderline when two patrolmen, John Gillis and Arthur Scrivener, heard gunfire. The pair followed the sound of the shot and came across Nájera and company and immediately decided that they were responsible for the shooting, probably intending to distract Gillis and Scrivener so that "aliens" could secure passage over the line. Nájera and his friends denied any such plot, but within seconds Gillis had slapped Nájera. Soon the El Paso police arrived; before they had time to intervene in any way, Scrivener had knocked Nájera down to the ground. Nájera, however, was bold enough to file a grievance with the police, which resulted the taking of statements from Scrivener, Gillis, Nájera, and Nájera's mother, all of whom attested to this sequence of events. When asked why he had slapped Nájera, Gillis replied, to "show him that we were not playing with him and for the purpose of finding out who had fired that shot."[42] For his part, Scrivener confessed that he had struck Nájera, claiming, however, that he had no choice but to protect himself given that there was a strong likelihood—not intimated by Gillis or anyone else—that he or one of the other young Mexican American men might have had a knife hidden in his hand.[43] The El Paso district director viewed this incident as severe enough to recommend that Gillis, who was dragging "this Service into disrepute," be met with a "severe letter of admonition." For Scrivener, however, who "viciously struck the boy and knocked him down," termination from the Border Patrol by the end of the month was suggested.[44] Scrivener's immediate superior, El Paso's chief patrol inspector, clearly believed that irascible men like Scrivener were doing a disservice to the Border Patrol and reinforcing its negative image. He wrote to the El Paso district director that Scrivener was "a person of very high temper and one who, it is believed, has demonstrated his unfitness for this class of work."[45]

Patrolmen also incurred animosity by causing disruptions at the homes of local Anglos. In early December 1924, for instance, two motorcycle officers, A. H. Jolly and William J. Farnsworth, ostensibly out to monitor roads and railroads, fired at a covey of quail near the Detroit Ranch in Rincon, New Mexico. In the same vicinity several days later, Farnsworth shot a house cat, alleging that he thought it was a fox. This so angered the ranch's owner, Mr. Pearce, that he demanded that the two patrolmen stay away from his place. While it is unclear whether Farnsworth was dismissed, he was relieved of motorcycle duty and both men were admonished that "promiscuous shooting" would "not be tolerated."[46] During the late 1920s and 1930s district directors were constantly investigating the indiscretions and abuses of Border Patrol personnel, as they received an unremitting stream of letters, newspaper articles, and internal complaints of misbehavior on the part of patrolmen.[47]

For these reasons, the Border Patrol had no choice but to expel many of its recruits, thus amplifying an already escalating turnover rate. While the Border Patrol did enlarge its force on both the northern and southern boundaries, from 472 men the first year, to 875 in 1929, to over 1,000 in 1934, district directors regularly bemoaned the dearth of qualified personnel and equipment and asserted that the starting salary of $1,680 was too low to interest the best candidates.[48] In the first three months after its establishment, the Border Patrol registered a 25 percent loss in employees: "so fast did resignations occur that the registrar soon became exhausted and consent was obtained to make temporary appointments."[49] This predicament continued unabated into the late 1920s: 25.4 percent in 1927, 28.7 percent in 1928, and 20.5 percent in 1929.[50] Moreover, many applicants were rejected, even after having passed the time-consuming civil service examination, because they consorted with the wrong kind, were known as drunkards, or had purported ties to contraband smugglers.[51] Others were turned away because they transgressed the Southwest's version of the Jim Crow color line. J. R. Jackson, for example, was not even granted a probational appointment because he was married to a Mexican woman and had purportedly "taken up the ways of the Mexicans and goes dirty and slouchy and associates with Mexicans most of the time."[52]

In addition, many who were accepted in the Border Patrol failed to show up for their assignment, exacerbating a situation of perpetual vacancies. Many patrolmen, instead of displaying violent temperaments, were unapologetically apathetic. For example, when asked about his training, Wesley E. Stiles told an interviewer, while chuckling, that he was told just to "catch aliens. That's what we were supposed to do," adding that in the Border Patrol's inaugural month of operations (August 1924), "we didn't do anything, we just wandered around town here." The only instruction he received was a slim book containing a copy of the 1917 Immigration Act.[53] Edwin M. Reeves, who made the cut in 1925 and was stationed in his hometown of El Paso, had joined the patrol out of a desire for excitement, but found himself given few orders and told merely to apprehend "aliens."[54]

These problems troubled middle managers like Perkins, who endeavored to imbue the agency with the stamp of federal professionalism. Despite the apathy, insubordination, and retention and recruitment dilemmas, Perkins remained optimistic that crass frontiersmen could eventually be made into well-mannered patrol officers through repeated inculcation of hierarchy, self-discipline, and adherence to the Border Patrol's motto,

"Honor First." From the Border Patrol's inception, this process of civilizing and remasculinization was tied to mastering marksmanship and a daily routine of calisthenics, both of which were given a boost in 1934 when the Border Patrol Academy was founded in El Paso and a more rigorous training regime was implemented.[55]

The Protean Masculinities of the Border Patrol

Attempts to domesticate the Border Patrol into a well-managed outfit unfolded alongside the transformation of Mexicans into illegal aliens. Intertwined with these overlapping processes were complex patterns of gender contestation that were reshaping understandings of the nation, the family, and "race" in the United States. The Border Patrol was an apparatus deployed in and for state formation and through which the limits of nationhood were demarcated and disputed. Examining the Border Patrol as a gendered project can illuminate the social and cultural production of masculinities in the United States in the early to mid-twentieth century and, in particular, can highlight novel frameworks for capturing the connections between paternalism and patriotism and the emergence of a "benevolent" welfare state in the 1930s. As recent critical scholarship has argued, masculinity is not a static essential condition but rather emerges out of an ensemble of temporally and spatially specific social practices that traverse the arenas of sexuality, reproduction, labor, and culture. Usually defined relationally in opposition to femininity, masculinity is one of the most potent modalities of social organization in patriarchal systems.[56] Examining normative, embattled, and transitional masculinities can reveal many of the operational principles of bounded polities, above all, nations. In his extensive work on fascism in Europe in the interwar era, George Mosse has demonstrated the insidious symbiosis of masculinity and nationalism in the construction of hegemonic regimes of both rule and consent.[57] Interpreted as a gendered project, the Border Patrol encapsulates the conflicted configurations of masculinity that arose in the United States in the early to mid-twentieth century.

Although more than 80 percent of Border Patrol recruits only knew common and skilled labor before wearing their federal badge, the mythology of the agency was firmly rooted in a romanticism of the Texas Rangers. Formally organized in 1873, the Rangers were a band of mounted

Anglo "mobile trouble shooters" known for taking the law into their own hands and aggressively pursuing "frontier justice."[58] First formed to run Apaches and Comanches either back into Mexico or onto an ever enlarging reservation system, when Anglo farmers and merchants gradually gained control of land in the Southwest, the Rangers' focus shifted from the putative depredations of "hostile" Indians to the perceived abuses committed by Mexican "outlaws" against their private property. From 1915 to 1917, the Rangers were critical to protecting a new commercial order and antagonizing a "race war" in Texas's Rio Grande Valley.[59] Hundreds of Mexicans were killed and many others complained to Mexican consuls about the Rangers' brutalities.[60]

As "frontier cowboys" unleashing Manifest Destiny through conquest and colonization, the Texas Rangers expressed the late-nineteenth-century ethos of primitive masculinity. As argued so perceptively by Gail Bederman, primitive masculinity was borne of the contradictions of modernization. While many middle-class Anglo men looked toward mechanization, urbanization, and industrialization as the beacons of progress in the 1890s and 1900s, they also experienced anxieties because of these changes. Neurasthenia, a catch-all diagnostic label for conditions ranging from complete physiological enervation to sexualized overexcitability, consumed men such as William James and Theodore Dreiser.[61] One of the most commonly prescribed cures for this nervous disorder was a temporary sojourn to the "Wild West," where manhood could be restored through embracing and embodying savagery. By bareback riding, hunting and shooting game, trailing Indians, and occupying the transitional zone between barbarism and civilization, a man's vital energies could be equilibrated. No one performed this rebirth better than Teddy Roosevelt, whose stints as a hunter, sheriff, and cowboy in the Dakota badlands catapulted him from an effete and asthmatic East Coast dandy into a hardy, rifle-toting cowboy. Eschewing the nineteenth-century Victorian code of restrained manhood, Roosevelt helped to spawn a construct of masculinity that revolved around the body as a site of physical aesthetics and virility.[62]

When the Border Patrol was created in the 1920s, it was invariably described in terms of primitive masculinity and, above all, as a continuation of the Texas Rangers. Indeed, the anointed "grandfather" of the Border Patrol, revered in two popular publications, was Jefferson Davis Milton, one of the original Texas Rangers. After chasing Apaches, Milton had resigned from the Rangers in the 1880s to work as a deputy sheriff, customs inspector, El Paso's chief of police, and Wells Fargo messenger. In 1904 he joined the Immigration Bureau, was bestowed a badge, and soon became known as the legendary "one man Border Patrolman."[63]

The Border Patrol also replicated their borderlands predecessors—the Texas Rangers, *rurales*, and cavalry—by seeking to become proficient in the putatively Native American art of tracking or "sign-cutting." As the INS deputy commissioner stated in 1934, "There is one angle to the work of the Border Patrol which links it with the Indian fighters of the early days. The science of tracking is constantly called into use by inspectors. Broken reeds on a river bank may tell the plain story of the landing of a smuggler's boat."[64] By cultivating an instinctual connection to the Southwestern topography, patrolmen perfected their latent primordial capacities for hunting and capture. Many patrolmen referred to this perception as a "sixth" or "super sense" and claimed they had learned it, directly or derivatively, from American Indians.[65] In one book dedicated completely to "sign-cutting," an ex-patrolman profiled one of California Imperial Valley's "greatest trackers." Once a dude rancher, Apache fighter, and reservation range rider, Fred D'Albini led Border Patrol tracking efforts in Arizona and California in the 1920s and 1930s. Albini claimed that his mentor had been a Papago Indian. According to Albini, to be an effective tracker, "you have to have eyes"—to read clues like gum wrappers, barely discernible footprints, and trampled vegetation.[66] Revealing the racialized assumptions about body types that circulated among early patrolmen, Albini averred that a "fugitive's nationality" usually could be ascertained because "a Mexican walks heavy on the outside of his feet. When he walks, he puts his foot down on the heel first and then rolls off it—Indians will do that too, Whites and blacks usually put their feet down flat."[67]

By "playing Indian," patrolmen participated in the well-honed rituals of performing and appropriating otherness in order to differentiate themselves as civilized by being able to purposefully cannibalize the primitive. The Border Patrol was an adult extension of the Boy Scouts and the Seton Indians, founded in the early twentieth century to mold young boys into maturity through scouting, nature study, wilderness trips, and survival games.[68] By "playing Indian," patrolmen sought out the childlike, natural, and intuitive sides of themselves, which could then be harnessed in the name of border surveillance. This gendered practice, as scholars have suggested, strengthened "U.S. hegemonic manhood" in the early twenti-eth century as "white men used their 'Indian' to fabricate and lay claim to western landscapes as sites of white American masculine power."[69]

If patrolmen were extolled for their primitive masculinity, they were also enjoined, as Perkins's reconnoitering of the Laredo and San Antonio branches demonstrates, to obey their superiors, exhibit self-discipline, and observe the organization's code of conduct. Patrolmen were expected to be successful military personnel and to have learned lessons about outsmart-ing and defeating the enemy from World War I. The Border Patrol high-lighted its military acumen by deploying techniques of surveillance that had been finessed along the U.S.-Mexico border during preparedness cam-paigns as well as on the European front. Specifically, emphasis was placed on defending the border not just by monitoring the one-dimensional line that stretched from the Gulf to the Pacific Coast, but by developing a "de-fense in depth" vision and conceiving of the landscape as a series of inter-locking zones.[70] While clearly akin to tracking, "defense in depth" drew heavily from a strategic logic that revolved around ideas of subterfuge, covert operations, and cryptography. In the post–World War I context of the Red Scare, this often meant that patrolmen were called on to act as spies. As one glowing account of the Border Patrol stated, "When the patrolman turns Sherlock Holmes, it is difficult indeed to recognize him, for he may be in the guise of a fisherman, tourist, immigrant or smug-gler."[71]

The Border Patrol's simultaneous embodiment of primitive mascu-linity and disciplined militarism is best illustrated sartorially. Inspired by the Canadian Mounted Constabulary and the U.S. cavalry, the agency's forest-green uniforms were, in the words of the INS commissioner gen-eral, "sacred," not only symbolizing "authority, the law's majesty, and all the power of the Federal Government" but constituting an external set of signs that were "intuitively recognized and scrupulously observed."[72] For the most part, the Border Patrol uniform replicated that of the peacetime officers—consisting of army breeches, a single-breasted sack coat, field boots, and a Sam Browne leather belt.[73] According to Perkins, the latter two accessories "completed the military appearance of the uniform."[74] This martial image, however, was complemented and transgressed by the quintessential marker of the Southwestern cowboy, the Stetson hat.[75] Memoirs, articles, and dime accounts of the Border Patrol frequently em-bellished descriptions of patrolmen by commenting on their Baden Powell

Stetsons. In the magazine *Frontier Stories*, for example, an author first informed his readers that patrolmen were "far snappier than the famous Texas Rangers," adding that they wore "Baden Powell Stetsons, olive drab blouses, and breeches, shining puttees."[76]

Reading patrolmen's clothing semiologically, as codes of signification, reveals a story of conflicted masculinities.[77] The Stetson, for example, symbolized the patrolmen's ties to the "frontier" past of Texas Rangers and Mexican *vaqueros*. Patrolmen eschewed the standard martial ideal in another way, by refusing the single-action 1917 Colt .45 revolvers they had been issued. Many members of the Border Patrol viewed these World War I leftovers as clumsy and antiquated, choosing instead more "western" Remington and Winchester rifles. As a gendered project, the Border Patrol was defined simultaneously by primitive masculinity and the martial ideal, two configurations that were intimately intertwined and replete with tensions.

Both these constructs of masculinity were complicated by the devastation of World War I, which left many soldiers shell-shocked and skeptical of the glory of warfare.[78] Thus, by the time the Border Patrol was created, the configurations of masculinity on which it was based were already giving way. Indeed, by the 1920s, as several feminist historians have argued, the winning of female suffrage, the "domestication of politics," and the expansion of an increasingly male-dominated welfare state helped to realign the interior coordinates of the family.[79] On one hand, many men, responding to what they perceived as an emasculation of the political arena, turned their attention to the home, schools, and churches and strove to reassert the supremacy of the father in child rearing and socialization.[80] On the other, many men sought to invent a novel normative masculinity by drawing starker lines between themselves and, in George Mosse's term, their "countertypes."[81] This kind of negotiation can be seen in the emergence of suprapatriarchal and racialist movements such as the Ku Klux Klan or evangelical fundamentalism. More broadly, the articulation of a new construct of masculinity was also linked to the institutionalization of scientific racism in 1920s immigration laws, the popularity of eugenic sterilization laws, and mounting alarm among parents and psychologists over homosexuality.

In the throes of these changes, and especially with the coming of the Great Depression, the Border Patrol began to rely on an emergent masculinity—the benevolent father protector—that resonated with an incipient welfare state and partially resolved the contradictions between primitive masculinity and the martial ideal. This genre of masculinity was spoken through a language of male "feelings of sympathy" that drew on long-standing tropes of the father as kind protector and functioned in concert with prevailing patterns of racialization and nationalism. In their memoirs, many patrolmen entrusted with "defending the line" along the Mexican border from the 1920s to the 1950s appealed to the emotion of compassion to describe their duties as "guardians of the gate." In *Desert Trackers,* for example, Peter Odens explained, "it may perhaps be corny to say that these officers have feelings just as those whom they have to apprehend. But it should be pointed out that today, many of them are family men who well understand why circumstances such as the great disparity in wealth between the United States and Mexico would force men and women to seek employment on this side of the border."[82] In his autobiography, Perkins dates his sense of compassion for "aliens" to his initial encounters with Chinese immigrants in Arizona in the years after 1910. Aware that the Chinese faced continuous persecution in Mexico, he stated dolefully that "they come so far, and their wants were so few in a land of so much opportunity."[83] Many patrolmen related to Mexican men as breadwinners and fathers; in an oral history interview, one offered, "I have to say that most of them were honest, reliable people. They were hungry and just wanted a job."[84]

This compassion was, above all, an emotive patriotism that undergirded the image of patrolmen as caring and courteous federal agents who professionally maintained the nation's boundaries. In the context of a burgeoning discourse of the welfare state, which stigmatized dependency and only valorized reproduction insofar as it perpetuated the white American family, immigration officials and patrolmen often cast their activities of seizure, arrest, and deportation in paternal terms. It is quite telling that in "The Mission of the Border Patrol," INS deputy commissioner Wixon closed his essay by evincing sympathy with the "honest, industrious alien whose only offense has been his illegal entry into the United States." Despite this benevolent gesture, however, Wixon went on to claim that although such an "alien" might not be overtly dangerous, his entrance and settlement in the country would necessarily lead to disruption and familial disintegration. Speaking hypothetically, Wixon proposed the following scenario: "In the natural course of events, he marries an American citizen, establishes a home, becomes the father of American-born children. Then comes his arrest on deportation charges."[85] Once excluded, this "alien" would be forced to abandon his wife and children, who, in dire straits, would only have the state to turn to. Therefore, feelings of sympathy and defense of the nation's borders were one and the same; it was imperative to debar such interlopers before "they had sunk their roots into this country and given hostages to fortune in the shape of American-born wives and children."[86]

By the 1930s, familial metaphors were regularly employed to describe the Border Patrol and by patrolmen to represent themselves. As several scholars have shown, the solidification of racial lines between Anglos and Mexicans was interpenetrated with forcible maintenance of the white family in the early 1900s. By the 1930s, an incident that occurred in Arizona, in which Irish orphans in the copper towns of Bisbee and Morenci were physically removed by an Anglo posse from the homes of their legal adoptive Mexican parents, had become common practice. Now the Border Patrol stood literally and figuratively at the defensive edges of the family-nation.[87] In the 1930s, against the tides of skyrocketing unemployment, plummeting marriage rates, and a dramatic decline in the birthrate, which fell below the replacement level for the first time in U.S. history, the Border Patrol fought to preserve the imagined racialized cohesion of the "American family."[88]

*   *   *

When the Border Patrol was established in 1924, it found its footing on ground that had been trod by the Texas Rangers and frontier vigilantes, the early immigration service "line-riders," the myths of Apache and Comanche warriors, romantic images of the brash and regal Mexican vaqueros, and the U.S. cavalry. Out of these earlier incarnations of masculinity and boundary maintenance emerged the repertoire for the manufacturing of the Border Patrol. Created during a transitional moment of gender systems, the agency relied on the enactment of primitive masculinity. In addition, however, the Border Patrol's standardized uniforms, code of conduct, and call for discipline contributed to a consolidation of the martial ideal. These two intertwined masculinities coexisted uneasily beside one another, complementing each other and clashing as the Border Patrol spearheaded the transformation of the Mexican into the emblematic illegal alien and haphazardly enforced a nebulous set of immigration laws that left Mexicans in a gray area of classification. Competing masculinities were also at play when immigration officers such as Clifford Perkins, taking orders from Washington, D.C., sought to domesticate and federalize unruly recruits into a "healthy, coordinated outfit" capable of engendering "a considerable amount of public confidence."[89] The fractured binary of the ethos of primitive masculinity and the martial ideal was triangulated and partially muted when the Border Patrol cast itself as the guardian of the white American family-nation. By the 1930s, this new persona—benevolent protector of the body politic—had become a crucial staple of the Border Patrol as a gendered and racialized project, swinging into action during the repatriation of hundreds of thousands of Mexicans during the Great Depression, and, even more strikingly, during Operation Wetback in 1954, when the deportation of persons of Mexican origin was conflated with anticommunism and the prerogatives of the national security state.

Notes

1 I. F. Wixon, "The Mission of the Border Patrol," U.S. Department of Labor, Immigration and Naturalization Service (INS) Lecture No. 7, 19 March 1934, 5.

2 See Alexandra Minna Stern, "Buildings, Boundaries, and Blood: Medicalization and Nation-Building on the U.S.-Mexico Border," *Hispanic American Historical Review* 79:1 (1999): 41–81.

3 See Floya Anthias and Nira Yuval-Davis, *Racialized Boundaries: Race, Nation, Gender, Colour and Class and the Anti-Racist Struggle* (London: Routledge, 1992); Geoff Eley and Ronald Grigor Suny, eds., *Becoming National: A Reader* (New York: Oxford University Press, 1996); and George L. Mosse, *The Image of Man: The Creation of Modern Masculinity* (New York: Oxford University Press, 1996).

4 See Klaus Theweleit, *Male Fantasies*, 2 vols. (Minneapolis: University of Minnesota Press, 1987–1989); and Gloria Anzaldúa, *Borderlands/La Frontera: The New Mestiza* (San Francisco: Spinster's/Aunt Lute, 1987).

5 See Ana María Alonso, *Thread of Blood: Colonialism, Revolution, and Gender on Mexico's Northern Frontier* (Tucson: University of Arizona Press, 1995).

6 See Eric Michael Schantz, "All Night at the Owl: The Social and Political Relations of Mexicali's Red-Light District, 1913–1925," *Journal of the Southwest* 34:4 (Winter 2001): 549–603.

7 See Anzaldúa, *Borderlands*; and Marjorie Garber, *Vested Interests: Cross-Dressing and Cultural Anxiety* (New York: Routledge, 1992).

8 See Thongchai Winichakul, *Siam Mapped: A History of the Geo-Body of a Nation* (Honolulu: University of Hawai'i Press, 1994).

9 Victor Zúñiga, "Nations and Borders: Romantic Nationalism and the Project of Modernity," in David Spener and Kathleen Staudt, eds., *The U.S.-Mexico Border: Transcending Divisions, Contesting Identities* (Boulder: Lynne Rienner, 1998), 39. Also see Pablo Vila, *Crossing Borders, Reinforcing Borders: Social Categories, Metaphors, and Narrative Identities on the U.S.-Mexico Frontier* (Austin: University of Texas Press, 2000).

10 See David J. Weber, *The Spanish Frontier in North America* (New Haven: Yale University Press, 1992).

11 See David Montejano, *Anglos and Mexicans in the Making of Texas, 1836–1986* (Austin: University of Texas Press, 1987).

12 See Robert M. Utley, *Lone Star Justice: The First Century of the Texas Rangers* (Oxford: Oxford University Press, 2002).

13 See Timothy J. Dunn, *The Militarization of the U.S.-Mexico Border, 1978–1992* (Austin: CMAS Books, 1996).

14 See Joseph Nevins, *Operation Gatekeeper: The Rise of the "Illegal Alien" and the Making of the U.S.-Mexico Boundary* (New York: Routledge, 2002), chap. 2.

15 See Stern, "Buildings, Boundaries, and Blood."

16 See Erika Lee, "Enforcing the Borders: Chinese Exclusion along the U.S. Borders with Canada and Mexico, 1882–1924," *Journal of American History* 89:1 (June 2002): 54–86.

17 See Mark Reisler, *By the Sweat of Their Brow: Mexican Immigrant Labor in the United States, 1900–1940* (Westport: Greenwood, 1976).

18 See "Seraphic Report regarding Conditions on Mexican Border, 1906–1907," case file 51423/1, reel 1, microfilm, Records of the Immigration and Naturalization Service (INS), record group 85 (RG 85), National Archives (NA), series A, part 2, Mexican Immigration 1906–1930.

19 Stern, "Buildings, Boundaries, and Blood"; Howard Markel, *When Germs Travel: Six Major Epidemics that have Invaded America since 1900 and the Fears they have Unleashed* (New York: Pantheon, 1994).

20 See National Archives at College Park (NACP), USPHS, record group 90, central file 1897–1923, file 1169, Laredo, Texas, and general subject file 1924–1935, Domestic Stations, Laredo and San Antonio, Texas.

21 See Mae M. Ngai, "Illegal Aliens and Alien Citizens: United States Immigration Policy and Racial Formation, 1924–1945" (Ph.D. diss., Columbia University, 1998).

22 See Mae M. Ngai, "The Architecture of Race in American Immigration Law," *Journal of American History* 86:1 (1999): 67–92; John Higham, *Strangers in the Land: Patterns of American Nativism* (New York: Atheneum, 1973).

23 Ngai, "Illegal Aliens and Alien Citizens," 129–32.

24 See Ngai, "Illegal Aliens and Alien Citizens"; George J. Sánchez, *Becoming Mexican American: Ethnicity, Culture, and Identity in Chicano Los Angeles, 1900–1945* (New York: Oxford University Press, 1993); Francisco E. Balderrama and

Raymond Rodríguez, *Decade of Betrayal: Mexican Repatriation in the 1930s* (Albuquerque: University of New Mexico Press, 1995).

25 United States Border Patrol, "History of United States Border Patrol," 4 (official history), General Archives, United States Border Patrol Museum (USBPM), El Paso, Texas.

26 Wixon, "The Mission," 2.

27 Ngai, "Illegal Aliens and Alien Citizens," 134.

28 Ibid, 171.

29 Ibid, 117.

30 U.S. Department of Labor, Bureau of Immigration, "General Order No. 49," 16 March 1925, included as appendix in "Immigration Border Patrol," Committee on Immigration and Naturalization, House of Representatives, 75th Cong., 2d sess., 15 January 1930 (Washington, D.C.: GPO, 1930), 28.

31 U.S. Congress, House of Representatives, "To Establish a Border Patrol," Hearing before the Committee on the Judiciary. 69th Cong., HR 9731 (Washington, D.C.: GPO, 1926), 32.

32 Clifford Alan Perkins, *Border Patrol: With the U.S. Immigration Service on the Mexican Boundary, 1910–1954* (El Paso: Texas Western Press, 1978), 1.

33 Cmdr. Alvin Edward Moore, *Border Patrol* (Santa Fe: Sunstone Press, 1988), 6.

34 Interview with Edwin M. Reeves, 25 June 1974, tape # 135, Institute of Oral History (IOH), University of Texas at El Paso (UTEP).

35 Murphy J. F. Steen, *Twenty-Five Years a U.S. Border Patrolman* (Dallas: Royal, 1958).

36 Ibid, 16.

37 Kelly Lytle, "Entangling Bodies and Borders: Racial Profiling and a History of the U.S. Border Patrol, 1924–1955" (Ph.D. Diss., University of California, Los Angeles, 2002).

38 Perkins, *Border Patrol*, 102.

39 Ibid, 102.

40 Ibid, 109.

41 Ibid, 110.

42 Statement of John Q. Gillis, taken by Nick D. Collaer, Chief Patrol Officer, 14 May 1927, 55509/25A, INS, RG85, NA.

43 Statement of Arthur G. Scrivener, taken by Nick D. Collaer, Chief Patrol Officer, 14 May 1927, 55509/25A, INS, RG85, NA.

44 El Paso District Director to Commissioner General of Immigration, 23 March 1927, 55509/25A, INS, RG85, NA.

45 El Paso Chief Patrol Inspector to El Paso District Director, 16 May 1927, 55509/25A, INS, RG85, NA.

46 Patrol Inspector in Charge (Perkins) to El Paso District Director, 9 January 1925, 55509/25, INS, RG85, NA.

47 Complaints against the Border Patrol were endemic in Southwestern newspapers in the years 1928 to 1930.

48 U.S. Congress, House of Representatives, Committee on Immigration and Naturalization, "Immigration Border Patrol." 75th Cong., 2d sess., 15 January 1930, (Washington, D.C.: GPO, 1930), 4.

49 U.S. Department of Labor, Bureau of Immigration, *Annual Report of the Commissioner General of Immigration the Secretary of Labor* (Washington, D.C.: GPO, 1925), 15.

50 "Memorandum of Facts Relating to Immigration Border Patrol, Immigration District No. 25," 23 November 1926, 55496/572, INS, RG85, NA.

51 U.S. Department of Labor, Bureau of Immigration, *Annual Report of the Commissioner General of Immigration the Secretary of Labor* (Washington, D.C.: GPO, 1930), 37.

52 Patrol Inspector Perry to El Paso Patrol Inspector in Charge, 9 February 1925, 55509/25, INS, RG85, NA.

53 Interview with Wesley E. Stiles (Wesley C. Shaw, Interviewer), January 1986, tape #756, IOH, UTEP.

54 Interview with Reeves.

55 See Clement David Hellyer, *The U.S. Border Patrol* (New York: Random House, 1963).

56 See R.W. Connell, "The Social Organization of Masculinity," in Stephen M. Whitehead and Frank J. Barrett, eds., *The Masculinities Reader* (Cambridge: Polity, 2001), 30–50; and R.W. Connell, *Masculinities* (Berkeley: University of California Press, 1995).

57 See Mosse, *The Image of Man*.

58 James B. Gillett, *Six Years with the Texas Rangers, 1875–1881* (Lincoln: University of Nebraska Press, 1976 [1925]), xiii.

59 Montejano, *Anglos and Mexicans*, 117–28.

60 Ibid.

61 See Gail Bederman, *Manliness and Civilization: A Cultural History of Gender and Race in the United States, 1880–1917* (Chicago: University of Chicago Press, 1995).

62 Bederman, *Manliness and Civilization*; Richard Slotkin, *Gunfighter Nation: The Myth of the Frontier in Twentieth-Century America* (New York: HarperPerennial, 1993); E. Anthony Rotundo, *American Manhood: Transformations in Masculinity from the Revolution to the Modern Era* (New York: Basic Books, 1993); and Michael Kimmel, *Manhood in America: A Cultural History* (New York: Free Press, 1997).

63 Hellyer, *The U.S. Border Patrol*, 20.

64 Wixon, "The Mission," 8–9.

65 See Moore, *Border Patrol*; Hellyer, *The U.S. Border Patrol*; and Steen, *Twenty-Five Years a U.S. Border Patrolman*.

66 Peter Odens, *The Desert Trackers: Men of the Border Patrol* (Yuma, Arizona, 1975), chap. 3.

67 Ibid.

68 See Philip J. Deloria, *Playing Indian* (New Haven: Yale University Press, 1998); Michael Rosenthal, *The Character Factory: Baden-Powell and the Origins of the Boy Scout Movement* (New York: Pantheon, 1986).

69 David Anthony Tyeeme Clark and Joane Nagel, "White Men, Red Masks: Appropriations of 'Indian' Manhood in Imagined Wests," in Matthew Basso, Laura McCall, and Dee Garceau, eds., *Across the Great Divide: Cultures of Manhood in the American West* (New York: Routledge, 2001), 123.

70 See "Marfa Sector Border Patrol," D87.92.12, Marfa Sector folder, General Archives, USBPM.

71 "Thrilling Adventures with Uncle Sam's Border Patrol," *Arizona Daily Star*, 26 April 1931, microfilm of file 55598/459E, INS, RG85, NA.

72 Committee on Immigration and Naturalization, "Immigration Border Patrol," 28.

73 See "Immigration Border Patrol," 15–25; Randy Steffen, *The Horse Soldier, 1776–1943*, vols. 3 and 4 (Norman: University of Oklahoma Press, 1979).

74 Perkins, *Border Patrol*, 91.

75 See David Dary, *Cowboy Culture: A Saga of Five Centuries* (New York: Avon, 1981).

76 Eugene Cunningham, "The Border Patrol: Forty Men, from El Paso the Gulf—But Oh What Men!," *Frontier Stories* 8:5 (August 1928): 87–88, series A, part 2, microfilm of file 55598/459C, INS, RG85, NA.

77 Roland Barthes, *Elements of Semiology* (New York: Hill and Wang, 1964); and Tammy M. Proctor, "(Uni)Forming Youth: Girl Guides and Boy Scouts in Britain, 1908–39," *History Workshop Journal* 45 (1998): 103–34.

78 See Kimmel, *Manhood in America*.

79 See Paula Baker, "The Domestication of Politics: Women and American Political Society, 1780–1920" in Linda Gordon, ed., *Women, the State, and Welfare* (Madison: University of Wisconsin Press, 1990), 55–91; and Seth Koven and Sonya Michel, eds., *Mothers of a New World: Maternalist Policies and the Origins of the Welfare State* (New York: Routledge, 1993).

80 See Kimmel, *Manhood in America*.

81 See Mosse, *The Image of Man*.

82 Odens, *Desert Trackers*, chap. 2.

83 Perkins, *Border Patrol*, 24.

84 Interview with Ben A. Parker (interviewer: Douglas V. Meed), 25 July 1984, tape # 661, IOH, UTEP.

85 Wixon, "The Mission," 11.

86 Ibid.

87 See Linda Gordon, *The Great Arizona Orphan Abduction* (Cambridge: Harvard University Press, 1999).

88 See Wendy Kline, *Building a Better Race: Gender, Sexuality, and Eugenics from the Turn of the Century to the Baby Boom* (Berkeley: University of California Press, 2001).

89 Perkins, *Border Patrol*, 100.

Conclusion

Borderlands Unbound

I see a whole generation
freefalling toward a borderless future
incredible mixtures beyond science fiction:
>   cholo-punks, pachuco krishnas
>   Irish concheros, butoh rappers, cyber-Aztecs,
>   Gringofarians, Hopi rockers, y demás . . .
—GUILLERMO GÓMEZ-PEÑA, "Freefalling Toward a Borderless Future"[1]

The U.S.-Mexico borderlands are marked by a history of violence and accommodation. Overlapping two nations and several historiographical realms, the field of borderlands history is similarly contested. Its heterogeneous foundations render futile any attempt to impose a monolithic historiographical genealogy on the field. As we discovered at the symposium for this book hosted by the Clements Center for Southwest Studies, scholars based in Chicana/o, U.S. West, and Latin American history often think differently about borderlands history and its significance. Chicana/o historians, in many ways, have made the largest and most obvious impact on the study of the borderlands, and their legacy can be seen clearly in these essays. Yet this collection is a child with a diverse heritage and several parents. Ongoing dialogues in Latin American history about nation building, U.S. imperialism, and modernity have informed the essays in this book, as have debates north of the border about Frederick Jackson Turner's frontier thesis, the notion of the West, and the incorporation of ethnic histories into regional and national history.

Although none of these fields has developed in isolation from the others, the U.S.-Mexico borderlands offers a particularly fertile meeting ground on which to sustain and deepen these conversations. This scholarly meeting ground is not without its politics. The transnational approach represented by many of the essays in this volume builds on and responds to a dynamic social movement questioning the benefits of globalization for the world's poor and disenfranchised. Not all the essays in this book address these issues directly, but it is hard to imagine any of them being written outside the context of the NAFTA debates, the Zapatista rebellion, and the anti–affirmative action crusades and anti-immigration legislation of the 1990s, all symbols of an enduring tension between the crossing and reinforcing of boundaries. As students of borderlands, we are very much a product of our times.

The essays in this volume show that although one finds continuity throughout the nineteenth- and early-twentieth-century borderlands, something had changed by the 1930s. The international boundary had become more of barrier, policed on the north by the U.S. Border Patrol and increasingly governed by restrictive immigration laws and xenophobic cultural practices. Yet as nation-states patrolled the borderlands, investment connected the region to an ever-expanding network of markets and trading relationships, prompting people to cross the line more frequently. The border would continue to gain importance as a transshipment point between nations, and—with Mexico's Border Industrialization Program and the rise of foreign investment in the 1960s—as a site of manufacturing and industrial assembly plants. The implementation of NAFTA in 1994 simply formalized relationships that had already been around for years, but it also reflected the ever-growing tempo of globalization, a process that, while not wholly new in the ways it connects and transforms far-flung peoples and places, has begun to profoundly change how we see our place in the world. "While few U.S. localities have remained completely unaffected by globalization," writes Claudia Sadowski-Smith, "border areas and cities have become some of its foremost staging grounds," with real consequences for the way we now experience and understand borderlands.[2]

U.S. communities that sustain cultural, political, and economic ties to Mexico (as well as other parts of Latin America) are proliferating in places as diverse as Boston, Los Angeles, Portland, and Iowa City. The 2000 U.S. census suggests that Hispanics are the fastest-growing population in North America, that whites no longer constitute a numerical majority in California, and that Texas is poised to go the same way in the near future. In Mexico, transnationalization is carried on the backs of returning migrants, who bring with them money, culture, and expectations from the United States, whereas the proliferation of Anglo-American expatriate communities in such places as San Miguel de Allende, Guanajuato, have resulted in dynamic—if often relatively bounded—cultural migrations of a different kind. Meanwhile, the inexorable march of multinational corporations and U.S. consumer markets into Mexico further blurs the borders between these two nations.

This does not mean that the border is no longer important. As we have seen in the wake of September 11, 2001, with the rise of new efforts to control entry into the United States and track the movement of "non-resident aliens" across U.S. soil, national distinctions are alive and well. And as immigrants from Mexico and the rest of Latin America have begun to move more systematically from the borderlands into communities all across the United States, the border itself has begun to move, in a sense, to the heart of the nation. This is reflected not only in new efforts by the state to track tourists, visitors, and recent immigrants across national space—thereby interiorizing the work of patrolling borders—but also in a shift of cultural and racial borders traditionally associated with the edges of the body politic to the centers of national space. Rubén Martínez, who has lived between Mexico City, Los Angeles, and San Salvador, sums up the existential crisis of such "borderized" identities: "I stand at the center—watching history whirl around me as my own history fissures: my love shatters, North and South, and a rage rises from within as the ideal of existential unity crumbles. I cannot tell whether what I see is a beginning or an end. My quest for a true center, for a cultural, political and romantic home, is stripped of direction."[3]

The field of borderlands history, in the long run, can help us better understand our place in a world characterized by the making and unmaking of borders. Even those who do not live near an international boundary are increasingly aware of living in a "fissured" world that is only partially contained by the nation. Borderlands history offers alternative narratives that get to the heart of this complex world. The boundaries that were mapped around emerging nation-states in the nineteenth century were modernity's dreams for a coherent, politically bounded horizontal community. On the ground, the reality was a lot muddier than the vision imagined by cartographers in Mexico City or Washington, D.C., yet the idea took hold, and national identity emerged as one of the strongest relationships of the twentieth century. Yet the reality of the nation was never fixed; many people lived in a world that slipped, ghostlike, in and out of the national narratives we tell about them. Perhaps now, as we find our own national foundations contested in new ways, we are in a position to recover this hidden historical legacy, and give it new meaning.

As we stand at the continental crossroads today, we can only imagine what brave new world awaits us. Will the ghosts of borderlands past teach us how to be new world border crossers, will they nurture greater transnational understanding, or will they lead us to more sobering conclusions about the endurance of nations, states, and the violence that often accompanies the policing of difference? One thing seems certain. If we let our historical narratives chart a wider variety of paths across national borders—both as a way to transcend these borders and to learn more about them—we will be in a better position to engage the enormity and complexity of our world. And if the essays in this collection offer any insight about entering this transnational historical terrain, it is simply that it is a space that thrives on open-ended frameworks and narratives. In the end, the continental crossroads finds its greatest potential as a meeting place rather than a bounded domain of scholarly inquiry. In the spirit of these new transnational dialogues, we invite you to join us in the borderlands and participate in its making.

Notes

1 Guillermo Gómez-Peña, "Freefalling Toward a Borderless Future," in *The New World Border: Prophecies, Poems and Locuras for the End of the Century* (San Francisco: City Lights, 1996), 1.

2 Claudia Sadowski-Smith, "Border Studies, Diaspora, and Theories of Globalization," in *Globalization on the Line: Culture, Capital, and Citizenship at U.S. Borders*, ed. Claudia Sadowski-Smith (New York: Palgrave, 2002), 6.

3 Rubén Martínez, *The Other Side: Notes from the New LA, Mexico City and Beyond* (New York: Vintage, 1992), 3, on borderized identities. Also see various works by Guillermo Gómez-Peña.

Contributors

GRACE PEÑA DELGADO is Assistant Professor of History in the Chicano and Latino Studies department at California State University, Long Beach, and is completing a manuscript on the Chinese in the U.S.-Mexico borderlands.

KARL JACOBY is Associate Professor of History at Brown University and the author of *Crimes against Nature: Squatters, Poachers, Thieves, and the Hidden History of American Conservation* (2001). He is currently working on a history of ethnic relations and identities in nineteenth-century Arizona.

BENJAMIN JOHNSON teaches history at Southern Methodist University. He is the author of *Revolution in Texas: How a Forgotten Uprising and Its Bloody Suppression Turned Mexicans into Americans* (2003) and coeditor of *Steal This University: The Rise of the Corporate University and the Academic Labor Movement* (2003).

LOUISE PUBOLS is Historian at the Museum of the American West at the Autry National Center in Los Angeles. Her current projects include a reinterpretation of the Autry's permanent galleries covering the U.S. West to 1865, and an exhibition on the reality and romance of California's Mexican era. She is revising her dissertation, "The de la Guerra Family: Patriarchy and the Political Economy of California, 1800–1850," for publication.

RAÚL RAMOS is Assistant Professor of History at the University of Houston and is completing a manuscript on identity formation and nationalism from the late colonial Mexican through the early American period in San Antonio and the Texas-Mexican borderlands. He has also been a fellow at the William P. Clements Center for Southwest Studies at Southern Methodist University.

ANDRÉS RESÉNDEZ is Assistant Professor of History at the University of California, Davis, and is the author of *Changing National Identities at the Frontier: Texas and New Mexico, 1800–1850* (2004).

BÁRBARA O. REYES is Assistant Professor of History at the University of New Mexico, where she teaches courses on Chicana/o history, borderlands, and immigration history. She is completing a manuscript tentatively titled "Private Women/Public Lives: Gender and Space in the California Missions."

ALEXANDRA MINNA STERN is Associate Director of the Center for the History of Medicine and Assistant Professor of American Culture and Obstetrics and Gynecology at the University of Michigan. She has written numerous articles on the history of race, gender, science, and medicine in the United States and Mexico, including "Buildings, Boundaries, and Blood: Medicalization and Nation-Building on the U.S.-Mexico Border, 1910–1930," *Hispanic American Historical Review* 79:1 (February 1999), which won the 2000 Berkshire Conference of Women Historians Article Prize. Her monograph *Eugenic Nation: Medicine, Race, and Sexuality in the United States, 1900–1970* is forthcoming.

SAMUEL TRUETT is Assistant Professor of History at the University of New Mexico and is the author of *Transnational Dreams: Transforming the U.S.-Mexico Borderlands* (forthcoming). He has also been a fellow at the William P. Clements Center for Southwest Studies at Southern Methodist University.

ELLIOTT YOUNG is Associate Professor of History at Lewis and Clark College and is the author of *Catarino Garza's Revolution on the Texas-Mexico Border* (Duke University Press, 2004). His articles have appeared in *Mexican Studies/Estudios Mexicanos*, *Western Historical Quarterly*, and *Southwestern Historical Quarterly*. His current research focuses on Chinese migrations in Cuba, Mexico, and North America, 1847–1940.

Index

126, 131, 168–169, 218, 245, 261,
273, 304, 326; California Republic,
67; Californios, 23, 67–70, 75–79,
84–86
Calles, Plutarco, 18
Camarillo, Albert, 3
Cameron County, Texas, 277, 283, 286,
288
Canada, 183, 201
Canadian Mounted Constabulary, 314
Canales, José Tomás, 279–283, 286,
289–292
Cananea, Sonora, 18, 198–199, 249–
258, 260
Canary Islanders, 42
Canclini, Nestór García, 12
Canton, China, 183
Cantú, Adelair and Ignacio, 286
Cárdenas, Lázaro, 19
Carr, Barry, 8
Carranza, Venustiano, 228
Carrillo, Juan Miguel, 99–100, 102
Carrillo, Luís, 77
Carrillo, Mariano, 99–103
Carrillo, Nicolasa, 99
Carrillo, Pedro Catarino, 77–80
Carter, Alabama, 216
Castañeda, Antonia, 5
Castañeda, Carlos E., 3
Castas, 42–43, 225–226
Catholic Church, 107–108, 138–139,
143, 166, 186, 281, 301; Dominicans,
97, 104–105, 108–110; Franciscans,
42, 104; Jesuits, 104; missions, 39,
41–42, 53, 58, 69, 71–72, 75, 97–112
Cawshatta, 55
Cerruti, Mario, 8–9
Ceylon (Sri Lanka), 167
Cherokee, 54–58, 126
Cherokee Phoenix and Indian Advocate,
130
Cheyenne, 131–134

Chicano/a: history, 2–6, 10, 12, 325;
Movement, 3
Chihuahua, Mexico, 13, 16–18, 40, 47–
49, 56, 126, 131, 135–136, 143, 163,
186, 258–259
China, 22, 155
Chinese Bureau. See U.S. Chinese
Bureau
Chinese Exclusion Act, 172, 184–185,
302, 307
Chinese exclusion laws, 173, 183–188,
191–192, 195–198, 202
Chinese identity, 185–191, 202
Chinese immigrants, xi, 13, 21, 172–
173, 183–202, 302, 316
Chinese Six Companies, 186
Chinese workers, 19
Choctaw, 126
Citizenship, 274–276, 284, 291–293;
Mexican, 185
Ciudad Juárez, Chihuahua, 303
Civilization and barbarism, 166–173
Civil rights, 274, 278–282, 291
Clark, V.M., 200–201
Cleveland, Grover, 224
Cleveland Gazette, 214
Clifton, Arizona, 18
Coahuila, Mexico, 13, 44–45, 47, 126,
186, 246
Colegio Superior de Comercio, 109
Colonialism, 97–98, 127, 154–155, 158,
164–170, 173–174, 276; colonial
domination, 103–105, 109
Colorado, 273
Colored Mexican Colonization Com-
pany, 218
Columbia Patriot, 125
Columbus, Christopher, 1
Comanche, 11, 37–58, 122, 126–128,
134–135, 312, 317
Comanche Treaty of 1822, 52–54
Combs, Franklin, 123, 127

Samuel Truett is an assistant professor in the
department of history at the University of New
Mexico. Elliott Young is an associate professor of
history at Lewis and Clark College. He is the author of
Catarino Garza's Revolution on the Texas-Mexico Border
(Duke University Press, 2004).

Library of Congress Cataloging-in-Publication Data
Continental crossroads : remapping U.S.-Mexico
borderlands history / Samuel Truett and Elliott
Young, eds.
p. cm.
Includes index.
ISBN 0-8223-3353-8 (cloth : alk. paper)—
ISBN 0-8223-3389-9 (pbk. : alk. paper)
1. Mexican-American Border Region—Historiography.
2. Mexican-American Border Region—Social
conditions.   3. Mexican-American Border Region—
Ethnic relations.   4. Ethnicity—Mexican-American
Border Region—History.   5. United States—
Relations—Mexico.   6. Mexico—Relations—United
States.   I. Truett, Samuel.   II. Young, Elliott.
F786.C67   2004
972'.1—dc22   2004004074